>> LITERARY COMPUTING AND LITERARY CRITICISM

>>   *edited by*

R O S A N N E G. P O T T E R

University of Pennsylvania Press · Philadelphia · 1989

upp

LITERARY COMPUTING

>> *and*

LITERARY CRITICISM

>> *Theoretical and Practical*

Essays on Theme and Rhetoric

Permission is acknowledged to reprint material from the following sources:

George Bernard Shaw, extracts from *Mrs. Warren's Profession, Major Barbara,* and *Heartbreak House.* Reprinted by permission of the Society of Authors.

Donald Ross, Jr., "Differences, Genres, and Influences," *Style* 11, 3 (1977): 262–73. Reprinted by permission of the University of Arkansas.

John B. Smith, "Computer Criticism," *Style* 12 (1978): 326–56. Reprinted by permission of the University of Arkansas.

Richard W. Bailey, "The Future of Computational Stylistics," *ALLC Bulletin* 7, 1 (1979): 4–11. Reprinted by permission of the Association for Literary and Linguistic Computing.

Passages from the preface also appear in Rosanne G. Potter, "Literary Criticism and Literary Computing: The Difficuties of a Synthesis," *CHum* 22, 2 (1988): 91–97.

Excerpts from *Literary Detection and Document Identification,* copyright © 1978 by Andrew Queen Morton, reprinted with the permission of Charles Scribner's Sons, an imprint of Macmillan Publishing Company.

Library of Congress Cataloging-in-Publication Data
Literary computing and literary criticism : theoretical and practical
  essays on theme and rhetoric / edited by Rosanne G. Potter.
      p.   cm.
  Includes bibliographies and index.
  ISBN 0-8122-8156-X
  1. English literature—History and criticism—Data processing.
2. English literature—History and criticism—Theory, etc.
3. English language—Style—Data processing. 4. Style, Literary—
Data processing. 5. Criticism—Data processing. I. Potter,
Rosanne G.
PR21.L58 1989
820'.28'5—dc19   88-38159
                                CIP

DESIGN: Adrianne Onderdonk Dudden

Dedicated to
    Bernice Powers Giuditta
and
    Harry A. Giuditta

CONTENTS

ACKNOWLEDGMENTS

I thank the contributors who wrote beautifully clear essays; David Sauke who designed the beautiful, clear charts; Art Evans, who had faith in this project; Iowa State University, which enabled my computing endeavors with funding and, more importantly, with interdisciplinary human support: from Jim Hoekstra, who wrote the COMP STYLE programs in PL/1, from Leroy Wolins, who did the statistics, from Kathy Shelley, who helped with the SAS programs. Working with specialists from many different disciplines has been constantly challenging and stimulating; it made me willing to assemble and guide the work of the community of scholars represented in this collection.

I most sincerely thank the people who taught me to believe in a community of scholars: Sister Mary Anthony Weinig of Rosemont College, Jim Kaufman and Jim Kinneavy at the University of Texas.

I also thank the people who got me started in computing: Helen Jo Hewitt at the Humanities Research Center of the University of Texas, Jim Hoekstra at Iowa State University, Joe Raben, editor of *Computers and the Humanities*. And I do not forget Elder Olson, who taught me about the structure of drama at the University of Chicago.

And, most of all, I thank Bill McCarthy, my strongest supporter, my editor, my colleague, and my husband.

FIGURES

TABLES

PREFACE

The mystiques of computer science and literary criticism differ considerably. These disciplines appear to stand at opposite extremes of knowledge—one rooted in facts, the other rooted in ideas; one focusing on the replicable, the other on the unique. This book consists of essays written and selected to demonstrate that computing, the ultimate tool of late twentieth-century life, can be effectively applied to basic questions of literary criticism.

The assertion that computers can be useful tools in literary study is, of course, no longer controversial. Constructing large critical editions or dictionaries, collating variant readings from different texts, concording entire corpora of prolific writers, deciding questions of disputed authorship by using indices of style so minute that they escape the most attentive reader—all of these activities, and numerous other equally complex tasks, now are routinely performed by computer methods; in fact, very few of these projects get funded without computers. The practice of computing is widespread and little disputed in these supporting areas of literary study. Essays about the utility of editorial or textual applications have therefore been excluded from this collection. This book confronts the more controversial question of what literary computing offers to literary criticism.

Several quotations from John B. Smith's 1978 essay, "Computer Criticism" (published in *Style* in Fall 1978 and included in this volume as chapter 2), will help to map out the shared ground between computing and criticism. Smith's analysis of twentieth-century criticism allowed him to assert that "the mainstream of recent critical thought has moved steadily, inexorably, toward greater formality and toward the notion of a 'science' or 'sciences' of criticism." Smith notes trends in the work of the Russian Formalists, the London School, the Prague Structuralists, the New Critics, and the French Structuralists which, taken together, form a "pattern of development in twentieth-century criticism." Smith's essay attempts to place Computer Criticism within the context of these other, more generally accepted, forms of criticism. His arguments do not imply that computer-aided criticism will supplant other, less "scientific" kinds of criticism. Literary computing does not, for instance, replace New Criticism's emphasis on the text as the central focus of study; indeed, it permits the closest possible examination of textual surfaces. Literary computing so little disputes structuralism that it in fact discloses structures invisible to the unaided eye. To all these types of critical discourse, what literary computing offers is evidence, precision of measurement and widely-accepted (in the hard and social sciences) standards of validity. All these services or supports should, on the face of things, be of interest to traditional criticism; they are not replacements or supplantings of other methods but aids to the more convincing implementation of those methods.

Despite the cogency of arguments by Smith and others, literary computing still remains outside the recognized mainstream of literary criticism. It has not been rejected, but rather neglected. Lack of interest in computer criticism can be traced to the three principal factors. (1) The preparation of literature students generally omits scientific training; thus, most critics feel inadequate in the face of essays or books based on statistical assumptions or computational technology. (2) On the opposite end of the spectrum, those who, for whatever reason, move into the technical treatments of texts very rapidly fall into the jargon of those technologies, thus rendering their research results inaccessible to their colleagues. (3) Since there is little payoff in attempting to do criticism when fellow critics do not understand it, most critics who originally sought computer means to achieve literary critical goals very frequently turn away from criticism.

The final stage of this declension finds literature PhDs moving into computing centers or departments of Computer Science to gain recognition for their work. This process can, I believe, be stopped if computer-aided researchers write with a literary critical audience in mind. Essays that explain their scientific methods and inferences adequately will make literary computing accessible to the general critic and will fulfill needs and extend possibilities for all formalist and structuralist schools of criticism. When Computer Criticism takes its logical place in the development of twentieth-century criticism, more computer-using critics will probably choose to stay in literary studies.

Whether in the future or now, according to Smith, one of the major implications of Computer Criticism is

> an altered concept of proof and what constitutes demonstration of a literary hypothesis. Because the computer requires coherent, formal rules/procedures to move from level to level within its stratified structure, abstract assertions remain closely linked to, if not coincident with, patterns within higher strata. Since a study progresses by developing successively higher strata in terms of patterns within lower strata, generalizations, no matter how abstract, can be traced back through the various levels to actual textual features and/or to closely observed primary responses. (39)

The close link between the text and the proof of a literary hypothesis described by Smith means that new critical concepts, like "pervasiveness and adequacy," can be tested before assertions are made. As Smith says:

in addition to offering confirming examples, the critic may indicate the pervasiveness of that feature or pattern; by offering a comprehensive description of the features considered for the particular focus of the study (for example, a comprehensive list of themes for a thematic analysis), the critic may address the question of adequacy of a particular assertion with regard to any specific combination of features. Thus, the computer offers the critic additional verificational concepts through its ability to address the entire text synchronically. (39)

Verification, though not a concept new to literary criticism, certainly represents a shift in focus away from brilliance of insight and assertion toward the detailed testing of scientific experimentation. Since the computer can both find and count all occurrences (and map areas of non-occurrences) of particular features, inductive proofs based on example are more typical than more traditional deductive proofs from authority (e.g., of earlier critics or one's own responses). Objective treatments of texts frequently involve not only finding examples of features, but also counting them and comparing the results with known facts about language. Things counted produce sums; the existence of new sums encourages comparison with other sums; statistical analysis follows almost inevitably. Only the presence of critical judgment saves the research from veering off into number juggling. It is easy to see why the linking of a text-centered criticism with a numbers-based analysis is not common. The usual impact of numbers on texts is reductionist. All of the beautiful specificity of figures of speech can get lost when each detail is represented by a number. A balance must be carefully maintained between acquired scientific methods and critical values.

A precise study of the language of literature results in two different levels of insight: the confirming and the redefining. Computing critics find it reassuring to discover that counting and analyzing features of texts very frequently leads to the confirmation of insights that other critics have presented. One would, however, be suspicious of this kind of evidence if it were all that was found; one might rightly wonder whether the researchers might simply be ransacking the texts to find proofs for their favorite positions. One need have no such suspicions when confirming insights are balanced by redefining ones.

The writers of the essays collected here routinely draw inferences from the data that would not have been predictable without the minute attention to detail made possible by the technology. Once formulated by the push of the data, these insights redirect researchers to new structural understanding of the text, the genre, or the period. (Readers interested in examples of this phenomenon should notice particularly the essays by John Smith, Paul Fortier, Nancy Ide, Julia Waggoner, and Rosanne Potter.) These previously unconceived directions can then be confirmed by the scientific test of replication in another sample. (Readers interested in replication would be especially interested in the essays by Donald Ross, Jr., Barbara Stevenson, and Joel Goldfield.) The tendency to be directed by the data lures computing critics on in their search for explanations of how literary texts work. The contributors to this collection know that new and valid insights emerge from each new test and each new sample; since we are all critics, we also know that some of these insights are more important than others.

THE AUDIENCE FOR THIS BOOK

This book is addressed to two kinds of researchers. The first, and by far the larger, group are those literary critics who have considered computing as a method of answering significant factual questions. They may not have followed this impulse because they consider themselves mathematically or technologically incompetent. These critics may check into the existence of concordances to their primary texts, and probably know that computers are being used for various large editing jobs (the Jefferson papers, for example), but are not interested either in creating a concordance or in constructing a critical edition; they imagine, therefore, that the computer can do nothing to advance their work. If they have ever wanted the evidence to support a position they "knew" was true about a text, if they have ever wondered what would emerge if they could look at all the instances of "something" in a work, these critics are leaning toward computing.

This book is also addressed to a much smaller group, those computer critics who have become so involved in computing as an end in itself that they have forgotten their original critical aims. Many readers of criticism do not know what can be done with computing because, until now, most literary users of computer technology have not written the essays they could have written about their work. Beautifully clear essays about literary critical data have gone unwritten because of the necessity of using a generally accepted scientific style to meet the standards of reviewers (usually specialists in fields other than literary criticism) at the journals interested in computer research. As a result, many computer critics have written themselves out of the range of their natural audiences. We, the contributors to this volume, hope to prove to these computer-using writers that high standards of objective text-handling can be maintained while writing accessible essays.

To meet the needs of both groups, each of the essays included here formulates the kind of questions that could easily be raised by any intelligent reader about a text. Each essay describes where the critic began, what knowledge was sought, why the decision was made to use computational methods. These matters may be brought up at the outset or raised as needed; regardless, the main body of each essay presents the critical insights made possible by using the power of computing.

THE STRUCTURE OF THE BOOK

This collection consists of twelve pieces: reprints of classic essays written in the late 1970s by three of the founding fathers in this field; and new essays written in 1987/88 by nine contemporary researchers, some well known and some just beginning in the field of computational criticism. The essays have been selected on the basis of several important principles: they treat authors (except for Gobineau) whose writings will be familiar to most readers; they treat texts from French, English, and American literature; they represent a variety of theoretical frameworks, and approach their texts looking for a variety of features—semantic and thematic, syntactic and rhetorical; they make assertions about genres, periods, authors, or individual works. They have been written under very strict stylistic guidelines: intelligibility and readability have counted more than the authority provided by dense statistical and linguistic terminology. Most of these writers cite their earlier published works; statisticians and linguists will find the rigorous descriptions of processes in those essays or (in briefer form) in the appendices.

The essays are arranged in three categories: those on theory, especially hypothesis testing; those on theme, all of which proceed from some form of semantic analysis; and those on rhetoric, all of which depend on syntactic analysis. It was not obvious when I began soliciting and inviting essays in the general field of literary criticism that they would fall into these categories. I had expected some broadly descriptive essays on the qualities of different genres or periods (having myself written essays in the early eighties about the qualities of syntax in drama across an eighty-year period), but at the moment most critics who are doing serious literary computing are contrasting one or two writers, comparing two or three works by the same author, or concentrating on one work at a time. The most extreme example of the present-day concentration on one author is J. F. Burrows's 1987 book on Jane Austen's novels, *Computation into Criticism* (Oxford: Clarendon Press), a 255-page book complete with sixteen tables, thirty-three graphs and two figures on

> eight personal pronouns, six auxiliary verb forms, five prepositions, three conjunctions, the definite and indefinite articles, and four other words ('to', 'that', 'for', and 'all'). (1)

Following patterns established in the earliest computer-assisted author-attribution studies, Burrows's concentration on function words proves once again how critically revealing this approach can be when applied to a known author. Although very different from the thematic or rhetorical focus of the contributors to this volume, Burrows's work shows that much of critical interest can be derived from the study of what may seem to be empty words.

Richard Bailey, John Smith, Donald Ross, and Barbara Stevenson provide a critical, historical, and statistical background for the essays that follow. Bailey and Smith place the field of computational stylistics or computer criticism in the context of earlier schools of criticism; Ross provides an example of how objective critical tools enabled the evaluation of previous scholarship; Stevenson provides both some basic information about the terminology of statistical analysis and some cogent warnings about the uses of this methodology by critics. Paul Fortier, Joel Goldfield, and Nancy Ide, the writers interested in thematic analysis here, collect and map the occurrences of words across several works (or one long work) by one or more writers. They then draw their conclusions either from contrasts of image density at crucial moments in the plots or from comparisons of similar patterns across works. Julia Waggoner, Eugene Green, Eunice Merideth, Ruth Sabol, and I, the writers involved in one way or another with rhetorical analysis, look for syntactic features and focus on speech, reported speech, or narrative voice in an attempt to see how the manner of expression influences judgments of characters by readers. This structuring of the essays makes the book readable not only on an essay-by-essay or author-by-author basis, but also in sections, or from cover to cover.

Following are detailed descriptions of the essays that also identify those which are accessible to novices, as well as those which are predicated on some statistical knowledge.

THE ESSAYS

The collection begins with Richard Bailey's classic analysis of "The Future of Computational Stylistics," originally published by the *Association for Literary and Linguistic Computing Bulletin* in 1979. Bailey divides "applications of the computer to problems of style" into three generic types: those that focus on data retrieval, those that attempt to construct models, and those that formulate explicit hypotheses and test them against empirical evidence. These divisions allow him to discuss the imminent demise of concordance-building as an ultimate product of research, the limitations of Markovian models in literary criticism, and the problems with a potential "scientific poetics." Bailey's wide reading in various schools of criticism allows him to place each kind of application in an historical context of scholarship and criticism. This essay both summarizes the most important achievements of computer-using scholars until 1978 and points out, with amazing prescience, the directions that computational stylistics would follow in the next ten years.

John B. Smith's "Computer Criticism" (cited by Bailey and published in *Style* [Fall 1978]) specifies that the exact link between computer criticism and the major schools of criticism of this century is their common concept of structure: "the notion of a horizontal, material text over which various abstract strata are projected." Early in the essay Smith explains how the text appears to the computer and what this means for the builder of lexicons and concordances or the collator of variant texts. Those new to computing should certainly read this part of the essay. Smith uses examples from his own work to demonstrate various increasingly complicated ways of representing frequency data, relationships between themes, and distribution of thematic clusters across whole works by using ever more sophisticated statistical analysis. He asserts that once critics make "the conceptual move to consider the text from a functional point of view and to consider 'meaning' as originating from the reader's interaction with features and patterns within that text" they are ready for "the variety of relational possibilities" offered by computing. The conclusion focuses briefly on his reasons for seeing Computer Criticism "as an emerging school in its own right." In an addendum, Smith also gives a demonstration of the kinds of questions that critics must ask, and answer, to probe their own assertions and assumptions and translate them into the very explicit definitions that computers demand. This addendum should be read by anyone trying to focus insights into precisely formulated, answerable questions. For readers new to computer criticism, Bailey's and Smith's broad accounts of the field in general are meant to serve as orientations before plunging into an early example of practical computer criticism.

Donald Ross's classic "Differences, Genres, and Influences" (also published in *Style* [Summer, 1977]) argues for developing a history of styles, an account of how texts were written at various times. This call for a broad-based account of how language has been used during different periods and within different genres, has not yet produced the sort of research in English that Ross hoped for. (French analysts of style, as we shall see, are much closer to what Ross envisioned.) In this essay Ross clarifies what would be required; he describes what kinds of instruments would have to be devised before a true history of styles could be said to exist. As an example, Ross transcribed Josephine Miles's extensive surveys of English-language poetry to "computer cards and calculated various ratios, period averages, and other statistical relationships to suggest how word-class data can help with the history of style." Ross has charted these relationships into very readable figures that pack a great deal of syntactic information into a small space; they merit detailed study by anyone interested in syntactic changes over time in English-language poetry. Ross draws attention to the difficulties of building up a history of styles from many accounts of smaller data sets. He insists that though these accounts must be provisional, they can be revised as more information becomes available if the presentations "have complete data so that other specialists may build on previous work without duplication."

Many writers on the subject of computational stylistics argue that we will not have a standard for measuring the styles of individual authors until we can describe the stylistic characteristics of all written language. Others acknowledge the truth of this assertion but, wishing to do research in the meantime, avoid this problem by describing the imagery, themes, linguistic characteristics, or syntax of a limited number of texts by one or two writers. Those who work in fields like French studies (where important external tools like frequency dictionaries exist) can measure an author's stylistic deviations from standards established for specific periods and genres. Basic differences of scope exist between working inductively up to generalizations from examples within a small corpus and working deductively down from generalizations about language to inferences about an author. The choice of methodology to follow depends in large measure, though not completely, on whether basic facts about the language have been systematized in generally accepted research tools; critics obviously cannot choose to use a frequency dictionary if none exists for their language. Nevertheless, I see considerable value in both inductive and deductive approaches, and include exponents of both.

Barbara Stevenson starts "Adapting Hypothesis Testing to a Literary Problem" with a provocative question: whether the "marriage of statistics and literary criticism, known as computational stylistics, does work." Stevenson discusses adapting statistical hypothesis testing to the literary problem of authorship attribution. She begins by giving a brief summary of the history of stylometric studies; the summary mentions both specific stages in the development of stylometry and principles that should guide such study. Stevenson focuses on the proper ways, given the qualities of language, to form an hypothesis, to collect random data from the population to be tested, to select a test that fits the data, and to understand how the commonly used chi-square test works. The essay ends by proposing some solutions to the problems raised by trying to treat language data as if they were independent. Stevenson describes how simulation studies on the numbers generated from literary texts might lead to more dependable results, but her essay closes with a call for skepticism. This essay confronts the potential problems inherent in the most common of statistical tests, chi-square analysis, and as such should be enlightening to all critics interpreting, or attempting to use, statistical tests in literary computing.

Paul Fortier's "Analysis of Twentieth-Century French Prose Fiction: Theoretical Context, Results, Perspective" situates his work in the context of new theories of literature of the past twenty-five years. All of Fortier's writings since the early 1970s have been designed to analyze the process whereby a novel produces its effect on the reader. Fortier uses the computer to foster more objectivity in the study of fiction, but as a critic he is firmly in control of the end product through his personal judgment. The computer, with its ability to compare texts and synonym dictionaries, to calculate frequencies and distribution, adds new information, but Fortier asks traditional questions like "How is literary effect achieved?" He takes from psychological criticism an interest in repeated images and use of vocabulary to evoke common themes like death and warmth; however, he uses the gathered information not to reconstruct the author's subconscious but (once the thematic structure of the text has been identified) to deduce how theme and other formal characteristics of the text like plot and characterization produce literary effects.

Joel Goldfield's essay, "Computational Thematics, a Selective Database, and Literary Criticism: Gobineau, Tic Words, and Riffaterre Revisited," enters the lists in a famous critical dispute between Leo Spitzer and Michael Riffaterre about the use and significance of "tic words" in the writings of Arthur de Gobineau. (Riffaterre defines "tic words" as "linguistic tips of a psychological iceberg"; they "repeat at striking frequencies.") Goldfield's purpose is to "refine and apply the quantitative aspect of Riffaterre's approach to another work by Gobineau to discover any significant quantitative and stylistic value in the tic word group." While presenting his work on Gobineau, Goldfield also discusses what he calls computational thematics: the building of an adequate textual base for thematic computing without having access to the entire machine-readable text. He explains how he decides what to include, how to group words into conceptual groups, how to test for their significant presence or absence, and how to interpret the results for use in literary criticism. Goldfield uses frequency data (from a frequency dictionary divided chronologically by genre) as a standard against which to measure major repetitions or omissions within and between the six novellas contained in Gobineau's *Nouvelles asiatiques*. He demonstrates with great specificity how the statistical tests work on the tic word data.

Readers who already know basic statistical terminology, or who have read Barbara Stevenson's extremely useful explanation of the chi-square test, will recognize many of the terms assumed by Goldfield's work (null hypothesis, expected vs. observed, significance level). Goldfield's essay moves to a somewhat more complicated statistical level when he applies the central limit theorem to what he calls "phatic" and "emphatic" word data. This research, along with that of Ross and Stevenson, exemplifies the ways in which earlier critical disputes can be objectified applying the scientific standard of replication. Goldfield accepts Riffaterre's intuitive collection of tic words so that he can submit it to rigorous testing against newly available information about the characteristics of literary speech in Gobineau's period. This essay exemplifies Ross's description of how a history of styles is built up; earlier insights by Riffaterre are here revised in light of newly available information about literary language used in the period 1850–79. Ross, Stevenson, and Goldfield all build on the work of earlier scholars by demonstrating what statistical analysis can add to our understanding of its validity.

Nancy Ide's "Meaning and Method: Computer-Assisted Analysis of Blake" begins the concentration on English-language literature that characterizes the balance of the book; the essay's thematic focus, however, connects it to the earlier essays on French literature. The statistical level achieved here (even though much has been submerged for this presentation of Ide's Blake data) is the most sophisticated in this collection. The essay defines the critical issues by focusing on a basic anomaly of *The Four Zoas:* the "fragmentary and often transitionless narrative of the poem" does not prevent readers, even those unfamiliar with Blake's symbols, from having a clear perception of what the poem is about. Ide finds that a close investigation of Blake's images, their frequencies, and their distribution across the poem reveals broader semantic patterns which uncover the real shape of this long prophetic work. When it became clear that images related to specific themes appear at decided points in the poem, Ide could assert that they act as significant vehicles for conveying meaning in the poem. The patterns of distribution also collectively reveal configurations which differ from standard critical descriptions of the structure of the poem. Frequency distributions and statistical measures show distinct patterns of density that provide evidence for a five-part rather than the traditionally accepted three-part structure of the poem. What is clear from this study is that thematic analysis based on the frequencies of images can reveal organizational principles in a literary work. Thus, highly sophisticated statistical analysis enables a kind of insight into structure that was not previously possible. This analysis, like all the others described in this collection, was not automated. At each stage the researcher as critic must intervene, deciding what to make of the evidence accumulated and what the tests reveal that the researcher knows to be true about the text, even as the tests uncover facts that were previously unnoticed.

Before moving from the essays on theme by Smith, Fortier, Goldfield, and Ide, we should note that all four focus on word-level data. Since words are discrete, very sophisticated statistical analysis can be applied to the numbers generated by counting them; equally sophisticated graphic representations of the number of occurrences can also be drawn against a stable line representing the length of a text. On the other hand, the essays on rhetoric by Waggoner, Green, Merideth, Sabol, and Potter look at sentence-level data. Some syntactical features, since they are also tied to simple markers (like the word "that" in nominal complement *that*-clauses or the question mark in questions), present no more challenge to computer searching than any other single string of characters. Other features that have clear markers, for instance negatives in English, can be handled with the aid of some rather complex searching procedures. One can define all the letter combinations that usually indicate negating (*no, un-, non-, -n't, dis-, in-,* etc.), then cover the words where the prefix is not a negative (like "unity" or "infuse") with a stopword list, and come out fairly close to the mark. Imperatives and other features that can take many forms present either a massive challenge for a parsing program or a minor bit of hand-encoding drudgery. Eventually, those who devote all their energies to computer analysis of language will devise methods for automatic text parsing. In the meantime, most computer-assisted critics do not expect artificial intelligence to find most of the syntactic features easily recognized using human intelligence. These critics just type the text into the computer's memory along with specific markers for each complex syntactic feature.

The most important difference between the word-level critics interested in thematics and the sentence-level critics interested in rhetoric is that words are easier to define than sentences, so the numbers are firmer on one side of the divide than on the other. The essays about semantic or thematic issues tend to rely on statistical analysis and graphic representation more than the essays about syntactic or speech-act issues, which rely on discussions of the rhetorical dimensions of attributed speech or narrative discourse.

The difficulty in syntactical parsing of texts has resulted in various *faute de mieux* methods of finding the particular items sought by different critics. At the simplest level one encodes only the sentences containing the items sought; more sophisticated methods include either selecting from the items found by preexisting software or designing one's own software. Eugene Green uses the first solution— essentially hand-encoding; Ruth Sabol follows the second, using concordance programs designed at the University of Wisconsin. My students, Julia Waggoner and Eunice Merideth, also follow this second method; they use programs and concepts designed at Iowa State University. However, Waggoner uses no statistical tests, and Merideth uses statistical methods different from those in the package. Designing programs to find exactly, and only, what the individual critic seeks, as I have done, might seem to be the final stage in gaining control over the computer's output. It is only the beginning. Other, far more complicated linguistic coding of language, of course, can be done. However, thus far only linguists and others interested in the characteristics of language as language have devoted themselves to these heavily labor-intensive, abstract codings word by word as they are typed into computer memory. Though these five critics use substantially different approaches to the stylistic features that interest them, they only *begin* to present all the ways of performing rhetorical analysis with syntactic features.

Julia Waggoner's "*Samson Agonistes:* Milton's Use of Syntax to Define Character" concentrates on Milton's methods of using syntax to define Samson, and to differentiate him from all the other characters, especially Dalila. Although Waggoner does not move beyond simple numerical analysis, she finds that the concepts derived from my research on syntax in modern drama can be applied to a very much earlier literature's methods of defining character in a poem. A close analysis of the lines found and sorted by the computer allows Waggoner to see previously unnoticed aspects of how Milton creates character. Waggoner assumes that Samson is dominant; she then looks at the syntax that usually correlates with dominance. Her work elucidates the techniques used by Milton to define Samson as a weak, demoralized character and then turn him into a strong, heroic character. In the process of her investigation, she discovers exactly where the software does not adequately provide for certain qualities of Milton's syntax. His sentence length does not easily fit into the defined units designed for the shorter sentences of twentieth-century drama. Milton's extremely high use of definitions, and his almost nonexistent use of fragments and pauses, also point to stylistic qualities of seventeenth-century dramatic poetry; these byproducts of her research could be investigated in follow-up work.

Waggoner's work demonstrates that literary critics can use the insights of pre-existing software packages to approach texts in new and revealing ways. By borrowing simple techniques for rearranging text and an already-proven concept (like the correlation between dominance and a cluster of syntax), Waggoner can make quite interesting assertions about a text without any knowledge of or support from statistical analysis. This essay, designed for Miltonists, should also encourage critics contemplating the move from traditional stylistic analysis to computational stylistics.

Eugene Green's "Speech Acts and the Art of the Exemplum in the Poetry of Chaucer and Gower" contrasts "force of expression" in carefully matched exempla from *Confessio Amantis, The Legend of Good Women, The Man of Law's Tale, The Physician's Tale,* and *The Wife of Bath's Tale.* After gathering sentences with potential speech act verbs, Green carefully distinguished genuine speech acts from inapplicable verbs and built a database of commands, promises, and requests. In order to build the database, Green had to code the entries as performative verbs, imperatives, and miscellaneous verb phrases (which function as speech acts). Encoding the speech act verbs forced Green to make difficult choices and to begin forming rules about what constitutes a command, promise, or request. Even though he did not, in this round, expect the computer to find these speech act verbs in the texts, he began to make attempts at defining the forms of Middle English words that would have to be sought if a program were to do the syntactic searching. After computer sorting of the sentences into groups, Green applied statistical analysis and found that the poets' instances of commands, promises, and requests yield no significant differences. His analysis, however, abetted by computer sorting, enables him to find that, within their comparable exempla, Chaucer and Gower vary significantly in their modes of expressing speech acts. In instances of deception, in moments depicting a woman at risk or in search of a goal, or during the utterance of an apostrophe, Chaucer relies primarily on the direct expression of a speech act, while Gower prefers to report it. Green closes by generalizing about the relationships between the two stylistic patterns and the poets' separate moral and aesthetic perspectives.

Eunice Merideth's essay, "Gender Patterns in Henry James: A Stylistic Approach to Dialogue in *Daisy Miller, The Portrait of a Lady,* and *The Bostonians,*" demonstrates that a study of simple syntax can reveal gender differences between characters in a piece of fiction. Merideth chose these three novels centered on women to avoid the predictable strength of men in major roles and weakness of females in minor roles. She contrasts the speech of the major female character and that of the minor male character who interacts with her. Merideth starts with the assumption that socially defined gender characteristics correlate with assigned speech habits. Chi-square analysis shows significant differences between male and female use of the features which correlate with dominance. The speech of males is direct, clear, and commanding; that of females is weak and submissive. The three novels chosen for this study feature thematically strong women (James calls them heroines), yet the language assigned to them tells quite a different story. Their speech is polite and uncertain, while the men, all secondary characters, use the language of dominance. The sorted lists of dialogue produced by the programs also provide Merideth with evidence about semantic features that emerge in a contrast of male and female self-definitions.

C. Ruth Sabol's "Reliable Narration in *The Good Soldier*" uses three products of the Wisconsin Old Spanish Dictionary Project to test the reliability of Ford Madox Ford's narrator. Her assertions, grounded in the work of theoretical linguists like Paul and Carol Kiparsky, Marc Rosenberg, and Deirdre Wilson, depend on linguistic evidence garnered from a concordance, a verbal index, and a field of reference. She proves that Dowell, the narrative voice in the novel, is a reliable narrator by analyzing eleven situations where Dowell uses nominal complement *that*-clauses; this analysis contrasts the level of factual knowledge asserted by Dowell with other information coming to readers from the implied author. This study provides a method, no longer based on intuitive judgments, for deciding whether a narrator is reliable or unreliable; the availability of computer evidence gathering, in combination with a linguistic system for categorizing the factive or world-creating qualities of verbs, has made this objective study possible. As Sabol says, "only a thorough semantic analysis of the truth conditions of a narrator's assertions can give a reader hard evidence of a narrator's reliability or unreliability."

Since concordances may be the computer-generated tool most commonly available, many critics will find the computer criticism practiced by Sabol quite accessible. Using a concordance does not require learning programming or statistical analysis; it necessitates only a guiding theoretical framework, which provides a clear sense of what information is sought, and a willingness to seek the words that signal the possible sources of evidence. As it happens, Sabol has a great deal of technical experience, but in her essay the application of rhetorical terms from Wayne Booth and of truth-condition terms from the theoretical linguists is far more basic to the argument than her knowledge of the scientific disciplines. What computing offers to this kind of criticism is a certainty that no evidence is being missed; previous intuitive criticism could not be absolutely sure.

My own essay, "Changes in Shaw's Dramatic Rhetoric: *Mrs. Warren's Profession, Major Barbara,* and *Heartbreak House,*" is a longitudinal study of plays written in 1893, 1905, and 1916. I assert as a critical first principle that Shaw has problems with resolutions. The research looks at the ways Shaw uses the elements of length (of scenes and of acts), of cast size (per play and per scene), and of syntax (assigned to characters) to end his plays more successfully. The central concept that emerged from my earlier study of twenty-one English-language first acts was that dominance was both the character trait most clearly correlated to syntactical choices and the one most clearly recognizable by readers. The second part of the essay applies this insight to an understanding of how the rhetoric works—or fails to work—on audiences in the crucial scenes in each of the three plays. This essay is about the kinds of things that become visible about Shaw's stagecraft if one begins to look at representative texts functionally, as Smith has put it, "considering 'meaning' as originating from the reader's interaction with features and patterns in the text." (31)

One of the clearest conclusions to draw from all these essays is that the current state of computational stylistics reveals many laborers tilling their own fields deeply rather than attempting to look across many fields to make generalizations about genres or periods. All of these critics are primarily interested in specific works by specific authors. We are dealing here not with computer scientists showing off what the machine can do, nor with statisticians choosing random samples to make generalizations about how language works, but with critics pursuing literary questions with the aid of computer text analysis and, frequently, using statistical analysis as a second new tool.

A COMMON SCIENTIFIC CONTEXT

We, the contributors to this volume, have all had the experience of finding both what we were looking for and what we did not expect. To my way of thinking, this common experience shows that we are in the artful world of original scientific experimentation. Like chemists who carefully construct their series of successively excluding tests only to make their greatest discoveries inadvertently, we place ourselves in an overall context of carefully designed experiments and then look at the results until a pattern coalesces before our eyes. Paying attention, being willing to reformulate hypotheses when the evidence leads in new directions, and following what at first appear to be only threads of inferences until they become tightly woven patterns—these are the mental requirements for literary critics who wish to recognize the new knowledge that computer treatments of texts can reveal.

Literary criticism may be at a crossroads, a moment when vision is extended into scientific areas, not just to ransack them for useful metaphors but to use their ways of seeing in order to see better *what literary critics are interested in seeing.* This last point is crucial, crucial because it is so often lost in the excitement of seeing what statisticians see. What we need is a principled use of technology and criticism to form a new kind of literary study absolutely comfortable with scientific methods yet completely suffused with the values of the humanities. That is what this collection of essays attempts to offer readers.

Oxford, England
April 18, 1988

>> *Part I*

THEORY AND HYPOTHESIS TESTING

>> 1

The Future of
Computational Stylistics*

R I C H A R D   W.   B A I L E Y

It is a real pleasure for me to have the opportunity to speak this morning at King's College, partly because I am glad to join you in recognizing the important work that Professor Roy Wisbey has accomplished here, and partly because it gives us an occasion to recall the research done at King's in the 1950s by Maurice Wilkins and Rosalind Franklin on the problem of the structure of DNA molecules. I would like to explore possible parallels between our humanistic enterprise in investigating language and literature with computer assistance and their inquiry into a purely scientific question of the biological and chemical basis of life. One parallel immediately presents itself in the role of apparatus in both kinds of research: Wilkins and Franklin could not have accomplished what they did without the development of X-ray diffraction techniques, and a great many things we now attempt in stylistics could not be sensibly undertaken without the help of the computer.

Let me give an example that will remind us of just how far we have come in the quarter century of work with computers in our field. In early November of 1978, James Joyce and John Nitti arranged an exhibit of machines at the annual meeting of the Midwest Modern Language Association in Minneapolis. Part of the display was designed to illustrate the work of the Hispanic Seminary of Medieval Studies at the University of Wisconsin, and Professor Nitti provided a demonstration that excited many of the scholars who attended the meeting: it began with a standard electric typewriter equipped with an optical character element, continued with a reader processing the typed pages of transcript from manuscripts with the lines of input successively displayed on an adjoining CRT terminal, and ended with the processed text (in concordance form) stored in a bank of microfiche and selected by fiche and image number either by manual retrieval through a sequence of addressing keys or by automated means through programs in a central processor. One of the visitors to the display, a young assistant professor with a degree from a major university in the United States, regarded the equipment with considerable interest and understanding. When she finally reached the end of the row of machines, she told us that she wished a friend of hers could know of such techniques. He is still at work on a dissertation, she said, in which he is preparing a concordance to the prolific writings of a contemporary author *by hand!*

What a sad story! No one should be awarded a graduate degree for such donkey work, and the circumstances that allow such a project to be undertaken without the routine assistance of a computer suggest that at least some academic advisors are morally culpable in their ignorance of the present state of the art in our field. To encourage students to waste their intellectual abilities in this way is profoundly wrong.

Unlike this graduate student, Wilkins and Franklin were fully aware of the most current technology, and Franklin improved the diffraction technique until she could produce the clearest pictures then made of the DNA molecule. As a biochemist has pointed out to me, their work was made possible because the structure of inquiry in their field was then, as now, hierarchical. By common consent, molecular biologists in Europe and America decided to concentrate their varied energies on a particular set of bacteriophages, and hence the results that were derived in various laboratories enabled information to accumulate progressively toward a solution of the problem of the structure of DNA and the means by which genetic information is replicated. A prior condition for such cooperation was laid in the agreement by the leading scientists in the field, Sir Lawrence Bragg, Linus Pauling, and Max Delbrück, that the question of the molecular structure of DNA was ripe for investigation and that the tools of inquiry were available to allow worthwhile speculations to be made. Some of these tools, such as special X-ray machines and centrifuges to isolate molecules of DNA were mechanical, and some, like the mathematical techniques through which it is possible to interpret the varying angles of reflection of the X-rays bouncing off the DNA specimens, were intellectual. The task of the scientists was thus concentrated on making the best use of available equipment and knowledge; the real intellectual work of science could proceed because good minds devoted themselves hierarchically to the problems involved.[1]

I would like to believe that computational stylistics is approaching a similar state of readiness for a parallel kind of essential discovery about the nature of literary language, and it is certainly true that we have available some very powerful techniques for analysis. But certain elements apparent in the research investigating the structure of DNA are clearly lacking. Computational stylistics, for one thing, is not usefully hierarchical, and there is no general agreement about the kinds of problems that should become the focus of our collective attention. Our machinery is powerful enough to make rapid measurements and computations at a reasonable cost, and many brilliant scholars spend at least part of their time engaged in making intelligent use of what is already known. Yet there is hardly any agreement about either proximate or ultimate goals, and perhaps too little rigorous criticism of the applications that have been made or are now proposed.

Application of the computer to problems of style can be conveniently divided into three generic types: one in which data retrieval is primary, a second in which models (or fragments of models) are constructed, and a third in which explicit hypotheses are formulated and tested against empirical evidence. For the most part, our achievements have been in the first of these domains, and dozens of research projects in Europe and North America make efficient use of large bodies of data as an adjunct to the production of dictionaries, linguistic atlases, variorum editions, and the other conventional products of scholarship that can now be carried out more thoroughly and carefully than ever before. Essential as these works are to the field of language and literature, they occupy the same place as do their hand-made predecessors, merely an adjunct and aid to the real work of criticism.

We continue to assume that the computer gives the scholar a powerful lever to multiply the force of intelligence against the resistant material of interpretation. Our harmless electronic drudges ought to free us for an intellectual engagement with the text, or at least enable us to carry on that work with greater perspicacity and thoroughness. No one could doubt that Spevack's concordance to Shakespeare is immeasurably superior to Bartlett's or that the Ingram and Swain concordance to Milton's English poetry is vastly better than Bradshaw's. Yet these better tools have not made us better workers. Concordances and similar works, after all, provide for only a restricted, though respectable, set of critical problems. The first of these involve external filiations of a text, studies of sources and influences; the second, internal matters of structure. Both profit immensely from a convenient data retrieval system. But the kind of research that can be carried out with the aid of such a system is limited and very often tangential to the major preoccupations of literary scholars and critics. If we project into the future the needs of scholarship for more such systems, it seems reasonable to assume that the demand for them is nearly satisfied. Most of the major authors in English and American literature and all of the texts of Old English and Ancient Greek are now supplied, even though there is considerable variation in the quality of the finished products. The use of the computer for making such automated data systems will wither away once we have encoded every author and text of interest to scholars. In fact, it seems reasonable to predict that in ten years no more concordances and textual data bases will be produced as terminal products of research.[2]

The presumptive use of concordances involves a primitive approach to the internal structure of literary texts. Concordances and word indexes, after all, are essentially first-order rearrangements of texts based on the occurrence of lemmas. All of the intellectual work must be provided by the user in one of two forms: the first, an analysis of various senses of key words as a clue to distinctive meaning in the text (for example "good" in *Paradise Lost*) derived from our identification of important themes and ideas in a work and verified by matching and counting instances of a given lemma or set of lemmas; and the second, the creation of a map to the patterns of meaning manifested by the repetition of words or words from a semantic set (for example, all the words that articulate water imagery in *The Tempest*). Such uses of computer-generated tools assist in the formulation of discoveries not otherwise easily made, discoveries like Caroline Spurgeon's that Shakespeare associates dogs with candy or verification of more exciting interpretations of image patterns like those found in Cleanth Brooks's analysis of *Macbeth* in *The Well-Wrought Urn*. Of course concordances and indexes are not necessary to such efforts, but they reduce the labor of exploring nascent ideas about the text and assist scholars in verifying more mature ones. Concordances provide useful help, and if the need for the critic to hold all of the text in mind is not much reduced by them, at least they make it possible to explore an intuition that might otherwise necessitate a laborious and error-prone multiple re-reading of the text.[3] Yet such tools belong to an earlier and more innocent day of literary research. Though they have their origins in antiquity, the modern interest in their preparation arose in the mid-nineteenth century, first as a result of the "higher criticism" of the Bible and then, by extension, to the texts of classical antiquity and finally to modern literature. The concordance (and similar aids) are limited in their application, not so specific that we can use them only to explore water imagery or parallel passages, but not so general that they bear usefully on a wide range of critical questions, ones having to do with substance and purport as well as usage and form.

Much more interesting for stylistics than data retrieval systems is the growth of model building in literary study generally, though perhaps only a few scholars would recognize that their criticism constitutes such an activity. In fact, many critics like to pretend that their observations are shaped by texts alone, not by theoretical assumptions about the nature of literary language. Yet no observations in the humanities or the sciences are free of presuppositions, and the implicit theories of the past have now been articulated in works like Frye's *Anatomy of Criticism* or Hirsch's *Validity in Interpretation*. It is not surprising that computer-assisted criticism mirrors these theories, and much of what has been accomplished recalls the innovative methods of I. A. Richards and his followers in the movement toward the "close reading" of texts that excited young scholars half a century ago. As Susan Wittig has recently pointed out, "the computer as an adjunct in literary analysis has been used consistently within what we are beginning to recognize as the limited conceptual framework of New Criticism."[4] Since New Criticism was implicitly formal, it is no surprise that it is now being made explicitly so with the assistance of the computer.

"Close reading" derives, as Wittig says, from a view of the text as a linear string of words and patterns. It presumes a Markovian model of reading, a process in which authors and interpreters move through a continually branching network of choices, *this* word and not these others; *this* filling of a metrical position and not others that are possible; *this* choice of a parallel syntactic structure rather than another. Though Markov models were persuasively rejected by Chomsky as inappropriate to the specification of linguistic competence, they may be quite useful in the analysis of the decoding of literary texts. The assumption of a Markov chain, in fact, is inherent in a whole variety of formalist-structuralist criticism: in the notion of defamiliarization of Russian formalism, its extension in the concept of "foregrounding" in the Prague School, and in the idea of varying degrees of surprise in the criticism of Riffaterre or Enkvist. The concordance and its natural uses depend largely on the notion of a text as an aggregate of repeating and varying elements, and the linear organization of the text is largely ignored except for occasional observations of the density or clustering of repetitions. Markov models, on the other hand, give primacy to the ordering of the text as a sequence of events, and the critic is obliged to add to a statement of segmentation and classification a description of the syntax of choices occurring one after another.

Only in a few instances have Markov models been explicitly developed in computer-assisted literary analysis, and in exploring them we may only be in the position of bringing critical insight from the late nineteenth into the early twentieth century. To accept the necessity for doing so is to condemn our criticism to re-living the intellectual past·and to making a stately progression toward the "limited conceptual framework of New Criticism" with a time-lag of about half a century. But groping our way through this past may not be an entirely useless enterprise. Formalist-structuralist criticism does provide a relatively explicit model subject to automation in which the syntagmatic chain and the associative relations that bear on choices within it are susceptible to formal definition. A fully developed model of this kind would represent the text as a linear sequence with distinctive syntactic rules into the slots of which are inserted elements selected from the network of associations that derive from the patterns offered by the language of a given time. Its simulation by computer would be no mean or unrewarding achievement.

For such an enterprise to succeed, we need to learn a great deal about a variety of related fields that have much to offer computational stylistics, even though formal models in many of them are partial and tentative. Artificial intelligence, for instance, is a domain of study with evident bearing on literary analysis, particularly that branch concerned with "knowledge representation," but a brief extract from a recent research report sufficiently indicates both the ambitions and the present condition of the field.

> We are in the position of attempting to codify all the knowledge of the world. . . . It is our belief that the best way to get at such knowledge is to forge ahead by creating primitives, and subsequently testing these primitives for their use as the basis of inference rules and as the basis for the development of understanding programs. We are currently working on developing a system of computer programs to understand newspaper headlines and stories based on the social ACTs and their respective inference rules.[5]

Evidently enough, mechanical models of "knowledge representation" are a long way from providing insight into the meaning of Dante or Shakespeare.

Nonetheless, there are other domains of study that offer more promising assistance, especially if we take a moment to define the organization of patterns that inhere in literary works. Some of these are linguistic: syntax, semantics, phonology, and text structure. Others derive from literary study: allusion, connotation, reference, and figuration. A third set emerges from psychology: mediation, sublimation, substitution, and transference. Presumably each of these strata of meaning has a distinctive organization subject to formalization by means of ordered rules, lattices, networks, fuzzy sets, directed graphs, catastrophe theory, or other schemes provided for our use by mathematics. As John B. Smith points out in an excellent survey of work in computer criticism, "the array of models or concepts of structure that the computer offers the critic as available analytic tools is truly stunning; the possibilities are limited only by our willingness to explore the unfamiliar".[6]

On the other hand, it would be a profound mistake to begin by searching out one or another of the proferred mathematical models to see what can be revealed about our subject. As Stephen Smale writes:

> Good mathematical models are not generated by mathematicians throwing models to sociologists, biologists, etc., for the latter to pick up and develop. . . . Good mathematical models don't start with the mathematics, but with a deep study of cer-

tain natural phenomena. Mathematical awareness or even sophistication is useful when working to model economic phenomena, for example, but a successful model depends much more on a penetrating study and understanding of the economics.[7]

Smale's warning applies even more forcefully to the study of language and literature where models and model building are relatively novel and often naive.

Is such a program of research reasonable and appropriate at this time? I believe that it is, and yet it cannot be realized without recalling that ours is an essentially humanistic enterprise. Colin Martindale has recently asserted that "computer studies of literature have been . . . rather atheoretical,"[8] and he suggests that "humanists are not trained to think in terms of operationalizing and measuring theoretical constructs."[9] In these claims, I believe that Martindale is largely correct, but it would be a mistake for proponents of the kind of "scientific poetics" he espouses to embrace his conclusion that "those who practice scientific poetics are—or ought to be—negative in their attitudes toward traditional humanism, since it in large part consists in the production of what from a positivist point of view can only be called nonsense."[10] Such a proposition does not contribute very usefully to ongoing discussion, particularly insofar as it distracts attention from the best products of traditional humanism, those that have added immeasurably to our understanding of literature however insufficiently "operationalized" and formalized they may be.

If one movement toward a scientific poetics suggests a narrowing of vision, another (that formulated in the Moscow-Tartu version of semiotics) ought to enlarge our concept of computational stylistics. Despite their many ramifications, the underlying principles of this approach to sign systems are not difficult to grasp, and they are well illustrated by excerpts from recent translation of major theoretical papers: "culture is information"[11]; "from the viewpoint of contemporary cybernetics and semiotics, man can be described as a mechanism that performs operations on signs and sign sequences"[12]; "man is a decipherer and proceeds from a natural disposition to regard any message as meaningful"[13]; "in every collective there exists some environmental norm in accordance with which a circle of semioticized facts is chosen and held in common by the collective"[14]; "a sign can only be an aesthetic sign in relation to a norm."[15] Ideas like these reflect basic points of consensus among Soviet semioticians and parallel other well-known trends in the analysis of symbolic behavior.

With proper use of formal modeling systems, semiotic approaches to culture, including the nature and function of literary language, are likely to profit from the use of the computer. Soviet semioticians have pointed to such possibilities for more than a decade, but they have been hampered by two factors: one, infrequent opportunities to make extensive use of powerful machines; and the other, an unfounded faith in the power of communication theory to provide the formalization of semiotic information. In their view, meaning is transmitted in discrete and sequential "bits" and modulated to reduce "entropy." Such an analogy is attractive in many respects, but it rests ultimately on the notion that "culture" is a well-defined set of discrete information systems invoked in the process of semiosis and open to explicit and exhaustive characterization by the investigator. In my view, communication theory does not constitute an adequate basis for empirical research.[16] Nonetheless, the theoreticians of the Moscow-Tartu school have made a major contribution to knowledge, particularly in their observations on the three types of relations that are central to the organization of meaning: "subtextual meanings, textual meanings, [and] functions of texts in a cultural system."[17]

Beyond the possibilities opened to us by efficient data retrieval and explicit modeling systems, computational stylistics has made successful use of hypothesis testing in ways that are instructive for traditional scholarship. In a sense, hypothesis testing emerges from the use of first-order rearrangements of literary and linguistic data, well illustrated in John B. Smith's maps of imagery in Joyce's *A Portrait of the Artist as a Young Man.*[18] By deriving graphic representations that resemble topographic maps, Smith is able to show the peaks and valleys of image clusters in Joyce's novel, at the same time confirming the traditional view of "epiphanies" in the novel and providing a three-dimensional model of the text space to help the reader "see" the literary work in a new way.

Other and more familiar instances of hypothesis-testing emerge in authorship studies or attempts to specify the chronology of an author's works. In this domain, computational stylistics has provided some of its most persuasive scholarship, and it is not surprising that studies of this kind have attracted the approbation of traditional scholars. One such case is illustrated by Daniel L. Greenblatt's use of metrical evidence to settle the authorship of the seventeenth-century English poem, "The Expostulation."[19] Another is found in Anthony Kenny's excellent study of Aristotle's *Ethics* and *Metaphysics*. It is worth noting, however, that Kenny's technique parallels that of Rudolf Eucken on the same problem in 1866. Because Eucken perforce relied on hand counts of Aristotle's particles and connectives and was so restricted by the "prevailing scholarly dogma," he lacked confidence in his results and was unable to solve the attribution problem.[20] Kenny succeeded where Eucken failed because he could rely on the computer to provide an exact inventory of features in a large body of data and could make use of statistical hypothesis-testing methods that were unavailable in the mid-nineteenth century. Such work is properly welcomed by humanists because it extends accepted methods and confirms the kind of hypothesis that is familiar in conventional scholarship.

As Michael Polanyi points out in *The Tacit Dimension,* our knowledge and even our view of framing questions about the natural world arises not from within ourselves (in the sense used by Plato in the *Meno*) but from the "society of explorers" to which we belong. The ALLC is such a society, but we need to do much more to make our studies hierarchical in the sense that Wilkins and Franklin belonged to a hierarchical in the sense that Wilkins and Franklin belonged to a hierarchical society devoted to the discovery of the structure of DNA. We need more agreement about the right kinds of questions to ask now, better understanding of the methods (both mechanical and intellectual) by which they may be answered, and greater cooperation among the colleagues whose various kinds of expertise in data management, model building, and hypothesis testing are essential to our success. Above all, we need to proceed from the achievements of humane scholarship in the past and reject counsel to construct an autonomous "scientific poetics" that cuts us off from our roots.

Notes

*This essay was originally presented at the Association for Literary and Linguistic Computing Fifth International Meeting, Friday, December 15, 1978, King's College, University of London; it appeared in the *ALLC Bulletin* 7 (1979):4–11.

1. L. D. Burnard regards a hierarchy as incompatible with humanistic scholarship. While grateful for his explanation of his views at the ALLC meeting, I believe that much humanistic research now presumes a hierarchy of increasing understanding and think that computer-assisted studies are especially dependent upon collaborative efforts toward the solution of well-defined problems.

2. In his address to the ALLC meeting, Professor R. Wisbey dissented vigorously from my prediction.

3. In discussion, Dr. P. Boyde (St. John's College, Cambridge) asserted that there are considerable personal insights to be gained from the hard work of enumerating features by hand. I share his belief and do not imagine that worthwhile results can be achieved without a profound knowledge of the texts we study.

4. Susan Wittig, "The Computer and the Concept of Text," *Computers and the Humanities* 11 (1978):211.

5. Roger C. Schank and Jaime G. Carbonell, Jr., *The Gettysburg Address: Representing Social and Political Acts* (New Haven, Conn.: Yale University Department of Computer Science, Research Report 127, 1978), 61.

6. John B. Smith, "Computer Criticism," *Style* 12 (1978):326–56; this volume Chapter 2.

7. Stephen Smale, Review of E. C. Zeeman, "Catastrophe Theory: Selected Papers, 1972–1977," *Bulletin of the American Mathematical Society* 84 (1978):1365. D. G. Higman was kind enough to bring this reference to my attention.

8. Colin Martindale, "Sit with Statisticians and Commit a Social Science: Interdisciplinary Aspects of Poetics," *Poetics* 7 (1978):276.

9. Martindale, 278.

10. Martindale, 280.

11. Ju. M. Lotman, "Problems in the Typology of Culture," in *Soviet Semiotics,* ed. Daniel P. Lucid (Baltimore: Johns Hopkins University Press, 1977), 213.

12. V. V. Ivanov, "The Role of Semiotics in the Cybernetic Study of Man and Collective," in *Soviet Semiotics,* 28.

13. Ibid., 32.

14. V. N. Toporov, "The Semiotics of Prophecy in Suetonius," in *Soviet Semiotics,* 158.

15. B. A. Uspenskij, "Semiotics of Art," in *Soviet Semiotics*, 172.

16. See Richard W. Bailey, "Maxwell's Demon and the Muse," *Dispositio* 1 (1976): 293–301.

17. Ju. M. Lotman and A. M. Pjatigorskij, "Text and Function," in *Soviet Semiotics*, 132.

18. In addition to the examples included in Chapter 2 of this volume, Smith's monograph on James Joyce illustrates a variety of image maps.

19. Daniel L. Greenblatt, "Generative Metrics and the Authorship of 'The Expostulation'," *Centrum* 1 (1973): 87–104.

20. Anthony Kenny, *The Aristotelian Ethics: A Study of the Relationship between the Eudemian and Nicomachean Ethics of Aristotle* (Oxford: Clarendon Press, 1978), 73. See also Kenny's "A Stylometric Study of Aristotle's Metaphysics," *ALLC Bulletin* 7 (1979): 12–21.

>> 2

Computer Criticism*

JOHN B. SMITH

Computer applications for language and literature studies have generally fallen into two major groups: those in which the computer was used to produce through textual manipulation conventional aids for future research (dictionaries, concordances, etc.) and those in which the computer was used in the actual analysis of specific works of literature (thematic analyses, stylistic studies, etc.). The former group has, in general, been viewed as beneficial or, at least, inevitable; the products that have resulted have been familiar and their value apparent. The latter group of applications has presented certain problems. These studies have often been based on initial assumptions that are unfamiliar and developed through techniques that seem more mathematical than literary.[1] In such cases the critic has had to supply an intellectual context for his study, relating it to conventional critical approaches, or risk losing his reader. Preferable to statements of context on an *ad hoc* basis would be a general awareness of the assumptions and methods inherent in computer-assisted studies of literature and the relations such studies have to major areas of conventional critical thought. Of greater consequence, however, would be the increased awareness of critics that this new critical methodology is available for use on a wide variety of problems. As late as 1973 Paul de Man wrote:

> It can legitimately be said . . . that, from a technical point of view, very little has happened in American criticism since the innovative work of New Criticism. There certainly have been numerous excellent books of criticism since, but in none of them

have the techniques of description and interpretation evolved beyond the techniques of close reading established in the thirties and forties.[2]

The computer, properly and sensitively applied, offers the literary critic a rich collection of new techniques that may help to meet de Man's challenge.

In the remarks that follow, I shall consider three aspects of computer studies of literature. I shall look at exactly what one does in using the computer to study language. I shall try to identify a mode of criticism that arises from using the computer, which I term *Computer Criticism*. Finally, I shall try to show that this mode of criticism is closely related to the major critical developments of this century.

Let me confess at the outset that I am uncomfortable with the term, *Computer Criticism*, for it suggests that somehow it is the computer that does the criticism. Nothing could be further from the truth. The role of the computer is to gather the information the critic asks for, to display or present the information, or to apply some analytic model to the information. As with any mode of criticism, assimilation and interpretation take place in the mind of the critic. One might argue that the computer is simply amplifying the critic's powers of perception and recall in concert with conventional perspectives. This is true, and some applications of the concept can be viewed as a lateral extension of Formalism, New Criticism, Structuralism, and so forth. On the other hand, when the computer is used extensively in an analysis it can influence the questions one asks of a text and the way one sees the text and its meanings. It is at this junction that the computer can lead to a linear, rather than lateral, extension of Formalist/Structuralist thought.

A survey of recent criticism is not necessary; however, since my thesis is based on the assumption of a particular pattern of development within twentieth-century criticism, I shall pause briefly to outline that perspective. In my view, the mainstream of recent critical thought has moved steadily, inexorably, toward greater formality and toward the notion of a "science" or "sciences" of criticism (these assertions are probably two sides of the same coin). In this country, the movement begins, at least in earnest, with the New Critics and their attempts to break criticism out of the philological mold, to remove the encumbrance of authorial intention (an epistemic impossibility), and to center the critical response on the language of the work itself. Similar intentions lie behind the earlier Russian Formalists. Concentrating more on linguistics, rather than on diction or rhetoric, they sought to distinguish the language of literature, viewed as a coherent system of linguistic traits, from other language/mental activities. They were most successful in their thematic studies (such as those of Propp), where their analyses really began after language per se was left behind and they were able to deal with the structure of symbols/categories derived from language. A necessary step toward formality is the awareness of the relativity of models or critical perspectives; this important step in the progression toward greater formality was provided by, among others, the Chicago Aristotelian critics. Stressing the necessity for critical pluralism, they liberated the work of literature from the particular critical statement just as the New Critics had liberated it from the author. More recently, Formalism has moved one step further in the Structuralists' view of a literary work, itself, as a semiotic structure. The full implications of regarding the literary work as a sequence of signs, as a material object, that is "waiting" to be characterized by external models or systems, have yet to be realized. Inherent is the possibility for defining content by formal rules of association, contiguity, and syntax; inherent is the possibility of defining aesthetic response by similar formal rules.

The potential of Structuralist thought has not been realized for two reasons. First, in spite of statements that Structuralism is really only a method, it is not methodical enough; Structuralists have never codified a set of methods or techniques that is adequate and general enough to accommodate close, sophisticated analyses of a variety of specific literary works. Second, their concept of structure has been overwhelmed by the notion of *linguistic* structure. There is no reason to believe, and in fact numerous reasons to believe otherwise, that segments larger than the sentence are structured in a form similar to the structures within a sentence. The next logical step in this progression toward greater formality would be a mode of criticism based on a coherent set of techniques that includes linguistic models but that goes beyond to include *any* concept of structure that is potentially useful for characterizing linear sequences of signs.

The progression toward the concept of a science of criticism is probably another manifestation of the movement toward greater formalism. The New Critics, while often using "the scientist" as a whipping boy in their efforts to distinguish the rich, connotative language of poetry from merely descriptive language, nevertheless endorse a mode of criticism that would be more precise, systematic, structural, i.e., "scientific." The Russian Formalists were more direct: as William Harkins has observed, they quite consciously saw themselves as "trying to create a literary science."[3] While not calling criticism a "science" per se, Northrop Frye has forcefully described the *scientific* aspects of contemporary inquiry:

> It seems absurd to say there may be a scientific element in criticism when there are dozens of learned journals based on the assumption that there is, and hundreds of scholars engaged in a scientific procedure related to literary criticism. Evidence is examined scientifically, texts are edited scientifically. Prosody is scientific in structure; so is philology. Either literary criticism is scientific, or all these highly trained and intelligent scholars are wasting their time on some pseudoscience like phrenology.[4]

Similarly, Robert Scholes has identified the "scientific" aspect of criticism with the "cumulative" aspect of scholarship,[5] a practice prescribed by McKerrow in

1952 and now expected by virtually every serious journal. A final, and perhaps extreme, view of criticism as a science is that of Roland Barthes stated in "Science Versus Literature."[6] Barthes not only identifies a scientific mode of criticism present in French Structuralist/Semiological Criticism, but asserts that the emerging field of semiology will constitute a "meta-language" (by which he means a meta-science involving both perspective and method) that will eventually include and absorb the sciences proper.

This brief overview of the Structuralist/Formalist tradition and the related movement toward a science of criticism has omitted reference to social, psychological, and phenomenological criticisms. There have, of course, been partial attempts to bring Marxist and Freudian criticisms into the domain of Structuralism. It is my belief that this trend is likely to increase and that social and psychological approaches will make a substantial, permanent impact only to the extent that they can be incorporated into a formal consideration of the text itself. As for phenomenological approaches, when neurophysiology and psychology finally merge and we have an operatively defined gestalt psychology, perhaps phenomenological criticism, too, can move toward a Formalist base.

Before attempting to infer the intellectual perspectives that constitute Computer Criticism, I shall describe briefly for the reader unfamiliar with the internal operation of the computer how the computer can be instructed to deal with texts.

TEXTUAL PROCESSING

In principle, a computer is a very simple machine. It is a symbol manipulator that can recognize 256 codes or characters.[7] These codes, which may be thought of as being ordered from zero to 255, can stand for numbers, letters of the alphabet, or practically anything that one wishes to associate with them. They may be considered separately, as is usually the case for language processing, but they can be considered in groups in order that numbers larger than 255 can be represented or texts with more than 256 characters (texts with a variety of fonts) can be represented.

Computers operate sequentially: they can look at two characters, compare them to see if they are equal, see if one is higher or lower than the other in alphabetic sequence, or move them from one place to another. For numbers, the computer does the same things but it may also add them, subtract them, multiply them, divide them. Using these basic operations one can describe procedures that can be applied to a text to do something useful and, eventually, to do something interesting.

Before such a procedure can be applied to a text, however, the text must be presented to the computer in a form that it can recognize; unfortunately this is normally not in the form of a physical book. Usually the text must be typed onto cards or, preferably, typed directly into the computer memory using a keyboard terminal. Texts are normally typed virtually as they appear in the printed book—one textual line per card or one textual line per terminal line—except that special characters are inserted to denote unusual features of the text; for example, one may mark italics by typing, say, a pound or hash sign (#) immediately before or after the word to inform the computer that this word is of a different font and to notify it to mark it accordingly. With most textual material and with many sets of conventions, the encoded text can be read both by the computer and by the human being without great difficulty.

After the text has been encoded it must be "read" by the computer. For cards, this is done by a card reader, a device that examines each column of each card, in order, to determine which of the 256 characters is represented. For texts typed directly into the computer through a terminal, this is done through a statement which is typed on the terminal but which the computer recognizes as a command rather than as more text. To read the text and to process it, the computer requires a detailed sequence of instructions or program; this can be written by the analyst, but there are an increasing number of such programs available. These may be stored in the computer's program library and simply called by the analyst when required.

As far as the computer is concerned, the text will appear as one long sequence of characters, starting with the first, continuing from card to card or line to line, to the last. It is usually preferable to segment the text into recognizable units: words, sentences, paragraphs. Each segment, however, must be described to the computer in terms that it can "understand"; for example, a word might be described to the computer as a sequence of nonblank characters bounded on the left and right by blanks. The situation can get a bit more complicated for abbreviations, words before commas, the last word in the sentence; but by careful planning and through a set of encoding conventions that anticipates such difficulties, the computer can be trained to recognize a word within the stream of characters. Similarly, it may be given a set of instructions or rules to recognize sentences, paragraphs, chapters. Once the text has been prepared and the computer instructed to recognize its particular features, the computer may then be used to produce a variety of conventional aids, such as a lexicon, a collated text, or a concordance.

To produce a lexicon, the computer might be told to extract each word from the running text and to place that word in a list, one word per line. The computer would then be instructed to sort the vocabulary into alphabetical sequence. This can be done by instructing it to start at the top of the list, compare adjacent pairs of words, exchange them if they are in reverse alphabetic sequence, or, if not, proceed to the next pair. By going through the list over and over again until no pair is out of sequence, the computer can eventually determine that the list is in alphabetical order. From the sorted vocabulary, it may then be instructed to run through the list and print a lexicon or dictionary of the text along with each word's frequency of occurrence for the critic's examination.

If two editions of a text are processed, one placed in one list and the other in a second list, the computer can be used to collate the two. That is, it can be instructed to compare the first word in each list and repeat the process. If they are not identical it can then move down one list until the words match or if that doesn't work move down the second list. In some cases the comparison can be a bit tricky, requiring a jump ahead and comparisons both backwards and forwards within both lists; but the computer is far more accurate than the human eye, particularly for texts representing different type settings.

To produce a concordance, the computer must recognize not just words but also sentences. The words may be placed in one list and the entire sentence for each word placed in a second, wider, but corresponding list. The list of words is then sorted, but whenever a pair of words is exchanged in the list, alphabetically, the corresponding sentences are also rearranged. When the word list is in alphabetical order a concordance could be printed by having the computer move down the list, printing each word and its corresponding sentence. The resulting concordance could be complete, or it could be selective, providing contexts for only a specific set of words supplied by the critic. The computer could even be instructed to print a concordance for only those sentences in which particular combinations of words appear.

In the remarks that follow, where I shall be dealing with computer materials that may be less familiar, I shall not burden the reader with discussion of *how* the particular aid was produced; I shall concentrate more on describing the product itself, the assumptions that have led to it, and its implications for literary research and critical perspective.

COMPUTER CRITICISM: MATERIALIST VIEW OF A TEXT

As we would anticipate, the computer's "awareness" of a text is quite different from that of a human reader. For the human being, the text "exists" on at least three different levels: the medium (ink marks of particular shapes on paper), the signifier (the character or letter *A*), and the signified (the meaning "*A*"). While we normally are not conscious of these levels—indeed, we normally deal with aggregates of such characters in the form of words, phrases, concepts—we can, if we need to, distinguish among medium or form, the signifier, and the signified.

These distinctions do not exist for the computer. As we saw in the previous section, the computer's total "awareness" resides in its ability to distinguish among a small (256) set of codes or states; the only physical dimension of these is the configuration of electrical impulses that constitutes them. All "awareness" is relational: one state "higher" or "lower" than another (*A* higher than *B* in alphabetic sequence).

Because the computer is a sequential processor of symbols, there is a notion of linearity and segmentation inherent in its design. The concept of linearity is fundamental to the "stream" of characters that it receives from outside—through the card reader or terminal. When the computer "reads" the text, it normally removes extra blanks in the typed lines and stores the text as a long, continuous string of characters, beginning with the first word and ending with the last. The fundamental segment is, of course, the character. Since each character is represented by one of 256 states, there is no variable spacing: all characters occupy equal space in the sequence and all are segmented from one another. Segmentation in the linguistic sense must be defined for the computer formally and functionally: the sequence of nonblank characters between blanks, or some equivalent definition. If these segments, words in this case, are moved to a list where each slot is of equal width, this transformed list version of the text becomes a text of equally spaced segments analogous to the character-level defined text. Thus, the items in the list, words, become the fundamental units or states and are usually dealt with by the computer as "wholes"; and the text considered as a sequence of words emerges with the same material characteristics as the text viewed as a sequence of characters.

The notion of signified is therefore missing from the text considered as a sequence of words just as it is missing from the text considered as a sequence of characters. When the computer "reads" a text, the three levels—the physical, the signifier, and the signified—collapse into the single stratum of the signifier: the sequence of characters or internal states of the computer. The process is necessarily and formally reductive but not as limiting as it may first appear. While the computer can deal only with *encoded* material, there is no reason that physical as well as semantic characteristics cannot be encoded into symbol sequences parallel to the textual sequence. One way of doing this is to envision the text as a list of equally spaced characters or, more likely, words, as described in the last section, but to divide that list into two columns: one for the word and a second for the designation of specific characteristics of the word. Thus, characteristics such as physical segmentation (page, line, position within the line), font, and so forth, can be encoded as separate sequences of symbols parallel to the actual textual items. Similarly, semantic relations such as synonymity, oppositeness, can be encoded in still another symbol sequence (or if necessary, several such sequences), and the text "viewed" by the computer as three or more parallel symbol sequences; unlike the human being, however, the computer cannot infer any relation or order among these separate sequences unless that relation is supplied by the researcher. So considered, the text becomes for the computer a material, linear sequence of symbols with, perhaps, additional parallel sequences. Of course, it makes no difference whether we "view" the text as a list running from top to bottom (as described) or whether we, mentally, turn it on its side and "view" it as running from left to right. The latter would result in the category columns becoming strata that are parallel to and "above" the textual sequence. I shall refer to the latter "view" below, particularly when discussing *hierarchical strata*.

Since the computer can deal only with formal relations among characters, words, or other segments, the researcher must provide all concepts of "meaning"; this is usually done through a system or systems of categories. Since the computer *can* produce a dictionary or lexicon, we may assume that the researcher has at his disposal an alphabetized list of the words that occur in the text under consideration. One type of categorization is obtained by dividing or partitioning the dictionary. That is, the researcher might read down the dictionary and divide the vocabulary into words that suggest sensory impressions (images) or words that carry content (as opposed to some list of functors); similarly, the researcher may wish to designate a number of such categories, as appropriate for a thematic analysis, in which the vocabulary of the text is divided into a number of separate categories. The computer, in its capacity as symbol manipulator, could then be instructed to establish a parallel symbol sequence and mark each word according to which group or category it fell into. For example, the researcher may select for the theme *fire* the words *burn, burned, burning, fire, heat, hot;* and, for *water, damp, water, watery, wet.* A broader study might deal with all content words but ignore, in its semantic emphasis, syntactic variability indicated by suffix. An appropriate category system for such an analysis, instead of having twenty or thirty categories, could employ several thousand, with each category standing only for a single root-group (*hope, hoped, hoping,* etc.) and containing only a half-dozen or so members. From the standpoint of the computer, it makes no difference whether the vocabulary is divided into two categories, thirty categories, or several thousand, nor does it matter what the rationale is behind the particular categorization scheme: all such relations can be handled analogously.

This notion of category, dependent on the concept of a dictionary alone, is not sufficient for many studies. For example, the configuration of characters *r o s e* may signify a flower, as appropriate for an imagery study; but it may also describe an action—he *rose* from his chair. Here context must be taken into consideration. Since the computer *can* produce a concordance, we may assume that the researcher has at his or her disposal a concordance as well as a dictionary. Consequently, the concept of category can be refined to include linear, diachronic relations as well as dictionary-based, synchronic relations defined for *every* occurrence of a given configuration of characters.

Since words in the same category would be marked by the same symbol(s) in the parallel signified column of the text list, the computer by being instructed to consider that column can regard a number of different word forms as equivalent. Consequently, it could look for paradigm-like sequences or patterns of categories in which, on the textual level, the elements of the paradigm could be any word contained in the appropriate category. If the categories indicate synonymous groups, the logical configurations of categories might be regarded as themes or content—the General Inquirer, an early and still the best known content analysis program, defined content precisely in this way: the logical configuration of conceptual categories of words.[8] If the categories indicated parts of speech, the paradigm can indicate syntactic structures; thus, the computer might locate most prepositional phrases by locating all category sequences of preposition followed by a noun, within so many words.

Once a category paradigm has been defined and the particular instances of its occurrence located, a third sequential level can be established, above that of the text and its parallel category level(s), in which the elements are those particular configurations: a specific thematic combination of words or a specific syntactic structure. Of course, this stratum could be viewed as just a second-order stratum of categories; so viewing it, we can imagine defining paradigms among *those* elements to derive still higher levels of abstraction. The process could be continued indefinitely.

In retrospect, we have seen that the text can be formally segmented in a step by step manner such that each higher segment is defined in terms of units at the next lower level, ranging from the character to the entire work considered as a whole and by extension to the corpus. For each level of segmentation, parallel strata of symbols representing both physical and conceptual aspects of the text may be established. These may refer directly back to the textual sequence itself, and are hence logically lateral to one another, but they may also be established hierarchically by referring directly to an intermediate stratum (category of categories, categories of syntactic forms, etc.). Concepts of form, structure, and meaning relate to patterns along, across, and among these various strata.

CONVENTIONAL CRITICISM: MATERIALIST VIEW OF A TEXT

The concepts of autonomy of art, materiality of the text, and primacy of category to define and characterize form are also central for Russian Formalism as well as its second generation in Prague. As Victor Erlich has observed, the autonomy of art for the Formalists ranges "from the autonomy of the individual poetic word *vis-à-vis* its object to the autonomy of the literary work of art with regard to reality."[9] At the level of word or figure, the Russians placed considerable emphasis on liberating the word from its fixed conventional connotations so that its full richness could be seen.[10] On a more general level, Skaftymov demonstrated that characters in the narrative, actions in the plot, and, indeed, the philosophic dimensions of the fictive universe must be considered first as components organized within a formal autonomous aesthetic structure before substantive extrapolation can be attempted.[11] The concept of category, also, is both pervasive and varied in its manifestations. To reveal the universal narrative structure of a collection of fairy tales, Vladimir Propp reduced the texts of a collection of some 479 tales to sequences of basic actions or *functions*. Since Propp's *function* represents an action described in the narrative, each function could be related to a set of configurations of words or phrases. Thus Propp's functions could be viewed as a second- or, possibly, third level category stratum within the general framework of Computer Criticism, and his familiar symbolic representation of thematic structure would be the sequence of categories or symbols within that stratum.[12] The "bootstrap" hierarchical structure encouraged by Computer Criticism, in which categories of higher strata are defined in terms of patterns of elements in a lower stratum, is more directly analogous to the three level thematics of A. A. Reformatsky. He distinguishes among *themes,* "the simplest static unit of plot construction," *motif,* a set (usually two) of themes joined by a verb; and *plot theme,* units composed of combinations of themes and motifs.[13] *Theme* could be viewed as a first-level set of categories; *motif,* as a logical configuration of themes, would be a second-level set of categories; and *plot themes,* as combinations of themes and motifs, would be a third level set of categories. Because Reformatsky is primarily interested in narrative sequence, he often in practice collapses these logically distinct categorical strata into a single symbol sequence to represent narrative structure. More important, particularly in later Structuralist thought, is the concept of metonymy. In distinguishing between figures of speech natural for poetry and those natural for prose, Roman Jakobson distinguishes between the relation of comparison inherent in metaphor and logically contiguous substitution inherent in metonymy. The latter, when considered methodologically, is an example of semantic category: the collection of textual items used individually to stand for the set.[14]

New Criticism shares several basic perspectives with Computer Criticism, but does not come as close as Russian and Prague Formalism. The concept of a materialistic text is apparent in Ransom's ontological concern for the *poem as object,* a predominantly holistic perspective in which sound and meaning must be joined phenomenologically by the critic.[15] Ransom's perspective is made much more concrete and applicable in Wellek and Warren's delineation of perceptual strata. They divide the text into: (1) the sound stratum, euphony, rhythm, and meter; (2) the units of meaning which determine linguistic and stylistic structure;

(3) image and metaphor; (4) mythic level of poetic symbols; (5) the fictive world; (6) the system of genres inherent in literature; (7) the evaluative domain; and (8) the historical context of the work.[16] While their delineation of strata has been useful for students of literature, their emphasis is historical and comparative rather than methodological; consequently, although the basic perspective is similar to the overall hierarchical strata of Computer Criticism, the analogy cannot easily be extended further. Perhaps the closest approximation to a New Critical methodology is Caroline Spurgeon's earlier categorization and tabulation of Shakespeare's images,[17] although her biological extrapolations were, of course, contrary to New Critical principles. To the extent that her images can be described formally, her identifications and tabulations can be accommodated by Computer Criticism.

More directly related to Computer Criticism's assumptions of a material text and the notion of categorical strata is French Structuralist criticism, perhaps best summarized in Roland Barthes's "The Structuralist Activity." Most Structuralists claim at least all of the arts as their domain, while their near kin, the Semiologists, claim all knowledge; consequently, when Barthes addresses first the object of scrutiny and, next, its dissociation into parts from which collections (paradigms) are formed, he does so for areas other than literature:

> The goal of all structuralist activity, whether reflexive or poetic, is to reconstruct an "object" in such a way as to manifest thereby the rules of functioning (the "functions") of this object. . . .
> The structuralist activity involves two typical operations: dissection and articulation. To dissect the first object, the one which is given to the simulacrum-activity, is to find in it certain mobile fragments whose differential situation engenders a certain meaning; the fragment has no meaning in itself, but it is nonetheless such that the slightest variation wrought in its configuration produces a change in the whole; a *square* by Mondrian, a *series* of Pousseur, a versicle of Butor's *Mobile*, the "mytheme" in Lévi-Strauss, the phoneme in the work of the phonologist, the "theme" in certain literary criticism—all these units . . . have no significant existence except by their frontiers: those that separate them from other actual units of the discourse . . . and also those which distinguish them from other virtual units, with which they form a certain class (which linguistics calls a *paradigm*). This notion of paradigm is essential, apparently, if we are to understand the structuralist vision: the paradigm is a group or reservoir—as limited as possible—of objects . . . ; what characterizes the paradigmatic object is that it is, *vis-à-vis* other objects of its class, in a certain relation of affinity and dissimilarity. . . . The dissection operation thus produces an initial dispersed state of the simulacrum, but the units of the structure are not at all anarchic: before being distributed and fixed in the continuity of the composition, each one forms with its own virtual group or reservoir an intelligent organism, subject to a sovereign motor principle: that of the least difference.[18]

Illustrative of Barthes's view of the text as "mobile fragments" and his insistence on the primacy of category (paradigm) for critical analysis is Tzvetan Todorov's

Grammaire du Décameron, in which he proposes a specific instance (Grammar of Narrative) of a universal grammar appropriate for all conceptualization. Similar to Propp's study of Russian folk tales, Todorov's study is a highly abstract study of narrative sequence after the text has been transformed into several strata of categories. He first distinguishes among textual segments: stories, sequences (complete "little tales"), propositions (basic narrative sentence), and parts of speech. He next reduces all actions to these verb categories and all attributes to the other categories. He then proposes a transformational grammar of narrative to accommodate the individual tales. Both the statement of principle and the illustrative example emphasize a critical perspective based on a segmented text of functional units that may be grouped in various ways in order to define relational patterns. Computer Criticism shares this perspective but is a bit more inclusive; that is, it demands neither Barthes's concept of the smallest possible set or Todorov's specific categories. The two differ most in the matter of structure itself, to be discussed in the two succeeding sections.

The Formalist group closest to Computer Criticism is the London School, centered in J. R. Firth but most thoroughly and articulately developed by M. A. K. Halliday. Firth and Halliday use the concept of *exponent* to define the substantive within a categorical stratum and to connect the various strata. Halliday, who borrows the concept from Firth, states the relation as follows:

> Exponence is the scale which relates the categories of the theory, which are categories of the highest degree of abstraction, to the data. . . . Each category can be linked *directly* by exponence to the formal item. This has then to be related, in turn, to the substance. . . . When grammar reaches the formal item, either it has said all there is formally to be said about it or it hands it over to lexis.[19]

Lexis, for Halliday, is the *set* of substantives that occupy the places in the sequence of categorical units within a stratum; at the lowest, or most delicate, level this consists of the orthographic or phonemic symbols. Larger units—words, phrases, syntactic patterns—are produced by formal patterns of textual co-occurrences, called *collocations,* which may be enumerated to form *sets.* There is thus a direct correspondence between the Firth/Halliday notion of sets and the Computer Criticism concept of *states* that constitute textual items; both share the view that subsequent categorical strata can be defined by formal delineation of patterns within a lower level; both establish correspondences between strata, one by the concept of exponency, the other through the concept of location and co-occurence. These and other similarities will be explored further in the discussions of structure below.

Thus several recent structuralist schools share the assumptions of an autonomous, material text; they encourage examination of the text with the aid of stratified levels of conceptual categories; they differ widely, however, in the formality with which such strata are defined and linked to one another. The computer demands an extraordinarily explicit degree of definition simply to function; consequently, it encourages a much more formal description of conceptual categories and relations. But since categories and strata must be defined functionally, Computer Criticism can accommodate the basic critical perspectives of all these groups. These structuralist schools have all been limited by the lack of a developed methodology and the impracticality of applying their perspectives to large, full length texts. The computer, with its ability to accommodate a variety of conceptual points of view through functional generality and its ability to handle large texts with comparative ease, offers the possibility of removing these encumbrances and permitting the application of structural hypotheses to actual works of a substantial nature. At this stage of considerations, the Computer Criticism perspective can be merged with conventional Formalist/Structuralist perspectives by regarding it as a compatible methodological adjunct.

COMPUTER CRITICISM: CONCEPTS OF STRUCTURE

Computer Criticism, while compatible with conventional Formalist/Structuralist criticisms, may eventually be seen as a separate school because of its expanded concept of abstract structure and the resulting shift in the critic's conceptualization of the text and its meanings. Structuralism has been dominated by the concept of linguistic form, particularly the mathematical notion of the transformation; Computer Criticism, by viewing the text as a functional, material sequence of symbols, may employ linguistic models when appropriate, but it has developed or adopted a number of nonlinguistic models that fit its functional view of the text. These models have usually been of two kinds: those that describe or predict patterns of occurrence along the "horizontal" textual axis (the text viewed as one long sequence of words, ticker-tape fashion) and those that develop patterns of co-occurrence among vertical strata to produce still higher, more abstract generalizations or category sequences. To give the discussion of structure illustrative content, I shall develop it in the context of thematics with specific examples taken from a study of James Joyce's *A Portrait of the Artist as a Young Man*. Of course, theme is just one type of secondary stratum that can be defined. By using different principles of categorization, identical structural patterns would have radically different meanings. Additionally, the segment of text over which the pattern is defined can greatly alter the interpretation of patterns. Where the primary focus is on the sentence, the patterns that result are likely to be viewed in the context of linguistics; for segments of paragraph length, the patterns are more likely to be seen in the context of discourse analysis. Thematics usually adopts the primary segment of the entire text and uses *themes* as categories consisting of metonymic collections of words. (The collections of words relating to *fire* and *water* mentioned above can serve as examples, but the general notion of category can accommodate other definitions as well.) Were a structural description of an author's entire canon developed, we might approach Northrop Frye's concept of contextual criticism.

Designation of the theme or category, as was seen in Spurgeon's study of Shakespeare, draws the critic's attention to the functional equivalence of the words or units of the category; Computer Criticism provides the further possibility of describing the form or "behavior" of the theme over the entire text. That is, we may count the number of times the category appears and by comparing this value with similar totals for other thematic groups gain some partial insight into its relative prevalence and, perhaps, importance. If the text is segmented on the physical level into segments of equal length (say, 500 words) and subtotals for each segment computed, the resulting values may be used to produce a distribution of the theme over the text (see Figure 1: a distribution of the theme *fire* for Joyce's *A Portrait of the Artist as a Young Man*). In such a drawing we may not only confirm critical impressions of thematic density, we may see exactly the proportional concentration in one section of the text as compared with another.

While a distribution of a theme can be regarded as a structural description of that theme, Computer Criticism can go one step further and employ models that *characterize* that distribution. That is, the critic may not only display the actual

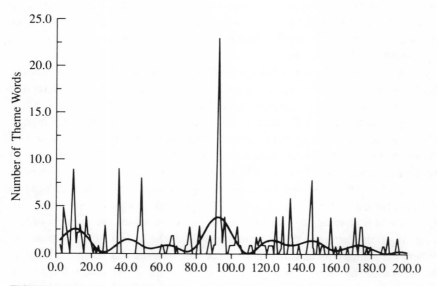

FIGURE 1. Distribution of the theme *fire* in *A Portrait of the Artist as a Young Man*. Linear words × 500 FIRE/HEAT

distribution, but may also uncover the underlying form or dynamics of that distribution and compare it with similar analyzed distributions. By regarding the diachronic sequence of words as analogous to the unitary progression of time, the critic may employ a variety of analytic models, known collectively as time series analysis, to characterize the distribution. One such model is Fourier analysis.

To apply Fourier analysis to the distribution of a category or theme, the critic must view the distribution as analogous to a wave over time, such as a graph of a sound wave over some period of time. If the sound wave has definite maximum and minimum frequencies, as would a sound wave carried over a telephone, it is a remarkable mathematical fact that no matter how irregular the wave appears, it can be reproduced by combining a definite number of flowing, perfectly regular (sine and cosine) waves of different frequencies and amplitudes/heights. By picking only the most important waves (those with the greatest amplitudes), adding them together, and ignoring the rest, one can produce a "smoothed" transformation of the original distribution in which the form and major dynamics of the theme are readily apparent. Further, a distribution of the amplitudes (actually, a function of the amplitudes) of the smooth waves can be regarded as a formal description of the complexity of the theme; a thematic distribution with only eight important terms or rhythms might be considered less "complex" than a distribution with sixteen. Thus, the critic may use the computer to draw attention to the variety of words connoting a theme, to compute its frequency of occurrence, to display its form or behavior over an entire text, and to characterize that form. The techniques described could also be employed to consider a variety of themes and the resulting materials used for comparative purposes.

The concept of distribution is a diachronic, "horizontal" concept of structure that characterizes patterns along one of the vertical strata described earlier; a different concept of form or structure is the collection of synchronic relations among a number of such distributions. Synchronic patterns of interrelation are essentially patterns of co-occurrence; these patterns may produce direct interpretive results, or they may serve as elements to derive more general "hyperthemes" of greater abstraction and complexity. For example, in Joyce's *Portrait,* a great deal is revealed about Stephen by the *combination* of themes and images that flow through his mind. In Chapter 1, he seldom recalls the pleasant and secure hearth fire of home without recalling the dreadful fall into the cold waters of the ditch; other combinations abound. A number of models are available for determining such patterns of co-occurrence: one I have found particularly useful is factor analysis or, more specifically, principal component analysis. To use it in the context cited above, the critic would determine a section of text—possibly the entire text—in which he or she feels that thematic interaction is relatively consistent. By next dividing that portion of the text into small, uniform physical segments (perhaps 100 words) and by computing distributions on the basis of those segments for all themes or categories to be considered, he may use principal component analysis to determine specific clusters or groups of themes that consistently occur close to one another. With this information he may return to his concordance or to the text to explore the specific thematic significance suggested by these patterns of interrelation.[20]

The result may be a direct interpretive statement; it may also be a higher, more abstract level of thematic combinations (themes whose elements are thematic clusters). Once this stratum is defined, it becomes subject to examination and characterization using all of the concepts of structure described. One possible approach is the consideration of thematic progression. To pick up the example from Joyce, while much is revealed about the development of Stephen's mind by considering the combinations of themes that occur in his consciousness, more is revealed in the *changes* in such associative relations that develop over the course of the novel. To trace structures such as the developing network of associations among themes, I shall describe two approaches. The first, employing a technique known as the state diagram, is rather simple to apply; the second, known by the acronym CGAMS, at present requires rather specialized computing equipment but is more powerful. State diagrams are used in automata theory to designate the particular configurations or states of a theoretical computing machine, the history of the "machine," or the permissible transitions from state to state. This is done by representing the states as a set of points and the transitions by lines or arrows between the points. The technique can be used to reveal the developing structure or network of thematic associations by representing each theme by a point and indicating the associative relations between themes as lines joining the appropriate points/themes. More specifically, one could have the computer mark each theme or, perhaps, cluster of a theme (a cluster could be a section of text in which, say, three words in the same theme occur within 100 words of one another).

The progression from theme to theme or from cluster to cluster can be traced by drawing and numbering the lines from appropriate point to appropriate point. close thematic interaction will be revealed in points close to one another in the diagram and by those having a number of lines joining them. An example of a thematic network of this sort is shown in Figures 2 and 3, representing two versions of the same basic text, in this case, a folk sermon.[21] While the diagram itself represents a synchronic structure for the entire text, the diachronic progression from theme to theme can be traced: locate START; find the path marked 1; move to the next point or theme; find the path marked 2; move to the next theme. Used singly, diagrams of individual texts reveal the specific thematic progressions in that text; diagrams for several texts can be used in combination for comparative purposes to approach questions such as thematic complexity and the relation of thematic structure to other aspects of the work.[22]

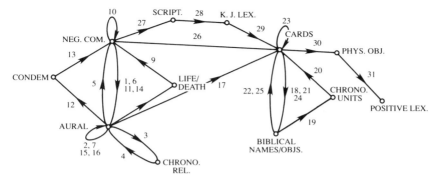

FIGURE 2. Thematic structure of DOC I

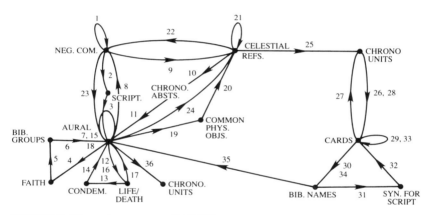

FIGURE 3. Thematic structure of DOC II

When the critic wishes to explore the dynamics of thematic interaction over a long text, the computational system CGAMS may be more appropriate.[23] CGAMS, while most useful for deriving a macroscopic representation of thematic relations, may also be used for close inspection of specific thematic relations within a smaller textual segment. The system produces a pictorial representation of the relations between a selected set of themes on television-like screen (see Figure 4, a representation of some half dozen themes in Chapter I of Joyce's *Portrait*). The basic picture resembles an aerial view of a mountain range in which there is a peak for each theme. The height of a peak represents the relative prevalence of that theme for the section of text under consideration. The horizontal distance between peaks represents the proportional diachronic distances in the text between those two themes relative to similar distances for all other theme

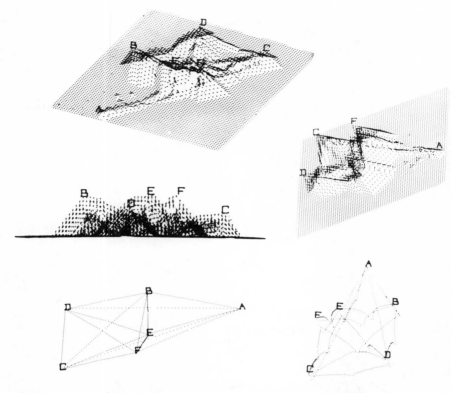

FIGURE 4. CGAMS images of thematic relations, Chapter I of *Portrait*

pairs. The slope of the facet between two themes/peaks indicates whether the two themes tend to be a stable distance from one another (for example, nearly always ten or twelve words apart), resulting in a sharp, abrupt facet, or whether the distances vary considerably (sometimes two or three words apart, sometimes twenty or thirty words apart), resulting in a sloping facet. The perspective on the "mountain range" may be changed by turning dials so that the critic can zoom up and look down on it from above, move down and look at it from ground level, or assume any other position he wishes. By producing an entire picture for, say, the first 1000 words of the text, another, cumulative, picture for the first 2,000 words, another for the first 3,000, through the entire text, one can note in the progression of pictures the way in which themes grow and shift in relation to one another over the diachronic course of the work.

The basic view of the peaks resembles a fishnet laid over mounds of sand; to gain a closer, more detailed perspective of the exact pattern of thematic interaction for a section of text, the researcher may remove the "fishnet" and examine the specific information on which the picture is based. Thus, CGAMS can portray the structural dynamics for selected themes from a micro-perspective as well as a macro-perspective.

I have argued elsewhere that in Joyce's *Portrait* the personality of Stephen remains constant between moments of epiphanal transition (the pandybat episode, the encounter with the prostitute, the confession, the encounter on the beach).[24] At these moments of epiphany, however, what *exactly* changes is the pattern of associations among images manifest in changes in the pattern of proximity of images in the text. The careful reader will, of course, notice certain shifts in proximity and association, but CGAMS marks the exact place where shifts occur, reveals the precise nature of the shift relative to other thematic relations, and indicates the relative importance of the shift. It does so in the form of an actual visual representation that can be used for demonstrations or for comparisons with similar representations of thematic activity in other textual sections.

Diachronic distributions, Fourier analysis, principal component analysis, state diagrams, and CGAMS are all models that may be used to explore thematic structures and relations. These same models could be used to examine different strata; for example, applied to a stratum of syntactic categories, they could be used to document shifts in syntactic patterns in a text (see the discussion of Halliday's study of *The Inheritors* in the section that follows). However, these are only a few of the concepts of structure that the computer makes practical to apply to extended texts. Once the critic makes the conceptual move to consider the text from a functional point of view and to consider "meaning" as originating from the reader's interaction with features and patterns within that text, the computer offers a wide variety of relational possibilities. In addition to the models or concepts of structure described here, there are numerous other possibilities. For example, additional parametric and formulaic possibilities exist that permit comparison of the distribution of a textual feature against some preestablished distribution or against an expected distribution of that feature based on earlier patterns of occurrence within the text; authorship studies typically have employed relational models of this kind. In short, the array of models or concepts of structure that the computer offers the critic as available analytic tools is truly stunning; the possibilities are limited only by our willingness to explore the unfamiliar.

CONVENTIONAL CRITICISM: CONCEPTS OF STRUCTURE

Most of the formalist schools of criticism discussed have used a stratified view of the text as the basis of their concept of form or structure. Summarizing the theoretical assumptions of the Russian Formalists, Tzvetan Todorov observes: "The concept of form produces and is then fused with the concept of function. Analysis of form . . . leads to the identificaton of its function, i.e., the relation between its various components. Its components . . . are connected by algebraic signs of co-relation and integration . . . : horizontal relations of distribution and vertical relations of integration." [25] The concept of vertical strata is most strongly associated with Shklovsky's metaphor of "staircase" construction. Erlich comments on Shklovsky's concept: "The principle of juxtaposition, Shklovsky asserted, is especially pertinent to the short story, the most 'artful' fictional genre. In short stories and novelettes the aesthetic effect rests more often than not upon deliberate exploitation of various types of contrasts and incongruity. These range from a 'realization' of a pun in terms of narrative structure through a motif of misunderstanding to that of a collision between two codes of morals." [26] While Shklovsky's staircase structure necessarily embodies a horizontal narrative medium, it emphasizes the effect of modulated vertical tensions and attractions among the various denotative and connotative strata parallel to the text.

A concept of structure shared by Shklovsky and his *Opojaz* associates that emphasizes the horizontal dimension of a text is that of retardation. Closely related to the factors producing staircase structure, retardation is the effect of delay in the narrative of episodic development relative to what might be expected if one simply stated the sequence of narrative events without digression, supplementation, or embellishment. By noting the relation between suspense and retardation, the Formalists suggest the possibility of developing a formal explanation of aesthetic response or behavior; unfortunately, they did not pursue this lead to the point of developing a practical, general methodology. Similarly, integration of vertical and horizontal concepts of structure was foreseen by the Russian Formalists, but the development of specific methods or models for achieving this was only partially realized. A. A. Reformatsky, we saw, established several distinct strata of categories, denoting theme, motif, and so forth, parallel to the textual sequence. Propp went two steps further to formulate comparable symbol sequences for a number of narratives and to deduce the inclusive underlying structure shared by all such sequences under omission or simple transformation. The concept of structure in both, however, is the unidimensional projection of strata into a single sequence of symbols. Pattern or form must still be inferred through observation of repeated sequences of symbols or symbol groups.

The Russian Formalists' concept of structure was extended by the Prague Structuralists in two major respects. With their emphasis on aesthetic theory and aesthetic response, they made important contributions toward establishing normative patterns; second, they were able to define more clearly the functional strata operating in a literary work and to demonstrate the value of this perspective by actually tracing structural patterns within and across the various strata.

The relations between normative expectation and variation is most thoroughly developed by Jan Mukařovský in considering the relation between standard language and poetic language:

The function of poetic language consists in the maximum of foregrounding of the utterance. Foregrounding is the opposite of automatization. . . . The standard language in its purest form, as the language of science . . . , avoids foregrounding. . . . In poetic language foregrounding achieves maximum intensity to the extent of pushing communication into the background as the objective of expression and of being used for its own sake; it is not used in the service of communication but in order to place in the foreground the act of expression, the act of speech itself.[27]

Mukařovský goes on to suggest that since non-normative language can be perceived only against a background of standard language, the aesthetic effect of poetic language is determined in large part by patterns of transition between the two:

Foregrounding arises from the fact that a given component in some way . . . deviates from correct usage. . . . The simultaneous foregrounding of all components is therefore unthinkable.[28]

Having observed that the transition from aesthetically indifferent speech to aesthetically colored speech can occur quite rapidly, often in the same sentence, Mukařovský concludes that the structure of such transitions and juxtapositions constitutes the aesthetic structure of the work.

The work of poetry forms a complex, yet unified, esthetic structure into which enter as constituents all of its components, foregrounded or not, as well as their interrelationships. . . . The predominancy of the esthetic function in poetic language, by contrast with communication speech, thus consists in the esthetic relevance of the utterances as a whole.[29]

To become a practical method of analysis, this view must be supported by a description of normative language. A functional model for normative stylistic traits has recently been proposed by Lubomir Doležel, a member of the Prague School now at the University of Toronto.[30] Doležel suggests that the investigator begin with a large collection of statistical measures for a text. Among these, he can determine empirically those that represent objective factors of language in general and hence remain constant throughout all texts (distributions of graphemes and phonemes); those that vary widely in all texts and, thus, represent subjective factors (distributions of specific content words); and, finally, those that range within certain limits over a number of texts and hence represent context sensitive or "subjective-objective" characteristics (sentence and word length distributions). Under this taxonomy, Doležel proposes that we may determine empirically not only normative values for a variety of statistical measures but an adequate set of distinctive features for characterizing a spectrum of styles over a variety of authors and subjects. While Doležel does not specifically say so, it is clear that the computer affords the only practical way to apply his model to a text of any substantial length. To the best of my knowledge, this had not been attempted.

The second major contribution by the Prague Structuralists in the continuing development of a stratified concept of structure is contained in the rather recent and controversial paper by Jakobson and Lévi-Strauss. Whereas numerous Structuralists have suggested the possibility of analyzing literary works formally in terms of complex relations within and among a number of linguistic strata, Jakobson and Lévi-Strauss have demonstrated the validity of this view by exhaustively examining a sonnet by Baudelaire. Beginning with the rhyme scheme, they factor out the phonic, syntactic, and semantic levels, and the patterns and relations within each. However, it is in the complex relations across these strata that the poem presents the most difficulty; it is within the interpretive domain, several levels removed from the text, that the various levels are drawn into a coherent whole as they contribute to a highly generalized theme of dialectic tension and resolution.[31]

The notion of structure most prevalent in New Criticism is that of "organic unity," relating part to whole, defined primarily in terms of metrical relations and image patterns. Caroline Spurgeon's classification and cataloging of Shakespeare's imagery has already been mentioned; the concept of structure, however, contained in that work is that of category and frequency. By classifying images and then counting the members of the various classes present in each play, she draws our attention to the tone-setting, often substantive, backdrop of verbal figures. Questions concerning combinations and patterns among categories, not her concern, were raised by later New Critics. For example, Cleanth Brooks, in his discussion of imagery in *Macbeth,* concentrates on two predominant patterns: images of clothes and concealment and images denoting babies. He goes beyond Spurgeon's method, however, by showing that it is the *interaction* of these two groups that underscores and comments upon the major action and theme of the play. Macbeth's ill-fitting garments, like adult clothes on a child, make him ridiculous in his present circumstances; the naked babe, paradoxically, suggests the strength of historical continuity that eventually crushes Macbeth's vain hopes. While it is the interweaving of these two image groups that results in the complex, multi-faceted semantic structure that attracts the critic's attention, the concept of structure involved is still that loose construct "organic form," suggested by combination and juxtaposition.

Wellek and Warren, describing the levels of existence of a text, present an interpretive stratification somewhat similar to that described above. As we noted above, they describe some eight interpretive dimensions. Within each stratum, they discuss the historical background of critical concern and often suggest approaches that could lead to methodological formality. For example, in discussing the level of euphony, rhythm, and meter they note Tomashevsky's statistical methods as well as other acoustic approaches; in their discussion of stylistics they similarly note the possibility of a stylistics based on normative values and a set of distinctive features. However, in their attempt to be suggestive rather than critically dogmatic, they stop short of advocating any specific methodology beyond recognition of these factored strata.

Within French Structuralist criticism the notion of structure has centered primarily on concepts of *linguistic* structure, with several notable exceptions. For Barthes, structure means primarily patterns of recurrence and association:

> Once the units are posited, structural man must discover in them or establish for them certain rules of association. . . . What we discover in every work of structural enterprise is the submission to regular constraints whose formalism . . . is much less important than their stability; for what is happening . . . is a kind of battle against chance; this is why the constraint of recurrence of the units has an almost demiurgic value: it is of the regular return of the unit and of the association of units that the work appears constructed. . . . Form, it has been said, is what keeps the contiguity of units from appearing as a pure effect of chance.[32]

The best known application of Barthes's concept of structure is his study *S/Z*. Barthes divides a short story by Balzac, entitled "Sarrisine," into some 561 textual segments or "lexies," each of which represents Barthes's judgment of the smallest portion of the narrative that carries "meaning." He then factors this "meaning" into five vertical planes or "codes" parallel to the horizontal sequence of lexies. Each code represents a different relation among the narrator, the subject matter of the text, and the culture. Barthes's method of application is to work his way through the story, lexis by lexis, commenting on the portion of his experience as highly informed reader drawn into focus by the various codes. The result is a brilliant but highly idiosyncratic reading. Associations and patterns of repetition are observed and discussed but are limited to the patterns Barthes happens to notice through his polarizing critical apparatus. There is no attempt at formality or reproducibility.

Todorov's analysis of structure in the *Decameron* is based on the concept of the transformation: individual tales are shown to be derivable from a general, paradigmatic form.[33] By demonstrating that all tales can be derived from a small number of paradigms through a set of basic transformations, Todorov shows that there exists a narrative generative grammar analogous to a Chomskian-style generative grammar for some specific set of sentences. While Todorov does extrapolate on the mental factors involved in composing large tale sequences, he does not attempt any systematic analysis of his paradigm sequence or its macroscopic structure.

More recently, Paul de Man has suggested the possibility of adopting the concept of a lattice structure for literary analysis. After noting the scarcity of new techniques for literary study ("There certainly have been numerous excellent books of criticism since, but in none of these have the techniques of description and interpretation evolved beyond the techniques of close reading established in the thirties and forties" [34]), he considers a passage from Proust from a rhetorical perspective. Concentrating on metonymic patterns of association as opposed to the more conventional assertions carried by metaphor, de Man foresees the possibility of a truly comprehensive Structuralist methodology:

> The further text of Proust's novel . . . responds perfectly to an extended application of this deconstructive pattern: not only can similar gestures be repeated throughout the novel, at all the crucial articulations or all passages where large aesthetic and metaphysical claims are being made . . . , but a vast thematic and semiotic network is revealed that structures the entire narrative and that remained invisible to a reader caught in naive metaphorical mystification. The whole of literature would respond in similar fashion, although the techniques and the patterns would have to vary considerably, of course, from author to author. [35]

Such networks of associations have been partially realized through considerations of selected passages in the work of Genette (particularly in *Figures III*), Greimas, and other Semiological critics; however, it has been impractical to explore such associative patterns for full length works.

The Formalist school whose concept of structure most closely resembles the stratified concept implicit in Computer Criticism is that associated with Firth. The comparison is closest not in the relation between the term, structure, as I have used it in this essay and as it is formally used by Firth and Halliday; rather, the comparison must be drawn between what I have called structure and the concept of the total language construct or model found in the London School. As mentioned above, Firth begins with a material text: either a sequence of characters or a sequence of sounds. He then suggests a succession of levels, each abstract but each growing out of a materialist consideration of the symbol sequence comprising a lower level, that culminates in a *context of situation*. Inherent in the levels of this outer domain is the possibility of a behavioralist theory of language which Firth anticipates in one of his final essays in his appeal for the aid of psychology and psychiatry in linguistic description. [36] Because of his untimely death, Firth was unable to complete the model that he had sketched; much of this job, fortunately, has been done by M. A. K. Halliday, particularly in the area of syntax. Halliday's elaborations have dealt primarily with levels ranging from text to sentence structure. *Structure,* as formally defined by Halliday, is an "arrangement of elements ordered in 'places'." Thus, *structure* is a "horizontal" concept; actual description of that horizontal order, however, is not addressed by Halliday. Relations across levels, referred to as *exponency,* are the relations between category designators and the lower level members that constitute them; while rules govern the general form of one level relative to those lower than it, specific procedures for deriving higher levels are not developed.

Nevertheless, Halliday has shown the strength of this stratified view of language as a tool for literary and stylistic analysis in his study of William Golding's *The Inheritors.*[37] Choosing several sizable samples distributed over the text, he establishes a level of syntactic pattern and parses each sentence in the samples. Through frequency counts he establishes what are really syntactic collocations to show that these patterns inform/constitute the growing conceptual awareness of the central character. The implication that the theme of growing mental complexity is, itself, an outer sequential level of the novel that could potentially be formally linked through exponence down through numerous intermediate levels to the material text is an exciting, perhaps frightening, possibility. Halliday does not take this last step, however, probably because of the impracticality of doing so through conventional methods.

A central aspect of the concept of structure for each of these critical schools is the notion of a horizontal material text over which various abstract strata are projected. The Russian Formalists identified such strata with the expectation of alternative narrative possibilities. The play on the reader's sense of anticipation was addressed more formally by the Prague Structuralists as they envisioned the development of actual probabilities of occurrence for textual items that would constitute normative patterns against which poetic variation could be perceived. For both New Criticism and the French Structuralists, secondary levels serve to focus the reader's attention on specific intrinsic and extrinsic dimensions of the text. While Barthes is more rigorous in the application of his framework than the New Critical practitioners, he makes no attempt to establish a true Formalist methodology. The group that comes closest to doing so is the London School, especially in the elaborations by Halliday. There, formal rules govern the form of individual strata relative to their relation to the lower level elements that constitute them; however, procedures to develop specific higher strata are left to the adoption of available linguistic models.

To describe relations along and across strata, these Formalist/Structuralist critics have relied primarily on the concepts of the transformation, the paradigm (including patterns derived through omission and repetition of elements), and, to a far lesser degree, the lattice. These are all powerful models, but the time required to apply them by hand has limited their value for examining actual extended texts. Computer Criticism, because of its functional generality, can accommodate both the stratified perspectives of these groups and the basic relational models they have employed. As we have seen, however, it can go further. It can add to the store of models a far wider collection than has been used in conventional criticism, and it can apply these models to extended, full-length texts quickly and easily. Consequently, Computer Criticism is not just compatible with traditional Formalist/Structuralist schools; their perspectives may be viewed in their functional dimensions as special cases of the more general perspective of Computer Criticism.

CONCLUSION

In the introduction to this paper, I stated that I would address three major issues: the cognitive perspective of the text and its meanings inherent in computational analyses, the relation between this perspective and major schools of Formalist and Structuralist criticism, and, finally, the identification of this perspective as an emerging school in its own right. While I have suggested throughout how Computer Criticism goes beyond conventional schools, I have focused most directly on the first two issues. Let me now address this last assertion more directly, but in doing so let me acknowledge that I shall ultimately have to beg the question. That is, I shall look at some three major implications that suggest a shift in perspective, but a shift will in fact be seen only after it has taken place in the mind of the critic. The situation is analogous to Thomas Kuhn's "scientific revolution": a shift in intellectual perspective that can be recognized only after it has taken place within the individual.[38]

A major thrust of interpretive criticism has traditionally been an enriched, expanded aesthetic and emotional response to literature. By knowing more about a work, its historical and biographical contexts, as well as the responses and insights of sensitive, informed readers, we can, in turn, understand and respond to the work more fully ourselves. Computer Criticism offers the additional opportunity to refine our awareness of our responses to the text. Instead of using secondary strata to represent only intrinsic patterns within the text, such strata may be used to record extrinsic factors. For example, in considering the text of a performance of a play, we could observe the various responses of the audience (it watched quietly, it laughed quietly, it roared with laughter, it gasped) among a variety of behavioral/temporal factors. By considering textual features in conjunction with observed responses we can gain a clearer sense of the affective dynamics of the theater.[39] Similarly, it may be possible for a reader to record his own encounter with a text, the thoughts and images evoked, and the nature of his emotional responses. Similar configurational analysis could lead to a clearer awareness of the phenomenology of one's reading experience. Although the techniques to actually achieve precise, sensitive results are only appearing on the distant horizon, we can see, nevertheless, their possibility. When more fully developed, we may be able to bring phenomenological criticism into the domain of Formalism and Structuralism.

The second major implication of Computer Criticism is an altered concept of proof and what constitutes demonstration of a literary hypothesis. Because the computer requires coherent, formal rules/procedures to move from level to level within its stratified structure, abstract assertions remain closely linked to, if not coincident with, patterns within higher strata. Since a study progresses by developing successively higher strata in terms of patterns within lower strata, generalizations, no matter how abstract, can be traced back through the various levels to actual textual features and/or to closely observed primary responses. As we would anticipate, the computer can locate each occurrence of a particular configuration. Consequently, the traditional modes of demonstration that have relied on authority (both previous critical statements as well as references to one's own responses) and citation of examples are expanded to include the additional concepts of pervasiveness and adequacy. That is, in addition to offering confirming examples, the critic may indicate the pervasiveness of that feature or pattern; by offering a comprehensive description of the features considered for the particular focus of the study (for example, a comprehensive list of themes for a thematic analysis), the critic may address the question of the adequacy of a particular assertion with regard to any specific combination of features. Thus, the computer offers the critic additional verificational concepts through its ability to address the entire text synchronically.

Finally, there is the distinct prospect of a discovery procedure for interpretive generalizations. At present and for the foreseeable future the computer will be used as an investigative tool under the close control of the critic. But as the critic becomes familiar with the products it generates, he may begin to apply analytic models used in one context to different contexts. For example, he may employ by analogy transformational models originally developed for syntactic analyses to thematic configurations by adapting the categories and the specific form of particular rules; indeed, this has already been done, as was described in Todorov's study of the *Decameron*. The functional nature of the stratificational system of Computer Criticism, however, makes this and other extensions by analogy virtually routine. As an experienced rider controls his horse with ever more subtle commands, so the critic may control the exact routines of the computer with more latitude. That is, he may develop "metaprograms" that can extend a structural model defined in terms of the categories of one stratum to the categories of another in an effort to discover combinations and configurations that could not be foreseen; automatic indexing merged with automatic theorem-proving would offer a primitive analogy. These speculations are, of course, highly tentative; but we can see enough substance in the current state of computer development to mark their outline.

At this stage, however, it is not important whether one views Computer Criticism as a separate school of criticism or whether one views it as a collection of techniques that can be used in conjunction with conventional perspectives. If one adopts the latter position, the computer can be viewed as a powerful ally, to consider interpretive questions with a detail and clarity that has been impractical until now. If one accepts the former position, a number of new questions emerge that offer the excitement and risk of the unknown and the untested. Regardless, the computer is a resource for critical inquiry that is limited only by our imaginations.

ADDENDUM

Most of the preceding discussion has dealt with theoretical aspects of Formalism, Structuralism, and Computer Criticism, or with abstract concepts of structure and form. It may be useful for the reader unfamiliar with the computer to see how a critical assertion might be handled by the computer. It is important to realize, however, that it is the critic, not the computer, who provides the intellectual context for the study, interprets the information produced by the computer, and forms the critical insight.

As with any critical mode, a study using the computer must begin with a strong initial hypothesis or question. In its initial formulation the problem should be cast in a familiar context, using conventional terminology. Similarly, the study must justify itself within conventional critical values; it must be worth doing in its own right and not simply something that *is* done because the computer *can* do it.

Once the hypothesis has been formulated in this manner, the critic must translate the hypothesis from substantive terms (as described above) to operative or functional terms. As with any translation process, there is great opportunity for distortion and error. The critic must be extremely judicious to insure that the operative definition of the hypothesis closely fits the substantive definition.

There is no set way in which this translation can always be made; however, an approach that may be useful is for the critic simply to probe his own critical assertions and assumptions, repeatedly asking himself, "What, *exactly*, do I mean by ———?" For example, take the rather obvious assertion that the first chapter of Joyce's *Portrait* is structured by the tension between the themes of *fire* and *water*. To demonstrate this with the aid of the computer would involve several translation steps. The critic might engage himself in an imaginary dialogue similar to the following:

1. Q. What, *exactly,* do you mean by the themes, *fire* and *water?*
A. Well, by *theme,* I mean a group of words or phrases, mostly images, that denote or suggest a basic concept or experience. Obviously, the theme of *fire* will be those words or phrases that suggest fire or heat and the theme *water* will be those words or phrases that suggest water, wetness, and, in this context, coldness.
2. Q. Fine, but *what* words or phrases suggest fire or water? To the computer, they all look alike.
A. I mean specific words like *burn, burned, burning, fire, hearth, heat.* For water, I mean *cold, ditch, spit, water, watery.*
3. Q. Now that you have translated the term, *theme,* from a substantive term (a group of words or phrases that suggest the same basic concept or experience) to a functional term (a *list* of specific words or collocations of words) recognizable by the computer, can you take the next step and clarify what you mean by the relation *tension* when you say that *fire* and *water* are in a state of *tension?*
A. *Fire* is usually related or associated in Stephen's mind with thoughts of home or other pleasant memories; conversely, *water* is associated with his terrible fall into the ditch. Although these two themes carry dialectically opposite connotations, he seldom recalls one without his mind jumping to the other. It is this constant, ironic juxtaposition or association between basically opposite themes that constitutes *tension.*
4. Q. Fine, but what do you mean by the statement that the chapter is *structured* by this relation of tension between the themes of *fire* and *water?*
A. That's a little harder because to say that the chapter is *structured* by this relation means several things. It means that this dialectic juxtaposition occurs frequently; it occurs at fairly regular intervals; and it is "fundamental" in some respect to other thematic relations. That is, it occurs in a variety of thematic contexts; and other major themes, while relating to this pair, do not occur with the same regularity or with the same diversity of context.
Q. Let's take them one at a time. How can you show that these two themes occur close to one another frequently?
A. I could divide the text into, say, 100-word intervals, have the computer tally up all of the *fire* words for each such interval, and then have it draw a picture or graph of this distribution over the chapter. By comparing this with a similar distribution of *water* words I can tell both the prevalence and the consistency of association of these two themes.
Q. Fine, you killed two birds with one program, but how are you going to show that this relation is more "fundamental" than other thematic relations?
A. First, I'll have to define *all* the themes that I feel are "major," just as I did in step 2; but then I'll have to show that these are less "prevalent" and less "pervasive" than fire and water and that they are oriented in some way to the fire/water dialectic. If I graph *all* of these themes, I can compare their distributions with those of *fire* and *water* for "pervasiveness." If this relation turns out to be true, then I can look at the section of text where these other themes seem to be important and see if they are in some way related to *fire* and *water.*

5. Q. How are you going to get the computer to tell you how these themes are related to *fire* and *water?*

A. I *can't,* but the computer *can* tell me where to look. Thus, it points me to the *right* places and it can tell me whether I have looked at *all* the places.

The substantive hypothesis having been translated into functional terms and the computer having been used to gather and display information and to explore various structural relations, it is then incumbent upon the critic to assimilate this information, to place it in context, and to synthesize his "interpretation." Obviously, the computer can only strengthen, not replace, his critical judgment. The final results of the inquiry should be expressed, once again, in the vernacular of the profession. To do this, the critic must translate in reverse the relations, patterns, and structures he has discovered on the functional level back into meaningful critical assertions. The computer should recede into the background, leaving behind the unencumbered thesis, but a thesis that rests firmly on a body of specifiable assumptions and demonstratable textual relations. It is this joining of the deductive, critical response of the researcher with the empirical methodology of the computer that makes it possible to envision a science of literary criticism that is powerful but not reductive, sensitive but not simplistic.

Notes

*This essay originally appeared in *Style 12* (1978):326–56, and in an expanded version in *Formalization in Literary and Discourse Analysis,* ed. Sally Sedelow and Walter Sedelow (The Hague: Mouton, 1979).

1. See Sally Yeates Sedelow, "The Computer in the Humanities and Fine Arts," *Computing Surveys 2* (June 1970):89–110; R. L. Widmann, "Computers and Literary Scholarship," *Computers and the Humanities 5* (Sept. 1971):3–14.

2. Paul de Man, "Semiology and Rhetoric," *Diacritics 3* (Fall 1973):27.

3. William E. Harkins, "Slavic Formalist Theories in Literary Scholarship," *Word 7* (August 1951):184.

4. Northrop Frye, *The Anatomy of Criticism* (Princeton, N.J.: Princeton University Press, 1957), 8.

5. Robert Scholes, *Structuralism in Literature* (New Haven, Conn.: Yale University Press, 1974), 77.

6. Roland Barthes, "Science Versus Literature," *Times Literary Supplement* (Sept. 1967), reprinted in *Structuralism: A Reader,* ed. Michael Lane (London: Jonathan Cape, 1970), 410–17.

7. I shall discuss the computer and its functions for language analysis in the context of large IBM machines. These remarks can be interpolated for other computers.

8. Philip J. Stone, Dexter C. Dunphy, Marshall S. Smith, and Daniel M. Ogilvie, *The General Inquirer: A Computer Approach to Content Analysis* (Cambridge, Mass.: MIT Press, 1966).

9. Victor Erlich, *Russian Formalism: History and Doctrine* (The Hague: Mouton, 1955), 177.

10. Erlich, especially his discussion of Shklovsky in Chapter 10.

11. Erlich, 176–77.

12. V. Propp, *Morphology of the Folktale,* 2nd ed. (Austin: University of Texas Press, 1968), especially Chapter 2.

13. A. A. Reformatsky, "An Essay on the Analysis of the Composition of the Novella," trans. Christine School, in *Russian Formalism,* ed. Stephen Bann and John E. Bowlt (New York: Barnes and Noble, 1973), 88–89.

14. Roman Jakobson, "Randben Rkugen Zur Prora des Dicktus Pasternak," *Slavische Rundschan* 7 (1936): 357–74; these concepts are discussed by Erlich, 177–78, 200.

15. John Crowe Ransom, "Wanted: An Ontological Critic," in *The New Criticism* (Norfolk: New Direction, 1940), 297–301.

16. Rene Wellek and Austin Warren, *Theory of Literature,* 3rd ed. (New York: Harcourt, Brace, and World, 1956), 157.

17. Caroline F. E. Spurgeon, *Shakespeare's Imagery* (Boston: Beacon Press, 1958).

18. Roland Barthes, "The Structuralist Activity," in *Critical Essays,* trans. Richard Howard (Evanston, Ill.: Northwestern University Press, 1972), 214, 216–17.

19. M. A. K. Halliday, "Categories of the Theory of Grammar," *Word* 17 (1961): 270–71.

20. For a more thorough discussion of models useful for illustrating and characterizing thematic structures see "Thematic Structure and Complexity," *Style* 9 (Winter 1975): 32–54.

21. For a detailed description of this study see Bruce A. Rosenberg and John B. Smith, "Thematic Structure in Four Fundamentalist Sermons," *Journal of Western Folklore* 34 (1975): 201–14.

22. For a full discussion of a formal notion of thematic complexity appropriate for thematic structure similar to that represented by state diagrams, see "Thematic Structure and Complexity."

23. John B. Smith, "Computer Generated Analogues of Mental Structure from Language Data," *Proceedings of IFIP '74* (The Hague: North-Holland, 1974): 842–45.

24. John B. Smith, "Image and Imagery in Joyce's *Portrait:* A Computer-Assisted Analysis," in *Directions in Literary Criticism: Contemporary Approaches to Literature,* ed. Stanley Weintraub and Philip Young (University Park: The Pennsylvania State University Press, 1972), 220–27.

25. Tzvetan Todorov, "Some Approaches to Russian Formalism," trans. Bruce Merry, in *Russian Formalism,* ed. Stephen Bann and John E. Bowlt (New York: Barnes and Noble, 1973), 11.

26. Erlich, 212.

27. Jan Mukařovský, "Standard Language and Poetic Language," in *A Prague School Reader,* ed. Paul L. Garvin (Washington: Georgetown University Press, 1964), 19.

28. Ibid., 65.

29. Ibid.

30. Lubomir Doležel, "A Framework for the Statistical Analysis of Style," in *Statistics and Style,* ed. Richard W. Bailey and Lubomir Doležel (New York: American Elsevier, 1969).

31. Roman Jakobson and Claude Lévi-Strauss, "Charles Baudelaire's 'Les Chats'," in *Issues in Contemporary Literary Criticism,* ed. Gregory T. Polletta (Boston: Little, Brown, 1973), 372–89.

32. Barthes, "The Structuralist Activity," 217.

33. Tzvetan Todorov, *Grammaire du Décameron* (The Hague: Mouton, 1969).

34. Paul de Man, "Semiology and Rhetoric," 27.

35. Ibid., 32.

36. J. R. Firth, "The Treatment of Language in General Linguistics," in *Selected Papers* (Bloomington: Indiana University Press, 1968), 209.

44   « JOHN B. SMITH

37. M. A. K. Halliday, "Linguistic Function and Literary Style," in *Literary Style: A Symposium,* ed. Seymour Chatman (London: Oxford University Press, 1971), 330–68.
38. Thomas Kuhn, *The Structure of Scientific Revolutions* (Chicago: University of Chicago Press, 1962).
39. For an example of such a study, see John B. Smith and Bruce A. Rosenberg, "Rhythms in Speech: Formulaic Structure in Four Fundamentalist Sermons," *Computer Studies in the Humanities and Verbal Behavior* 4 (Fall/Winter 1973): 166–73.

>> 3

Differences, Genres, and Influences*

DONALD ROSS, JR.

Most histories of literature are not about literature—they are about the people who produce it, or about the ideas that it contains or fails to contain. Only a history of styles treats literature as a fine art. This history looks at the language of literature. It is produced by disassembling the work into its several linguistic and rhetorical structures. Such dissection upsets many students of literature because descriptions of a style's bits and pieces tend to bore, not to "sing," and they rarely lead to massive re-evaluation of the works scrutinized. The difference between doggerel and great poetry is a set of variations in style. The linguistic elements of which each set is made are much the same; the elements have no intrinsic aesthetic value. A stylistic analysis will not necessarily reveal if a work is good, pretty, or successful.

Literary history is in a bewildered state—a group of scholarly endeavors with no explicit or fixed methodology. Most works under that rubric are chronologically arranged series of authors' biographies, usually with a focus on working conditions and reading lists. (The Oxford series is a fine example.) Other works make up yarns about the thematic or moral content of a group of writings and talk of "growth" and flowering, or of a battle between originality and the forces of repression; or, more fancifully, they treat a country's literature as a person—"inquiring . . . exploratory . . . delighting in adventure . . . humanitarian." [1] Neither the biographies nor the content analyses have to do directly with literary art. If the first group were to include hack writers and eloquent politicians, the picture of authors' motives, interactions, and triumphs would be even more complete. A description of contents and moral attitudes is essentially a history of ideas limited to texts which are declared "literary." It is a truncated account because of that limitation, especially since ideas are seldom a poet's or novelist's main strength or concern.

Theories of causality are rarely made explicit. The connections among events seem generally to be Hegelian and abstract. Every relevant occurrence is assumed to be universally and immediately transmitted to all readers and certainly to all contemporary writers, who scrutinize as closely as any graduate student. When high prestige is given to originality, writers who use an invention are "trendy" or imitative, while those who do not use it are conservative, old-fashioned. Somehow the history becomes a tool for expressing critical judgments.

Much of what is said about the "history of literature" really has to do with the legitimate need to use extra-literary, historical information to improve the interpretation of literary texts. This "historicism" is not often related to the history *of* literature or *of* style.

When we talk about the methods used to institute a history of style, it is important to put up some borders around the word "style." The act of *reading* a text is quite separate from that of *studying* or analyzing one. When I take the commuter bus home, I can (and do) look out the window, get off at the right place, and notice when the bus seems crowded—I both use the facility and like or dislike the ambience of the ride. In a different mood I might analyze other features of the same trip—question the logic of the bus route, count the passengers who get off at each stop, even notice how soon before an intersection the driver puts on the turn signal. Chances are, when I analyze the ride, I won't enjoy the scenery as I did when only a passenger. My analytic mood gives other pleasures—more intellectual and rational. The "content" of the bus ride and its "style" are inextricably mingled, but noticing one blinds me to the other, and discussing one in detail precludes a simultaneous discussion of the other. So it is with analysis of style.

"Style" is restricted to the analysis of the language used in a piece of writing. Any text is a complex object, with a wealth of observable features, the relations among which are "surface" structures and are parts of the author's writing performance. A grammar picked to describe and analyze such structures should be appropriate to that task—a parsing grammar rather than a generative grammar is more fruitful for describing the syntax of existing texts, for example.

A stylistics based on the text as a linguistic object excludes two other areas of inquiry—the styles of text-production and of text-reception. Eventually enough information might be gathered about the language of many works, and psychological laws might exist concerning the relationships between an element of language and the mind which produced it. No such laws have yet been formulated in a way that can be tested, especially for dead authors. Direct, unambiguous inferences from a text into the author's personality are not possible, and the whole issue is clouded by one person's ability to parody another's style or successfully to contrast the language of fictional characters within a single work. Recall that *Huck Finn* has not only different styles but even different dialects. "Affective" stylistics, the account of how texts are received, has its own snags: we know very little about when and how readers respond to style. Norman Holland has suggested that the range is quite wide.[2] We know even less about which features of style struck the attention of average or expert readers of past ages. Most stylistic commentary has been vague, general, or metaphorical—Swift is "strong," Pope "graceful." A history of receptions cannot be written.

WHAT STYLISTICS MIGHT BE

Style descriptions should be based on explicit, objective methods consistently applied. They need a way both to acknowledge and then to avoid historical changes in the language, to notice that *mee* and *me* are spelling variants of the same word with the same meaning, or that *makest* and *makes* serve the same syntactic function. Ultimately some features of the language need to be compared over centuries, as would be true in a history of sonnets. Metrics, a traditional part of the literary curriculum, can serve as an example. In metrics a few observable features of language are isolated—usually the relative locations of stressed and unstressed syllables and pauses within the line. Some system translates the locations into a mapping code and generalizes about the translation by a specialized, technical vocabulary. A line might be mapped as x′ x′ x′ x′ x′ or labeled as "iambic pentameter." Once a mapping code is decided on and texts are analyzed, one can count the frequencies of each type of line to formulate generalizations, even refined ones such as "lines with inverted first-feet are nearly all in the octaves."

What does a metrical study do? It tells about a purely aesthetic dimension of poetry, particularly about the phonetic rhythms which transmit the meanings. Metrics also can show relations among an abstract or ideal pattern, the general "background" pattern of the genre, and any "foregrounded" elements of the particular poem. Beyond that small compass, metrics divulges little—it cannot reveal what the poem means, predict a poem's success with an audience, or say anything about the poet's mind. Meter is one level of the poem's art, not the only one, nor the most important. Understanding it is interesting, amusing, and challenging. The underlying metrical patterns and variations are real and present in every poem, but most readers do not consciously observe them. Still fewer people, most of them literature teachers, must notice them, and few of those must say something about them.

Metrics is typical of the kind of linguistic description that is useful for stylistics. The mapping languages and methods of generalization will differ when the focus is on syntax, vocabulary structure (lexis), semantics, or those rhetorical figures that depend on language, but the main strategy will be the same.

A proposal may now be offered: a history of style will be an account of how (some) texts were written at different times. The word "account" is intended to chart a path between an unselective chronology and a narrative which has a plot line and a purpose. A chronology of how everyone wrote would be the perfect source from which the account would be drawn, but only a minute fragment of such a chronicle has ever been published by literary researchers. Experienced readers and scholars have a large amount of the relevant information in their memories and can rely upon it for intuitions and judgments that are often accurate and helpful. If everything goes well, stylistics should account for some critical and explanatory judgments and discredit others, and it may provide better-informed ones in the future. Since individual components of a language and the structures which combine to make up a style have no intrinsic literary value, no valid way exists to rank styles, or to predict success or failure, or to define categorically "good" or "bad" styles.[3]

I intend to avoid the issue of determining what separates non-literature from the Real Thing. For a history of style, a literary text can be any one which has been so labeled, either on traditional, aesthetic, or arbitrary grounds,[4] or just by an author's declaration. Most existing studies have treated belles lettres or non-literary writings such as military dispatches, but not much between. Text selection can be subjective; since so little work has been done, any place is a good one from which to start. Not all the features of each text will be included in the description, but the more there are, the richer will be the historical account. It is obvious that statistical descriptions are necessary when the number of texts and number of features become large. Stylistics in the immediate future will be limited because it takes so much time to assemble descriptions, and because linguistic and rhetorical theories do not give ways to describe all the relevant features of style. It would be helpful, for instance, to have a convincing way to generalize about the syntactic forms and the semantic contents of metaphors.[5]

Commentary about style is a permanent part of literary study—indeed, it may be central to an interest in literary artistry. The challenges to the writing of histories of style are considerable. Some features are normal (or predictable) because of the language at the time a work is written. But, in striking contrast, many of the features normal to a genre are independent of time; a ready example is the permanence of rhyme schemes in Italian and Shakespearean sonnets. Genres can be combined in a single work as well. Current studies of the novel strongly suggest that the style of dialogue is systematically different from the style of narration and that it is an error to mix data from the two sources.[6]

As histories of style are assembled, our students will have a body of information with which to make more substantial literary judgments and criticism. A concordance or word index will accurately show which semantic associations are present in a text. (See Andrew Crosland's article.[7]) The careful definition of a scale for interacting features such as "complexity" can let us determine where a particular work resides, and a full history of style lets us judge whether that work's complexity is typical of its genre. Even if the only result is to get people to read literature more carefully, the effort is worth the trouble.

SORTING OUT GENRES

Ezra Pound states in *ABC of Reading* that "most arts attain their effects by using a fixed element and a variable." Descriptions of style include both, and it is not easy to specify what is fixed by the language and by the genre (which the artist selected), and what are individual variations. The answers will be probability statements, not fixed definitions—some percentage of English nouns are preceded by articles; pronouns in stage drama are usually three times more frequent than in essays; the probability of finding a slant rhyme in one of Keats's Italian sonnets is .38, for a Shakespearean sonnet it is .74.

A brief review of three studies of style will illustrate various aspects of the current state of the methods. Two reminders are necessary—first, none of the studies treats all features of a full stylistic analysis; second, interpretation of the results will keep snagging on the issue of identifying genre.

One of the most extensive surveys of English-language poetry was conducted by J. Miles, who used thousand-line samples of two hundred English and American poets. The data she presents consist of counts of verbs (main, auxiliary, infinitival, participial, and copulative), nouns, and adjectives (including all determiners except for the articles).[8] Miles's studies also include a fair amount of content analysis, performed by keeping track of high-frequency lexical items for each era, but I will focus only on her study of syntax. I have transcribed the frequencies to computer cards and calculated various ratios, period averages, and other statistical relationships to suggest how word-class data can help with histories of style.

Miles's basic measure of literary "modes" is the ratio of adjectives to verbs—when the ratio is greater than about 1:2, poetry is called "phrasal"; when it is less than 0.9, it is "clausal." The middle range is "balanced." The picture which

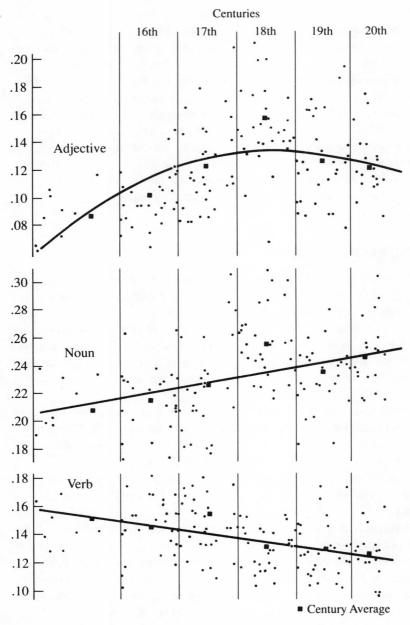

FIGURE 1. Adjective, noun, and verb proportions and regression lines.

results is a change from a ratio of 0.6 adjectives (to 1 verb) in the pre-1470 poets, 0.7 in the sixteenth century, 0.8 in the seventeenth, to 1.3 in the eighteenth, and then to a balanced 1.0 in the nineteenth and twentieth centuries. These data can be more fully exploited. I normalized the counts as proportions (i.e., percentages when multiplied by 100). These numbers are more uniform than the frequency-per-ten-lines; which is sensitive to vagaries in the number of words in the lines (from 4 to 11 in Miles's sample). In the graphs of Figure 1, the 150 English poets are placed by birth dates, the eras are marked, and era averages are shown as squares. General trend lines are drawn to a computed "fit" for all the observations. (Technically they are regression lines which are significant above the .005 level.) Adjectives and the nouns they modify are noticeably above the trends in the eighteenth century. Verbs tend to decrease linearly over the years, a fact which may be related to G. T. Wright's observations about the use of the simple present tense,[9] or by a decrease of time-marking auxiliaries. Miles's combining ratio links the peak adjective proportion to the decline in verbs. Had her data included prepositions, we could discover whether the variability came from clause subjects or objects, or from sentence-modifying prepositional phrases. An explanation for changes in the proportion of nouns can be proposed but not tested directly: in another data base that included word-class information for 94,000 words of poetry and 200,000 words of essays and novels, a very stable relationship is the *sum* of nouns and pronouns (29.7% of the words, S.D. = 1.6%). Miles gives no pronoun counts, but they may have generally decreased from nine to five percent since 1500.

The ratio of adjectives to verbs has the pattern of changes listed above, but it is not clear exactly what syntactic features it represents. It does not seem that a high ratio per se denotes the presence of "phrasal and coordinative modifications of subject and object . . . heavy modifications and compounding of subjects, in a variety of phrasal constructions." [10] This ratio does not treat the rising proportion of nouns at all. The ratio of adjectives to nouns, also shown in Figure 2, is a better index of changes in noun-phrase modifiers, and it is not sensitive to the varying proportions of nouns. The scatter plots of the ratios identify couplets (with triangles) and blank verse (with squares), since these genres comprise much of the seventeenth-century sample and contribute most to the eighteenth-century high points. A history of style must first give an account of which genres are used, and only then describe individual variables within each genre. For instance, what the novice sees first in eighteenth-century English verse is not that the ratios of adjectives to nouns or to verbs are high, but rather that most poems by famous (anthologized) writers are in couplets. Amid the efforts to write a history of style, we should not lose track of such gross and striking differences as those between Elizabethan and modern spelling, or between poetry and prose.[11]

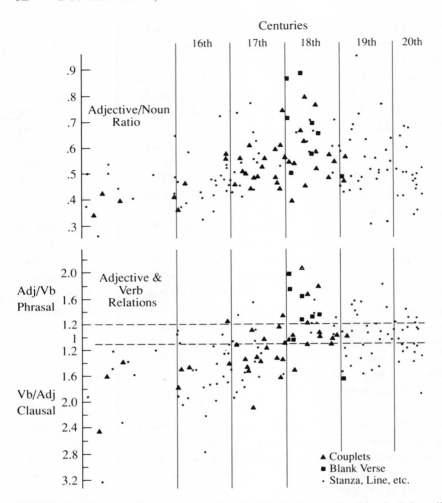

FIGURE 2. Adjective-to-noun ratios and verb-and-adjective relationships in "phrasal" and "clausal" poetry

Miles's data involve only three syntactic categories, so it is not clear what kinds of clauses are present, or what kinds of nominal and verbal phrases the clauses contain. I have analyzed a sample of English Romantic poetry with a more elaborate parsing strategy and more complicated word-class tagging. This computer-aided system also measures vocabulary structure, word length, and clause length, and it gives an extensive census of the types and constituents of all phrases. The current version of the program is still incomplete on identifying the types of clauses. The Romantic poetry sample includes Keats's odes and sonnets,

Blake's *Songs of Innocence and Experience,* most of Coleridge's "Conversation" poems, and two odes and random samples from *The Prelude,* I and II, by Wordsworth.[12]

This analytic procedure gives hundreds of observations for each poem, which are then combined and reduced to what seem the most fruitful and illuminating descriptors. These are arranged on linear scales to show relative distances as in the example of Figure 3.

A tentative explanation of the alignments is that the poems represent three genres. First Blake's *Songs* and Wordsworth's odes are at one extreme on most scales. To use the taxonomy of Wordsworth's 1815 "Preface," these poems are *lyric* in a pure sense of that word which suggests a song-like quality, a need for "an accompaniment of music" for their "*full* effect." They use relatively more verbs, more pronouns, and fewer modifiers such as adjectives, adverbs, and prepositional phrases. At the opposite end of the scales is *The Prelude,* with few verbs and many prepositional phrases and adverbs which probably help convey the poem's epic or expository contents. In the middle are the "Conversation" poems by Coleridge and Keats's sonnets and odes. In Wordsworth's formulation these are *idyls* that describe the "processes and appearances of external nature" and include "the epistles of poets writing in their own persons, and all loco-descriptive poetry." These genres are defined empirically, on the basis of underlying linguistic and stylistic patterns. They do not necessarily follow labeled genres—the odes by Keats are different from poems with the same label by Wordsworth.

After it is known how a genre contributes to the style of a work, then the individual styles can be compared. The most significant differences between the poems by Keats and Coleridge in the sample are that Keats uses fewer verbs, more coordinating conjunctions (especially in his sonnets), and fewer determiners. A history of style would, of course, be improved if it showed when one style influences another. Keats had a copy of Coleridge's 1817 anthology, *Sybilline Leaves,* within three months of publication,[13] but it is not known how closely he read the poems or whether he noticed differences between the ballad-like "Ancient Mariner" and other poems in the collection. Perhaps the best explanation is that both poets followed a longstanding iambic-pentameter tradition, Keats in rhymed stanzas and sonnets, Coleridge in blank verse. Unfortunately, no extensive data have been gathered from earlier works in iambic pentameter or from "idyls," so this idea cannot yet be tested.

In another study, I tried to account for Emerson's stylistic influence on Whitman.[14] The biographical evidence is extensive; records tell of visits and of public and private praise, and give similar useful material. It seems obvious that Emerson's rhymed "bardic" and stanzaic poetry had no positive impact on Whitman. However, by juxtaposing Whitman's free verse with passages of Emerson's *prose,*

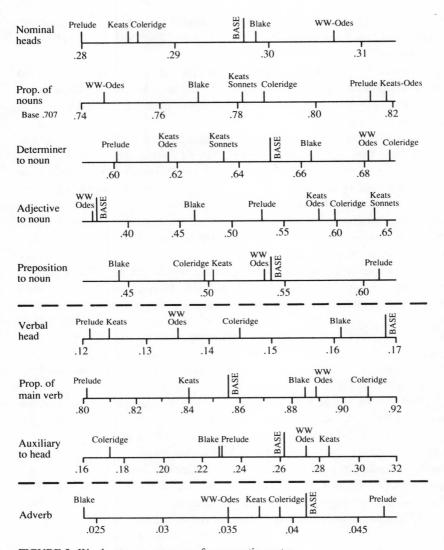

FIGURE 3. Word-category measures for romantic poetry

the critic can rather easily demonstrate stylistic connections. This is especially true in places where Emerson celebrates the wondrous potential for America or lists the attributes of the poet or scholar. As a test case I compared the final paragraph of "The Poet" with a passage of the same length and on similar topics from "Song of Myself." Metrical or rhythmic patterns, clause lengths, repetition-patterns of vocabulary, the use of conjunctions, parallelism, and a number of

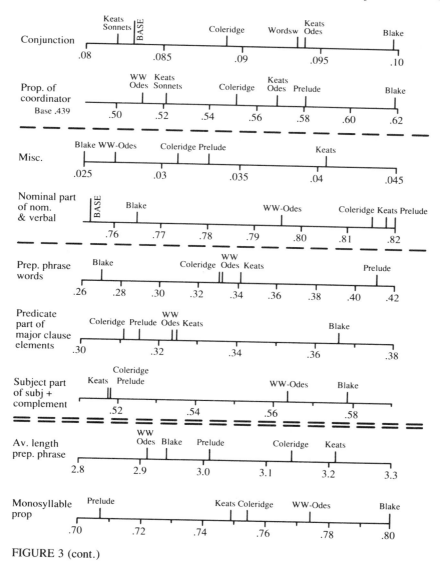

FIGURE 3 (cont.)

other features were quite alike. While the personal connection between the two men is clearly documented, it is possible that both styles derived from a common tradition—i.e., the style of public oratory in mid-nineteenth-century America. Emerson was a lecturer by profession, and Whitman toyed with the idea of becoming one.

Methodological problems in writing a history of style arise at each stage. Researchers directly involved must find ways to present the information clearly to teachers of literature who are neither interested in nor yet acquainted with technical mapping languages, or statistical arguments. The presentation must have complete data so that other specialists may build on previous work without duplication. Even though linguistic and rhetorical theories are imperfect and stylistic data sets are not yet large, the historian need not hesitate to formulate provisional accounts, perhaps for small periods of time or for less-used genres. When new facts become available, the old history can be revised or rejected. As this paper suggests, an account of the several genres is an integral part of the account of how texts were written. Ultimately, the means to discover and justify claims about the causal relations among styles may be formed. All writers in an era share more or less the same syntax, phonology, and so on—no one learns long words from Gibbon or short words from the Bible, or long sentences from Faulkner and short ones from Hemingway. Nevertheless, no one since Lyly is likely to have invented the combination of features that comprise Euphuism.

Notes

*This essay originally appeared in *Style* 11 (1977):262–73.

1. The quoted phrases are from "Address to the Reader," in *The Literary History of the United States,* Robert Spiller et al., 3rd ed. (New York: Macmillan, 1963), xx.

2. Norman Holland, "UNITY IDENTITY TEXT SELF," *Publications of the Modern Language Association* 90 (1975):821–22.

3. In an artificial situation, with inexperienced writers, as in a composition class or writing workshop, a law-giver can decide to forbid or encourage some features. It will look silly to give Hemingway low marks for short, choppy sentences, however.

4. An arbitrary exclusion would be an anthology with room for a short story by Conrad but no space for a novel by Dickens.

5. Some work has been done. For the semantic content of metaphor, see Archibald Hill, "Analogies, Icons and Images in Relation to the Semantic Content of Discourse," *Style* 2 (Fall 1968):203–27. For the relationship between syntax and metaphor, see Rosemary Gläser, "The Application of Transformational Generative Grammar to the Analysis of Similes and Metaphors in Modern English," *Style* 5 (Fall 1971):265–83. See also Leonard A. Podis, "'The Unreality of Reality': Metaphor in *The Great Gatsby,*" *Style* 11 (Winter 1977):56–77.

6. See, for example, M. B. Pringle and D. Ross, "Dialogue and Narration in Joyce's Ulysses," in *Computing in the Humanities: Proceedings of the Third International Conference on Computing in the Humanities,* ed. Serge Lusignan and John S. North (Waterloo: University of Waterloo Press, 1977), 73–84. See also Barron Brainerd, "An Exploratory Study of Pronouns and Articles as Indices of Genre in English," *Language and Style* 5 (1972):239–59.

7. Andrew T. Crosland, "The Concordance as an Aid in the Historical Study of Style," *Style* 11 (1977):274–83.

8. Josephine Miles, "Eras in English Poetry," *Publications of the Modern Language Association* 70 (1955):853–75, reprinted in *Essays on the Language of Literature,* ed. Seymour Chatman and Samuel R. Levin (Boston: Houghton Mifflin, 1967), 175–96, and *Eras and Modes in English Poetry* (Berkeley: University of California Press, 1964). My study uses data from the book. Others who use the data should be warned that the article

and its reprint contain nearly one hundred rounding-off or transcription errors, based on the counts which are given in *Eras and Modes*. Miles's counts end with zero, which represents between 7 and 12 (personal communication). The word categories are defined in *Eras* (251): "adjectives, nouns, and verbs—as distinguished from articles, pronouns, connectives, and most adverbs." Adjectives thus include all so-called determiners except *the* and *a(n)*, and some participles; nouns include gerunds; and verbs include auxiliaries, copulas, and infinitives. Miles's basic measure is the frequency of each class per line multiplied by 10. For problems with the texts Miles used, see William P. Williams, "Analytical Bibliography and the Historical Study of Style," *Style* 11 (1977):235–41.

9. G. T. Wright, "The Lyric Present: Simple Present Verbs in English Poems," *Publications of the Modern Language Association* 89 (1974):563–79.

10. Miles, 176.

11. C. B. Williams, "Mendenhall's Studies of Word-length Distribution in the Works of Shakespeare and Bacon," *Biometrika* 62 (1975):107–12, shows how a number of scholars have gone astray in the Baconian controversy by trying to compare prose and verse.

12. Donald Ross, "Stylistics and the Testing of Literary Hypotheses," *Poetics* 7 (1978):389–416. See also Ross, "The Use of Word-Class Distribution Data for Stylistics: Keats's Sonnets and Chicken Soup," *Poetics* 6 (1977):169–96.

13. John Keats to the Dilkes, 5 or 12 November 1817, No. 42 in *The Keats Circle: Letters and Papers and More Letters and Poems of the Keats Circle*, ed. H. E. Rollins (Cambridge, Mass.: Harvard University Press, 1965).

14. Donald Ross, "Emerson's Stylistic Influence on Whitman," *American Transcendental Quarterly* 25 (1975):41–51.

STATISTICAL APPENDIX

Listed below, for reference, are the basic statistical descriptions computed from Josephine Miles's data. Table 1 gives the average proportion (multiply by 100 for percentage) and standard deviation (variability) for the three word-classes, and the next part gives three ratios, for each century and for all the samples. Table 2 contains the basic results of correlation and regression analyses of the category or ratio as a function of time.

TABLE 1. PROPORTIONS AND RATIOS FROM MILES (BY CENTURY)

		British Poets						American Poets	
	All samples	to 15th	16th	17th	18th	19th	20th	19th	20th
No. of samples	200	10	30	30	30	30	20	30	20
Adjective Av. (S.D.)	.1239 (.0317)	.0868 (.0169)	.1011 (.0192)	.1234 (.0318)	.1582 (.0306)	.1277 (.0310)	.1234 (.0224)	.1207 (.0215)	.1251 (.0229)
Noun Av. (S.D.)	.2360 (.0340)	.2088 (.0224)	.2157 (.0257)	.2267 (.0387)	.2561 (.0254)	.2358 (.0343)	.2463 (.0262)	.2414 (.0288)	.2457 (.0383)
Verb Av. (S.D.)	.1351 (.0224)	.1507 (.0211)	.1454 (.0187)	.1528 (.0280)	.1301 (.0152)	.1285 (.0195)	.1267 (.0178)	.1249 (.0174)	.1267 (.0164)
Adj:Noun Av. (S.D.)	.525 (.1) (.110)	.418 (.077)	.472 (.090)	.542 (.093)	.620 (.113)	.545 (.127)	.505 (.097)	.503 (.082)	.513 (.072)
Adj:Verb Av. (S.D.)	.951 (.317)	.596 (.166)	.718 (.211)	.831 (.264)	1.245 (.336)	1.031 (.339)	.998 (.234)	.984 (.218)	1.003 (.206)
["Phrasal" distance]					−.803	−.970			−.997
Noun:Verb Av. (S.D.)	1.800 (.423)	1.411 (.241)	1.514 (.305)	1.515 (.302)	1.988 (.238)	1.870 (.347)	2.009 (.488)	1.979 (.418)	1.986 (.464)

TABLE 2. CORRELATION AND LINEAR REGRESSION PARAMETERS—RATIOS AS A FUNCTION OF TIME (BY CENTURY)

	British Poets							American Poets	
	All samples	to 15th	16th	17th	18th	19th	20th	19th	20th
Adj:Noun and year	r .16	.47	.22	.16	-.13	.01	-.44	-.08	.05
	F 5.09*	2.29	1.36	0.77	0.50	0.0	4.28	0.18	0.05
	B .0001	.0011	.0005	.0005	-.0005	.0000	-.0029	-.0002	.0003
	A .3312	-1.050	-.351	-.328	1.507	.487	6.000	.8588	-.0039
Noun:Verb and year	r .47	.46	.04	.19	-.22	.18	.19	-.18	.01
	F 55.96**	2.10	0.04	1.03	1.37	0.94	0.68	0.95	0.0
	B .0013	.0033	.0003	.0020	-.0018	.0021	.0063	-.0022	.0004
	A -.4070	-3.014	1.040	-1.728	5.064	-1.963	-10.048	6.024	1.148
Adj:Verb and year	r .38	.58	.17	.18	-.22	.12	-.17	-.23	.10
	F 33.01**	4.01	0.78	0.92	1.41	0.37	0.56	1.54	0.17
	B .0008	.0029	.0010	.0017	-.0026	.0013	-.0028	-.0015	.0014
	A -.3805	-3.272	-.7686	-1.867	5.644	-1.352	6.247	3.638	-1.658
No. of samples	200	10	30	30	30	30	20	30	20
Average date	1721	1357	1523	1617	1718	1816	1900	1814	1900

r = correlation coefficient
F = value in F distribution; df: 1 and sample-size minus 2
B = slope of linear regression; A = intercept
* = R or F significant at the 0.05 level; ** = significant at 0.01

Adapting Hypothesis Testing to a Literary Problem

BARBARA STEVENSON*

Many advocates of statistical interpretation believe that statistical hypothesis testing can objectively and accurately prove a hypothesis. Actually, researchers
routinely make decisions that involve subjectivity, and statistical tests make assumptions that some hypotheses may be unable to meet. This subjectivity com-
pounded with the stringent requirements of statistical testing can thwart the
application of hypothesis testing to literary problems. Although some brush aside
these obstacles, it is questionable whether this marriage of statistics and literary
criticism, known as computational stylistics, does work.

This controversy concerning computational stylistics is perhaps best exempli-
fied by the arguments over the validity of the statistical authorship test developed
by A. Q. Morton, which he has named *stylometry*. In 1984, *The Shakespeare
Newsletter* printed a series of articles by M. W. A. Smith attacking Morton's
proof that Shakespeare composed all of *Pericles*. Editor Louis Marder, noting
the statistical jargon pervading the articles, commented on the difficulty of com-
prehending fully Morton's stylometry and Smith's refutation (28). This issue of
the newsletter portrays perfectly the current status of computational stylistics: the
experts cannot agree on the ways statistics should be adapted to literary criticism,
and statistical novices are unable to understand the jargon of the experts.

Because computational stylistics is such a new field, many more years of experimenting will probably have to pass before the experts will be able to reconcile statistics with literary criticism. However, what can be done now is to educate novices about the principles and problems of adapting hypothesis testing to literary criticism so that they can understand the difficulties inherent in such stylistic experiments as stylometry.

FORMULATING THE HYPOTHESIS

In hypothesis testing, the first step is to formulate the hypothesis to be validated. The hypothesis for an authorship examination seems simple enough: did this particular author compose that particular text? However, this simplicity is deceptive.

For example, some critics question the existence of the entity known as the *author*, with some justification. An editor (or a scribe, if the text is an ancient one) may shape parts of an author's work in such a way as to render the style indistinguishable from one writer to the next in an authorship test. And, indeed, a single author may be several stylists in one.

Also, does each writer have a unique style, one that can be differentiated from everyone else's? Authorship tests assume that style does vary from person to person, and some experiments do support this assumption. In one experiment, seventy college students wrote nine themes during the span of eight months. The themes were gathered, and obvious identifiers, such as the students' names, were removed. Readers then tried to group the essays according to the student writers. Although the groupings were not totally accurate, the readers were able to group the majority of the papers correctly. Even though the experiment provided evidence that writing style consists of individual characteristics, the researchers could not precisely ascertain what traits differentiated the writers from one another (Miller, 120).

Even though studies suggest that people *do* write differently, research has not indicated *how* writing differs from one person to the next, and for stylistic studies like authorship tests this knowledge is indispensable. Many scholars believed—prematurely—that Mosteller and Wallace had uncovered the feature that distinguishes writers' styles. By counting the rates of occurrence of "content-free" function words, Mosteller and Wallace proved that Madison, not Hamilton, had composed the twelve disputed Federalist letters; that is, Mosteller and Wallace calculated the average number of times function words such as prepositions and conjunctions occurred. Shunning "content words" like *government* because the subject of the text determines the selection of these words, Mosteller and Wallace concentrated on words they believed were not so dependent on the content of the paper. One successful test revealed that Hamilton used *while* whereas Madison used *whilst;* all the disputed letters contain *whilst* (203–05).

Other researchers followed this model with little success. McColly and Weier, in their research on the *Pearl* poet, found that function words are not content-free as had often been assumed, but that in fact the rates of occurrence of function words seem to be dependent on the subject and style of the text (70). As Morton has observed, Mosteller and Wallace had only to match two authors' styles to yield their results, whereas the typical authorship experiment involves many possible authors (104).

Attempting to discover how authors' styles do differ, Morton counted such items as position of words in a sentence and collocations, which are pairings of words (like *to the*). Morton realized that the subject and style of a text could determine the author's choice of words, but he postulated that word position and collocations would vary from one writer to the next. To test this theory, Morton examined several novels by John Fowles, but could not establish consistent features for Fowles to form the basis for an authorship test (144–46). This failure, however, has not deterred Morton from continuing to advocate the validity of stylometry.

As these authorship examples show, formulating a hypothesis is tricky when the hypothesis itself relies upon unproven opinions, such as the belief that a certain feature will expose the author of a text. By contrast, formulating a hypothesis for an agricultural experiment seems much easier, not a surprising revelation since much of hypothesis testing originated in agricultural studies. A textbook example tells of a gardener who wanted to test a new fertilizer to ascertain if it were superior, equal, or inferior to the fertilizer he had been using. He began his experiment by formulating the *null hypothesis* that no (null) significant difference existed between the potency of the two fertilizers. After the tomatoes grew, the number of tomatoes grown with one fertilizer was compared to the number of tomatoes grown with the other. If a significant difference were to occur, then the null hypothesis would be rejected, and one fertilizer would be proven to be superior to the other one (Box, Hunter, and Hunter, 94).

The hypothesis for Morton's stylometry is not as straightforward as is this one for the agricultural experiment. Stylometry's null hypothesis assumes that no significant difference exists between the writing style of two texts, and, consequently, this lack of difference supposedly proves that the same person produced both texts. The null hypothesis rests upon the unproven assumption that word position and collocations do differ among writers. Because of the unproven assumption, it is impossible to interpret the results. Ideally the null hypothesis should not rest on any unproven assumptions.

DATA GATHERING

Once a hypothesis is formulated, the next step is to gather data randomly from the population to be tested. The data in an experiment consist of samples chosen from a *population,* which is a theoretically infinite group of items that share common characteristics. In the agricultural experiment mentioned above, the gardener wanted to test fertilizer on his particular variety of tomato plants. The specific plants tested were samples from the population of tomato plants of that variety.

Defining a population for literary studies poses difficulties. Whereas a tomato plant is a discrete, definable object, linguists have not been able to agree upon a satisfactory definition of such linguistic entities as a word, much less a satisfactory way of collecting and classifying them. In attacking Morton's stylometry, Smith asserted:

> The failure to mention straightforward but important definitions distinguishes Morton's work from scientific studies. Included in this category are the definitions of a sentence for positions testing, a collocation (for example, if a punctuation mark occurs between its two words is it still valid?), . . . and the determination as to whether or not elided words are incorporated in the counts. (Smith, "An Investigation," 355)

Literary texts do not strictly meet the two conditions of a population—being theoretically infinite and sharing common characteristics. Tomato plants can produce generation after generation, providing a seemingly infinite number of samples, so that gardeners can continually verify their conclusions about the best fertilizer. This replication is limited with literary experiments because a writer produces a finite number of works, and no more (Cox and Snell, 64).

A more serious setback lies with establishing the shared traits of the members of a literary population. As a result, those conducting authorship tests are faced with the quandary of what to include in the experiment. Most agree that it is best to try to get as homogeneous a sample as possible by not mixing radically different styles like prose and poetry. Mosteller and Wallace were successful when they used political prose pieces by Hamilton and Madison, but, in replicating Mosteller and Wallace's work, McColly and Weier discovered that even homogeneous works by the same author are at times rejected as being genuine in a statistical authorship examination (69).

Another difficulty in data gathering is deciding the proper way to select random samples. As the word *random* suggests, samples are chosen indeterminately, not according to some premeditated plan. Random sampling ensures that unbiased data are collected; only unbiased data will really indicate the properties of the population.

To sample randomly, the gardener investigating fertilizers randomly put the experimental fertilizer on some plants and the usual fertilizer on others. He decided on the random arrangement by placing cards from a shuffled deck in the same pattern as the garden. Those plants designated by red cards received the usual fertilizer and those plants represented by black cards received the new fertilizer (Box, Hunter, and Hunter, 94).

How do literary researchers select samples? By randomly choosing words, or sentences, or paragraphs, or something else? Essentially, the difficulty is that randomly selected linguistic features like words or sentences are not a microcosm of a text in the way that randomly selected plants are a microcosm of a species. The nonrandom arrangement of language into such categories as sentences and paragraphs makes sampling a perplexing problem. In addressing this problem, Alvar Ellegard discussed the necessity for large samples (7–63), while Morton surveyed the various approaches to sampling that scholars have tried through the years: *spread sampling* (for instance, choosing the fifth sentence on every other page) and *block sampling* (selecting sections from a long work), but none of these approaches are random (75–78). If possible, entire works should be included in the experiment, not just excerpts from works. After all, statisticians encourage the collection of large random samples to ensure that the properties of the entire population are represented in the experiment, and using entire works is the only way to ensure that all the features of the literary population are present.

SELECTING THE TEST

After collecting the data, investigators must select a statistical test that will fit the data and the problem. Many different tests have been created for many different sorts of problems, so it takes the expertise of a statistician to select an appropriate test for a problem. In selecting a test that suits his problem, Morton chose the chi-square formula because it tests for differences between two items, making it ideal for authorship work.

The underlying assumptions that specific tests make about the data must also be taken into consideration. Many statistical tests assume that data, when graphed, will fall into a particular pattern, such as the familiar bell curve (called the *normal distribution*). However, the frequency of a linguistic feature in a text perhaps will not fall into the perfectly symmetrical bell curve. The advantage of the chi-square test is that it permits data to take on an irregular shape.

Another assumption frequently made about data when using statistical formulas, including the chi square is *independence,* which means that the choice of an item to be tested is not influenced by any of the preceding choices. Yet again the nonrandom nature of language presents complications. Language is dependent, not independent (Cox and Snell, 64). It is much more likely, for instance, that after the word *from* a noun rather than a verb will appear.

How will this violation of statistical principles affect the outcome of the test? If the data have been counted correctly and meet the conditions of the test, the calculated results of the test should fall into a particular shape when graphed. For example, the results of a chi-square test should fall into a chi-square distribution, as pictured in Figure 1.

Even though all the data may be counted correctly and may be appropriate for the formula, the results may still be erroneous. Statisticians acknowledge this potential for error by arbitrarily setting what is called the *significance level,* which is the maximum amount of error that is acceptable for the particular experiment. Morton has recommended the conventional significance level of .05, which means that there is a maximum probability of 5 percent of being wrong when the null hypothesis is rejected. In other words, 5 out of 100 occurrences may be chance mistakes. When the computer (or statistician) performs the calculations, this 5 percent chance of error is figured into the results.

If the data are not independent, the significance level may be inaccurate, and the results, when charted, will fall into a distorted shape rather than the proper distribution. Figure 2 compares the chi-square distribution with its 5 percent chance of error with a slightly distorted shape, caused by the lack of independence, that has more than 5 percent chance of error.

When literary investigators set the significance level, they must realize that their results are perhaps skewed; instead of having a 5 percent chance of being wrong, they may actually be something like 15 percent wrong. All researchers, no matter what their subject fields, must admit that their results may be wrong, but, because of the heterogeneous complexity of their subject, literary researchers must be acutely aware of this shortcoming.

EXECUTING THE TEST

Once the appropriate statistical test has been selected, researchers then must adapt their literary problem to the particular formula. Morton's experiment with Sir Walter Scott illustrates this step. Morton decided to run a test to determine whether the passage of time and the onslaught of disease affect a writer's style, so he chose to consider Sir Walter Scott, who suffered from strokes. Morton selected samples from *The Antiquary,* written in 1816 before Scott's first stroke, and *Castle Dangerous,* written in 1831 after the strokes (134–35).

By applying the chi-square test, Morton ascertained that Scott used the word *but* as the initial word in a sentence at a consistent rate in each of the two novels,

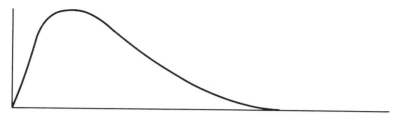

FIGURE 1. Typical chi-square distribution

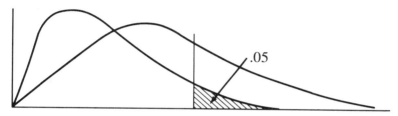

FIGURE 2. The 5 percent chance of error of a chi-square distribution compared with the chance of error of a distribution distorted by lack of independence

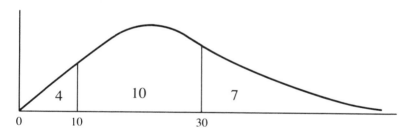

FIGURE 3. Distribution with observed values

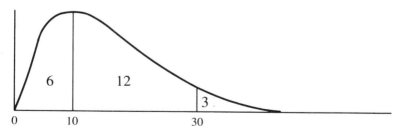

FIGURE 4. Distribution with expected values

so he decided to employ this as one discriminator of Scott's style. He then fitted these data into the chi-square formula. The *null hypothesis* of the chi-square test supposes that no (null) significant difference exists between the expected proportion of the items under consideration and the observed proportion. If Scott used "initial *but*" consistently, then a certain number of "initial *buts*" is expected to appear in each novel. This number is called the *expected proportion;* the actual number of "initial *buts*" appearing in the novels is called the *observed proportion.* (The appendix to this chapter shows the execution of the chi-square test.)

The result from the chi-square test is then compared with the significance level of .05, the recognized level of error mentioned earlier. If the calculated answer is *less* than .05, the null hypothesis is rejected because there is a 5 percent or less chance of error when rejecting the null hypothesis. In other words, a significant difference probably exists between the expected and the observed proportions. If the answer is *higher* than .05, then the test fails to reject the null hypothesis because there is a more than 5 percent chance of being wrong if the null hypothesis is rejected. Therefore, the test supports the idea that no significant difference exists between the expected and observed proportions. Being conscious of possible error, statisticians do not say that they have proven a hypothesis; instead, they say that they have failed to disprove their hypothesis.

In Morton's chi-square test on Scott, the result is .1, which is higher than the significance level of .05. Since .1 is higher than .05, Morton did not reject his null hypothesis; he maintained that Scott used this linguistic feature consistently. Morton ran a total of 26 such stylistic tests on Scott and claimed that 19 proved consistent and 7 inconsistent.[1] From a statistical viewpoint, the hypothesis that Scott wrote consistently has *not* been proven because the significance level of .05 dictates that only 5 percent of the tests can be inconsistent. Five percent of 26 tests is 1 inconsistency. Instead of only 1 inconsistency, Morton's experiment has 7, and 7 inconsistencies out of 26 tests is approximately 25 percent, not 5 percent.

DRAWING CONCLUSIONS

When drawing conclusions, researchers naturally exercise their own judgment, thereby creating the potential for error. When drawing conclusions about Scott's writing style, Morton disregarded his own statistical results and decided that he had enough proof to suggest that Scott's style did remain stable over time. Morton justified his decision by saying, "The examination starts from a text and it should always end with the text; the statistics are only a useful summary description of what an author is doing" (141). Yet in other parts of his book, Morton made such statements as "stylometry is a science and a powerful one" (39), suggesting that statistics can definitively prove hypotheses. Such contradictions invalidate much of Morton's work; he seems to follow the rules of statistical testing only when they support a hypothesis favored by him.

Despite Morton's assertion that stylometry is "scientific" and "objective," hypothesis testing does entail a certain amount of subjectivity, as evidenced by the potential for error acknowledged in the significance level. In addition, researchers must be careful to avoid hasty generalizations. In Morton's test on Scott, all the chi-square test has shown is that Scott used "initial *but*" at a consistent rate in two novels; that this consistency proves that the writing style of Scott, and by extension all authors, remained unaffected by time and disease is a leap in logic made by Morton.

Morton made a similar leap in his experiment with John Fowles. Morton selected Fowles because he represents one of those authors who are fond of changing writing styles. Morton insisted that even when authors try to disguise their writing style, stylometry can still detect consistent features of which the author is unaware. Morton analyzed Fowles's novels *The Collector, The Magus,* and *The French Lieutenant's Woman,* each written in a radically different style from the others. He was unable to uncover linguistic habits common to all of these works, but that did not deter him from advancing stylometry as a valid test. After finding consistent features within each novel, Morton expressed this inference:

> It can therefore be argued that what Fowles does is change his habits with his literary form but not within it. So the examination does confirm the starting hypothesis that, for writers in an uninflected language, the placing of words in preferred positions or in collocations offers a range of tests of authorship, the application of which within any literary form is straightforward but the comparison of different forms is complicated. (146)

Morton committed two hasty generalizations: he assumed that one Fowles novel can represent all novels that Fowles will write for that particular genre, and he generalized his findings to all writers of uninflected languages. Because of the danger of committing hasty generalizations, responsible scientists urge constant replication of experiments.

Aside from the usual pitfalls of reasoning errors, investigators have to be aware of the special circumstances discussed before: independence and randomness. The failure to meet such assumptions for the statistical formulas may distort the results. The crux of these difficulties is that statistical tests were designed for experiments in agriculture and other such "hard" sciences, and stylometric experiments force these tests onto problems for which they were never designed.

SOLUTIONS

Despite these inherent problems, literary critics should not abandon hypothesis testing, because it offers valid quantitative data—when properly applied. When reading a text, a person sees thousands of words, seemingly without a pattern. In stylometry, a computer counts linguistic features, and statistical tests establish general traits of the writer's language that the unaided human eye cannot discern. Here lies the strength of a stylometric study: it can illuminate general trends from quantitative data. However, because of its limitations, the adaptation of hypothesis testing to a test of authorship seems inappropriate. If researchers use stylometry, they are faced with an absolute hypothesis: a particular writer either composed the text or not; an author either writes consistently or not.

For literary criticism, hypothesis testing works better where there is not an absolute right or wrong answer. For instance, Louis Milic, in *A Quantitative Approach to Jonathan Swift*, used his data to draw conclusions about Swift's literary style, such as describing Swift's fondness for lists consisting of three items. Since Milic was interested in general trends rather than an absolute yes-or-no answer (except in the one chapter where he attempted an authorship test), the disparity between statistics and stylistics did not affect his results dramatically.

In contrast, stylometry seems to place too many demands upon hypothesis testing, as Morton's work with Scott illustrates. When comparing the "initial *but*" in *The Antiquary* and *Castle Dangerous,* Morton got a level of .1. Since this is higher than the significance level of .05, he did not reject his null hypothesis, but instead maintained that Scott used this linguistic feature consistently. But is there much difference between .05 and .1? To answer this question, Van Brackle and I performed what statisticians call a *sensitivity study* to determine whether the formula being applied is resistant to small changes in data. While in the samples from *Castle Dangerous* Scott used the "initial *but*" twenty times, we supposed that "initial *but*" appeared eighteen times instead, and we ran the chi-square test again, getting a result of .03 (a significant difference). By changing the number of "initial *buts*" by two, we got a result opposite to Morton's, illustrating that Scott comes close to being different in the two texts. Thus, for this particular case stylometry is overly sensitive to small changes in data. Although classical statisticians arbitrarily select a significance level and stick to it resolutely, such an approach does not work well here.

To avoid some pitfalls, researchers may want to limit the use of hypothesis testing to describing general stylistic traits as opposed to proving absolute hypotheses. Nevertheless, the success of some authorship studies, in particular Mosteller and Wallace's, suggests that hypothesis testing could be expanded to applications other than just general descriptions. Before this expansion can happen, the difference between language and statistics needs to be reconciled. Perhaps the resolution lies with simulation studies, which can verify the accuracy of a statistical test used in a particular situation.

When scientists are faced with such problems as having to perform experiments on data that exhibit dependence instead of independence, they perform simulation studies to determine whether the dependence skews their results. Simulation studies applied to literature could perhaps reveal specifically how the lack of randomness and independence in literary texts affects statistical testing.

For stylistic studies probably the best simulation technique is resampling. As the name *resampling* implies, samples from the literary texts being examined are chosen and tested over and over again. If the results deviate from what is expected, the test is probably invalid; if results meet expectations, the test probably works.

No one, as far as I know, has performed such a simulation study on literature. A. Q. Morton, in *Literary Detection* (35–39), and Anthony Kenny, in *The Aristotelian Ethics* (90), claim that lack of independence is not a problem. To prove their point, they both divide their samples of text into groups and perform a chi-square test on these groups to show the groups' consistency with each other. But their tests are not sufficient to prove their point; resampling requires *hundreds* of complicated chi-square manipulations, not just one simple test (see, for example, Geisser, 320–28).

What follows is a description of a hypothetical resampling study that could be done with A. Q. Morton's test of Scott's use of *but* as the initial word of a sentence in *The Antiquary*. First, a random sample of several chapters from *The Antiquary* are chosen. The chi-square value is calculated for "initial *buts*" for each of the selected chapters. Then, *hundreds* of random samples are selected from these chapters, and chi squares are calculated for all of these random samples.

In the second step of resampling, these calculated chi-square values constitute the observed occurrences. These chi squares are then grouped in intervals according to their size. For instance, four chi squares may fall in the 0–10 interval (let us say the values are .3, 2.8, 7.2, and 9.0); ten chi squares may fall in the 10–30 interval; and seven chi squares may fall in the 30 or larger interval. The size of the interval is arbitrarily dictated by the statistician.

Figure 3 illustrates what the distribution with these observed values may look like.

Next, a computer with a statistical software package like SPSS can calculate the number of chi-square values *expected* (versus the *observed* ones in the previous paragraph) to fall into each interval. The computer may calculate that six of the total number of chi squares should fall between 0–10, twelve should fall between 10–30, and three should fall in the 30 or larger interval.

Figure 4 depicts the true chi-square distribution based upon these expected values. A new chi-square test is performed for each of the intervals, using the observed and expected values mentioned above. Let us say that there are four observed occurrences in the 0–10 interval and that the computer gives the expected occurrence of six. With these two numbers, the new chi-square test is done. The process is repeated for each interval.

Finally, all these newly calculated chi squares are added to form one large chi-square. The computer then is asked to give the significance level that corresponds to this large chi square. If the significance level is less than .05, the resampling test indicates that the chi-squares just calculated probably correspond to the true values in the chi-square distribution. In other words, the lack of independence in the literary text probably does not disrupt the chi-square test. Thus, Morton's tests on Scott are most likely accurate. If, on the other hand, the significance level is higher than .05, the resampling test suggests the opposite conclusion: the lack of independence of the literary text invalidates the results of a chi-square test, and the work done by Morton should be viewed skeptically.

Until a simulation study can verify the accuracy of such literary hypothesis tests as stylometry, critics should view these tests skeptically. In the interim one possible solution is to set the significance level at a more stringent level like .01, although this increases the chance of rejecting the null hypothesis when it is actually true. And even if the problem of independence could be solved, there are still other problems with adapting statistical testing to literary criticism which this paper does not even explore. In short, literary critics should approach computational stylistics with trepidation.

Notes

1. Aside from the test with "initial *but,*" however, Morton did not include the other tests in *Literary Detection.* Because of such oversights as this and because of the many errors that appear in the book, M. W. A. Smith, in "An Investigation of the Basis of Morton's Method of the Determination of Authorship," argues that Morton's claims for stylometry remain unsubstantiated.

*Statistical information furnished by Lewis Van Brackle.

References

Box, George E. P., William G. Hunter, and J. Stuart Hunter. *Statistics for Experimenters: An Introduction to Design, Data Analysis, and Model Building.* New York: John Wiley & Sons, 1978.

Cox, D. R., and E. J. Snell. *Applied Statistics: Principles and Examples.* London: Chapman and Hall, 1981.

Ellegard, Alvar. *A Statistical Method for Determining Authorship: The Junius Letters, 1769–1772.* Gothenburg Studies in English 13. Ed. Frank Behre. Gothenburg: Acta Universitatis Gothoburgensis, 1962.

Geisser, S. "The Predictive Sample Reuse Method with Applications." *Journal of the American Statistical Association* 70 (1975): 320–28.

Kenny, Anthony. *The Aristotelian Ethics: A Study of the Relationship between the Eudemian and Nicomachean Ethics of Aristotle.* Oxford: Clarendon Press, 1978.

Marder, Louis, ed. "Stylometry: The Controversy Continues." *The Shakespeare Newsletter* 34, 3 (1984): 28, 33.

McColly, W., and D. Weier. "Literary Attribution and Likelihood-Ratio Tests: The Case of the Middle English *Pearl* Poems." *Computers and the Humanities* 17 (1983): 65–75.

Milic, Louis. *A Quantitative Approach to the Style of Jonathan Swift.* The Hague: Mouton, 1967.

Miller, George A. *Language and Communication.* New York: McGraw-Hill, 1951.

Morton, A. Q. *Literary Detection: How to Prove Authorship and Fraud in Literature and Documents.* New York: Scribner's, 1978.

Mosteller, Frederick, and David Wallace. *Inference and Disputed Authorship: The Federalist.* Reading, Mass.: Addison-Wesley, 1964.

Smith, M. W. A. "Critical Reflections on the Determination of Authorship by Statistics. Part 1." *The Shakespeare Newsletter* 34, 1 (1984): 4–5.

———. "Critical Reflections on the Determination of Authorship by Statistics. Part 2." *The Shakespeare Newsletter* 34, 3 (1984): 28, 33.

———. "An Investigation of the Basis of Morton's Method for the Determination of Authorship." *Style* 19, 3 (1985): 341–58.

APPENDIX: EXAMPLE OF ADAPTING HYPOTHESIS TESTING TO A LITERARY PROBLEM

Illustrated below is the chi-square calculation of *but* as the first word in a sentence in *The Antiquary* and *Castle Dangerous*. With this chi-square test, Morton is trying to prove that Scott uses "initial *but*" at a consistent rate. The chi-square calculation below has been done manually, for illustrative purposes, but statisticians routinely use computers for such calculations.

1. Formulate the null hypothesis, which is for the chi-square test a supposition that no (null) significant difference exists between the expected proportion and the observed proportion.

Morton's null hypothesis. Sir Walter Scott used *but* as the initial word in a sentence consistently in *The Antiquary* (written before he suffered strokes) and in *Castle Dangerous* (written after his strokes).

2. Use the null hypothesis in the statistical test.

First Step. Calculate the expected occurrences. Expected occurrences of initial *but* in a Scott novel = proportion of the novel's total occurrences of *but* × occurrences of initial *but*.

CALCULATIONS OF OBSERVED OCCURRENCES

	As first word in sentences	In all other positions	Total
The Antiquary	123	276	399
Castle Dangerous	20	70	90
Total	143	346	489

For example, *The Antiquary*'s expected initial *but* occurrences = (total *buts* in *The Antiquary* [399] ÷ total *buts* in *The Antiquary* and *Castle Dangerous* [489] × total initial *buts* in *The Antiquary* and *Castle Dangerous* (143).

CALCULATIONS OF EXPECTED OCCURRENCES

	As first word in sentences	In all other positions
The Antiquary	(399 ÷ 489) × 143 = 116.68	(399 ÷ 489) × 346 = 282.32
Castle Dangerous	(90 ÷ 489) × 143 = 26.32	(90 ÷ 489) × 346 = 63.68

Second Step. Calculate the chi-square values.

(observed − expected)^2 ÷ expected = chi-square
(123 − 116.8)^2 ÷ 116.8 = 0.34
(276 − 282.32)^2 ÷ 282.32 = 0.14
(20 − 26.32)^2 ÷ 26.32 = 1.52
(70 − 63.68)^2 ÷ 63.68 = 0.63

Third Step. Add the chi-square values.

0.34 + 0.14 + 1.52 + 0.63 = 2.63

3. Execute the test.

First Step. Determine the degrees of freedom.

(number of books − 1) × (number of word positions − 1) = degrees of freedom
(2 − 1) × (2 − 1) = 1

Second Step. Consult the chi-square table. The table is organized according to chi-square values and degrees of freedom. To determine if his chi-square value of 2.63 shows a significant difference or not, Morton checks the chi-square table to find this number's corresponding significance level. If the resulting significance level is lower than .05, the test shows a significant difference between the expected and observed proportions.

The table reveals that Morton's significance level for the chi-square value of 2.63 is .10 (no significant difference).

4. Draw conclusions.

Therefore, Morton's test fails to disprove his null hypothesis that no difference exists between the rates of initial *but* in *The Antiquary* and *Castle Dangerous*.

>> *Part II*

THEME AND SEMANTIC ANALYSIS

>> 5

Analysis of Twentieth-Century French Prose Fiction:

Theoretical Context, Results, Perspective

PAUL A. FORTIER

On a number of occasions I have described my software for aiding computer studies of thematic structures in French literature (Fortier 1974a; Fortier and Mc-Connell 1973, 1975, 1976), and I have also reported the results of such studies. In this essay, I want to situate my work within the great flowering of theory of literature which we have seen in the past quarter-century. It seems useful to start from first principles, with a definition of literature, and then sketch the various movements in literary criticism which impinge on the topic.

LITERATURE AND THE NOVEL

We know that human societies existed before the discovery of metal working, before the invention of agriculture, before any of the technologies which we take for granted today were even imaginable. We have no evidence that any human society ever existed without literature. Anthropologists have observed and recorded the oral literature of societies in which writing is not practiced. Indeed, there is strong evidence to suggest that some of our great written works of literature—the Homeric epics, the Pentateuch—were originally oral literature. Thus it is clear that literature is an integral part of human existence—a reflection of the fact that we are cultural beings.

Several disciplines study aspects of the human condition. The medical sciences have produced vast amounts of information on the biological side of our existence, helping us to understand better the functioning of our bodies. Sociology, anthropology, political studies, and certain branches of history have developed coherent explanations of our modes of existence as social beings. Literary criticism seeks to expand our knowledge of ourselves as cultural beings. Its legitimacy is founded on the same principle as the biological and social sciences: the effort to understand ourselves is a worthy human activity.

In the vast and varied domain of literature, I have chosen to study the novel, which is a late development in the history of literary genres. Since the inception of the novel in the sixteenth century, it has been a printed prose text produced, with very few exceptions, by a single author. Although some critics speak of "profundity" and of the "ineffable" in novels, the reality is that a novel is an artifact, a series of black marks on a surface, which for convenience has been cut into sections and bound sequentially. Like other artifacts in the modern world, the novel functions within the market system. In Canada, a paperbound novel costs about as much as a case of beer, and a clothbound one roughly the same as a bottle of liquor.

Produced by an author, this *artifact* in turn is intended to *produce* effects outside itself, the most basic of which is to be bought. Curiously enough, this is the rarest effect produced by novels. A very few novels are widely liked, and become best-sellers. An even smaller number attain notoriety through their scandalous aspects. The vast majority are greeted with indifference on their publication, and never recover from it. With the passage of time even best-sellers, more frequently than not, sink into the oblivion of indifference. Some novels are consigned to oblivion by a hostile public, but usually no such external pressure is necessary. My interest is trying to determine what it is that permits some few novels to escape the oblivion which is the designated fate of most of the individual texts in this literary genre. Since I look for the source of this literary survival in the texts themselves, I find myself integrated into a cultural activity: literary criticism.

Literary Criticism

It is quite probable that as long as there has been literature there have been people explaining and commenting on it. As with so many things in our culture, we can find in Aristotle an early formulation and example of literary criticism. Aristotle's *Poetics* describes the literature of his time, distinguishing the various genres being practiced, explaining the characteristics of each, suggesting what is more or less important in each, using concrete examples to formulate theories which explain why some works are more successful than others. This *descriptive* criticism has changed little over the intervening millennia. Not just book reviews, but a large proportion of learned articles and the overwhelming majority of our teaching hours as professors of literature, are devoted to just this type of literary criticism. Indeed, no matter how advanced or rarefied, all literary criticism starts from a description—explicit or implicit—of the literary phenomena.

These phenomena are, however, almost impossible simply to describe; one describes from a perspective—certain things are important, others are less so; certain relations are worthy of note, others are passed over. One's perspective is determined partially by choice, partially by what one has inherited from a critical tradition. The French critical tradition has formed much of my outlook, and I believe that it is reasonable to sketch its main tenets.

French critics in the late Renaissance and early modern period used Aristotle's *Poetics* not as model for criticism but as a recipe for literary works. Less theory of literature than cookbook, the *Poetics* was the lynchpin of a school of prescriptive criticism. For instance, Corneille's *le Cid* was condemned by contemporary critics because it did not conform to the description of a tragedy in Aristotle (Gasté); in spite of this, the play went on to become a classic of French literature.

Critics of Corneille's time, and for the following two centuries, also considered it their duty to point out to the author any errors he might have made in grammar or language usage (see, for example, Voltaire, *Commentaires*). Although we are reluctant to admit it, a strong prescriptive streak lurks in most of us professors of literature. When we correct our students' essays, we go through them and mark the grammatical errors, check for misreadings of the text being interpreted, look for holes in the logic, and so forth. It is very easy to transfer these habits to our reading of literature and begin suggesting where the author might have done better, rather than explaining the function of what he or she has done. These lapses are usually well camouflaged, since prescriptive criticism has been generally discredited since the early nineteenth century.

About the time that prescriptive criticism was reaching the last stages of intellectual decadence, a new approach to literature was growing up. The historical study of literature is part of the nineteenth-century phenomenon of nationalism, and has as its aim the development and propagation of the nation's literary heritage (Jauss). This approach governs the teaching and study of literature to this day. Our courses present literature in terms of historical periods—eighteenth-century novel, nineteenth-century poetry, twentieth-century theatre. We define ourselves as specialists in the literature of a given historical period as well. A large amount of this is vestigial. Few of us today consider ourselves the handmaidens of nationalism.

Be that as it may, the problems with the historical approach to literature have become progressively more obvious. No one is going to profess to teach bad literature, but the historical method requires that one study things in a temporal continuum. Thus we find ourselves teaching and studying literary genres during periods when they were in decadence—eighteenth-century theatre and poetry in France are a case in point. A more serious problem arises from the type of history which provides the model for literary history—positivist history. This theory of history holds that coherence is immanent in the historical process. Thus once one has collected the facts—which are discoverable through close examination of documentary evidence—one can relate them to one another in a simple cause and effect relationship to discover "the truth" about what is being studied (Voltaire, Préface à *l'Essai sur les moeurs*). Professional historians have not taken this approach seriously for about a century.

Positivist literary history, as it is still practiced today by a few holdouts, stresses the process of production of the work of literature. It amasses all imaginable facts about the life and times of the author. In these facts it tries to find the causes or sources of every aspect of a literary text (e.g., Lancaster). Anything that cannot be explained by this type of cause and effect relationship is shunted aside either as irrelevant or as the effect of inspiration and beyond the ken of mere mortals.

The problem with this method is that it works equally well on good literature, texts like *Andromaque* which have stood the test of time, and on bad, like Pradon's version of *Phèdre*. This approach cannot show any difference between the works of the great classic playwright Pierre Corneille and those of his brother Thomas, who also wrote plays but without ever achieving literary stature. In short, positivist literary history—which has had at least a part in the training of virtually every critic practicing today—is, in the final analysis, unable to come to grips with the literary aspect of literature.

The reason for such failure seems clear. Once the positivist perspective has been chosen, the critic can find solid facts only in events, usually biographical, lying outside the structures of the text itself. Perhaps justly wary of impressions and personal reactions to the text, the positivist ends up on the periphery rather than at the heart of the study of literature. Computer analysis, as will be shown later in this essay, can provide all of the facts concerning the texts themselves that even the most exigent positivist could demand. But positivist literary criticism was already in the wane long before computer processing of literary texts was technically feasible.

As the deficiencies of positivist literary history became progressively clearer from the beginning of this century, many alternative approaches to literature have grown up. They can be conveniently grouped under three headings: formalist criticism, psycho-criticism, socio-criticism.

Contemporary Critical Theory

Formalism The Formalist school of literary criticism has two main branches: Russian Formalism and American "New Criticism." Both branches have had their practitioners in France as elsewhere, although the Russian school has had considerably more influence in France and so will be the only one discussed here. The hallmark of the Formalist approach is a stress on the text as independent reality, something to be examined and analyzed in and for itself, without the application of external criteria. A curious phenomenon can be observed in the practical application of these theories to literature. Formalists tend to work on form as commonly understood—words, sounds, rhyme, meter—in poetry only (Brik, Tomachevski). When they work on prose, their attention is focused on a curious hybrid which can be called "the forms of content". Propp's *Morphology of the Folktale* is one of the earliest examples of this. It categorizes the plot elements of all Russian folktales under a series of rubrics such as "The hero leaves home," "The hero returns," and is able to analyze the text in terms of the appearance or non-appearance and the ordering of these elements.

At their best, Formalist studies of novels provide brilliant insights into the workings of the texts; at their worst—and this tendency seems to be predominating—they spin ever subtler and ever more opaque taxonomies of literary phenomena, and seem more interested in developing new terminology than in explaining literature (Genette, "Discours"). This hypertrophy of technical language divorced from an underlying technology seems a clear sign of intellectual decadence.

Psycho-Criticism Parallel to Formalist criticism, and not unrelated to it, one can place psycho-criticism. Sigmund Freud commented on literary texts as a type of clinical phenomenon, and in France a number of critics, notably René Laforgue and Marie Bonaparte, followed in the master's footsteps. Even today one comes across the occasional book or article which relates literary texts to some putative psychosis suffered by the author; the concept of a healthy, well-adjusted author seems foreign to this type of criticism (see Pacaly). In any case, literary concerns have been replaced by medical ones.

Charles Mauron, Jean-Pierre Richard, and Jean-Paul Weber have developed a subtler, and more satisfying, application of Freudian theories to literature. Their aim is to reconstruct an author's "mental universe" from his/her writings. They begin by looking for repeated themes—like warmth, violence—and habitual groupings of themes in the author's complete works. Once these constants have been determined, they can be related back to childhood traumas which can be documented from the author's biography in order to discover the underlying principle which governs the whole literary production.

Although elegant in theory, this approach has some problems in practice. The first and greatest weakness lies in the definition of themes. One starts out with a clear, precise definition. The theme becomes broader in scope as progressively more details are quoted in support of the point being made. The Freudian practice of free association contributes to a still wider inclusiveness. More and more elements are subsumed under the theme, until the vagueness is such that virtually everything can be included in it. Perhaps the most extreme example of this intellectual flabbiness can be found in Jean-Paul Weber's study of Vigny (33–90), in which the theme of the clock ends up including not just time and fate, but everything long and/or pointed like the hands of a clock; everything round like the face of a clock; everything cyclical, including the cycles of nature because of the cyclical motion of the hands; everything mechanical, because a clock is a machine; and all manifestations of violence, because of the clockwork in a time bomb.

A second difficulty with psycho-criticism lies in the importance placed on childhood traumas. The type of incident used—for example, the purchase of a new clock by the child-author's parents (Weber, 33–49)—is so banal that one must posit similar experiences on the part of hundreds of people who did not go on to become authors, let alone great ones. It requires no small leap of faith to believe that such incidents are the fundamental causes of literary greatness.

A final difficulty arises from the fact that this approach is applied to the author's complete works, usually including her/his published correspondence. This flies in the face of basic facts. We know that great authors write good books and poor books. Flaubert's marginally successful historical novel *Salammbô* seems a strange source of information on the causes of his brilliant literary success in *Madame Bovary*. Literary works have their own internal coherence. Observation shows, for instance, that the image of the sun has a completely different symbolic value in *l'Étranger* from what one finds in *la Chute*. Moreover, in *la Peste* not only is this image different again, but it also changes value in the course of the novel (Fortier 1977).

So, basing one's interpretation of an author's entire literary output on the premise that it is possible to discover symbolic constants in it very frequently leads psycho-critics into grave difficulty. A recent psycho-critical study of Camus (Gassin) presents a more balanced and judicious treatment of the literary works than is found in the pioneers of the movement. It is worth noting that Gassin made extensive use of a computer-generated concordance in carrying out his analysis.

Socio-Criticism Lukács's efforts to elevate Marxist literary criticism above the level of simplistic polemics has found a number of echoes in France. The way was prepared by Jean-Paul Sartre's (1948) doctrine of "engaged literature," which stressed the fact that literature is a social phenomenon; it is produced in the context of a given society and it has its effect on that society. Goldmann, like Lukács, insisted that an individual is incapable of creating an entirely new structure; the author, an individual, of necessity finds structures in his society and expresses them in literary works. Roland Barthes put into circulation the term "écriture" to designate that aspect of a text which the author fashions in order to please a potential public.

The concept of literature as a social phenomenon—rather than the product of genius or some ineffable inspiration—is quite appealing. At its best, socio-criticism fosters brilliant insights into literary works. But it does not always avoid banality, and sometimes it is so dependent on abstruse economic concepts as to be impenetrable (Goldmann, 279–324). Not all practitioners of socio-criticism manage to avoid the temptation to slip into social or political commentary in the guise of discussing literature (Leenhardt). Even Lukács, in applying his approach, ends up condemning writers whose eminence is such that the reader has more serious doubts about the critical method than about the literary value of authors such as Beckett (57, 93, 99, 128–29, 144–45), Joyce (93, 99, 164), or Proust (68–70, 131). More fundamentally, socio-criticism has not come to terms with the fact that in a given historical period hundreds of authors are integrated into a certain nexus of social structures, but only a very few will produce great literature.

Stylistics Elements of both the Formalist and the socio-criticism schools are combined in the stylistic approach of Michael Riffaterre. According to Riffaterre the aim of any work of literature is communication, in the sense of modifying the perception of the reader. More precisely, a literary work must oblige the reader to pay close attention to its own form and content. The means of forcing the reader to pay attention is style, which therefore is defined as what focuses the reader's attention. Riffaterre has shown a great subtlety and frequently is most convincing when he applies his approach to individual texts, although his work is almost entirely limited to poems.

A COMPUTER-AIDED APPROACH TO LITERATURE

Background

My work since the late 1960s has had as one of its goals to integrate the application of computers to literature into the critical theory which has been sketched out above. From my training in history, and in the historical approach to literature, I draw the distinction between facts and interpretation, and hold to the concept that interpretation must build on and integrate the facts. From the Formalists, I draw a stress on the text. I consider it the primary authoritative source of facts on which to base an interpretation, and like most Formalists I refuse to accept, until demonstrated, the concept that what holds for one text also explains other texts. This means, to begin with, that whenever possible when studying a work of literature I make constant use of two documents: a copy of the text, and a concordance to the text. These basic principles also serve as a foundation for a more fully developed use of computer technology.

From the Freudians I have borrowed the concept of theme. I try to correct the amorphous nature of their use of the concept of theme by reference to a principle of socio-criticism. The latter theory reminds us that literature is a social phenomenon, but the language out of which the literature is formed is also a social phenomenon. If one reflects on the second fact, one realizes that society has produced documents—synonym dictionaries—which show what words are related to a given theme, not just in the mind of a single imaginative critic, but for the whole society. I have directed the development of software to draw up word lists from synonym dictionaries and compare these lists to texts which have been specially prepared to facilitate computer processing. Over the years, a number of novels have been prepared, and synonym data for several hundred themes has been recorded.

My analysis of a text includes, of course, examination of plot and characterization. The computer analysis shows me that the frequency of a given theme is highest on certain pages of a text. I can determine the stage of plot development at that point, note what characters are important there, and where they are in their evolution. All of these facts can then be integrated in the form of an interpretation of the text. I have done this for texts by Céline, Beckett, Malraux, Robbe-Grillet, and Gide. I am presently working on Sartre's *la Nausée*.

Origins: Camus

The above-mentioned approach, as might be expected, evolved gradually. It grew out of my early study of Camus. Because of this author's great popularity in North America as well as in Europe, there was an enormous bibliography on him. But, as I read through this material, I was struck by the dearth of proof or demonstration—as distinguished from opinion—to be found in the generally laudatory writings on Camus as a thinker and as an artist. I set out to evaluate him as a novelist, with the working hypothesis that the source of his success could be discovered by carrying out precise analyses of his novels and of the short stories in *l'Exil et le Royaume*. Very rapidly I found that I was counting words in these texts in order to establish the importance and distribution patterns of the themes whose structural interrelationships I soon came to see as the cause of the works' aesthetic success. These initial studies were facilitated by a word list for *l'Exil et le Royaume* which was originally prepared at the University of Besançon using mechanical card sorting equipment.

Several hypotheses were proven by this work. First and foremost, precise analyses of themes proved useful in preparing literary studies (Fortier 1973a, 1973b, 1977). On the other hand, close attention to themes reveal something disconcerting for biographical or psychological criticism. In *l'Étranger* and in "Le Renégat," a short story from *l'Exil et le Royaume,* the sun is thematically associated with violence, to the point that it could be called an objective correlative or symbol of violence. In *la Chute,* however, the sun functions as a symbol of death. One finds several references to the "plague sun" as a murderous force in *la Peste,* but the sun is also associated with joy at the end of the novel, a function which it also has in "La Pierre qui pousse" (*l'Exil et le Royaume*), in which the sun is a sign of fraternity as well as joy. Similarly, the sea symbolizes life and joy in *l'Étranger* and *la Peste,* but is quite clearly associated with ambiguity and death in *la Chute* (Fortier 1977).

The importance of these discoveries becomes clear when one realizes that Camus had a well documented personal love of the sea and bright sunshine, feelings rooted in his Algerian childhood and adult sufferings as a tubercular living in the cold, dank cities of Paris and Saint-Étienne. The biographical and psychological justification for assigning a permanent value to the themes of sun and sea in Camus's work is thus overwhelming; the texts, unfortunately, do not permit such action. Clearly then, as I studied other works, I would have to deduce the significance of themes from the texts themselves, and my experience with Camus showed me that, although counting words evoking themes was absolutely necessary for determining thematic structures, such counting was not only tedious, but extremely error-prone. Computer processing speeds up and improves the accuracy of the theme analysis.

Development: Céline

The next text to which I turned my attention was Céline's *Voyage au bout de la nuit* (1932), a picaresque novel with philosophical overtones. The main character and narrator, Bardamu, joins the French army just before the First World War, and is subjected to wartime conditions both at the front and in Paris. He escapes to become a trader in the African jungle, but catches a fever and is sold as a galley slave on a vessel going to the United States. After a sojourn there, he returns to France, becomes a doctor and practices medicine in Rancy, a Parisian slum. He ends up as interim director of a madhouse in Vigny, just outside Paris. This text is generally considered to be one of the most pessimistic and depressing novels of our century.

In analyzing Céline's novel, I used a computer-generated concordance to trace the frequency and distribution of individual words evoking themes like love, death, water, or vegetation. To decide which words should be included in a list for a given theme, I relied primarily on my own knowledge of the language, supplemented by consultation of synonym dictionaries. Quite rapidly the basic structure of the novel became clear (Fortier 1981a). The first three sections of the novel (War, Africa, U.S.A.) create a vision of totally unacceptable conditions for human existence, in settings which to the French reader are both exceptional and exotic. The same themes which created these conditions reappear in the second half of the novel—this time in the unremittingly banal context of a Parisian slum—and they are juxtaposed and interrelated in such a way as to form structures almost identical to what was found in the first sections. The basic message is clear: the generalized senseless violence of war, the paroxysm of biological forces seen in Africa, the dehumanizing conditions of a 1930s auto plant, are only slightly exaggerated manifestations of the conditions which render life untenable, every day, for most people. This pessimism is all the more forceful because it is embodied in the overall structure of the novel, rather than simply stated.

Similar phenomena can also be found at a less general level. For instance, the theme of violence is evoked most frequently not in the war chapters of the novel, but in the African section. This fact is striking because war necessarily implies violence, but biological forces dominate in Africa. Violence, thus, is primarily associated, not with an exceptional historical phenomenon (war), but with the inescapable biological aspect of our human condition. The structure of the violence theme thus contributes to the strong aura of pessimism which characterizes the novel.

Several aspects of the novel help to heighten the importance of this sort of structure. In the war section, Bardamu describes almost lightheartedly the effect of a shellburst on two soldiers: one is decapitated, the other, literally ripped open. But when he has to go to his regiment's improvised slaughterhouse shortly afterward, he becomes physically sick with disgust. Analysis of the themes characterizing the description of the slaughterhouse shows that they echo those used to evoke conditions at the front on numerous occasions. So Bardamu violently rejects a paradigm of war rather than a single, if striking, incident. Similarly, he becomes wild with fear after seeing a shooting gallery in a carnival, saying that the whole world is a shooting gallery. In point of fact, the description of the carnival concession does include all the themes which the novel associates with war, both at the front and behind the lines. So Bardamu's reactions are profoundly justified by the thematic structures, although the other characters in the novel see them as cowardice or madness.

Towards the end of the novel, Bardamu hires a nurse, Sophie. His descriptions of her beauty contain strong overtones of revulsion, an ambivalence which one critic cites as an example of Céline's "fundamental perversity" (Beaujour,

178). But on the level of theme, Sophie is integrated into a myth of feminine beauty which had earlier attracted Bardamu to America—where he had suffered greatly. More than a hundred pages before the description of Sophie, Bardamu had debunked this myth, showing that it was related to the biological forces whose evil effects he had seen in Africa and in Parisian slums. Here, precise information about themes explains Bardamu's ambivalent attitude in terms of the structures of the novel, without having to fall back on complexes which Céline might or might not have had.

Another powerful contribution to *Voyage au bout de la nuit*'s depressing aura can be found in the author's skillful placement of image-packed visionary descriptions. These passages contain *in ovo* all the important themes for a given part of the novel, and usually these themes interrelate to form a structure analagous to what is found in the larger part of the text. Such a passage opens the novel as a whole; such a passage is also to be found at the beginning of each of the six major sections of the novel, and in many subdivisions of these sections. In fact, it is possible to demonstrate (Fortier 1974b) that this use of preparatory prophetic vision also characterizes Céline's doctoral thesis (1924), as well as his subsequent novels *Mort à crédit* and *Guignol's Band*.

Céline—consciously or not—used this technique to add an impression of inevitability to the pessimism of the text; all the horrors which are presented in detail had been predicted or suggested ahead of time. This novelistic technique can equally well suggest something about the structure of the author's political outlook. The novelistic structure puts the perfection of the striking image before the detailed exposition which logically justifies it. Perfection is in the past, and day-to-day events develop from it. In other words, the structure of images and themes in these novels is reactionary.

Historians of literature have had a problem with Céline. He is usually considered to have been a flaming left-wing radical in 1932, at the time of the publication of *Voyage au bout de la nuit*. Then, in 1936, he inexplicably began spouting anti-semitic and pro-fascist ideas. No known important event in his life or experience justified such a fundamental change. Ironically, a computer approach, oriented primarily towards the texts, and not at all seeking biographical information, shows that as early as 1924 Céline's writing had a reactionary structure. Thus, a simpler and more elegant biographical criticism is fostered by a computer analysis.

Extension: Malraux

The experience with *Voyage au bout de la nuit* suggested the advantages of a more systematic analysis of themes. Although I had had good results drawing up *ad hoc* lists of words likely to evoke themes, deriving these words from synonym dictionaries presents the advantage of better reflecting the linguistic phenomena and reducing the element of personal impression. The counting and housekeeping aspects of theme searches could profitably be transferred from hand work on paper to computer processing, where it belonged.

Although I did not realize that it would take as long as it did, I was aware that I was embarking on a long-term project entailing both the development of computer software and considerable data entry. Given the realities of career progress evaluation in a university setting, I saw the necessity for some small, short-term projects to keep my publication rate at a reasonable level. So, when bits of research support became available on occasion, I had texts input for a number of novels by Malraux and for a play by Beckett, *En attendant Godot*, in order that computer-generated concordances would be available to me.

Although tangential to my main line of research, work with these texts does suggest a characteristic of computer-aided work, so perhaps the reader will excuse a brief list of what was done. From the concordances, I was able to produce an article on Beckett's play (Fortier 1971), about which more will be said later. In Malraux's *La Voie royale* I traced the interplay of the themes of art, the absurd and history to suggest the mythic dimensions of the novel (Fortier 1973c). The importance of historical forces in *Les Conquérants*, and the novel's critique of attempts to overcome the absurd by political action to be found in the novel were the subject of a recently published article (Fortier 1985a). On another occasion I traced the theme of mythomania through all of Malraux's novels (Fortier 1979). I have also suggested that Malruax's first attempt at writing a novel, *La Tentation de l'Occident*, contains a clear exposition of the themes which are important in his writings during the rest of his life: the menace of irrational forces, the vision of the dissolution of accepted values, the desire for an ideology capable of integrating all aspects of reality, the prime importance of the individual, and art as transcending history (Fortier 1985b).

All of these studies were, without a doubt, facilitated because I could make frequent use of a concordance while writing them. It might even be possible to say that their production was speeded up if the time spent producing the concordance were not counted. It cannot be claimed that they make a lasting contribution to the integration of computer methods into literary studies. All were written using the standard discourse of academic literary criticism; none proposes anything radical from the point of view of methodology. In fact, it would be an astute reader indeed who could deduce that these studies owed anything at all to computer technology. As more and more concordances are produced by computer and take their places on library shelves, it may well be that the added speed and accuracy which have always been promised as a product of computer methods will be realized, but that the computer's contribution will be as invisible as it was in my articles on Malraux and Beckett. Indeed, we may well be witnessing this phenomenon at the present time, without being able to identify it.

Testing: Robbe-Grillet and Beckett

At the same time that these studies were being prepared, work was going forward on developing a computer system for thematic analysis. One part of the system prepares texts, reducing their words to standard dictionary forms—rather than spelled forms—and stores them in a format permitting rapid and efficient computer searches. Another set of programs gathers words from synonym dictionaries and reduces them to a single alphabetical list of words evoking a given theme, under conditions fostering the greatest care and accuracy. A final program compares the list of theme words to the prepared texts and produces a variety of reports showing the frequency and distribution of the evocations of the theme in a text. (The reader interested in the technical aspect of this process will find details in Fortier and McConnell 1975.)

After the new system was written, thoroughly tested, and revised, a number of theme lists were drawn up, and Robbe-Grillet's *la Jalousie* was prepared for further processing. This novel reflects the thoughts of an invisible narrator as he mulls over the circumstances surrounding a trip to town taken by his wife and an over-solicitous male neighbor, leaving the narrator alone on his plantation. Several times, the narrator recalls various incidents preceding or following the trip, but each time they change a bit. It is impossible to reduce these incidents to a linear chronology, because their order varies on the different occasions when they are recalled. The reader quickly realizes that in reading this novel one is seeing—from the inside, as it were—the tortured meanderings of a jealous mind as it attempts to arrive at a certainty which is both impossible to achieve and also avoided because it would bear an unacceptable message.

The computer system was able to produce in minutes frequency and distribution profiles for each of the important themes in the novel. But the theme profiles did not lead to an acceptable interpretation of the text. After some reflection I discovered why. My approach took for granted that profiles could meaningfully be expressed in terms of the pages of the text, because an unexpressed axiom expected plot and character development to be essentially a linear progression from the beginning to the end of the text. *La Jalousie* reflects the twists and turns of a tortured mind rehashing the same incidents several times, and so lacks such a lineaɪ progression. In fact, Robbe-Grillet stated several times that he had constructed his novel purposely in such a way that its incidents could not be reduced to a single chronological order.

Once this was established in my mind, I was able to use the computer system to trace in detail how Robbe-Grillet uses themes, showing the internal contradictions in their presentation, contradictions too frequent and too systematic to result from chance or authorial inattention. The anti-structural character of the themes in this novel, like the equally disconcerting plot and character presentation, lead necessarily to confusion, irritation, and a refusal to accept evidence, which are characteristic of the emotion of jealousy (Fortier 1981b).

Computer processing gave me two clear advantages in studying *la Jalousie:* it obliged me through weight of evidence to reject an erroneous original hypothesis, and it provided ample material to demonstrate the viability of a new way of looking at the text. This was not the first time that I had derived such benefits from using the machine.

In my study of Beckett's *En attendant Godot* (Fortier 1971), a concordance had enabled me to trace down a number of contradictions in the text—mainly centered around its chronology. Here again, instead of showing me how to resolve seeming contradictions, the evidence convinced me that these contradictions were a fundamental aspect of the play. A bit more digging revealed an enormous number of hesitations or pauses in the dialogue (more than a hundred); again, I could demonstrate that the text was generating uncertainty rather than clarity. Godot, mysterious, unidentifiable, unrevealed in the play, could with equal probability—or lack of it—be identified as God, death, a slavemaster, or an employer. The common element in all of these potential identities of Godot is that he would confer a definite form on the amorphous existence of Vladimir and Estragon. Pozzo and Lucky can be related to this structure, as examples of a form of existence which the main characters reject. The latters' tenacity in waiting for Godot thus becomes explicable because he will save them from their own formlessness.

My experience with both of these texts shows an advantage of computer work which is too easily overlooked. I approached both of these texts with working hypotheses and the intention of resolving apparent contradictions. I took it for granted that these mid-twentieth-century texts had a coherence more proper to literature of an earlier age. To use an expression of Robbe-Grillet's, I was judging them by criteria inherited from our grand-parents' time (Robbe-Grillet 1963, 28). Had I been working only from notes and impressions, I would probably have managed to stress certain elements of the texts, overlook others (probably not even consciously), and explain away still others using the tricks of dialectic which Potter calls "dancing on the ceiling" in her article in *Computers and the Humanities* (92). After all, one of the most eminent critics of Robbe-Grillet uses just this mixture of selectivity and brilliant argument to reduce *la Jalousie* to Balzacian linearity (Morrissette, 111–40).

The use of the computer saved me from my own initial enthusiasm. The machine furnished overwhelming evidence that my original approach and hypotheses were dead wrong. What might have been a few minor details to explain away in a set of notes taken by hand turned out, because of the very unselectivity of computer processing, to be so overwhelmingly important that they had to take a preeminent place in the final interpretation. Because the machine works on the surface of the text, and is not influenced—as note-taking is—by the state of mind of the person examining the text, it forces the critic to examine the text on its own, not the critic's, terms. It is difficult to underestimate the importance of this phenomenon, given the structure of certain of our professional activities.

At the present time specialists rise to eminence in literary criticism as a result of the opinion of their peers. When a respected colleague expresses opinions concerning the texts, these opinions become accepted. A new critic, whether a younger colleague or someone moving into a second specialty or subdiscipline, is obliged to work within the framework of existing opinion. What is missing from this whole process is the concept of fact or proof. The computer can provide demonstrations of verifiable textual phenomena, whose existence can be established independently of the critic who is explaining them. As such information becomes widely available, we can look forward to a new structure in the academic critical establishment—one which distinguishes clearly between fact on the one hand and opinion on the other, and gives pride of place to those practitioners who best account for the former.

Confirmation: Gide

Some of my work on Gide's *l'Immoraliste* can serve as an example of this new type of interpretation. Michel, the main character and narrator of the novel, contracts tuberculosis on his honeymoon in North Africa. He recovers his health thanks to the devotion of his wife Marceline. The couple returns to France via Italy, but Marceline falls ill and Michel takes her to Switzerland to help her get better. But he is unable to stay in one place, and they leave for Italy, then North Africa again. There, worn out by travelling, Marceline dies.

The plot of *L'Immoraliste,* summarized above, simply presents a case of almost pathological egotism. My study of thematic structures in the novel reveals a different way of interpreting the text. Quite early in the novel, as a result of his illness, Michel forms a personal mythology. He associates sickness with the themes of confinement, boredom, weakness, cold, ugliness, fear, and death. Sickness thus has strong negative connotations: it is to be avoided at all costs, as are manifestations of those themes associated with it. Health has positive connotations; it is associated with goodness, love, beauty, warmth, water, strength, joy, light, vegetation, life, and (in the latter part of the novel) violence. The ambivalent theme of order is associated with health in the first half of the novel, and with sickness in the second.

In terms of his personal mythology, Michel's actions are perfectly consistent. When Marceline falls ill, he tries to place her in an environment conducive to health as he sees it. After obliging his increasingly sick wife to travel from France to Switzerland, to Naples, back to Rome, and to Naples again, Michel finally takes her to North Africa. He is charmed by the beauty he finds there. Then he notices Marceline and asks: "Why is she coughing when this weather is so beautiful?" ("Pourquoi tousse-t-elle par ce beau temps?", 465). Thus, dramatic tension in the novel results from the existence of two contradictory sources of coherence for Michel's actions, one based on plot, the other on theme structures.

This interpretation was developed using frequency and distribution profiles for the themes in question, produced by my computer programs. In collaboration with Professor Paul Bratley, I took the frequency and distribution tables which had been used in the interpretation and subjected them to a number of simple, straightforward statistical tests—correlations, clustering, and multidimensional scaling (Bratley and Fortier). These techniques belong to what is called descriptive statistics, and, as distinguished from inferential statistics, do not rely on any definition of what literary structures should or might be. This distinction is important, because the presuppositions required by inferential statistics are usually unacceptable when a text is studied from a literary point of view. I believe that the article written with Bratley shows that *l'Immoraliste* does in fact contain a strongly dualistic structure generated by the disposition of the themes mentioned earlier. Although the statistical article is short and easy to follow, it will reach a small audience, because—for the time being at least—very few literature scholars can find the time to read a statistical study of literature. (A presentation of the same material, using the accepted discourse of literary criticism, supplemented by a few charts and tables, has been published in the series *Stanford French and Italian Studies* [Fortier 1988].)

PERSPECTIVES FOR THE FUTURE

It would, of course, be premature to think that the computer's capacities have been fully utilized. Judiciously used, the machine offers the means for producing precise and fruitful analyses of texts—which can be expressed using traditional language, or descriptive statistics, or both. I believe, however, that more can be done. Riffaterre, in examining how an author modifies the perceptions of the reader, makes frequent use of the concept of surprise (30–31, 57–60, 78–79, etc.). He shows time and again how a certain verbal context is set up in a text and how elements which are incongruous in this context are precisely the ones that command the reader's attention and orient his/her reactions. Of necessity, Riffaterre examines this phenomenon within single works, usually poems. The practical problems of determining readers' expectations as they begin a work of literature seem insurmountable to Riffaterre (52–54).

A monumental work published recently in Sweden suggests that Riffaterre's pessimism is no longer entirely justified. Gunnel Engwall's *Vocabulaire du roman français* shows the frequency and distribution of 500,000 words drawn from twenty-five best-selling novels published in France between 1962 and 1968. By combining these data with my synonym dictionary lists, it is possible to determine which words would be striking and which would seem more or less normal to a reader of novels in a very recent period. This, of course, is properly applied not to individual words, but to the semantic groupings which comprise literary themes. Many practical aspects, as well as interpretation and theoretical ramifications, remain to be worked out. Some advanced statistical techniques will also need to be brought to bear on the problem. Computer-aided study of literature is thus not only fully in the mainstream of French literature studies; it shows good promise for expanding the capacities of these studies beyond what had hitherto been considered possible.

ACKNOWLEDGMENTS

This research has been supported by the Social Sciences and Humanities Research Council of Canada under the following grants: S70-1561, S71-1933, S72-1650, W74-0453, S76-0734, 451-77-520, 410-81-0856, 461-84-0137, 451-85-4921, and 461-85-0047.

References

Aristotle. *Poetics*. Trans. H. S. Butcher, ed. Francis Fergusson. New York: Hill and Wang, 1961.

Barthes, Roland. *Le Degré zéro de l'écriture*. Paris: Seuil, 1953.

Beaujour, Michel. "Temps et substances dans *Voyage au bout de la nuit*." *Cahiers de l'Herne* 5 (1965): 173–88.

Bonaparte, Marie. *Edgar Poe*. Paris: Denoël et Steele, 1933.

Bratley, Paul and Paul A. Fortier. "Themes and Variations in Gide's *l'Immoraliste*." *Empirical Studies in the Arts* 3 (1985): 153–70.

Brik, O. "Rhythme et syntaxe." *Théorie de la littérature*. Trans. Tzvetan Todorov. Paris: Seuil, 1965.

Camus, Albert. *L'Étranger*. 1942. *Théâtre, Récits, Nouvelles*. Ed. Roger Quilliot. Bibliothèque de la Pléiade. Paris: Gallimard, 1962.

———. *La Peste*. 1947. *Théâtre, Récits, Nouvelles*.

———. *La Chute*. 1956. *Théâtre, Récits, Nouvelles*.

———. *L'Exil et le Royaume*. 1957. *Théâtre, Récits, Nouvelles*.

Céline, L.-F. *La Vie et l'oeuvre de Philippe-Ignace Semmelweis*. 1924. *Oeuvres*. 5 vols. Ed. Jean A. Ducourneau. Paris: André Balland, 1966–69. Vol. 1.

————. *Voyage au bout de la nuit*. 1932. *Romans*. Bibliothèque de la Pléiade. Paris: Gallimard, 1962.

————. *Mort à crédit*. 1936. *Romans*. Bibliothèque de la Pléiade. Paris: Gallimard, 1962.

————. *Guignol's Band*. 1952. *Oeuvres*. Vol. 2.

Engwall, Gunnel. *Vocabulaire du roman français (1962–68): Dictionnaire des fréquences*. Data Linguistica. Stockholm: Almqvist & Wiksell, 1984.

Fortier, Paul A. (1971). "Beckett émule de Gide." *L'Esprit Créateur* 11, 3:55–66.

————. (1973a). "Le Décor symbolique de 'l'Hôte' d'Albert Camus." *French Review* 46:535–42.

————. (1973b). "Création et fonctionnement de l'atmosphère dans 'Le Renégat' d'Albert Camus." *PMLA* 88:484–95.

————. (1973c). "Structuration mythique de *la Voie royale*." *André Malraux: Visages du romancier*. Ed. Walter G. Langlois. Paris: Minard, 41–53.

————. (1974a). "From Objectivity to Convenience: Information Processing for Literary Study." *Information Processing 74*. Ed. J. Rosenfeld. Amsterdam: North-Holland, 846–50.

————. (1974b). "La Vision prophétique: Un procédé stylistique célinien." *L.-F. Céline: Pour une poétique célinienne*. Ed. Jean-Pierre Dauphin. Paris: Minard. 41–56.

————. (1977). *Une Lecture de Camus*. Paris: Klincksieck.

————. (1979). "Mythomania and Malraux." *Mélanges Malraux Miscellany* 11,2:13–19.

————. (1981a). *Le Métro émotif: Étude du fonctionnement des structures thématiques dans* Voyage au bout de la nuit *de Céline*. Paris: Minard.

————. (1981b). *Structures et Communication dans* la Jalousie *d'Alain Robbe-Grillet*. Sherbrooke: Naaman.

————. (1985a). "L'Action et l'absurde l'expression mythique dans *les Conquérants*." *André Malraux 6: Les Conquérants 1. Critique du roman*. Ed. Christiane Moatti and Walter G. Langlois. Paris: Lettres Modernes. 125–49.

————. (1985b). "L'Expression mythique dans les romans de Malraux." *Mélanges Malraux Miscellany* 17:28–36.

————. (1988). *Décor et dualisme:* L'Immoraliste *d'André Gide*. Stanford French & Italian Studies. Saratoga, CA: Anma Libri, 1988.

Fortier, Paul A. and J. Colin McConnell. 1973. "Computer-Aided Thematic Analysis of French Prose Fiction," *The Computer and Literary Studies*. Ed. A. J. Aitken, et al. Edinburgh: Edinburgh University Press, 167–81.

————. (1975). *THEME: A System for Computer-Aided Theme Searches of French Texts*. Winnipeg: Department of French and Spanish, University of Manitoba.

————. (1976). "Computer-Aided Analysis of French Prose Fiction: II. Analysis of Texts and Preparation Costs." *The Computer in Literary and Linguistic Studies*. Ed. Alan Jones and R. F. Churchhouse. Cardiff: University of Wales Press. 215–22.

Freud, Sigmund. *Délire et rêve*. 1907. Paris: Gallimard, 1931.

————. *Essais de psychanalyse*. Paris: Payot, 1948.

Gassin, Jean. *L'Univers symbolique d'Albert Camus: Essai d'interprétation psychanalytique*. Paris: Minard, 1981.

Gasté, Armand. *La Querelle du* Cid: *Pièces et pamphlets publiés d'après les originaux*. Paris, 1898.

Genette, Gérard. "Discours du récit." *Figures III*. Paris: Seuil, 1972.

Gide, André. *L'Immoraliste*. 1902. *Romans, Récits, Soties, Oeuvres lyriques*. Ed. Y. Davet and J.-J. Thierry. Bibliothèque de la Pléiade. Paris: Gallimard, 1958.

Goldmann, Lucien. *Pour une sociologie du roman*. Paris: Gallimard, 1964.

Jauss, Hans Robert. *Toward an Aesthetic of Reception*. Trans. Timothy Bahti. Minneapolis: University of Minnesota Press, 1982.

Laforgue, René. *L'Échec de Baudelaire*. Paris: Denoël et Steele, 1931.

Lancaster, H. Carrington. *A History of French Dramatic Literature in the Seventeenth Century*. 5 vols. Baltimore: Johns Hopkins University Press, 1929–43.

Leenhardt, Jacques. *Lecture politique du roman* la Jalousie *d'Alain Robbe-Grillet*. Paris: Minuit, 1973.

Lukács, Georg. *La Signification présente du réalisme critique*. Trans. Maurice de Gandillac. Paris: Gallimard, 1960.

Mauron, Charles. *Des Métaphores obsédantes au mythe personnel: Introduction à la Psychocritique*. Paris: Corti, 1962.

Morrissette, Bruce. *Les Romans de Robbe-Grillet*. Paris: Minuit, 1963.

Pacaly, Josette. *Sartre au miroir: Une Lecture psychanalytique de ses écrits biographiques*. Paris: Klincksieck, 1980.

Potter, Rosanne. "Literary Criticism and Literary Computing: The Difficulties of a Synthesis." *Computers and the Humanities* 22 (1988):91–97.

Propp, Vladimir. *Morphology of the Folktale*. 2nd. ed. Austin: University of Texas Press, 1970.

Richard, Jean-Pierre. *L'Univers imaginaire de Mallarmé*. Paris: Seuil, 1961.

Riffaterre, Michael. *Essais de stylistique structurale*. Trans./ed. Daniel Delas. Paris: Flammarion, 1971.

Robbe-Grillet, Alain (1957). *La Jalousie*. Paris: Minuit.

———— (1963). *Pour un nouveau roman*. Paris: Minuit.

Sartre, Jean-Paul. *La Nausée*. 1938. *Oeuvres Romanesques*. Ed. Michel Contat and Michel Rybalka. Bibliothèque de la Pléiade. Paris: Gallimard, 1981.

————. *Situations II*. 1948. Paris: Gallimard.

Tomachevski, Boris. "Sur le vers." *Théorie de la littérature*. Trans. Tzvetan Todorov. Paris: Seuil, 1965.

Voltaire. *Essai sur les moeurs*. *Oeuvres Complètes*. Ed. Louis Moland. 52 vols. Paris, 1877–85. Vol. 11.

————. *Commentaires sur Corneille*. *Oeuvres Complètes*. Ed. Louis Moland. 52 vols. Paris, 1877–85. Vol. 31.

Weber, Jean-Paul. *Genèse de l'oeuvre poétique*. Paris: Gallimard, 1960.

>> 6

Computational Thematics, a Selective Database, and Literary Criticism:

Gobineau, Tic Words, and Riffaterre Revisited

JOEL D. GOLDFIELD

COMPUTATIONAL THEMATICS AND THE "TIC WORD" CONTROVERSY

In his study of the style of Arthur de Gobineau's *Les Pléiades* (1874), Michael Riffaterre devotes nearly an entire chapter to a thematic or conceptual grouping of "tic words," which I define below.[1] This conceptual word group of persistent verbal traits or mannerisms consists of the French equivalents of expressions like "assuredly," "certainly," "one must admit," "without doubt," and so forth. The controversy which the title of this section introduces lies in the stylistic significance of a group of words which Riffaterre defines as "tic words." For Leo Spitzer, they do not necessarily contain the intensity which Riffaterre attributes to them. Spitzer writes of Riffaterre's work on this subject:

> Do all these "stylistic effects on the language base" really illustrate "a break in habit, the product of an individual will reworking the common property of the language"? You, reader, and I, writing in French, would we not thus all be great stylists? . . . [If] we consider the "author's tics" as indicators of the "intensity" felt by the writer . . . they do not seem remarkable to me in the least.[2]

Riffaterre had contended that his goal was to adapt and "to reconcile the Spitzerian views with the methodical, down-to-earth, but sure, study of procedures conceived by the French School" (17). Spitzer quotes Riffaterre's statements to this effect in his review (68–69). My hypothesis is that we can refine and apply the quantitative aspect of Riffaterre's approach to another work by Gobineau (1816–82) to discover any significant quantitative and stylistic value in the tic word group while using some of Spitzer's analytical procedures to synthesize our findings.

Riffaterre's stylistic observations may shed light on the six novellas of the *Nouvelles asiatiques* (1876) as well, if I can assess Gobineau's quantitative and contextual use of these words.[3] In his scholarly *Gobineau, l'Orient et l'Iran*, Jean Boissel evaluates the *Nouvelles* as "one of the masterpieces of nineteenth-century exotic literature."[4] This and other testimony to the little-known nineteenth-century French work which has recently been the focus of graduate courses at the Sorbonne and at the Université Paul Valéry (Montpellier) helps to justify the attention given by the present study.

Tic words repeat at striking frequencies, according to Riffaterre (116). From my viewpoint, he seems to consider them linguistic tips of a psychological iceberg. After defining them, I would like to discover why they are used in their microcontexts, whether they always exert a negative influence on Gobineau's style, and what further significance they have. Riffaterre asserts that tic words are part of an intensification process that shapes a stylistic trait of Gobineau, a process that can be voluntary or involuntary:

> The effect . . . can come from unconscious repetitions which intensify, but which are only the involuntary result of the author's obsessions. Let us add that there is not necessarily any opposition between the conscious style and the unconscious style. . . .
>
> These repetitions are true *tics*. One hardly need emphasize the importance of the verbal obsessions to the stylistician; revelatory of the deep currents of thoughts, of the major ideas, and even of the idées fixes of the author, they can help us understand his conscious choices, his preferences for certain procedures or for certain expressions (116).

In this work, Riffaterre's logical analysis of Gobineau's style extends far beyond the intensifying nature of the tic words. Riffaterre avails himself of several stylo-statistical examples which rely on comparisons with often inadequate French prose norms established by Vander Beke in the latter's *French Word Book*, (see below) which possesses a base of 1,200,000 word occurrences.[5] These frequency comparisons are few, though they point to a technique that would facilitate the analysis of a topic dealing precisely with the cumulative effect of repetition.

Of particular interest as a cohesive, semantic group are words that Riffaterre studies on his pages 118 to 120. He maintains that these words, by their very nature, eliminate other possibilities. They are superlatives, adverbs of exclusivity (e.g., "never"), and expressions like "without limit," "without measure," "without . . . doubt," (*sans limite, sans mesure, sans . . . doute*). Add to these some apparently glib and frequent expressions meant to convince, such as "let us admit," "all in all," "in sum," (*avouons, en définitive, en somme*), and we may also have a few of the elements for a psycho-stylistic study. Riffaterre has a keen eye for some striking interconnections involving Gobineau's style: the meritocratic and aristocratic themes (9–10, 119) that are continually reemphasized in *Les Pléiades* and the concomitant vocabulary and rhetorical devices. The critic designates tic words which we can often read in emotional passages, where Gobineau the author is "asseverative," earnestly portraying his views or those of his characters. Spitzer highlights the tic words in his self-defensive reaction to Riffaterre's *Le style des "Pléiades"*:

> They [the tic words] do not seem remarkable to me: that an "asseverative" [*asséveratif*] being like Gobineau may write the adjective *absolu* 63 times in *Les Pléiades* and *fort* (p. 120) 25 times in one part of this work is not particularly surprising (27 exclamation points in one page are perhaps more significant and bring Gobineau closer to Céline) [The page reference to Riffaterre's work is Spitzer's].

Spitzer's jump from word counts to a reference relating the occasionally ranting and often irreverent Louis-Ferdinand Céline (1894–1961) to the prudish, miscegenistic, earnest, yet often reticent Gobineau is disturbing.[6] Gobineau was the author of controversial writings on racial development that are imbued with idiosyncratic mythology. In his fiction he is a curiously prudish Romantic realist. Céline was a gifted writer, pessimistic, but much more hateful, much more violent, and was a Nazi collaborator. Spitzer's association of the two is thus understandable, though tenuous. For his part, Riffaterre could also have specified whether he had looked up the adverbial or adjectival disambiguation (either semantic or grammatical distinction) of *fort* ("quite"). Additionally, he could have checked the origin of Vander Beke's database to see whether the constituent works were written and published in the mid-1800s. They were not. In fact, Vander Beke selected works which date from the late 1800s and early 1900s: many appeared more than a generation after Gobineau's death. According to information provided by a much larger French word frequency dictionary (see below), the total which Riffaterre gives for *fort* is completely normal for the period 1850–79 if one counts both grammatical functions; but if he is referring to just the adverb, it is remarkably high—a true tic word by standards I will discuss below. In any case, Riffaterre firmly states the relativistic effect of a text upon a reader: "One must verify if the points which caused the reactions are truly stylistic effects, not poorly understood effects of the language from another epoch."[7]

More important than the statistical validation of a frequency-oriented problem, we must ask ourselves *how* we know that Gobineau writes earnestly, under which conditions he portrays his characters in an emotional state, and *why* he expresses certain ideas. Once we integrate our thematic and stylistic findings with the ideas contained within the text, the holistic picture should appear. An understanding of this reconstructive, integrative process based on consistent research of the constituent words, linguistic elements, themes, and ideas of the text in combination with the secondary literature may facilitate an enlightened view of Leo Spitzer's criticism of Riffaterre.

One of the key elements to consider in a quantitative approach to style and thematic word groupings is repetition. I am also interested in the linguistic tendencies that might result in creative repetition in the *Nouvelles asiatiques*. Spitzer himself might take advantage of a stylo-statistical tool like computational thematics to this end if he were with us today. He wrote in 1955:

> Counting the percentage of abstract and concrete nouns or the repetitions of keywords in the works of certain authors is a task which, after all, does not prove to be any more difficult than the transformation of statistics into an affirmation of the nature of these authors. Subsequently linked to other observations made throughout the book, these observations will have a sure value.[8]

Spitzer adds here that one can develop adeptness at this process of making statistical observations and integrating them with other literary observations, but that "*cela ne va pas toujours sans ennui.*" Even when one uses the computer, this process does not always proceed without difficulty or "ennui," like any lengthy act of literary interpretation. One recompense is the wealth of details one gains on the path to literary synthesis, but one also needs a methodology to facilitate conceptual grouping of words, quantitative processing, literary interpretation, and display of the results.

METHODOLOGY

The basis of my methodology lies in strategically grouping words by their conceptual association, as in Table 1. If the associations Riffaterre or I have made are not valid, intuitively or as applied to the *Nouvelles*, the statistical results will probably be inconclusive or contradictory. Alternatively, if for inconsistent reasons these results are statistically significant, according to the guidelines specified below, we will probably learn when examining the appropriate contexts that our grouping was invalid. For example, where statistical results indicate a remarkably high density of certain word clusters, we will have to judge the significance of these words and their context to a recurring theme, philosophy, emotion, or stylistic trait. The computer allows us to test quantitative elements within a reasonably short length of time, but we must view the results critically.

TABLE 1. FRENCH-ENGLISH GLOSSARY OF RIFFATERRE'S "TIC WORDS"

abandonné	— ABANDONED	hargneux	— BELLIGERENT
abandonner	— TO ABANDON (not ref.)	heureux	— HAPPY
abandonner x	— (not past part.)	idée	— IDEA
absolu	— ABSOLUTE	illustre	— ILLUSTRIOUS
! absolument	— ABSOLUTELY	imagination	— IMAGINATION
admirable	— ADMIRABLE (ironic)	!incomparable	— INCOMPARABLE (exagg.)
admirable	— (not ironic)	incomparable	— (unexaggerated)
admirable x	— (all entries)	intéressant	— INTERESTING
admirer	— TO ADMIRE (ir.)	intéressé	— INTERESTED
admirer	— (not ironic)	intérieur	— INTERIOR
admirer x	— (all entries)	ironiquement	— IRONICALLY
adorable	— ADORABLE	!jamais	— NEVER; EVER
adoration	— ADORATION	joli	— FINE, NICE (ir.)
affection	— AFFECTION	joli	— PRETTY; NICE (unir.)
affectueux	— AFFECTIONATE	joli x	— (all meanings)
aimer	— TO LOVE	libre	— FREE
amant	— LOVER (nonsexual)	malheur	— MISFORTUNE
âme	— SOUL; SPIRIT; MIND	mesquin	— MEAN; PETTY
amitié	— FRIENDSHIP	mort (. . .)	— DEATH; DIE (etc.)
amour	— LOVE	*mot, en un	— IN A WORD
anéanti	— ANNIHILATED; OVERCOME	noble (adj.)	— NOBLE
anxieux	— ANXIOUS	noble (noun)	— NOBLE
assez	— ENOUGH	noble x	— (all gram. funct.)
! assurément	— ASSUREDLY	!nullement	— NOT IN THE LEAST
audacieux	— AUDACIOUS	orgueil	— PRIDE; ARROGANCE
au-dessus	— ABOVE	!parfait	— PERFECT; COMPLETE
*avouer	— AVOW; ADMIT	passion	— PASSION
bonheur	— HAPPINESS	pauvre	— POOR, WRETCHED
bourgeois	— BOURGEOIS	peut-être	— MAYBE
*brave	— BRAVE; "GOOD SPORT"	plus	— MOST
*bref	— IN BRIEF	presque	— ALMOST
canaille	— RABBLE	raison	— REASON (mental fac.)
céleste	— CELESTIAL	ravir	— TO DELIGHT
! certain	— CERTAIN	!réellement	— REALLY, ACTUALLY
charmant	— CHARMING	résolu	— RESOLUTE
coeur	— HEART; COURAGE	rêverie	— DAYDREAM(ING)
colère	— ANGER	!rien	— NOTHING
! comble	— HEIGHT (anger, etc.)	sangloter	— TO SOB
! complètement	— COMPLETELY	sentiment	— FEELING; EMOTION
coquin	— RASCAL(LY); ROGUE	!soit	— SO BE IT
coquine	— (feminine form)	*somme, en	— ALL IN ALL; IN SUM
*définitive, en	— ALL SAID & DONE	sphère	— SPHERE
différent	— DIFFERENT	sublime	— SUBLIME
doué	— GIFTED	!sûr	— SURE
*doute, sans (. . .)	— WITHOUT (. . .) DOUBT[a]	!surtout	— ESPECIALLY
éclater	— BURST	sympathie	— LIKING; AFFINITY
élite	— ELITE	tendre	— TENDER (adj.)
! emphatique	— BOMBASTIC	tendresse	— TENDERNESS
ému	— MOVED (emotion)	transports	— TRANSPORTS (joy, etc.)
! entier	— ENTIRE	!très	— VERY
! fort (adv.)	— QUITE, MOST	verve	— VERVE; ELOQUENCE
hardi	— BOLD, DARING	vie (. . .)	— LIFE (etc.)

[a]"sans doute," "sans aucun doute," "sans nul doute"

Note: In the interest of brevity, only the basic types and tic word definitions are given. An "x" following an entry indicates that it includes all definitions and forms. Multiple entries of the same indicate disambiguation; the absence of another translation indicates the same primary one as for the preceding entry but disambiguation according to the brief comment in parentheses. !—emphatic word; *—phatic word; (. . .)—etymologically and semantically related group of words.

I am thus using both inductive and deductive processes to undertake a stylo-statistical, thematic, and contextual analysis of a selected, controversial vocabulary group in Gobineau's *Nouvelles asiatiques* and in the novella *The Dancer from Shamakha* in particular. On the basis of these "Asian novellas," I have constructed a selective database—a special dictionary—for use as an elaborate thesaurus. By using the computer to analyze the location and frequency of certain conceptually related words, I hope to find the contexts most relevant to the themes under investigation in this study. I find the frequency and distribution of these word associations, then interpret the results by simultaneously considering the statistical results associated with these words in light of the contexts pinpointed by the study. The methodology will also suggest criteria for stylistic analysis and additional avenues for exploration.[9]

I follow two principal procedures, though not always in the order stated. First, one reacts to the text inductively and subjectively, listing single words without necessarily having a concrete reason for isolating them. The ultimate object is to discover some statistical basis for their possibly unusual use, either in the text or according to literary norms of the period (see below). One can then group the words by theme or concept. This is a type of word association which can be aided by a thesaurus, a standard dictionary, or a special dictionary, like one on regressive imagery, which divides an image or concept into its constituent parts.[10] To paraphrase Klaus M. Schmidt's analogy (788), a conceptual dictionary resembles the telephone book, where the white pages provide an alphabetical arrangement to search for head words ("lemmas") but the yellow pages offer alphabetically listed, conceptual entries containing their alphabetized constituents. We assume that all shop names, place names, and so forth, have been properly lemmatized, that is, categorized under the appropriate main entry.

In the next step of the procedure, I statistically evaluate the words' frequency of use by section and throughout the text. Other critics may or may not have isolated the same words I choose to study. Lastly, I interpret the findings after returning to the context of the words or group of conceptually-related words whose frequency of use has proved unusual, either statistically high or low.

Second, one reacts to the secondary literature (deductive), constructing categories or thematic groups of words based on themes or other ideas which critics have studied. Our colleagues' work provides us with many of the contextually important words which will populate our dictionary's database. The statistical results could clarify the reasons critics study particular words or passages. These tagged words may allow us to discover common bonds among many passages and themes. Alternatively, we may find certain themes to be mutually exclusive, a phenomenon called "inverse correlation."

In the first case, we can assume that the words in question are not related through any theme or other conceptual bond. We thereby construct a "null hypothesis" which states that there is no expectation of a statistically significant correlation for a particular group of words. However, should we find high frequencies (repetition) or low frequencies (omission), we should try to explain why. This interpretive process requires us to return to the context of the words in question, especially to the locations where they are quantitatively significant.[11] If certain words co-occur, that is, if the author often uses them in clusters, they are likely to be part of a conceptual group. Normally, these words do not appear in clusters: they are usually evenly distributed. If we compare this group with the results of similar research on the author's other works or on the works of his contemporaries, we may find common bonds or great differences in ideas, concerns, and styles that we may not have noticed before. This type of approach can provide a more objective corroboration of mainly intuitive perceptions. One advantage of literary computing and of computational thematics in particular is that once the researcher's strategies are programmed, they are consistently implemented by the computer.

Regarding the second procedure, the deductive one, we need not restrict the themes to those suggested by other critics. We can construct our own lexicon as a database for a lexicometric ("word-measuring") analysis. In any case, the computer is indispensable in assisting our organization of the entries and in statistically analyzing the quantitative use of words in a text. As the researcher and presenter of this study, I have to make *some* intuitive choices in grouping the tic words, but, in general, statistics allow me to evaluate the choices in a more circumspect and open way. I am modifying Leo Spitzer's "circular reasoning" in a manner which should allow me to posit a "stylistic fact," test it through statistical means, then draw some interpretive conclusions which integrate the quantitative and content material.[12]

Although I may have certain preconceptions at this point regarding the nature and identity of tic words in the *Nouvelles asiatiques*, only Riffaterre's choices appear here. However, the words he labels "tics" belong to at least three major groups, two of which seem closely related. We can call a special group of possible tic words in Gobineau's writings "phatic" in Peter Newmark's sense:

> The minor functions of language are diverse. The translator is concerned only with phatic language where phrases such as "of course," "naturally," "as is well known" (Stalin's phrase for what was not), "it need hardly be mentioned," "it is worth noting," "interesting to note," "important," etc. (usually "it" is not so)—German has many more (*ja, eben, gewiss, usw.*)—are used to keep the reader happy or in touch.[13]

Webster's Ninth New Collegiate Dictionary defines "phatic" as "revealing or sharing feelings or establishing an atmosphere of sociability rather than communicating ideas."[14]

Complementing the phatic category is another group of words that I will call "emphatic" words, words "marked by emphasis" (*Webster's*) or characterized by forceful expression. This group includes words like *jamais, nullement,* and *rien* ("never/ever," "not in the least," "[not] anything/nothing"). In using intensifying adverbs the author intensifies the entire thought. I detect both types of potential tic words in Riffaterre's choices. Both are weak in apparent secondary and tertiary definitions, thus in semantic richness, but they are often affectively strong. They stand out much like a physical tic, a seemingly random twinge or jerk of the finger, hand, or head, for example. The rest, which form a large third group, belong to many different thematic or conceptual categories. Table 1 lists the words of all three groups and indicates phatic and emphatic words.

To simplify the analysis of Riffaterre's findings as we might apply them to the *Nouvelles,* I shall concentrate initially on the two ostensible tic word subgroups: phatic and emphatic words.

Their semantic narrowness, yet potential narrative and stylistic effect, set them apart from entries which normally denote or connote love, life, and death, for example. Perhaps these words are tic words, perhaps not. Because the designation of phatic and emphatic terms is a subjective decision depending on readers' experiences, they should verify each word in my list. This verification of the database is admittedly easier for those who know the text and contexts in which Gobineau tends to use these words.

Should the statistical results we obtain below prove to be positively significant, then we can conclude that the words in question are most likely tic words. If the words in the tables do not belong in either group, then the collective results will probably be somewhat compromised. In order for these words to be considered tic words, I propose that only one condition must be met: statistically significant repetition. Statistically significant repetition in itself probably signals a use of these terms which Riffaterre calls obsessive (117). I do not believe, however, that this obsessiveness need be pejorative. In any case, phatic and emphatic words strike me as being promising candidates for the label "persistent," if not "obsessive," and the reader is free to assign them this latter quality as suggested by their contexts as well. This study will differentiate words which we might like to include by association or context in the tic word network from those which we can also statistically isolate as unusually repetitive.

DATABASE STRUCTURE AND STATISTICAL APPLICATIONS

Since we are using thematic or conceptual groups, we do not need an entire machine-readable text at our disposal in order to obtain complete results. Other researchers, such as Étienne Brunet in Nice and Robert F. Allen at Rutgers University, have used databases of complete, machine-readable texts in order to pinpoint all word occurrences and to perform statistical texts of various complexities.[15] One advantage I had in conducting this study was the use of an alphabetized printout of all words with their page locations in the *Nouvelles asiatiques*. But I did not have on-line access to the machine-readable text. I hope to show that use of a selective database with a complete list of occurrences is valid, helpful, and time effective in computational thematics. This efficient use of time should be of special interest to literary researchers who do not have optical scanners, which automatically scan and electronically duplicate the text on a computer disk or tape, nor time nor assistants to type in large texts.[16] Although this database requires some meticulous effort in organization and cataloguing, it is critical to the success of this method. We must include all occurrences of entries under study. Fortunately, there are long-term benefits, for we can reuse the database and the statistical and utility programs for sorting and word-processing in other studies.[17]

Now that we have defined a literary problem and established groups of words based on a common theme—phatic, emphatic, and other tic words—we must create a database that will allow the computer to calculate their distribution in the text. Once we analyze the results, we will know whether they are repetitious enough to qualify as tic words. Additionally, we will be able to locate quickly the pages where the thematic clusters or individual words are quantitatively significant. Then we can evaluate the contexts in question and draw some informed conclusions on Gobineau's use of these tic words in the *Nouvelles asiatiques*. Our results would eventually allow us to make some stylistic and thematic comparisons between the *Nouvelles* and *Les Pléiades*, given complete quantitative results on the latter. The addition and evaluation of other themes would allow us to compare further the author's style(s) and ideas as they appear throughout the six novellas and in other texts. The reference work we shall use for our comparison of lexicometric results with the literary norms of the period (1850–79) is the French frequency dictionary, *Dictionnaire des fréquences*, hereafter labeled "*Dictionnaire*."[18]

In order to compare the total number of occurrences of a word in a particular text with the normal frequency ("norm") for that word, we must proportionally adjust one norm to the other in the same way that one adjusts the numerical size of the lexical database of which it is a part. For example, whereas the *Nouvelles* consist of 105,093 word occurrences, the *Dictionnaire*'s frequencies are based on a hypothetical database of 100,000,000 word occurrences. This adjustment allows us to compare the frequencies from genre and other groupings of varied sizes. Alternatively, we could adjust the individual and combined frequencies of the words in our texts to some other norm, as the TLF team did in its frequency dictionary. Hereafter, I will usually refer to the adjusted normal frequency or frequencies of a word or group of words listed in the *Dictionnaire* as simply the

TABLE 2. NUMBER OF WORD OCCURRENCES IN EACH NOVELLA

Novella	Estimated:	Percent of total	No. of words
The Dancer from Shamakha	(DS)	20.65569%	21,708
The Illustrious Magician	(IM)	13.03581%	13,700
The Story of Gambèr-Aly	(GA)	16.79501%	17,650
The War of the Turkomans	(WT)	17.39468%	18,281
The Lovers from Kandahar	(LK)	16.52067%	17,362
The Travelling Life	(TL)	15.59814%	16,392
Nouvelles asiatiques	(NA)	100.00000%	105,093

"external norm." I have proportionally adjusted the *Dictionnaire*'s total for each word examined to reflect the smaller word occurrence base of 105,093 in the *Nouvelles,* including foreign words and proper nouns, which are normally eliminated from the *Dictionnaire*'s database. Given this final adjustment to a "common ground" total, we shall see below that since *The Dancer from Shamakha* is approximately one-fifth the length of the collection of six novellas (see Table 2), we must divide each external norm total for a particular word by roughly five. In so doing, we reduce the norm to reflect a smaller hypothetical database the size of the novella in question.

The *Dictionnaire* derives its frequency norms for the period 1850–79 from 147 literary works retyped into machine-readable form. The team of experts from the Trésor de la langue française ("TLF") lemmatized all words in the texts with the help of computer algorithms based on grammatical and syntactical rules of French. These 147 works yield a total of 12,596,788 word occurrences within a total corpus of 72,543,490 word occurrences (TLF's result) in the 1,002 publications whose words form the *Dictionnaire*'s database. There are 71,415 entries not including proper names and foreign words. Without these last two groups of words, the total number of occurrences as recalculated by Brunet (I, 22, note 2) is 72,273,552, still the largest textual database for literary research of any Western language, and perhaps of any language in the world.

Since Gobineau wrote and published the *Nouvelles asiatiques* in the mid-1870s, the nearest chronological division (1850–79) is a valid and useful one. My normative database uses figures based exclusively on the prose (novel, essay, short story) plus poetry word populations. There are 500,000 word occurrences in the poetry segment of the 12,596,788 occurrences for the literary period 1850–79. I decided that this lexical environment appropriately reflects a segment of the French literary public's potential lexical background.

There are many methods available for counting words, although researchers will find cause to debate what, exactly, constitutes a word or occurrence in many types of expressions.[19] By choosing six pages at random in each novella and counting the number of words per page according to the length of lines actually containing text, I am able to estimate the number of words per novella in Table 2. This table also provides all the novella abbreviations which I use in this study.

The statistical portion of computer-assisted content analysis is vital to the work of many literary critics publishing in this area. Literary scholars such as Alphonse Juilland, Charles Muller, and Étienne Brunet (see above) have even provided us with clear descriptions of how our quantitative use of words follows predictable frequency patterns according to the normal curve. The central limit theorem and its standard deviations ("z" scores) provide a simple yet valuable statistical tool for discovering unusual quantitative uses of words (high or low frequencies).[20] The theorem's easily-applied formula allows us to retain the sign, positive or negative, in our result. We shall see that this quality is extremely helpful in allowing us to recognize quickly the abundance or dearth of various thematic group or individual word populations. The formula is as follows:

$$z = \frac{\text{observed frequency} - \text{theoretical frequency}}{\sqrt{\text{theoretical frequency}}}$$

We subtract the theoretical (expected) frequency from the frequency we observe in the text, then divide this result by the square root of the theoretical frequency. The observed frequency of the word(s) under study in a text and the theoretical frequency must be part of equal, comparable databases, as described above. We can compare the 73 occurrences of *pauvre* ("poor") in the *Nouvelles* only against an expected normal frequency adjusted to the same type of database possessing the same number of total occurrences of all words. The expected frequency must be adjusted as though it came from a corpus of 105,093 word occurrences, not from one of 100 million. I have already adjusted the normal frequency of *pauvre:* a hypothetical total of 60.5 occurrences.

$$z = \frac{73 - 60.5}{\sqrt{60.5}} = \frac{12.5}{7.8} = 1.6 \text{ (standard deviations)}$$

Application of the formula shows that *pauvre* is not quite a tic word overall in the *Nouvelles asiatiques,* for its z-score falls below the threshold of +2. This figure represents a probability of 95.4% that the number of occurrences is unusually high or a probability of 4.6%, according to the French literary norm (1850–79), that its quantitative use is not unusually high. The deviation 1.6 corresponds to a probability of .110 or 11% (Muller, *Principes,* 198). This means that there is an 11 percent chance that this amount of repetition is normal or expected, 89% that it is not. Although 11 percent may intuitively seem fairly low, it is not low enough in matters of lexicometrics to consider the repetitiousness of *pauvre* significant overall in the *Nouvelles asiatiques* (see note 21).

As a test case for just one novella, let us examine the use of *pauvre* (all meanings) in *The War of the Turkomans*. Approximately 17.4% (.1739468 of 1) of all the word occurrences in the *Nouvelles* appear in this novella: 18,281 out of 105,093 occurrences (Table 6.2).

Adjusted norm × coefficient for the *WT* = expected frequency

60.5 × .1739468 = 10.52 occurrences.

We find 26 occurrences of this entry instead of a total close to the external norm of 10.52. The observed frequency seems substantially higher than the expected norm from an intuitive point of view, but we need to evaluate our results through a demonstrable model and method.

$$z = \frac{26 - 10.52}{\sqrt{10.52}} = \frac{+15.48}{3.243} = +4.77 \text{ (standard deviations)}$$

By consulting a table of probability for z-scores (Muller, *Principes,* 198), we find a probability of less than .0006%, a probability of .000006 out of 1, that this relationship between 26 occurrences and 10.52 is "normal" or "expected" ($z = 4.77$). The odds are over 166,667 to 1 or 99.9994% (100 − .0006) that Gobineau's repetitious use of *pauvre* is significant in this work of 18,281 word occurrences within the lexical environment of novels, essays, short stories, and poetry written and published between 1850 and 1879. None of the 147 works included in the *Dictionnaire*'s database appears to have divergent dates. For example, these works include no re-editions or printings published earlier than 1850.

Now we can question whether Gobineau's frequency of use of *pauvre* is somehow significant, either positively or negatively, in the *Nouvelles asiatiques* alone. Perhaps it is normal in the context of this work in general. In addition, we can examine its figurative use alone. This is impossible when we use the external norm, for the *Dictionnaire* does not disambiguate (differentiate) the contexts where *pauvre* means "poor" in the sense of "the poor/wretched soldier" and those where it means "poor/indigent." Using the null hypothesis, we will assume that the 20 occurrences of *pauvre* we observe in its figurative context are statistically insignificant. I call the expected norm the "internal" norm in the present case since we are comparing our observed results against a limited norm: one observed only in the literary work of which we are evaluating a part.

We may define the internal norm as the total number of occurrences of the word(s) in question divided by the relative length of the section in which they are found compared with the length of the whole text. We find the word *pauvre* ("wretched") 61 times in 105,093 words. Since the *War of the Turkomans* occupies 17.39468%, or about one-sixth, of the length of the *Nouvelles,* we expect to find this word:

$$61 \times .1739468 = 10.6 \text{ times.}$$

However, we find it 20 times.

$$z = \frac{20 - 10.6}{\sqrt{10.6}} = \frac{9.4}{3.26} = +2.9 \text{ (standard deviations)}$$

The z-score of $+2.9$ for *pauvre* ("wretched") in this novella in comparison with the expected internal norm is not as high as the one found for all occurrences and meanings relative to the external norm ($z = 4.77$). However, it is substantially higher than our threshold of $+2$. The corresponding probability of .004 means that there is a 99.6% chance, odds of 250 to 1, that this frequency has some underlying significance. In the *War of the Turkomans,* the quantitative and figurative use of *pauvre* justifies our calling it a tic word.

All the lexicostatistical problems we considered above are easily solved using a pocket calculator and a probability table. Readers can nonetheless anticipate the difficulties that may arise when there are hundreds of thousands of similar calculations for researchers to make when evaluating the distribution of many occurrences in a text. The element of energistics—of time, accuracy, and benefit—could take a heavy toll on our ability to understand and critique literature, our primary goal. The computer offers us an effective solution: the quick manipulation of lexicometric information to provide new ways of looking at where and, to some degree, how and why authors use certain words.

LEXICOMETRIC RESULTS AND LITERARY SYNTHESIS

In order to ascertain which entries qualify statistically as tic words, we can now focus our attention on the research of lexical statisticians, who call those words whose frequencies attain or cross the threshold of plus or minus 2 "key words" or "keywords." [21] The term does not necessarily imply a thematic power, simply a quantitative one. If thematically associated words cross the $+2$ threshold, we might call them "thematic keywords." I now use the expression "tic" in quotation marks when referring to words or expressions alleged by Riffaterre to be tic words but which I have not yet shown to be tic keywords.

Additional research shows that in comparison with the external norm there is a drastic reduction in phatic and emphatic tic words that qualify as keywords according to the internal norm. There are no emphatic tic words which appear frequently enough to be designated as keywords in *Dancer* and *Lovers*, but I find one emphatic keyword in *Magician, Gambèr-Aly (parfait)* and *Travelling Life (très)* and two in *Turkomans (fort, très)*. The only phatic tic words which qualify as keywords appear in *Turkomans (avouer)* and *Lovers (noble,* adjective and noun). According to the external norm, however, I find seven emphatic keywords in *Dancer,* five in *Turkomans,* three in *Magician* and four in each of the remaining three novellas. These may occur from two (*DS: comble*) to thirty-eight times (*LK: rien*). There are two phatic keywords in *Turkomans (avouer, en somme)*, none in *Lovers* and *Travelling Life* and 1 in each of the remaining novellas.

We can now start to apply our knowledge of Gobineau's stylistic use of phatic and emphatic words to reveal how he creates character. Judging according to Gobineau's stylistic tendencies as described above, we can tentatively conclude that he uses the tic words, intentionally or not, fairly evenly throughout the novellas, with the exception of *The War of the Turkomans.* Importantly, this is the only story recounted in the first person. By selecting certain tic words for unusual repetition, Gobineau creates a well-defined narrative voice and character for the likable but unfortunate Iranian soldier, "Aga."

In a broader light, of Riffaterre's 104 selections for *Les Pléiades,* 46 entries are tic keywords in the *Nouvelles asiatiques* according to the internal norm; 51 entries are tics according to the external, literary norm of the period. The number of entries qualifying as tic keywords increases when we judge his style by the norm which Gobineau and his literary contemporaries established. Nonetheless, if Riffaterre is correct in his assumptions concerning Gobineau's earlier work, *Les Pléiades,* the author modified his style significantly for the *Nouvelles* by either expanding his vocabulary and rhetorical repertoire or by more generally softening its tone or both. He has reduced the number of strident, emphatic "tic words" and tic keywords. Even when we evaluate Gobineau's use of the "tic" words according to the external norm, fewer than half qualify as tic keywords.

We can further develop a quantitative feeling for these results with the addition of figures from a separate tally I have made: whereas there are 601 occurrences (noncomparable lemmas excluded) of the appropriately disambiguated tic words in the *Nouvelles,* the adjusted norm of the period for these words is approximately 383 occurrences. To summarize, there are 218 more occurrences of these words than expected in Gobineau's work. Given that one of these words might occur 11 times in the novellas (*assurément,* "assuredly") instead of twice, or 108 times (*assez,* "enough") instead of the 55 times expected according to the literary norm, it is not surprising that we might sense a slant away from the zero degree of a supposedly typical French literary style, specifically, of a style found in works written in the 1870s.

We can only hypothesize about readers' impressions of the style Gobineau uses in these novellas. Naturally, for a reader of another century and background, the impressions or inner feeling for the norm or deviation from the norm might be quite different from our own. The opposition of Spitzer's mentalistic approach to Bloomfield's more mechanistic and behavioral one regarding these issues was a cause of friction between the two in the 1940s, and between Spitzer and Riffaterre in the late 1950s.[22]

Table 3 helps us focus on particular passages that should exemplify the style and context(s) where Gobineau consciously or unconsciously injects an abnormally high concentration of phatic and emphatic words. Most of them statistically qualify as tic keywords. Those on page 61 of *Dancer* are designated by an asterisk (external norm). One can observe the separate thematic clusters independent of contexts. They are bricks with no mortar, but often revelatory. Since some keywords' semantic depth or polysemous potential is weaker than others' ("all in all" versus "love," for example), as is the case with grammatical words and many phatic tic words, we might see these clusters as mortar without bricks. I attempt to provide an applied feeling for the usual number of keywords present, then concentrate on the exceptional cases, believing that the literary researcher working with statistics and a computer needs to return to the literary text as often as possible to facilitate the synthetic process. This procedure imitates the "to-and-fro" or "*va-et-vient*" one that Spitzer and Riffaterre advocate in their descriptions of stylistic analysis.[23]

The exceptional cases referred to in this table are almost always obvious in hindsight. The majority of pages containing Riffaterre's "tic" words yields three or fewer. Through additional research, I find that out of all sixty-four pages containing the text of *The Dancer of Shamakha* in the Classiques Garnier edition, forty contain three possible tic words or fewer. Forty-six pages yield four possible tic words or fewer. Eighteen pages, then, contain more than four possible tic words: fewer than one-third of the total number of pages in question. Therefore, pages containing more than four occurrences of these words are likely to be of greater initial stylistic and, perhaps, thematic interest in this area.

In our ever-narrowing semantic funnel, we can now focus on contexts that seem likely to provide interesting correlations with alleged tic words and tic keywords. This test, we must remind ourselves, is based on repetition or positive densities, not on unusual microcontexts or stylistic convergences such as rhetorical devices and unusual word associations. As an illustration of the next step in this methodology, we might first examine page 61 in *The Dancer from Shamakha*. This page contains nine phatic or emphatic "tic" words, the second-highest absolute frequency (real total) on one page in the *Nouvelles*. Page 61 also contains the highest total (Table 4 below) of the 104 words listed in Table 1. The location is Omm-Djéhâne's apartment. The Lesghy dancer is engaged in a heated

TABLE 3. PHATIC OR EMPHATIC "TIC" WORDS IDENTIFIED BY MICHAEL RIFFATERRE. Densest Pages or Passages by Novella According to the Internal Norm.

Dancer: (Total)

pp. 14–15 (7):	assez, nullement, fort (3), jamais, très.
21 (5):	en définitive, nullement, sûr, très, parfait, surtout.
27 (5):	fort, jamais, nullement, parfait, très.
28 (5):	assez, assurément, bref, jamais, sûr.
36 (6):	assez, avouer, fort, jamais, très (2).
61 (9):	avouer, *jamais (3), *nullement, *parfait, très (2).
63 (6):	fort (3), pauvre (2), très.
71 (7):	absolument, assurément, comble, jamais (2), pauvre, surtout.
75 (5):	assez (3), fort, jamais.

Magician:

98 (6):	absolument (2), sans . . . doute, jamais, pauvre, surtout.
103 (6):	bref, nullement, parfait, pauvre (2), très.
105 (5):	fort, pauvre, sûr, surtout, très.
110 (5):	assurément, jamais, sûr (2), très.

Gambèr:

130 (6):	assez, sans . . . doute (2), illustre, surtout (2).
131 (5):	assez (2), fort, jamais (2).
142 (5):	fort (2), jamais (3).
176 (5):	absolument, fort, nullement, très (2).
177 (6):	absolument, assez, bref, parfait, en somme, surtout.

Turkomans (Note high density):

185 (5):	assez, fort (2), jamais, très.
186 (6):	avouer, doute, fort (2), jamais, sûr.
192 (8):	absolument (2), fort, jamais (2), parfait, pauvre, sûr.
196 (7):	absolument, avouer, fort, jamais (2), pauvre, très.
205 (6):	assez, bref, jamais (3), pauvre.
211 (10):	absolument, assez, doute, fort (2), jamais, pauvre (2), en somme, très.
234 (9):	avouer (2), comble, sans . . . doute, fort, jamais, pauvre, sûr, très.

Lovers (Note reduced density and distribution over several pages):

243 (4):	assez (3), très.
245 (4):	assez, jamais (3).
251 (4):	jamais (3), sûr.
265 (4):	assez, surtout (2), très.
274 (4):	assez (3), jamais;
275–6 (6):	jamais, parfait; assurément, sans . . . doute, fort, pauvre.
278 (5):	assez (2), fort (2), jamais.
281–2 (6):	assez (2): jamais (3), parfait.
284–5 (8):	jamais (2), nullement, en somme; assez, avouer, jamais, nullement.
287 (4):	assez (2), jamais, surtout.

Travelling (Note generally lower "tic" word density):

298 (4):	pauvre (3), très.
302 (6):	assez, bref, nullement (2), surtout (2).
312 (6):	absolument, assez, fort, très (3).
316–317 (10):	absolument (2), assurément, très; avouer, sans . . . doute, jamais (2), pauvre, très.
321–323 (12):	jamais (2), nullement, très; illustre, jamais, en somme, très; jamais, pauvre, très (2).
325 (4):	assez, jamais (3).
329 (4):	fort (2), jamais (2).
333 (5):	jamais (2), sûr (2), très.

Note: A semicolon indicates the page division of a multiple-page passage. The number in parentheses indicates the total occurrences. I have included only words which seem to fall into the phatic or emphatic categories. An asterisk regarding p. 61 designates a tic keyword.

discussion with her cousin, Assanoff. She pleads with him to desert the Russian Army's engineering corps. His real name is Mourad; he is a Moslem who has tried to blend into an acceptable branch of Russian civilization in the 1800s. His female cousin, the last of his tribe, which was obliterated by Russian soldiers claiming the Caucasus, wants to return to her homeland and recover her true Lesghy identity with Assanoff as her husband. Calling upon the power of nostalgic folk music and using almost supernatural powers of persuasion and personal charisma, she has persuaded her cousin to desert, or so she believes. The following sentences contain most of Riffaterre's choices of "tic" words on page 61. The phatic and emphatic words appear in all capitals. Other "tic" words are italicized.

> ASSANOFF: You are really VERY pretty, I *love* you with all my *heart*. . . . Do you know French? . . .
>
> OMM-DJÉHÂNE: Mourad, son of Hassan-Bey, you should be ashamed! Forget these horribles thoughts FOREVER ["pour JAMAIS"]!
>
> ASSANOFF: I am a Tartar and NOTHING else, and I want to be only that. And may I be cut into ten thousand pieces if our children aren't PERFECT Moslems! But that's *enough* of reasoning!
>
> OMM-DJÉHÂNE: The Russians will NEVER see you again here. . . .
>
> NARRATOR: Once he was in the street, he was pleased with himself, pleased with his plans, and VERY much in *love* with his cousin, whom he found *adorable*. It must be ADMITTED, accustomed NEVER to follow more than one idea at a time, he had COMPLETELY forgotten his travelling companion . . . he didn't think IN THE LEAST ["NULLEMENT"] that Moreno was waiting for him. . . . (*DS* 61)

We might identify the adverb "enough" as an emphatic "tic" word here. In addition to the highlighted "tic" words, readers may have noticed a potential one that I did not list earlier, the adverb "really" (*vraiment*). Viewed with *nullement* and *complètement*, its context points to another possible emphatic word group, the French adverbs containing the *ment* suffix which corresponds to the adverbial ending "ly" in English.[24] Additional research on this group reveals that the standard deviation for these words is +2.4 compared to the internal norm and +10.7 compared to the external norm. Some describe movement—e.g., "brusquely," "suddenly,"—but can be separated from the more emphatic members of the group. On the whole, I conclude that this group of adverbs warrants contextual analysis in future studies, for these words carry emphatic and narrative power and play an important quantitative role in the *Nouvelles,* as further evidenced by their frequent appearance in novella quotations used in this essay.

I discovered yet another device that reinforces the emphatic nature of this passage: the exclamation point, which appears four times in the quotation above and in nearly consecutive sentences. We are not surprised, then, to find 13 exclamation points on page 61. In my study on the punctuation of the *Nouvelles asiatiques,* one can see that the total number of exclamation points, 1,116, is not at all unusual for French prose published between 1870 and 1879 (Goldfield, I, 54–56). In fact, the norm for a work of this length is 1,130 occurrences. However, compared to the norm of the entire French literary corpus examined in the *Dictionnaire* (1,002 works, 1789–1964), this is unusually high. The standard deviation is +17! This result gives us an objective standpoint from which to judge the role of exclamation points upon which Spitzer comments above concerning Gobineau and Céline. We might tentatively conclude that the prose of 1870–79, a period which covers the Franco-Prussian war, is emotional. In the context found on page 61 (*Dancer*), based on the 367 words contained therein, we would expect approximately 4 exclamation points. But there are 13, yielding a significant standard deviation of +4. The probability is approximately 16,667 to 1 against this number of exclamation points occurring in such close succession. From the statistics alone we may conclude that something of emotional interest is happening on this page, a fact which reinforces our tic word findings.

We can expand our knowledge of *The Dancer from Shamakha* and of page 61 in particular by consulting Table 4, which considers all or nearly all the "tic" words identified as such by Riffaterre in his chapter III, "*L'intensité*" ("Intensity"). Table 6.4 indicates all pages containing at least nine occurrences of these words, many of which, in my opinion, must be cross-referenced under other themes as well. Such is the case of "adorable," "affectionate," "love" (n.), "to love," and so forth (*adorable, affectueux, amour, aimer*). Of the sixty-four pages of text in *Dancer,* only two contain no occurrence of these 104 entries. These two "negative clusters" or omissions merit the attention that we will give them below.

The thematic results outlined in Table 4 also point out passages for comparison with page 61. On pages 30, 35, and 36, several unsavory Armenian and Asian characters discuss their plans and profits in the female slave trade. We read lines which approach preciosity such as the following ones which flow from the tongue of the corrupt prefect of police, Paul Petrowitch, concerning his colleague, Grégoire Ivanitch Vialgue: " 'This Armenian is ASSUREDLY a man of genius!' murmured Paul Petrowitch, raising his eyes to the sky and crossing his hands on his belly" (*DS* 30). After Grégoire has predicted an unlimited expansion of their business, Petrowitch adds: "I think so, [too,] my good, my PERFECT friend, and what's more (for I don't think only about my own property! I also take an interest in the HAPPINESS of my peers! I am, above all, a philanthropist!), look at what good we are doing!" (*DS* 30).

These "tic" words stand out as semantic "neon signs" for irony through exaggeration and logical opposition. The exclamation points appear again to reinforce the energy of the characters' ironic attitude. We see not far below that the narrator cannot or chooses not to hide his attitude toward such dealings, once

TABLE 4. THEMATIC GROUP: 104 ALLEGED "TIC" WORDS IDENTIFIED BY RIFFATERRE
Comparison of Lexicometric Results with the Internal Norm, Densest Pages or Passages by Novella in the *Nouvelles asiatiques*[a]

Page Total	Tic words
DS 26 (10):	adorable, amour, certain, charmant, doué, heureux, imagination, joli, parfait, surtout.
DS 30 (9):	assurément, au-dessus, bonheur, bourgeois, brave, différent, parfait, pauvre, presque.
DS 35–36 (19):	éclater, aimer, coeur, fort, heureux, joli, mort (2), sentiment, assez, avouer, charmant, fort,[b] joli,[c] malheur (2), tendre, très (2).
DS 43–44 (21):	abandonné, abandonner, aimer, bonheur, coeur (2), heureux, imagination, presque; amant, assez, avouer, brave, coeur, ému, en somme, imagination, malheur, presque, raison, tendresse.
DS 61 (12):	adorable, aimer, assez, avouer, coeur, complètement, idée, joli, nullement, parfait, très.
DS 62–63 (17):	bonheur, bref, comble, noble, pauvre, résolu; âme, fort (3), idée, malheur, pauvre (2), presque, rêverie, très.
DS 71 (9):	absolument, affection, assurément, coeur, comble, idée, imagination, pauvre, surtout.
DS 77 (11):	admirer, aimer (2), amitié, colère, fort, idée, joli, mort (3).
DS 78 (10):	aimer, âme, coeur, ému, heureux, mort, orgueil, pauvre, ravir, sans doute.

[a]There are 1,950 occurrences of these words in the *NA*, 349 of which are in *The Dancer from Shamakha*. Semicolons indicate page separations in the case of multipage passages.
[b]adverb
[c]ironic

Grégoire doles out the profits. "The two friends were plunged deep in calculations which, by their result, OBVIOUSLY caused great satisfaction to Paul Petrowitch. When all this *crooked dealing* ['*tripotage*'] had ended, the *worthy* prefect of police shouted for schnapps . . ." (*DS* 30, my emphasis). Through a matrix of "tic" words, Gobineau builds a network of emphatic signals to heighten the irony or emotion underlying his dialogues.

The same style and clusters of ironic oppositions can be found on pages 35 and 36 in the conversation between the large Armenian, Grégoire, and the plump, yet exotic dancer and madam of bellydancers, "Splendors of Beauty" (*Splendeurs de la beauté*).

The subject matter and style change radically, however, on page 43. These are still "tic" words, presumably, yet the mood has changed when the narrator alludes to Moreno: "Either as a result of morals or the greater delicacy and weakness of the IMAGINATION and of the HEART, there exist few men today whose HAPPINESS and vital force reside outside of themselves, in another being or in another thing" (*DS* 43). As in the *Pléiades*, Gobineau has started to make a statement of faith in vitalism, which maintains that life is not explainable by the laws of physics and chemistry alone. He thus implies that there is an escape hatch from determinism.[25]

Computational thematics helps highlight yet another passage in our investigation of vitalism in *The Dancer from Shamakha*, specifically on pages 62 and 63 (Table 4). Arthur de Gobineau reveals his own sense of atavism through Moreno, who exhorts Assanoff not to desert, but rather to remain loyal and honorable so as not to be shot like the latter's dead tribal elders:

> You're going away with bandits, with a loose woman, if I may be permitted to say. And from an elegant man, likable as you are, from a brilliant officer, born to be distinguished in all the salons, you are meditating becoming some sort of vulgar savage, good for shooting in the corner of some woods.
> —You're forgetting that my father was a vulgar savage, and that, specifically, he was shot as you say.
> —My POOR friend, I would be sorry to distress you, but, just because your father met that end, which is not enviable, you need not end up that way willingly. Look, Assanoff, let us be reasonable, if we can! Your father was a savage? Well, you are not. Where is the harm in it? Men cannot all resemble each other from generation to generation. (*DS* 62–63)

As one sometimes finds while using a thematic cluster approach, contextually important passages can sometimes be relatively poor in the theme words and keywords under investigation. We find this circumstance in the passage quoted immediately above. The personality and mood of the characters can, of course, influence many of the author's dramatic and stylistic decisions and, necessarily, vocabulary choices.

But the same computational study reveals a passage dense in keywords and theme words which thrust one of the novella's major themes, ethnicity versus assimilation, into the forefront. Most of page 63 contains an increasingly emotional analysis of Assanoff's situation that may actually reflect, in part, the intensity of his feelings. Moreno is an embodiment of the rational side of the narrator, as is Valerio in the final novella, *The Travelling Life*. Moreno is the friend referred to by the omniscient narrator while the latter probes Assanoff's state of mind:

> He had become VERY perplexed. He was bothered by the opposition of his friend. . . . Omm-Djéhâne had created the MOST vivid impression in his SOUL. . . . The truth was that the POOR Assanoff was not Russian, was not savage, was not civilized, but he was a little of all of these, and the POOR beings that transitional time periods and countries deform in that fashion are QUITE [*fort*] incomplete, QUITE miserable and are in store for more vices and UNHAPPINESS than virtues and HAPPINESS (*DS* 63).

We will not always discover phatic and emphatic "tic" words in emotional and thematic passages nor will results showing dense clusters of emphatic "tic" words guarantee the presence of an emotional passage, but Gobineau's use of these terms seems fairly consistent with Riffaterre's educated observations. We have seen that, on the one hand, they may veil or subdue certain convictions through irony or understatement. On the other, they may sometimes shatter the narrator's separating window of aloofness, as in the passage quoted above

TABLE 5. SIGNIFICANT LOW FREQUENCIES OF POSSIBLE "TIC" WORDS STUDIED BY RIFFATERRE.
All Words Have Standard Deviations Less Than or Equal to −2.

Significant low frequencies according to the *external norm* (1850–79):

DANCER	MAGICIAN	GAMBÈR-ALY
amour (3)		aimer (3)
		amour (3)
		peut-être (0)

TURKOMANS	LOVERS	TRAVELLING
âme (2)	très (6)	
amour (2)		

Significant low frequencies according to the *internal norm:*

DANCER	MAGICIAN	GAMBÈR-ALY
	fort [adv] (2)	aimer (3)
		amant (0)
		coeur [abs] (6)
		passion (0)
		peut-être (0)

TURKOMANS	LOVERS	TRAVELLING
amant (0)	fort [adv] (4)	
âme (2)	pauvre (3)[a]	
imagination (0)	très (6)	

Note: Novella short titles are in capitals. abs—absolute (concrete) sense; adv—adverb.
    Entries read: word entry [grammatical function or sense] (total)
[a]Context is "wretched".

(*DS* 63). We may by now suspect that an affective word like "poor" can be paired with certain ironical types of characters, like Grégoire Vialgue or Paul Petrowitch, with a self-pitying character like Aga (*WT*) or even with the narrator.

Detecting significant word omissions or low frequencies is one of the most useful processes in computational thematics but it is nearly impossible for the individual working manually. Without the associations provided by appropriate thematic categories as well, this procedure is absurd, however. We would not accomplish much by finding all the pages or sections where a randomly chosen word does not occur. There must be some purpose behind the search. A thematic or conceptual group is a prime target.

Out of the 302 pages of text in the *Nouvelles,* there are only 12 pages where no phatic and emphatic "tic" words appear. *The Dancer from Shamakha* contains two of these pages: 43 and 53. Furthermore, there are two other pages, 13 and 64, where none of Riffaterre's 104 "tic" words occurs. We might wonder about the significance of these omissions. To illustrate in a critical article what is *not* found in a text is no easy feat. Aside from reprinting entire pages, the best solution lies in describing the context in question which readers can then contrast with passages dense in "tic" words.

Page 13, only twenty-five lines long out of a possible forty, contains exclusively Moreno's initial encounter with Assanoff. Although the latter ends the page with an enthusiastic statement about his origins, terminated by an exclamation point, exchanges by both consist of relatively neutral introductions. The text on page 64 describes Omm-Djéhâne's cautious arrival at Assanoff's apartment, shared with Moreno. The Spanish exile is alone and reacts machine-like (*"machinalement"*) and coldly (*"froidement"*) to the Lesghy, who explains succinctly her intention to await her cousin Assanoff, her fiancé.

I provisionally conclude that an absence in the *Nouvelles* of the "tic" words Riffaterre had selected regarding *Les Pléiades* indicates either a neutral situation—one with little emotional impact—or, alternatively, a situation where the narrator's and character's emotions are deliberately limited, perhaps to heighten tension in surrounding passages. This second part of my theory proves true for page 64, for both pages 63 and 65 contain emotional outbursts. This type of suspenseful layering seems to be a dramatic trait of the *Nouvelles asiatiques;* examination of the twelve pages where the absence of phatic and emphatic words comes into play reveals five other similarly constructed situations (pages 43, 94, 208, 248, 327). In the interest of brevity, I summarize below these and other contexts lacking "tic" words. These appear to corroborate the layering pattern theory.

Pages 53 and 123 are highly emotional. Noble language characterizes the first one. The second consists mainly of short exclamations. These two contexts may imply that extremely emotional reactions preclude this "tic" characteristic, particularly in noble characters such as Omm-Djéhâne (*DS* 53) and Mirza-Kassem (*IM* 123). Page 87 is principally surrounded by mostly unemotional description and short monologues followed two pages later by increasingly emotional exchanges between the protagonist Mirza-Kassem and a mystical dervish. Pages 127 (*GA*) and 288 (*TL*) begin or end their respective novellas. Their descriptive context is generally unemotional. Preciosity surrounds page 144 of *Gambèr-Aly.* Pages 144 and 145 contain some unemotional description, but also a total of four adverbs ending in *ment,* many relatively rare words in French, and several ironic contexts that constitute a precious narrative style. Preciosity, at the expense of true love, is typical of this picaresque novella criticizing a group of roguish, conniving, lower-middle-class civil servants at the Persian court. My findings above concerning this group of adverbs support this conclusion.

CONCLUSIONS

A conclusion for literary critics to evaluate in contextually based research on Gobineau's style for narrative voices is that he is drawn to use the phatic/emphatic tic word group repeatedly in several circumstances:

1. wherever there is precious irony, as we observed in *The Dancer from Shamakha;*
2. in aggressive discourses;
3. as a usual part of flowery, Middle Eastern speech patterns (Afghan, Iranian, and Iraqi) as Gobineau interprets them.

The striking number of phatic tic words in many locations in the *Nouvelles asiatiques* reveals an important stylistic trait of Gobineau: he tries to bring a social, conversational quality into both his narrative and his dialogues. These words will normally co-occur with another theme, such as pessimism, or in oppositional relationships: of Western and Middle Eastern civilizations, of the city to the country, of the natural to the artificial. On the one hand, when we research deductively, where there is an unusually high concentration of phatic and emphatic words, we are likely to find a highly emotional passage. On the other, absence or near absence of these two word groups usually signals a non-polemical passage. When we work mainly inductively, if we find the thematic oppositions mentioned above but few phatic or emphatic words, the narrator is most likely referring to the above themes ironically or unemotionally. A context containing much romantic and noble vocabulary, such as in *The Lovers from Kandahar,* may also reveal few phatic and emphatic tic words. This novella exhibits a romantic and noble thematic power which overwhelms or neutralizes the author's tendency toward aggressive narrative passages. Judging by the results regarding tic keywords which I summarized for *The Illustrious Magician* and *The Lovers from Kandahar* in the preceding section, one might conclude that in Gobineau's *Nouvelles asiatiques* true love conquers most phatic and emphatic tics.

As can be seen in many of the cases developed above, there are two fundamental procedures that we can use consistently in computational thematics: induction and deduction. Our reasoning can proceed from individual words, groups of words (themes), or even groups of themes in our search for general principles that might explain concomitant stylistic techniques. This procedure enabled us to find phatic and emphatic tic words or phrases such as *assurément, certainement,* and *sans doute* ("assuredly," "certainly," and "without doubt") in high concentrations where the narrator or a character is ironic or very polite. These characters are probably Asians or "pseudo-Asians" in the *Nouvelles asiatiques,* especially in contexts where Western civilization's technology policies and moral values are being criticized. However, in *Les Pléiades,* which Riffaterre studies in depth with only occasional references to the *Nouvelles,* only Europeans or Westerners appear. I believe that the setting of the *Nouvelles* and the roles and language attributed to the Asians significantly modify Gobineau's tic word use. Gobineau perhaps gained psychological relief in the writing and publishing of *Les Pléiades,* which enabled him to subdue, somewhat, the aggressiveness of the *Nouvelles asiatiques.*

Gobineau does retain a significantly high number of tic words and phrases in the *Nouvelles,* which reflects his continued preoccupation with certain idées fixes. At the same time, under the microscope of the computer-assisted analysis, we see that Gobineau's use of these words is not by any means ubiquitous. Specific applications of inductive and deductive approaches, both quantitative and contextual, have allowed us to analyze the tic word group relativistically, but also concretely, using normative baselines created both by the text and by works of many authors of the same literary period. Fewer than one-half of Riffaterre's tic word selections for *Les Pléiades* qualify quantitatively as tics in the *Nouvelles asiatiques.* The nature of the characters and themes treated by each novella may heavily influence this result. Lastly, my interpretation of the results obtained through computational thematics shows that Gobineau's use of phatic and emphatic words and phrases does not seem indiscriminate. Rather, these elements partly characterize his style in association with specific types of characters and narrative situations.

Notes

1. See Michael Riffaterre, *Le style des "Pléiades" de Gobineau. Essai d'application d'une méthode stylistique* (Geneva and Paris: Droz and Minard, 1957), 116–63. Throughout this study, my comments within quoted passages appear in brackets.
2. Leo Spitzer, "Michael Riffaterre, *Le Style des Pléiades de Gobineau, essai d'application d'une méthode stylistique,* rev. of *Le style des "Pléiades" de Gobineau,* by Michael Riffaterre, *Modern Language Notes* LXXIII (Jan. 1958):72. All translations are mine.
3. All French quotations from this work are cited from Arthur de Gobineau, *Nouvelles asiatiques,* ed. Jean Gaulmier, biographical summary, preface, notes, and bibliography by Jean Gaulmier (Paris: Garnier Frères, 1965). All translations, including translations from other works quoted here, and tic word capitalizations are mine.
4. Jean Boissel, *Gobineau, l'Orient et l'Iran* (Paris: Klincksieck, 1973), 19.
5. George E. Vander Beke, *French Word Book,* Publications of the American and Canadian Committees on Modern Languages (New York: Macmillan, 1927), vol. 15.
6. See Jean Boissel, *Gobineau (1816–1882). Un Don Quichotte tragique* (Paris: Hachette, 1981); Pierre-Louis Rey, *L'univers romanesque de Gobineau* (Paris: Gallimard, 1981).
7. Michael Riffaterre, "Réponse à M. Leo Spitzer: sur la méthode stylistique," *Modern Language Notes* LXXIII (June 1958):476.
8. Leo Spitzer, "Stylistique et critique littéraire," *Critique* 98 (1955):598. My translation.
9. Concerning computer-assisted content and concept analysis, see the excellent article by Klaus M. Schmidt, "Concept versus Meaning. The Contribution of Computer-Assisted Content Analysis and Conceptual Text Analysis to This Disputed Area," in *Méthodes quantitatives et informatiques dans l'étude des textes. Computers in Literary & Linguistic Research,* ed. Étienne Brunet, 2 vols. (Geneva-Paris: Slatkine-Champion, 1986) 2:779–95.
10. See Julius Laffal, *A Concept Dictionary of English* (Essex, Conn.: Gallery Press, 1973).

11. For information on the laws of probability that linguists and lexical statisticians have proven reliable for vocabulary study, see Étienne Brunet, *Le vocabulaire français de 1789 à nos jours*, 3 vols. (Geneva and Paris: Slatkine-Champion, 1981); Pierre Guiraud, *La stylistique*, 8th ed., "Que sais-je" series (Paris: Presses Universitaires de France, 1975); J. D. Haygood, *Le Vocabulaire fondamental du français* (Paris: Droz, 1937); Alphonse Juilland et al., *Frequency Dictionary of French Words* (The Hague and Paris: Mouton, 1970); Charles Muller, *Principes et méthodes de statistique lexicale* (Paris: Hachette, 1977).

12. See Leo Spitzer, "Why Does Language Change? " *Modern Language Quarterly* IV (1943):431. Also see Spitzer's "Les théories de la stylistique," *Le français moderne* XX (1952):166.

13. Peter Newmark, *Approaches to Translation* (Elmsford, N.Y.: Pergamon Press, 1982), 22.

14. *Webster's Ninth New Collegiate Dictionary* (Springfield, Mass.: Merriam-Webster, 1983), 881.

15. See Brunet, *Le vocabulaire français* as well as his studies of the vocabulary of Giraudoux, Hugo, and Zola; Robert F. Allen, *A Stylo-Statistical Study of "Adolphe"* (Geneva-Paris: Slatkine-Champion, 1984).

16. One can obtain printouts of over 1,500 French texts from the American and French Research for a Treasury of the French Language (ARTFL) at the University of Chicago or the Institut National de la Langue Française (INaLF) in Nancy, France.

17. See Joel D. Goldfield, "Literary Computing in French on the UNIX System," *Méthodes quantitatives et informatiques dans l'étude des textes* 2:455–65.

18. Paul Imbs, director, *Dictionnaire des fréquences*. Vol. I: *Vocabulaire littéraire des XIXe et XXe siècles* (Paris: Klincksieck, 1971); Microfiche edition (Nancy, France: C.N.R.S.-INaLF, 1984). Volume III (variations in frequency) is unusable without the missing coefficients supplied by Brunet in his excellent *Vocabulaire de la langue française,* I:4, note 1 and p. 18, Table 3.

Paul Imbs, director, *Trésor de la langue française. Dictionnaire de la langue du XIXe et du XXe siècle (1789–1960)* (Paris: C.N.R.S., 1971). Hereafter I refer to this dictionary's lexical team or organization as the "TLF."

19. How many word occurrences should we count for the following expressions: *c'est-à-dire, grand-père,* and *d'abord?* The TLF team mentions this difficulty in the introduction to the *Dictionnaire* (xiv). ARTFL and INaLF provided the word count totals I use for the *Nouvelles.*

20. See Morris Hamburg, *Statistical Analysis for Decision Making* (Chicago: Harcourt, Brace, Jovanovich, 1977), especially 215–16. I thank Prof. Robert F. Allen of Rutgers University for this reference. Readers of French can refer to Charles Muller's *Initiation aux méthodes de la statistique linguistique* (Paris: Hachette, 1973) and to his *Principes et méthodes* for clear explanations of the French equivalent: the "*écart réduit.*" While Muller writes that the *écart reduit* is reliable for frequencies of at least ten (*Initiation,* 140), he cautions us about the application of this theorem to consistently low frequencies (*Initiation,* 137–42).

21. In French: "*mots-clés.*" Particularly in the 1950s, French lexicostatisticians often used a cutoff figure of 3 or even 3.5 for determining keywords. See Guiraud, 66. The standard deviation level of $+3$ or -3 represents a probability of .0027 or a 99.73% chance that the deviation would not normally occur as opposed to the "2" level, which represents .046 or 95.4%, respectively. Also see the quotation from Spitzer above ("Stylistique," 598).

22. See Leonard Bloomfield, "Secondary and Tertiary Responses to Language," *Language* XX (1944):45–55. Also see Leo Spitzer, "Answer to Mr. Bloomfield," *Language* XX (1944):245–51.

23. See Leo Spitzer, "Linguistics and Literary History," in *Linguistics and Literary History* (New York: Russell and Russell, 1962), 19–20.

24. See Brunet, I, 298–99 and Joel D. Goldfield, "Thèmes, style et vocabulaire dans les 'Nouvelles asiatiques' de Gobineau. Essai d'application à la critique littéraire d'une analyse lexicométrique assistée par ordinateur" (Ph.D. dissertation, Université Paul Valéry, Montpellier III, 1985, vol. 1, 243–50.

25. See George M. Spring, *The Vitalism of Count de Gobineau* (New York: Institute of French Studies, 1932).

>> 7

Meaning and Method:

Computer-Assisted Analysis of Blake

NANCY M. IDE

Blake, who among romantic poets is perhaps the most energetic proponent of unconstrained and imaginative expression, produced much poetry that explodes so violently on the page that it often strikes the first-time reader as absolutely without order or underlying plan. But Blake proclaimed in his preface to *Jerusalem* that "[e]very word and every letter is studied and put into its fit place,"[1] and the systematic and intricate organization in all his poetry inspired me to find some means to study his poems as formal entities. The computer provides that means. Like many literary analyses, my computer-assisted analysis of Blake's *The Four Zoas* raises questions concerning its definitions and methodology, but despite these problems the computer has enabled me to look at the text of the *Zoas* and see Blake at work as no one has before. My resulting idea of the structure of *The Four Zoas* solves some of the problems that have engendered critical debate concerning the poem's form and offers considerable insight into how the poem conveys its powerful thematic statements.

THE LITERARY PROBLEM

Perhaps the most widely held belief about William Blake is that serious study of his poetry requires familiarity with his intricate mythic system. Blake's mythic system borrows many familiar symbols from biblical and poetic tradition, but it is generously populated with symbols of his own invention. Each symbol in the system is associated with some aspect or property of human existence as Blake saw it and stands in relation to other symbols in the system on this basis. The system has been derived from the whole of the Blake corpus by Blake scholars, and its explication is the central subject of several seminal critical texts on Blake's poetry.[2] Once understood, this system can in theory be reapplied in order to unravel the meaning of specific poems within the Blake corpus. Although they only occasionally say so explicitly, most critics of Blake believe that without knowing the meaning of the symbols and the system of relationships in Blake's mythic system, only superficial understanding of his poetry is possible.

Among Blake's major prophetic poems, *The Four Zoas* is most pointedly concerned with the matter of Blake's myth; but unlike the others, it offers very little in the way of exposition and explanation of Blake's private vision of existence. In its essence the vision is abstract: it consists of states and qualities of human experience and relationships among them that characterize various stages of man's development. The abstraction is realized and communicated through the story of the myth of man's fall, his life in the fallen state, and his return to unfallen existence, which is told in its entirety in the *Zoas*. The complexities of the system underlying the story contribute to the obscurity of the narrative, and the presentation of the story of the myth without commentary to tie it to an external context complicates the narrative even further. Therefore, the fragmentary and often transitionless narrative of the *Zoas* offers problems even for seasoned readers of Blake. For novice readers, much of the narrative of the *Zoas* is virtually incomprehensible.

Curiously, despite difficulties with the narrative of the poem, the *Zoas* works as a poetic utterance even for novice readers. The powerful effect of the poem on first-time readers is often noted, and while details of the story may remain obscure, the poem's broader thematic statements are almost always well understood (something which is often not true of more conventional poetry). This simple fact has two very important implications for study of Blake's poetry: first, it demonstrates that familiarity with Blake's myth is not prerequisite to understanding his poetry; that far from constituting a self-referential collection of poems whose meaning is inaccessible to the uninitiated, Blake's poems speak each for themselves, and, more importantly, speak to shared experience and universal concerns. Second, it implies that meaning in the *Zoas* is conveyed by some means other than the narrative, since many beginners are capable of lucidly explaining the meaning of a specific episode even when the narrative seems to make little sense. This, of course, gives rise to a new question: if not primarily through narrative, how does the *Zoas* convey its meaning? Several critics of Blake have noted that meaning, especially in the prophetic poems, is conveyed somehow telepathically, primarily through other than narrative means. Beyond this, very little conjecture has been made concerning the ways in which Blake's poems, in S. Foster Damon's words, "seem to make sense long before they do." [3] The extra-sensory explanation tends to curb further discussion of the question of how Blake conveys meaning to his readers, so it is clearly not satisfactory; Blake must use some other means, and most would agree these means should be manifest within the text itself.

To determine Blake's vehicle for conveying meaning, one need only look through the Blake corpus and abandon the notion that Blake's symbolic language was primarily a private one. In doing so, one finds that the central semantic element in Blake's poetry, in the early *Songs of Innocence and of Experience* and throughout the prophetic poems, is clearly the image—not his private symbols and invented names, but rather images that abound in general and archetypal qualities and that have persisted in poetic tradition over several centuries. Blake's reliance on traditional and universal symbolism, even in his mythic system of associations, has been noted by Frye and other critics. Others—notably Josephine Miles—have pointed out in addition that Blake relies much more than other poets, and almost compulsively, on repetition of his relatively small and substantival vocabulary for poetic effect.[4] So, Blake's poetic language is not a private and largely inaccessible one, but rather one that is characterized by the repetitive use of common images such as fire and ice, light and darkness, clouds, worms, lions, lambs, morning and evening, upon which he can rely for consistent semantic effect. Blake's art is in manipulating the connotations and associations of these images to make his powerful poetic statements.

In most narrative poetry, images participate in both the surface meaning of the poem—that is, meaning at the literal level of the narrative—and in the "deeper" meaning of the poem that realizes the fuller implications of the poem's images. Even purely figurative images are generally analogical and therefore closely related to other images or entities in the poem. In the *Zoas,* however, the lack of literal meaning inhibits analogical associations. With surface meaning largely stripped away, the impact of an image is determined almost exclusively by the qualitative connotations and associations it has for the reader. For instance, when the reader encounters a passage such as

> From her bosom weaving soft in Sinewy threads
> A tabernacle for Jerusalem she sat among the Rocks
> Singing her lamentation.   (I, 5:6–8)

where no mention of "rocks" has preceded it and the scene has not been located in a landscape or visual scene of any kind, the lack of context and contact with the everyday world of our experience obstructs visualization; and so in encountering the image of "rocks" it is the qualities of rockiness—solid, hard, inert—that are impressed upon the reader. Thus, images in the *Zoas* are foregrounded because of the lack of narrative context, and the impact of their traditional connotations is substantially heightened. In places Blake repeats an image to enhance its effect, as in the following passage:

> The flames rolling intense thro the wide Universe
> Began to Enter the Holy City Entring the dismal clouds
> In furrowed lightnings break their way the wild flames whirring up
> The Bloody Deluge living flames winged with intellect
> And Reason round the Earth they march in order flame by flame
> (IX, 119:16–20)

Inasmuch as the narrative makes any sense in this passage, its meaning is obscured by the chanting of the central image. The ultimate meaning of the passage derives almost exclusively from the qualitative associations of the flame image.

It seems reasonable to regard individual images as independent semantic elements in Blake's poetry. In all language, broader and more complex meaning is conveyed by involving semantic elements in relationships with one another. Meaning at the literal level is achieved primarily through syntactic relationships among semantic elements. Other kinds of meaning—particularly meaning at the level of theme and other kinds of extra-narrative meaning with which literary language is substantially involved—can be established through spatial configurations—that is, through proximity and distance among semantic elements across a text.[5] To put it simply, the closer together two elements are in a text, the more their "meanings" or connotations intermix for varied or enhanced meaning. For example, in Blake's "The Sick Rose" the juxtaposition of images of rose and worm and the resulting intermixing of their connotations yields the poem's central thematic statement: The association of the images "rose" and "worm" binds the beautiful, the voluptuous, the emblem of joy and fertile life to the ugly, the parasitic, the emblem of the grave. The result is to convey the notion of the frailty, imperfection, and impermanence of life.[6]

In a poem as long as *The Four Zoas,* spatial relations among images can be manipulated to produce complex semantic effects. When syntactic relationships among images are obscured as they are in the *Zoas,* these effects play a significant role in determining the poem's overall meaning. Therefore I set out to determine spatial relations in the poem. Once spatial relationships were determined, broader patterns of interaction among images across the entire text were revealed that shed light on the structure of the poem. In turn, an understanding of the poem's structure revealed even more about the ways in which Blake conveys meaning in the poem.

In order to look at the spatial relations among the images in *The Four Zoas* and examine their patterns of usage, the location of every image in the poem and the frequency of its use across the text of the *Zoas* had to be determined. In a poem of over 42,000 words, simply identifying the images would be an enormous task if attempted by hand, and locating the occurrences of the images is virtually impossible. A computational solution was the only one possible for a task of this magnitude. The computer's powerful pattern-matching capabilities enabled rapid location of words in the text, and the computer easily generated graphic representations of the distribution for any identifiable item across the text. The key word here is "identifiable," for the computational solution is ideal only beyond the ability to define the semantic elements to be considered—here, images—as discrete patterns of characters. This presents not only computational problems but also purely literary ones.

THE COMPUTATIONAL SOLUTION

The computational solution to the problem of determining how Blake uses images for semantic effect in *The Four Zoas* required several steps. First, the images to be considered had to be determined and their locations in the text ascertained. Then, the pattern of distribution for each image had to be compared with those for all other images in order to determine spatial relationships among images, and significant patterns and fluctuations in the distributions had to be identified. Beyond this, significant groupings of images in specific passages as well as across the entire text had to be isolated in order to identify the poem's thematic dimensions and their components. Generalized patterns in image distribution that might lend insight into the structure of the poem also had to be identified.

The computer was used to find and compare words and other strings of characters and to apply statistical measures in order to get at various relationships and patterns among semantic elements in the text. Ironically, the step the computer could not perform is the first and seemingly most simple: determining which images to consider in the analysis. Given a text in machine-readable form, programs for computational analysis of language can recognize straightforward syntactic structures and identify very general semantic properties of words and sentences. However, none is sophisticated enough to handle the complexities of syntax or produce even vaguely satisfactory semantic descriptions of typical literary language, let alone that in a work as stylistically unconventional as *The Four Zoas*.

A detailed specification of the criteria for identifying an image—one that could be translated into computational terms—requires considerable understanding of semantic relations in a text. In literary usage, an image is defined to be "the reproduction in the mind of a sensation produced . . . by language."[7] A further distinction between literal images, adequately described by this definition, and figurative images, which "involve a 'turn' on the literal meaning of the words,"[8] is often made. The notion of a "turn on the literal meaning" is somewhat vague even for human intelligence. In computational terms, it might be specified as any noun or adjective found in any of several (fully specified) syntactic relationships with another noun or adjective, where the two are marked with normally incompatible semantic properties. This would be an extraordinarily simple and limited definition. It might help to identify "fire" in the phrase "fire in his heart," where designated semantic properties for the object of a prepositional phrase headed by "in" and modifying "fire" (for example, "non-body-part") are violated by "heart," but it would not identify images that function at both the literal and figurative levels, as many poetic images do. Even for purely figurative images, a definition of this sort is grossly inadequate.

The poem's images therefore had to be identified "by hand," but the task was not completely straightforward even when computational concerns were eliminated. My analysis required consideration of only those images whose connotations are accessible to all readers. Therefore, Blake's private images and symbols were not included, and only archetypal images with habitual and traditional connotations for most readers were considered. To determine which images satisfy this criterion, I used Cirlot's *Dictionary of Symbols,* which treats only those symbols that have persisted in use across time and cultures and bear some "intrinsic relation" to what they represent.[9] Further, I eliminated images such as "drown" and "smile" that participate in meaning primarily at the level of narrative. To consider the structure of ideas underlying the text, meaning at the level of narrative must necessarily be differentiated from meaning conveyed through extra-narrative devices—in this case, through connotations intrinsic to the images themselves. Therefore I included only figurative and not literal images, according to the definitions given earlier.

Although the computer was not used in deciding what constitutes an image in the analysis, computational concerns further constrained my definition of "image." To perform the analysis the computer had to be able to locate the images in the text; therefore, each image had to be specified as a uniquely identifiable string of characters that could be compared to strings in the text in order to determine when and where a match occurs. Additional questions were raised: do images consist of individual words? individual phrases? sentences? Are the words or phrases that constitute an occurrence of an image uniquely identifiable? These questions were more difficult to resolve satisfactorily than those addressed above, and the solution applied in this analysis was to consider only images that are instantiated as individual words. Looking at the text of the *Zoas,* it seems clear that many of the archetypal and "public" images that Blake uses are, in fact, individual words such as "cloud," "morning," "lion," "fire," and so on. More complex images in the *Zoas* such as "robes of blood," which might be considered a single image, actually partake of the meanings of their constituents—in this case, the meanings implied in both the garment image and the image of blood. Regarding individual words as isolatable images is consistent with the practice in many conventional analyses of Blake's poetry (and much other poetry), although conventional analyses can do so far less self-consciously. This and many of my assumptions about what constitutes an image in *The Four Zoas* may well be questioned; there is little critical agreement as to what constitutes an image, and it is doubtful that I have arrived at a universally satisfactory definition here. However, I believe that these assumptions are reasonable in the light of Blake's use of the words selected for the analysis.[10]

Once the substantial problems of defining an image in terms that satisfy both literary and computational criteria were overcome, the remaining steps in the analysis were straightforward. To avoid typing the entire text of the *Zoas* into the machine by hand, I obtained the machine-readable version that had been used to generate Cornell's concordance of Blake's works[11] from Cornell University. The text was edited to delete variants and special symbols used at Cornell in order to conform to the text of the *Zoas* as it appears in Erdman's *The Poetry and Prose of William Blake.*[12] For the next phase of the analysis, I used a prototype of the ARRAS text analysis system[13] to identify the images in the text by generating a "dictionary" listing of all of the words in the text and a full concordance, which provided a context for words whose meaning or use could not be determined from the list alone. The ARRAS program also enabled grouping words that constitute textual variants of a single image so that they could be regarded as a single entity in later stages of the analysis. Thus singular and plural forms and in some cases adjectival and verbal forms, as well as Blake's variant spellings for a given word-form, were collected and packaged together to constitute a computer-recognizable "image." In this way 167 images were defined. For each of the images, ARRAS was asked to generate a histogram-like graph of distribution across the text. Graphs were also generated for groups of images which fall into general categories—images of nature, the pastoral, labor, war, parts of the body, and so on.

In order to produce a meaningful distribution graph for any item across a text, the text must be divided into segments. The graph then shows how many times the item appears in each of the segments, in order, and the overall picture shows how the frequency of an image varies across the text. To generate its graphs, the ARRAS program divides the text into 2 percent segments, which means that, for the *Zoas,* each segment includes slightly over 940 words. Unfortunately, the program does not allow segmenting the text in any other way. The 2 percent divisions pay no regard to logical divisions within the text—in some cases this caused a sudden increase in the frequency of an image or images in a particular part of the text to be broken in two across two segments, thus obscuring the magnitude of the increase. Therefore, for each of the distributions a laborious comparison with the text was required, in order to ensure that significant patterns were not overlooked.

At this point in the analysis of images and their patterning in *The Four Zoas,* the graphs were examined by eye alone, and with considerable reference to the text itself, in order to determine the interplay among images from passage to passage in the text. This served as the basis for a detailed analysis of each passage in the *Zoas* in terms of the images and in view of larger patterns of distribution for images in the text.[14] The detailed analysis is the first to consider the *Zoas* primarily in terms of its images and provides significant insights into the way in which individual passages convey meaning, usually confirming or complementing prevailing critical assessments. However, in the process of examining the distribution of images over the entire text, several patterns that had previously gone completely unnoticed appeared. More importantly, a decided pattern in the distribution of all 167 images across the text suggested a structure for the work that is entirely different from any of the several underlying plans that have previously been proposed, all of which are based on details of the fragmentary narrative alone. These patterns clearly warranted more attention to determine their exact form as well as the significance of their patterning across the text.

The most important patterns revealed in the distribution graphs involve all of the images in the analysis. The first is the pattern of image *density*—that is, a graph showing variation in the number of images appearing in each of the fifty segments of the text. In order to discuss the patterns, it should be noted here that the nine Nights of the poem are far from equivalent in length; instead, Nights I through VI constitute roughly the first physical half of the poem, and Nights VII, VIII, and IX constitute the second half. (See Figure 1 for a graph of the configuration of the nine nights.) The number of images in the text peaks at three decided and symmetrically placed points—at the beginning of the poem, at the end of Night I, and continuing into Night II; in the physical middle of the poem, in

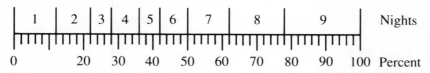

FIGURE 1. Positioning of the Nights in terms of the percentage of the text they cover.

Nights V and VI; and at the end of the poem in Night IX. At the two points falling between these three peaks, roughly in Night IV and in Nights VII and VIII, the number of images reaches its lowest levels. This five-part distribution of image density across the text is symmetrical around the physical midpoint of the text and is based overall on its physical rather than logical configuration. Here, ARRAS's disregard for the logical divisions in the text seems to have worked to advantage; had the text been segmented according to the logical divisions between Nights, this pattern might have been less apparent. A distribution for image *variety*—the number of *different* images in each segment of the text—shows a similar pattern of fluctuation. (See Figure 2.)

The distributions for many of the poem's important images follow from and provide supporting evidence for the five-part plan as well as give more insight into the nature of the overall pattern of image distribution. Many of these images appear in significant concentrations in each of the three areas of high image density, and only in these three sections of the poem. Other images appear in two of the three segments, and a few in only one. Very few images appear significantly in one or more areas of high image density as well as in an area of low image density, and, in fact, few of the images that do appear in one of the two areas of low image density appear in the other. All of this suggests that similar things are going on in the three areas of high image density, that entirely different themes and atmospheres prevail in the two areas of low density, and that the two areas of low density are themselves very different from one another.

The third interesting set of patterns of distribution involves collections of images that are thematically related. Images of the pastoral and images of labor were grouped together by hand, and collective distribution graphs were generated for each group. The two resulting graphs showed that each group's distribution undulated regularly across the text and in roughly complementary patterns. (See Figure 3.) That is, where the frequency of images of the pastoral is high, the frequency for images of labor is low, and vice versa. The undulation in frequency for these two sets of images is more rapid than that for image density as a whole and is relatively unrelated to the five-part pattern discussed above. In view of Blake's tenet concerning the necessity for alternation between labor and rest, this result is especially interesting; Blake apparently conveys this idea in the *Zoas* by embodying it in the patterns of distribution for images of labor and images of the pastoral rather than by stating it explicitly.

These patterns suggest a great deal about *The Four Zoas*, but all are based on subjective assessment of the distribution graphs. The "significant" shifts in frequency discussed above are judged to be significant by the human eye, not by any objective measure. I wanted to verify that the patterns so seemingly obvious in the distribution graphs were in fact "real." Verification was especially necessary for the overall pattern upon which the theory of the five-part structural plan for

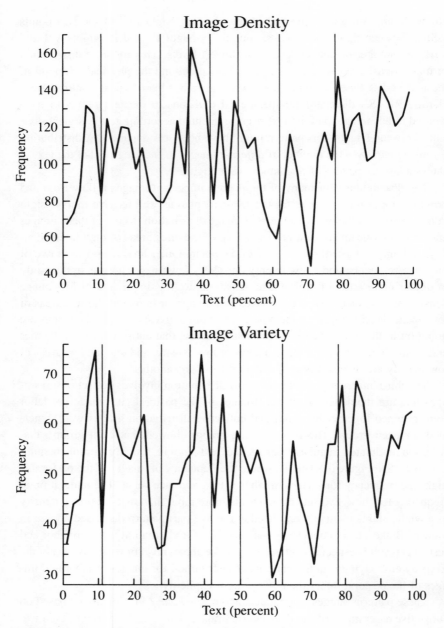

FIGURE 2. Distribution graphs for image density and variety.

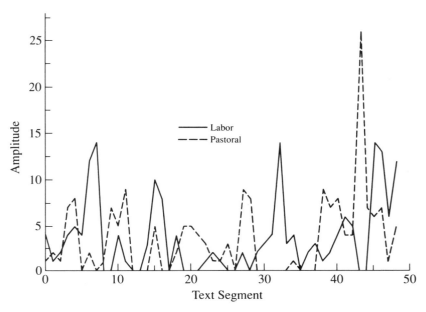

FIGURE 3. Images of the pastoral and of labor

the work is based. The theory flies in the face of current theory about the poem's structure; therefore, the more objective evidence there is to support it, the better. Furthermore, I was making judgments about the significance of an image's concentrations in the five segments, but before applying objective measures of significance, I had to verify the existence of the segments and establish the exact starting and ending locations in the text for each. Therefore, I turned to statistical measures to show that patterns in the variations in frequency of images over the fifty segments of the text could not have occurred by chance alone. Because I was interested in how images combined to form larger thematic units, a statistical means to determine the "relatedness" among images and to identify images that tend to cluster together was also necessary.

The analysis ran into difficulty in the search for a statistical measure that would help to verify patterns in the frequency data. Most measures of the significance of variance among values do not take into account an important fact: that the segments in the text are ordered—that is, they are sequential in time. Furthermore, very few methods have been developed to look at patterning across time-dependent data. The most appropriate measure I could find, after considerable search, was the time series analysis method used by economists to discover trends in data that show its "period" across time. I fed the data for image density and image variety to the time series analysis routine.[15] Time series analysis produces a graph showing how well the frequency in any given segment correlates with its frequency in segments that are one, two, three, or more segments away. Thus, if there is a pattern—that is, if the frequency of an image correlates well with not only its frequency in adjacent segments (as can be expected) but also in segments that are, say, five segments distant—the graph will show a rise in the correlation value at interval five. If the correlation repeats itself every 5 segments, a rise will occur at intervals 5, 10, 15, and so on.

Time series analysis revealed a decided pattern in the distribution of image density across the text of *The Four Zoas*. The "period" of the fluctuation in image density appears to be exactly 11 segments, for in the graph that is produced by the time series routine, peaks appear at intervals 11 and 22. The peak at 11 intervals is inverted—that is, it represents a negative correlation—and the peak at 22 intervals represents a positive correlation. (See Figure 4.) Both of these peaks are too high to be attributed to random or chance fluctuations in the frequency data. Thus, a pattern appears: when the number of images in a given

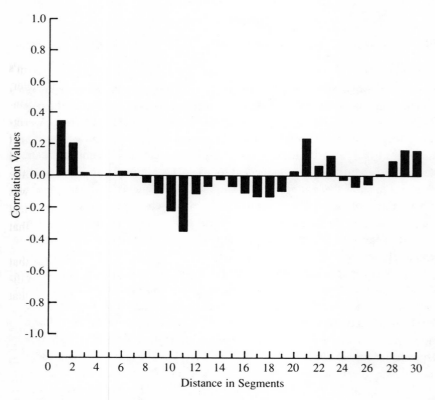

FIGURE 4. Autocorrelation function for image density

segment is very high, we can expect that 11 segments later it will be very low; and we can further expect that 22 segments later it will be high again. So, the time series analysis substantiates the claim for a five-part plan in the poem and determines each of the five parts of the poem to be roughly 11 segments in length. Curiously, the same pattern is not apparent in the data for image variety, nor does there appear to be a significant pattern of any kind in the distribution of image variety.

Statistical tests to determine which images cluster together and which can therefore be said to form thematic groupings are more readily available than tests to determine patterns in frequency data. Factor analysis routines can take the raw frequency data for the poem's 167 images (50 numbers for each image, indicating the image's frequency in each segment of the text) and generate a correlation matrix, which yields a value between -1 and $+1$ indicating the degree of relatedness between each pair of images. This matrix, in turn, can be used to perform a principal components analysis, which identifies groups of images that tend to cluster together in the text. This technique was applied to the frequency data for the 167 images being analyzed, and the results were not conclusive. Twelve image groups revealed themselves, but the strength of the images' involvement in the groupings in which they appear (the factor loading) is not overwhelming, suggesting that each image is actually involved in several weaker relationships rather than one very strong one. However, the groups identified in the analysis are interesting because they can be seen as representative of twelve themes with which the *Zoas* is generally concerned, as follows: (1) universal harmony vs. domination and base earthly concerns (*sowing, community, sky and the heavens, stars, torture, slavery, walls, dungeons, dust*), (2) power, strength in nature (*forest, birds of prey, eagle, earth*); (3) peace, domesticity, innocence, fertility (*sun, sheep, house, grasses and vines, dew, flowers, brook, garden, fruit*); (4) rigidity and entrapment (*iron, cliff, ice and freezing, valley, web*); (5) social power and earthly concerns (*horses, chariots, silver, royalty, arrows, castles*); (6) wrath and power vs. weakness (*tigers, lions, mountains, bulls, the winepress, children, boys*); (7) barrenness, lifelessness (*wasteland, desert, winter, plague, slime*); (8) abundance of life, especially reaping the abundance as a benefit of past labor (*harvest, reptiles, feast, milk, flies and insects, autumn, weeds*); (9) material concerns, hardness, activity with the intent to reduce multiplicity to unity (*gems, implements of war, tools*); (10) renewal of life (*buds and blossoms, morning*); (11) control vs. chaos (*geometric shapes, creatures of the sea [low life forms]*); (12) activity directed toward containment, restraint, control (*furnace, hammer, anvil, wheel, bellows*).[16]

To substantiate further my notion that the character of images in areas of low and high images differs, I combined the frequency data for each of the images in the twelve groups detailed above and generated distribution graphs for each thematic group. The distributions revealed that several of the thematic groups occur across the text in two- or three-part patterns, where incidences of high frequency correspond with areas of high image density. Other thematic groups showed concentrations in a single area of high image density. The exceptions to this were groups 9, 11, and 12: these factors are distributed such that they are primarily concentrated in the areas of lowest image density. (Factor 11 has one concentration in the first segment of the text where image density is high as well.) These distributions begin to give some insight into the differences in the character of images and overall semantic effects in areas of high and low image density: all three of these groups have to do with restraint and hardness, and two of them are indicative of activity. It is no surprise that image density decreases as the action in the narrative increases, since imagery is more predominant in descriptive prose. Thus the broadest suggestion of the data is that the text is structured according to a five-part plan, where the second and fourth segments are concerned with action (plot) and, thematically, with restraint and/or constriction of the viewpoint. This structure is, of course, in accord with the structure suggested by variations in image density across the text.

Performing simple correlations between frequencies for each theme group and image density as well as for each theme group and image variety further clarified the relationships among image density and the twelve thematic categories. With one exception, correlations between any theme and either density or variety are positive, which is to be expected since the occurrence of any image is contained in the data for density and variety. However, the correlations between themes 9, 11, and 12 and both density and variety were low-positive—under .2 in all cases—whereas the correlations for the rest of the theme groups typically exceeded .3. This bears out the evidence in the distribution graphs that suggests that these themes are predominant in areas of low image density and variety.

Correlations between the remaining themes and density and variety revealed some interesting relationships as well: themes 1 (universal harmony vs. domination and base earthly concerns), 2 (power and strength in nature), and 6 (wrath and power vs. weakness) are more highly correlated with both density and variety than any of the other theme groups, suggesting that they play a role in all three areas of the poem where image density and variety are high. Curiously, themes 3 (peace, domesticity, innocence, fertility) and 7 (barrenness and lifelessness) correlate well with density but not with variety. This suggests that these themes are extremely strong (accounting for high image density in the areas where they occur) but that they tend to occur in isolation, thus focusing the reader's attention on a single theme. The distribution graph for theme 3 shows that the theme occurs primarily in one location in the text, in the final area of high image density, at a point where other themes are almost completely absent. Theme 7 has a significant concentration in each of the three areas of high image density, but again, most other themes have low concentrations where it appears. This further suggests some expansion and contraction of semantic range *within* areas of high image density—a fluctuating pattern superimposed upon the broader undulations in image density and variety. Since these themes 3 and 7 are virtual opposites in meaning, it also suggests that the contrast and tension between the two play a central role in determining the thematic dimensions of Blake's apocalyptic vision in the poem's final movement.

CONSIDERATION OF THE RESULTS

The most exciting result of this analysis is that a new architectural plan for *The Four Zoas* can be proposed, one which, looking back at the text, makes a great deal of sense. The *Zoas* is a poem about man's fall, his subsequent existence in the fallen state, and his return to the harmony of unfallen existence. The earliest parts of the poem describe the events of the fall, and in this portion of the text an area of high image density appears; the next section describes progression to the depths of the fall, a portion of the text dominated by action and therefore one of low image density; the physical center of the poem deals with the depths of fallen existence, another descriptive and therefore image-rich section of the poem; the next section furthers the poem's action, concerns man's rise from the depths of fallen existence, and is the second area of low image density; the final section of the poem, characterized by the densest appearance of imagery in the poem and including literally all of the images that appear earlier, describes unfallen existence. Thus the poem consists of three largely descriptive portions separated by two sections more clearly characterized by action. The two areas of low image density contain fewer images than those of high image density, suggesting that the viewpoint is constricted in these areas of the poem. Again, this five-part structure is dependent on the physical rather than the logical configuration of the text, and this may account for the fact that it has apparently gone unnoticed among critics of Blake.

The results of the factor analysis suggest the broad thematic dimensions of *The Four Zoas* in the groupings of images it provided. However, as mentioned above, these grouping are relatively weak and do not reflect decided associations that are consistent over the poem. This result, however, is not surprising in the light of Blake's apparent manipulation of images in the text. That is, the distributions for the 167 individual images suggest that especially in each of the three areas of high image density, Blake uses the same image in different groupings. For instance, in the first section of the poem, the image "wine" is coupled with "blood," whereas it is associated in the middle section most significantly with "fire" and in the final section with images of low life forms and implements of torture. In each case, the adjacent images emphasize a different connotation of the wine image: its connotation of suffering is brought out by the blood image; the fire image emphasizes its connotaton of passion; and in the final grouping, the wine image's connotations of suffering, instinctual passion, and eternal life are predominant. This example demonstrates what I believe to be a major vehicle for conveying meaning in the poem: Blake's manipulation of the reader's perception of an image or group of images. When an image reappears in the poem, but with its context and therefore its meaning altered, the reader not only recalls the earlier appearance but is also made aware of the differences in his perception of the current instance. The consequence is the reader's awareness that perception is a dynamic and fluid process, which is one of the central tenets of Blake's philosophy. It is to be expected that image groupings in *The Four Zoas* are inconsistent over the text; the combining and recombining of image groups is a central semantic device. Like the distributions for images of labor and the pastoral, the manipulation of an image's meaning by altering its context conveys meaning not with explicit statement but rather by drawing the reader directly in to the process of making meaning.[17]

Apart from the results cited above and those discussed earlier in this paper, the analysis yielded considerable insight into the way that Blake uses images to convey meaning in *The Four Zoas*. Simply identifying the poem's images allowed for studying their character; the images fall very easily into seven general groups: nature images, images of animals, birds, insects, and so on; images of body parts; images of labor (weaving, farming, forging of metals); images involving metals and gems; images of war, slavery, and torture; and images of civilization and domesticity. The distributions of individual images showed that Blake often colors an entire passage by repeating a single image twenty or thirty times; this is true for the sea image at the beginning of the first area of low image density, in Night III, and for the image of fire in Night V and again at the beginning of Night IX. The distributions also showed that in the final section of the poem (Night IX), which deals with the apocalypse, all of the images that appear earlier in the poem, suggesting the comprehensive vision with which this portion of the poem is concerned.[18] Some of the results substantiate familiar generalities concerning Blake's style (such as his love of repetition), and others provide new information. Overall, this analysis constitutes the most comprehensive study of the imagery of Blake's prophetic poetry, and one of the most comprehensive studies of *The Four Zoas* to date.

One always wonders what the authors whom we dissect and analyze would think of the work we do. I cannot help but think that Blake, who forever urged new perspectives, would be somewhat pleased with my approach, and that the poet who adored the juxtaposition of opposites would find the application of Reason's tool to study of the fruits of the Imagination somehow appealing. Far from the antirational zealot he is often misconstrued to be, Blake advocated the harmonious balance of intellect and imagination. In applying quantitative measures to qualitative materials, we may create our own marriage of heaven and hell, and move beyond the confines of a single viewpoint to embrace a larger and more encompassing perspective.

Notes

1. *Jerusalem,* plate 3.
2. See, for instance, Northrop Frye's *Fearful Symmetry* (Princeton, N.J.: Princeton University Press, 1947) and S. Foster Damon's *A Blake Dictionary: The Ideas and Symbols of William Blake* (1965; reprint, New York: E. P. Dutton, 1971).
3. Damon, ix.
4. Josephine Miles, *Eras and Modes in English Poetry,* 2nd ed. (Berkeley and Los Angeles: University of California Press, 1964), 79.
5. Elements configured across a linear text can be said to be ordered in time rather than space; indeed, the application of the statistical method called "time series," which is described below, implies such a view of a text. However, although the distinction may be of interest in literary theoretical terms, it is irrelevant to the methodology described here: either view may be taken with no effect on the methods or interpretation of results.
6. See Michael Riffaterre, "The Self-Sufficient Text," *Diacritics* 3, 3 (1973) : 39–45.
7. Norman Friedman, "Imagery," in *Princeton Encyclopedia of Poetry and Poetics,* enlarged edition, ed. Alex Preminger (Princeton, N.J.: Princeton University Press, 1974), 363.
8. C. Hugh Holman, *A Handbook to Literature,* 3rd ed. (Indianapolis, Ind.: Bobbs-Merrill, 1972), 263.
9. Juan Eduardo Cirlot, *A Dictionary of Symbols,* trans. Jack Sage (New York: Philosophical Library, 1962), xxx.
10. A complete listing of the image categories and their contents appears in the appendix to this chapter.
11. David V. Erdman, ed., *A Concordance to the Writings of William Blake,* 2 vols. (Ithaca, N.Y.: Cornell University Press, 1967).
12. David V. Erdman, ed., *The Poetry and Prose of William Blake,* commentary by Harold Bloom (Garden City, N.Y.: Doubleday, 1970). My work predates the publication of the 1982 edition of *The Poetry and Prose of William Blake,* in which the arrangement of Night VII in the text of *The Four Zoas* is substantially different from that of the earlier edition. Although it would be interesting to replicate this analysis using Erdman's later text (as well as Night VIIb), I do not believe that the broad patterns of image distribution would differ significantly. In any case the arrangement of Night VII is conjectural, and no clearly superior version of the text has yet been identified.
13. Archive Retrieval and Analysis System (ARRAS), written by John B. Smith and distributed through Computer Textual Services, Inc., Chapel Hill, North Carolina. See John B. Smith, "RATS: A Middle-Level Text Utility System," *Computers and the Humanities* 6 (1972) : 277–83, for a description of an earlier version of the ARRAS program. See also John B. Smith, "ARRAS and Literary Criticism," in *La Critique littéraire et l'ordinateur / Literary Criticism and the Computer,* ed. Bernard Derval and Michel Lenoble (Montreal: Derval and Lenoble, 3390 rue Limoges, St-Laurent, Québec H4K 1Y1, 1985).
14. See Nancy M. Ide, "Patterns of Imagery in William Blake's *The Four Zoas* " (Ph.D. dissertation, The Pennsylvania State University, 1982).

15. For this phase of the analysis, I used the autocorrelation function in the Minitab statistical package.

16. Note that the thematic titles are based on connotations given for images in Cirlot's *Dictionary of Symbols*.

17. Unfortunately, I have not yet found a clearcut statistical measure of such *shifting* relationships among images that takes into consideration time dependencies implicit in the linear ordering of the text.

18. A fuller discussion of these results can be found in Nancy M. Ide, "Patterns of Imagery in William Blake's *The Four Zoas*," *Blake: An Illustrated Quarterly* 20, 4 (1987).

APPENDIX: LIST OF THE IMAGE CATEGORIES

Abyss	Cave	Face
Air	Celestial bodies	Feast
Animals	Chariot	Fire
Armor	Chain	Fish
Arrow	Children	Flood
Ashes	City	Floor
Autumn	Clay	Flower
Beast	Cliff	Foot
Bed	Cloud	Forehead
Bee	Cold	Forest
Bellows	Cows (goats)	Fountain
Bird	Crystal	Fruit
Birds of prey	Cup	Furnace
Black	Dark	Garden
Blood	Day	Garment
Body parts	Death	Gem
Bonds	Den	Geometric objs.
Bone	Desert	Girl
Bow	Dew	Gloom
Boy	Door	Gold
Branch	Dove	Grass
Brass	Dry	Grave
Bread	Eagle	Hair
Breath	Ear	Hammer (anvil)
Breeze	Earth (ground)	Hand
Briars	Earth (element)	Hard
Brook (spring)	Earth (planet)	Harvest
Bud	Elephant	Head
Bulls	Evening	Heart
Bush (leaf)	Eye	Heat

Horse
House
Ice (snow)
Infant
Insect
Iron
Knife
Lake
Lead
Light
Lily
Limb
Lion
Loin
Loom
Machinery
Maze
Measurement
Metal
Mill
Moon
Morning
Mountain
Music
Neck
Net
Night
Nose
Oak tree
Palace
Pastoral
Plague
Plow
Poison
Prison
Raven

Red
Religion
Reptile (bat)
River
Ruin
Rock
Roof (ceiling)
Root
Rose (flower)
Royalty
Sea
Sea creatures
Seed
Serpent
Shadow
Sheep
Shepherd
Shore
Silver
Skull
Sky
Slavery
Slime
Smoke
Social groups
Soft
Sow
Spear
Spring
Star
Steel
Storm
Structures
Summer
Sun

Sword
Tears
Tent
Tiger
Tongue
Tools
Torture
Tree
Trumpet
Valley
Veil
Vine
Vintage
Void
Wall
War
Waste
Water
Weapon
Web
Weed
Wet
Wheat
Wheel
White
Wild animals
Wilderness
Wind
Window
Wine
Winepress
Winter
Wolf
Womb
Worm

>> *Part III*

RHETORIC AND
SYNTACTIC ANALYSIS

>> 8

Samson Agonistes:

Milton's Use of Syntax to Define Character

J U L I A   W A G G O N E R

Critics frequently treat the characters in Milton's *Samson Agonistes* simply as figures from the Old Testament because they interpret the poem as though it were merely an extended account of the Samson story in the Book of Judges. Such an interpretation fails to address the differences between Milton's characters and those in the Bible. Other critics' interpretations are based solely on the perceived roles or functions of the individual characters. Again, this approach ignores the characters Milton created. My approach, however, is different: I have attempted to analyze the characters themselves through their use of syntax. Therefore, my understanding of the characters comes from the text itself and not from the Old Testament nor only from an analysis of roles.

When Milton wrote *Samson Agonistes,* he substantially altered the Old Testament story of Samson. Consider the number of significant ways in which Milton's story differs from the Biblical story. In the Old Testament an unidentified narrator provides a narrative of Samson's entire life, whereas in *Samson Agonistes* we experience only the last day of Samson's life with and through the characters. This shift focuses our attention on the characters and their relationships to each other. Furthermore, consider that Milton could have left the story in narrative form, put it in the present tense, and let the characters have their say, linking scenes with exposition, as he had done in *Paradise Lost.* However, he chose instead to present the story through dramatic dialogue: *Samson Agonistes* is composed of uninterrupted dialogue. Because Milton chose to rewrite the biblical story by letting the characters "speak for themselves," I believe it is only reasonable to examine the poem in terms of what the characters say, how they say it, and who says what to whom.

Examining "how they say it" requires a close analysis of the syntax that the characters use. I accomplished such an analysis using a computational stylistic package designed by Rosanne G. Potter (see appendix to this chapter). Potter's approach to plays and the character relationships in them is based on the assumption "that our expectations of characters are created in the same ways that our expectations of people in everyday life are created" (Potter 1980, 187). In drama, these expectations are created, for the most part, through the characters' syntax. Of playwrights' choice of that syntax Potter says:

> Every line in a part contributes to the structure that is character; every pattern of usage builds cumulatively toward the moment when character is created. This is not to say that a playwright sits down to his or her work with some preconceived notion that this character will specialize in exclamations and fragments while the next will use imperatives and questions excessively. But the type of character intended will, at some preconscious level, dictate the syntactical traits of the dialogue. (1981, 46)

Because of her approach to drama, Potter developed the COMP STYLE package to search for, count, and sort a number of identifiable syntactical structures. Using these programs, she has done extensive research on the dialogue in a number of plays. In her research she has identified a constellation of speech habits which correlates with the character trait *dominance* (1980; 1981; 1982). I was interested in what Potter's programs could reveal to me about the characters in *Samson Agonistes*.

But is this approach to *Samson Agonistes* justified? Can the characters in *Samson Agonistes*, a poem which, according to Milton, "never was intended for the stage," [1] be treated like characters in plays which were specifically written to be staged? Perhaps differences between this poetic play and dramas written for the stage are too great to permit approaching them in the same way. But I think not.

Milton's shift in focus, through his shift in genre, gives rise to two important questions: what is the nature of the relationships between the characters, and who is the dominant character? Because *Samson Agonistes* is composed strictly of dialogue, the answers to these questions must lie in the characters' speech. In order to understand the characters, then, we need to analyze their speech; therefore, I believe I am justified in using Potter's approach to drama with *Samson Agonistes*.

Having decided to use Potter's programs, I entered the text of *Samson Agonistes* on a mainframe system and ran the COMP STYLE package on it. I first

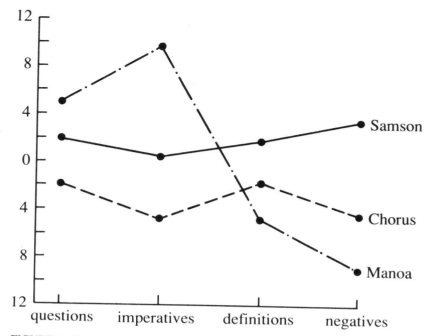

FIGURE 1. Character usage of the four variables

had to determine whether Milton uses syntax to define and differentiate characters in the poem. If he does not, then there is little that these programs can reveal about these characters. However, the data show that Milton does use syntax to define and differentiate his characters; each character uses differently four syntactical variables: questions, imperatives, definitions, and negatives. Figure 1 shows how the three major (defined by Potter according to role size) characters differ in their use of these variables.

As it can be seen from the graph, the characters are characterized by their use (or the lack thereof) of the four syntactical variables. We see, for example, that Manoa, Samson's father, is characterized by a relatively high use of questions and imperatives and a low use of definitions and negatives. Comparing characters, we see that relative to the other characters Manoa and Samson use significantly more questions and imperatives than the Chorus and that Samson uses significantly more definitions and negatives than Manoa and the Chorus. Since the characters' speech habits differ, we can tentatively assert that Milton uses syntax to create his characters.

In my analysis of this work, I decided to examine only four of the eleven variables in Potter's package. I was interested in these variables because Potter's research has shown that this cluster of variables (excluding negatives) is characteristic of dominant characters. I chose to include negatives because they play a significant part in how Dalila, Samson's wife in Milton's story, defines herself and her surroundings. Using Potter's objective approach, I hoped to support my critical intuition that Samson is the dominant character in the play. As such, Samson should "dominate" the other characters in his use of syntax, especially in his use of questions, imperatives, and definitions. In this paper, I will discuss these three variables, as well as Dalila's use of negatives, and how the major users of them differ in their usage.

The actual use of the variable "questions" by individual characters is shown in Table 1. We see here that Samson is the highest user of this variable and that he is followed in equal use by the Chorus and Manoa. However, when we look at the characters' use relative to each other (see Figure 1), we see that in proportion to his role size Manoa asks more questions than either Samson or the Chorus. Samson is, in proportion to his large role, the second highest user of the variable. How then does the use of this variable differ among these characters? To answer this question I looked beyond the numbers to the quality of the syntax. Analysis of the quality shows that Samson uses this variable more strongly than Manoa not just because he uses a larger absolute number but also because of the types of questions he asks.

Samson's questions are stronger than Manoa's. They can be categorized as those that examine, challenge, or accuse. Manoa's questions, on the other hand, can be categorized as those that express incredulity, ask for information, or are simply concerned with practical matters. The types of questions Samson uses are more aggressive than Manoa's; they frequently reflect the questioner's struggle with or against someone or something. In the play, such questions require the questioned to justify actions or assumptions to the questioner. Samson's questions (like his imperatives and definitions) follow the development of his regeneration and become stronger as the play progresses.

Early in the poem, especially in the opening monologue, Samson's questions neither challenge nor accuse. For the most part they simply complain. For example, the questions in the passage which follows not only allow Samson to

TABLE 1. QUESTIONS IN *SAMSON AGONISTES*

Character	Total lines	Question lines	Percent of questions spoken by all characters
Samson	158	33	42.8
Chorus	98	16	20.8
Manoa	68	16	20.8
Dalila	36	5	6.5
Harapha	18	4	5.2

complain about his plight but also give us information which illuminates Samson's condition by establishing the contrast in Samson between "what once I was, and what am now" (22):

> O wherefore was my birth from Heav'n foretold
> Twice by an Angel, who at last in sight
> Of both my Parents all in flames ascended
> From off the Altar, where an Off'ring burn'd,
> As in a fiery column charioting
> His Godlike presence, and from some great act
> Or benefit reveal'd to *Abraham's* race?
> Why was my breeding order'd and prescrib'd
> As of a person separate to God,
> Design'd for great exploits; if I must dye
> Betray'd, Captiv'd, and both my Eyes put out,
> Made of my Enemies the scorn and gaze;
> To grind in Brazen Fetters under task
> With this Heav'n-gifted strength?
>
> (23–36)

In another early, but brief, passage, Samson again uses questions to complain:

> O impotence of mind, in body strong!
> But what is strength without a double share
> Of wisdom?
>
> (52–54)

Despite the weakness of these questions, they do show that Samson is beginning to examine himself early in the play. Following the first passage quoted above, Samson speculates that he might be responsible for his present condition:

> Yet stay, let me not rashly call in doubt
> Divine Prediction; what if all foretold
> Had been fulfill'd but through mine own default,
> Whom have I to complain of but my self?
>
> (43–46)

Even though Samson appears to relapse a few lines later in his insight, this speculation shows that he is beginning to examine and search for a true understanding of himself. As the play progresses Samson's use of questions to complain decreases, and his use of questions to examine his assumptions increases.

These early complaining/plaintive examination questions are followed by more aggressive questions that challenge and accuse. Such questions typify those that Samson uses with Dalila, Harapha, and the Public Officer. In the Samson/Dalila scene, Samson sometimes uses the same question both to challenge and accuse Dalila. In the following question, for example, Samson raises doubts about Dalila's motives for marrying him, "Why then / Didst thou at first receive me for thy husband?" (882–83) since, as he points out, he was "Then, as since then, thy countries foe profest" (884). Samson accuses Dalila of having ulterior motives for marrying him since it is unlikely to him that Dalila would have married him, an enemy of her country, for love.

In another example of this more aggressive type of question, Samson challenges Dalila's explanation of why she told the secret of his strength to the Philistines (she has claimed at one point that it was feminine weakness, "incident to all our sex" [774]):

> weakness is thy excuse,
> And I believe it. Weakness to resist
> *Philistian* gold: if weakness may excuse,
> What Murtherer, what Traytor, Parricide,
> Incestuous, Sacrilegious, but may plead it?
> (829–33)

Samson concedes that it was indeed weakness but weakness for money not, as Dalila says, a feminine weakness. In challenging Dalila's explanation, Samson also accuses her of being no better than the worst of criminals.

Much of the same type of challenging and accusing is characteristic of the Samson/Harapha scene. This scene, though brief, is Samson's most aggressive, both physically and verbally. Samson challenges Harapha three times to physical combat; Harapha three times declines. Accepting the fact that Harapha will not fight physically, Samson begins to fight verbally. In the first of Samson's two questions in this scene, he challenges Harapha to prove his charge that Samson is a "Murtherer, a Revolter, and a Robber" (1180) by asking, "Tongue-doughtie Giant, how dost thou prove me these?" (1181). Harapha appears to argue reasonably that Samson is these things, but in his reply to Harapha's argument, Samson undermines the assumptions and clears himself of the charges. In his second question to Harapha, Samson accuses him of being a coward and a boaster, a man of words and not of deeds: "Cam'st thou for this, vain boaster, to survey me, / To descant on my strength, and give thy verdict?" (1227–28). Harapha has no reply to Samson's challenges (physical or verbal) and accusations except to say, "O *Baal-zebub!* can my ears unus'd / Hear these dishonours, and not render death?" (1231–32), which they evidently can, since Harapha exits just a few lines later without "rendering" death. Thus, we see that Samson, blind and fettered, emerges as a stronger character than Harapha, "The Giant . . . *of Gath*" (1068).

At the end of the play, Samson uses a series of questions directed to the Public Officer that also challenge and accuse. When Samson is ordered to appear before the Philistine Lords to entertain them with demonstrations of his strength, he asks the Officer:

> Can they think me so broken, so debas'd
> With corporal servitude, that my mind ever
> Will condescend to such absurd commands?
> (1335–37)
> . . . .
> To shew them feats, and play before thir god,
> The worst of all indignities, yet on me
> Joyn'd with extream contempt? I will not come.
> (1340–42)

After the Officer departs with Samson's message, the Chorus questions Samson's decision not to go; Samson replies with questions that accuse the Chorus of a lack of understanding and challenge it to re-see the nature of the Officer's request:

> Shall I abuse this Consecrated gift
> Of strength
> (1354–55)
> . . . .
> By prostituting holy things to Idols;
> A *Nazarite* in place abominable
> Vaunting my strength in honour to thir *Dagon?*
> Besides, how vile, contemptible, ridiculous,
> What act more execrably unclean, prophane?
> (1358–62)

From these examples we can see that although Samson's questions are relatively weak at the beginning, he begins as the drama progresses to use stronger questions that examine, challenge, or accuse. Although there are only two questions in the Samson/Harapha scene, they are strong questions because of their nature and because Harapha does not adequately reply to them.

Unlike Samson's questions, Manoa's are consistently weak; they neither challenge, accuse, nor examine. In his opening speech, however, Manoa appears to ask a number of challenging and/or accusing questions. In the following passage he appears to question the justice of God's laws and to challenge God's authority for granting his prayer for a son:

> O wherefore did God grant me my request,
> And as a blessing with such pomp adorn'd?
> Why are his gifts desirable, to tempt

> Our earnest Prayers, then giv'n with solemn hand
> As Graces, draw a Scorpions tail behind?
> For this did th' Angel twice descend? for this
> Ordain'd thy nurture holy, as of a Plant;
> Select, and Sacred, Glorious for a while,
> The miracle of men: then in an hour
> Ensnar'd, assaulted, overcome, led bound,
> Thy Foes derision, Captive, Poor, and Blind
> Into a Dungeon thrust, to work with Slaves?
>
> (356–67)

But as we consider this passage and examine the other types of questions that Manoa asks, then we see that these are neither truly challenging nor accusing questions.

Looking at the initial speech of the Chorus in conjunction with the initial speech of Manoa will help us to understand the nature of both. Upon finding Samson the Chorus exclaims:

> O change beyond report, thought, or belief!
> See how he lies at random, carelessly diffus'd,
> With languish't head unpropt,
> As one past hope, abandon'd,
> And by himself giv'n over;
> In slavish habit, ill-fitted weeds
> O're worn and soild;
> Or do my eyes misrepresent? Can this be hee,
> That Heroic, that Renown'd,
> Irresistible *Samson?*
>
> (117–26)

Because the poem begins after Samson's heroic deeds have been performed and because we, the audience, see him only as he "lies at random," it is necessary for Milton to establish immediately for us the contrast between Samson past and Samson present. Milton uses the Chorus and Manoa to do this through a high concentration of questions, positioned in their early speeches, which call attention to a dramatic change in expectations—for Manoa, from the greatness promised by the angel for Samson to Samson's current imprisonment; for the Chorus, from Samson's once "heroic" self to his present condition as one "carelessly diffus'd" and "past hope." In Manoa's first speech, we learn that Samson's birth was foretold to Manoa by an angel; his son was to be "Select, and Sacred, Glorious for a while, / The miracle of men" (363–64). This vision is then contrasted with the reality of Samson's situation—"Captive, Poor, and Blind." The Chorus's speech reinforces this change in expectations, too. They expected to see

"That Heroic, that Renown'd, / Irresistible *Samson*" (125–26), but instead they see him "As one past hope, abandon'd."

Milton almost exclusively uses the Chorus and Manoa to provide background information (especially early in the poem), underscoring the fact that in them we are not dealing with developed characters as much as we are dealing with functional characters. This is especially apparent with the Chorus, one of whose main functions is to introduce new characters to Samson, thereby moving the plot along. Rhetorically, therefore, these early questions of Manoa and the Chorus function to call attention to the catastrophic change in Samson rather than actually to challenge or accuse God of anything. Furthermore, unlike some of Samson's questions, neither the Chorus's nor Manoa's questions offer possible answers. Because of their mainly rhetorical function and because no answers are posited for them, the Chorus's and Manoa's complaining questions are weaker than Samson's.

The majority of Manoa's questions come at the end of the play when he wants to elicit information from the Messenger. After the Messenger arrives, Manoa plies him with one queston after another concerning Samson's death: "How dy'd he?" (1579), "by whom fell he, / What glorious hand gave *Samson* his deaths wound?" (1580–81), "Wearied with slaughter then or how?" (1583), and "Self-violence? what cause / Brought him so soon at variance with himself / Among his foes?" (1584–85). All these "plot-moving" questions are strictly information-eliciting questions. Though numerous, they are not questions characteristic of a dominant character.

In contrast to both Samson and Manoa, Dalila and Harapha ask questions to get themselves "off the hook." Neither of them asks many questions, six and five respectively, so it is significant that 33% of Dalila's questions and 80% of Harapha's are used to shift responsibility for their actions from themselves to someone else. Although they both ask questions which appear to accuse Samson of wrongdoing, they ask them not so much to accuse Samson as to minimize what they have done. Dalila uses "if it's okay for you, then it's okay for me" reasoning when she accuses Samson of weakness so that her actions will not seem "wrong":

> Was it not weakness also to make known
> For importunity, that is for naught,
> Wherein consisted all thy strength and safety?
> (778–80)

And Harapha appears to be charging Samson with murder:

> Is not thy Nation subject to our Lords?
> Thir Magistrates confest it, when they took thee

As a League-breaker and deliver'd bound
Into our hands: for hadst thou not committed
Notorious murder on those thirty men
At *Askalon,* who never did thee harm,
Then like a Robber strip'dst them of thir robes?
(1182–88)

Whereas it is true that Samson should not have revealed his source of strength to Dalila and, according to all appearances, did commit "notorious murder" on thirty "innocent" men, both Dalila and Harapha use their questions not to challenge, accuse, or try to understand but simply to justify why they did or did not do something (for Dalila, why she betrayed Samson, and for Harapha, why he will not fight Samson). The two use questions to avoid facing themselves; they shift the focus away from themselves to someone or something else.

Elsewhere, Dalila also uses questions to transfer the responsibility for her actions:

and the Priest
Was not behind, but ever at my ear,
Preaching how meritorious with the gods
It would be to ensnare an irreligious
Dishonourer of *Dagon:* what had I
T' oppose against such powerful arguments?
(857–62)

And, in a like manner, Harapha responds to the last of Samson's challenges to fight, saying: "With thee a Man condemn'd, a Slave enrol'd, / Due by the Law to capital punishment? / To fight with thee no man of arms will deign" (1224–26). Though it may be true that a "man of arms" would not fight a condemned man, Harapha uses this as an excuse rather than as a reason not to fight Samson. Samson has already challenged Harapha twice to physical combat, and it is only the third challenge that elicits this response from Harapha.

Thus a comparison of the kinds of questions the characters ask shows that Samson is the dominant user of this variable. Although early in the play Samson asks complaining questions, they are not as weak as they appear because Samson uses them to try to understand his present situation. Furthermore, Samson's questions become stronger, more aggressive as the play progresses, whereas none of the other characters' questions become stronger. The Chorus's and Manoa's questions are basically functional; Dalila's and Harapha's questions are weak because they use them solely to shirk responsibility for their actions.

Like questions, imperatives when used at a high level are part of the constellation of speech patterns of dominant characters. If we refer to Table 2,

TABLE 2.   IMPERATIVES IN *SAMSON AGONISTES*

Character	Total lines	Imperative lines	Percent of imperatives spoken by all characters
Samson	158	24	40.0
Chorus	98	9	15.0
Manoa	68	17	28.3
Dalila	36	4	6.7
Harapha	18	1	1.7

we see that Samson and Manoa are the highest users of this variable. Again, we need to look beyond the comparative proportion to the types of imperatives being used.

As Samson's faith is regenerated, we see the increasing strength of his imperatives. Early in the poem Samson hardly ever uses imperatives, and those he does use are relatively weak; however, in his exchanges with Dalila and Harapha, Samson uses imperatives frequently, and they are strong ones. After Samson's encounter with Manoa, his imperatives tell others what to do and usually require some type of response from the individual to whom they are addressed—they are too forceful to be ignored.

Samson's early imperatives reflect the "languish't" Samson, the Samson described by the Chorus "as one past hope." His attitude is that of resignation:

Spare that proposal, Father, spare the trouble
Of that sollicitation; let me here,
As I deserve, pay on my punishment;
And expiate, if possible, my crime,
Shameful garrulity. . . .

(487–91)

These imperatives are weak; one can imagine a slight wave of the hand accompanying them. Rather than actually having accepted the responsibility for his present situation, Samson seems to have resigned himself to it with the hope that he will be able to "pay on his punishment" and "expiate" his "crime" in that way. That he does not truly know the nature of his "crime" is reflected in his calling it a "shameful garrulity." Were this actually the case, we would sense the unfairness of the "punishment" just as much as Samson, the Chorus, and Manoa do, as reflected in their initial speeches quoted above.

Whereas in his early use the imperatives sound "tired," in subsequent scenes Samson's imperatives are forceful and commanding, full of energy. When Samson has been informed by the Chorus of Dalila's approach, he immediately responds with, "My Wife, my Traytress, let her not come near me" (725); the

Chorus can do nothing except to report, "Yet on she moves" (726). After Dalila addresses Samson, his reply to her is simply, "Out, out *Hyaena;* these are thy wonted arts" (748). This is not what Dalila expected. She had expected to find the "old" Samson, over whom she had control, but she now must immediately respond to Samson's dismissal of her so that she can try to "win" him back. She counters Samson's strong imperatives with a pleading one, "Yet hear me *Samson*" (766).

Throughout the rest of the scene, Samson's imperatives continue to tell Dalila what to do: "Take to thy wicked deed," "take no care," "Nor think me," "go with that," and "Bewail thy falsehood." Dalila's only other imperatives in the scene either tell Samson how to be ("Be not unlike all others, not austere" [815]) or require Samson's assent (Let me obtain forgiveness of thee, *Samson*" [909]; "Let me approach at least, and touch thy hand" [951]); Samson acknowledges neither kind of imperative. Dalila's exit is marked by Samson's relatively weak imperative directed to the Chorus which is, however, linked to his strong assertion about himself:

> So let her go, God sent her to debase me,
> And aggravate my folly who committed
> To such a viper his most sacred trust
> Of secresie, my safety, and my life.
>   (999–1002)

This passage not only shows Samson in control of the situation but also reflects a difference in the way Samson views his "crime." Earlier in the play, Samson viewed the violation of the secret of his strength as a result of garrulousness, a "shameful garrulity" he calls it. This description shows us that Samson did not see the enormity of his violation of the secret of his strength. However, by this point in the play, Samson recognizes just how serious the violation was. He did not merely reveal wherein lay his strength; he committed "his most sacred trust / Of secresie, my safety, and my life" to a "viper." Samson has come a long way in his understanding since the early lines of the play.

If Samson's imperatives were strong in the Samson/Dalila scene, they are even stronger in the Samson/Harapha scene. The Samson of this scene is anything but "languish't"; his imperatives no longer sound as if they were accompanied with a wave of the hand, and he no longer "lies at random." Somewhere Samson has risen to his feet, perhaps when Dalila "sailed" into view, and he is now ready for his most commanding scene.

There are more imperatives in this scene than in any other scene in the play. They are Samson's strongest, most active imperatives: "boast not," "let be assign'd," "put on," "add thy Spear," "Go to his Temple, invoke his aid" (1146), "answer thy appellant," "Come nearer, part not hence," "take good heed," "bring up thy van," and "Go baffl'd coward." To this whole barrage of imperatives, Harapha can reply with only one: "Presume not on thy God, what e'er he be" (1156). This line clearly shows that Harapha does not have control of this scene. In his earlier scenes, Samson has used imperatives which tell others how to be, which are relatively weak imperatives. Gradually, Samson's imperatives have become stronger; they now tell others what and what not to do.

The few other imperatives Samson uses before he leaves the stage are also commanding. As he decides to leave with the Philistine Officer, he says to the Chorus:

> Be of good courage, I begin to feel
> Some rouzing motions in me which dispose
> To something extraordinary my thoughts.
> I with this Messenger will go along,
> Nothing to do, be sure, that may dishonour
> Our Law, or stain my vow of *Nazarite*.
> (1381–86)

The strength of these imperatives lies in Samson's position of being able to provide comfort and assurance to those who had initially come to comfort him (183–86). So we can see an increasing strength in Samson's imperatives from the beginning to the end of the poem.

Manoa also uses a significant number of imperatives. He uses them frequently at the beginning of the play and at the end after Samson has left. Like Samson's, Manoa's imperatives become stronger as the play progresses, although they are never as strong as Samson's. Manoa's high use of imperatives shows us that he is dominant in particular scenes in the play. By looking at these scenes, we can see, however, why Manoa's "dominance" is not as dominating as Samson's.

At the beginning of the play, when Manoa first appears, he uses imperatives which look fairly strong and commanding but which really are not very strong. They are more like advice than commands: "Be penitent," "act not," "Reject not," "Believe not," "Repent the sin," and "be calm." All of these imperatives are directed to Samson. Through these advice imperatives, Manoa seems to be offering reassurance to a "hopeless" Samson. His dominance here exists basically because Samson is weak. Yet even in his weakness Samson undercuts Manoa's authority and the strength of his imperatives by choosing to ignore his father's advice. Thus, these imperatives are contextually represented as ineffectual.

Toward the end of the play, Manoa uses imperatives basically to demand information from others: "Tell us," "Relate by whom," "speak them out," "say first," "explain," and "give us [an account]." This particular group of imperatives is clustered toward the end of the play after Samson's death, and Manoa uses them to get information from the Messenger. The imperatives, therefore, function to move the story along and to create minor suspense as the Messenger's story unfolds. What Manoa's imperatives also show us is that in Samson's absence he is the dominant figure of this group.

At the very end of the play, after he learns of the destruction of Samson and the Philistines, Manoa assumes control of the situation, which is reflected in his use of these imperatives: "Come, come no time for lamentation now" (1708), "let but them," and "Let us go." This scene shows Manoa at his strongest, and we are left with a vision of Manoa leading the Hebrews off to the temple to find Samson's body.

Because Samson's imperatives are more direct, active, and forceful than Manoa's, and because they usually demand an immediate response of some type from the individual to whom they are addressed, Samson is the dominant user of this variable. He controls most of the scenes in the play, except the earliest and of course those after he has left the stage. Manoa's use of imperatives is weaker; his imperatives give advice (which require no active response) or seek information (which require only a verbal response).

The third, and last, syntactical variable characteristic of dominant speech is a high use of definitions. When we examine Table 3, we immediately see the problem that exists with this variable in the play. Virtually every utterance in *Samson Agonistes* involves some type of definition—of self, of other, of past or present situation. The problem is the sheer amount of data generated—in this case, almost the entire poem. (In the modern plays for which the COMP STYLE package was designed, less defining takes place so the output is more manageable.) Here the results show that Samson and Dalila define on a relatively similar basis, but Dalila does more defining than Samson. When we consider the size of her role, this becomes significant. Significant too is the fact that Manoa does the least amount of defining in the play. Because of the highly defined world of the play, Manoa, with his low amount of defining, is a reactor to the established reality rather than a creator of reality. Samson and Dalila, on the other hand, are the

TABLE 3. DEFINITIONS IN *SAMSON AGONISTES*

Character	Total lines	Definition lines	Percent of definitions spoken by all characters
Samson	158	147	39.2
Chorus	98	88	23.5
Manoa	68	58	15.5
Dalila	36	34	9.1
Harapha	18	18	4.8

major creators of reality in the poem because of their high use of definitions. The difference between Samson and Dalila lies not only in the nature of the realities they define but in why they define.

In looking at definitions, the worldview embraced in the poem becomes important. Since the worldview which underlies the poem is a Judaic one, any definition contrary to that reality is "wrong," and since Dalila is not a Hebrew but a Philistine, the reality she defines is bound to be the "wrong" one (and thus Samson emerges as the dominant character because his reality is the "right" one). But it would be a mistake simply to dismiss Dalila with this argument. Because Milton created her as a complex character, we should not dismiss her definitions on such grounds alone. Dalila, though, provides us with sufficient other grounds to discredit her definitions. Although Samson's view of reality is the "right" one in the context of the poem, he shows himself as dominant irrespective of his "right" reality—just as Dalila shows herself to be weak beyond the "wrongness" of her reality.

Most of Samson's defining at the beginning of the play is done for our benefit to establish the "what once I was, and what am now." Through the definitions of Samson and the Chorus, we also get the historical situation defined and through that the "right" reality and the "wrong" reality. Such definitions establish the principal issues of the drama.

Most of Samson's early definitions show him to be weak. As I have already pointed out, Samson's early definition of his "crime" is inaccurate. This "misdefining" is typical of Samson's early use of this variable. Samson uses his definitions to evade the responsibility for his actions, which he tries to shift to God. In the following passage, Samson is concerned not with his relationship with God, as he should be in the context of the poem, but with what members of his tribe think of him:

> Yee see, O friends,
> How many evils have enclos'd me round;
> Yet that which was the worst now least afflicts me,
> Blindness, for had I sight, confus'd with shame,
> How could I once look up, or heave the head,
> Who like a foolish Pilot have shipwrack't
> My Vessel trusted to me from above,
> Gloriously rigg'd; and for a word, a tear,
> Fool, have divulg'd the secret gift of God
> To a deceitful Woman: Tell me Friends,
> Am I not sung and proverb'd for a Fool
> In every street, do they not say, how well
> Are come upon him his deserts? yet why?
> Immeasurable strength they might behold

In me, of wisdom nothing more then mean;
This with the other should, at least, have paird,
These two proportiond ill drove me transverse.
(193–209)

Samson calls himself a "foolish Pilot" and twice a "fool." In the Judaic context of the poem, it is clear that Samson has not been foolish but negligent in keeping his vow, something he cannot blame God for. Samson's concern here for what others think of him demonstrates that he does not yet understand that his true concerns should be (in Milton's view) not with what men think of him, but with what God thinks of him.

But as the poem progresses, Samson's definitions become stronger in that they become more accurate and that he uses them to accept responsibility for his actions: "of what now I suffer / She was not the prime cause, but I my self" (233–34); "Nothing of all these evils hath befall'n me / But justly; I my self have brought them on, / Sole Author I, sole cause" (374–76). And he eventually defines accurately and precisely what it is that he has done:

Father, I do acknowledge and confess
That I this honour, I this pomp have brought
To *Dagon*, and advanc'd his praises high
Among the Heathen round; to God have brought
Dishonour, obloquie, and op't the mouths
Of Idolists, and Atheists; have brought scandal
To *Israel*, diffidence of God, and doubt
In feeble hearts, propense anough before
To waver, or fall off and joyn with Idols
Which is my chief affliction, shame and sorrow,
The anguish of my Soul, that suffers not
Mine eie to harbour sleep, or thoughts to rest.
(448–59)

From the middle of the play onward, Samson does not use language to cover up what he has done; rather, he admits responsibility for his actions by using language to discover Truth.

Because Samson's definitions progress from being evasive and "misdefining" and because, for the most part, as the play progresses Samson uses definitions to acknowledge and accept responsibility for his actions, he emerges as a strong definer in the play. Dalila, on the other hand, uses definitions strictly to redefine her "crime" so that she can shift responsibility for her actions elsewhere. Nowhere in her speech does she actually acknowledge or accept what she has done. Her initial speech is a *tour de force* in "misdefining":

With doubtful feet and wavering resolution
I came, still dreading thy displeasure, *Samson*,
Which to have merited, without excuse,
I cannot but acknowledge; yet if tears
May expiate (though the fact more evil drew
In the perverse event then I foresaw)
My penance hath not slack'n'd, though my pardon
No way assur'd.
                                        (732–39)
. . . .
If aught in my ability may serve
To light'n what thou suffer'st, and appease
Thy mind with what amends is in my power,
Though late, yet in some part to recompense
My rash but more unfortunate misdeed.
                                        (743–47)

It is quite an understatement for Dalila to label what she did a "perverse event" and a "rash but more unfortunate misdeed." And not only is everything "mis-defined," but Dalila thinks that "tears / May expiate" her crime, which shows that she has not acknowledged her responsibilty for Samson's blindness and imprisonment.

If we examine several other speeches of Dalila, we see the same tactic of using language to shift responsibility:

First granting, as I do, it was a weakness
In me, but incident to all our sex,
Curiosity, inquisitive, importune
Of secrets, then with like infirmity
To publish them, both common female faults. . . .
                                        (773–77)

Here again Dalila is understating what she has done; mere curiosity is seldom severe enough that a wife will knowingly endanger her husband's welfare. Furthermore, Dalila is trying to shift her responsibility for what happened by blaming her sex.

Some lines later Dalila tries another way of shifting the blame.

It was not gold, as to my charge thou lay'st,
That wrought with me: thou know'st the Magistrates
And Princes of my countrey came in person,
Sollicited, commanded, threat'n'd, urg'd,
Adjur'd by all the bonds of civil Duty
And of Religion, press'd how just it was,
How honourable, how glorious to entrap

A common enemy, who had destroy'd
Such numbers of our Nation . . .

(849–57)

Here she is trying to shift the blame to her countrymen, saying that they swayed her into believing that by betraying Samson she was doing a great honor to her country. Her argument of civil duty might carry some weight were it not for the fact that Samson was her husband first—a bond, theoretically, stronger than the civil bond. But her argument here is wrong for other reasons, too. Even were we to grant to Dalila the validity of her religion (which the poem does not), she does not act because of her religion or for patriotic reasons. Ultimately, it is not for the glory of Dagon or her country that Dalila betrays Samson but for Dalila's own glory, as she reveals:

But in my country where I most desire,
In *Ecron, Gaza, Asdod,* and in *Gath*
I shall be nam'd among the famousest
Of Women, sung at solemn festivals,
Living and dead recorded, who to save
Her countrey from a fierce destroyer chose
Above the faith of wedlock-bands, my tomb
With odours visited and annual flowers. . . .

(980–87)

Dalila defines away the political significance of her actions, revealing that her sole interest is in herself. The reality that she defines is without standards; it centers around herself and the gratification of her desires.

Besides weakening her definitions by using them solely to evade responsibility for her actions, Dalila defines her world and others by what they are not rather than by what they are (see Table 4). Dalila's initial speech is loaded with negatives ("I cannot but acknowledge," "displeasure," "without excuse," and "unfortunate misdeed"), which should immediately put us on our guard. The rest of her speeches are likewise filled with negatives and negative constructions: "It

TABLE 4. NEGATIVES IN *SAMSON AGONISTES*

Character	Total lines	Negative lines	Percent of negatives spoken by all characters
Samson	158	95	42.2
Chorus	98	50	22.2
Manoa	68	30	13.3
Dalila	36	25	11.1
Harapha	18	10	4.4

was not gold, as to my charge thou lay'st" (849); "Afford me place to shew what recompense / Towards thee I intend for what I have misdone, / Misguided" (910–12); "nor too much disapprove my own" (970); and "My name . . . / To all posterity may stand defam'd, / With malediction mention'd, and the blot / Of falshood most unconjugal traduc't" (975–79). And she tells Samson what not to do/be rather than what to do/be: "nor shouldst thou," "exact not," "Be not unlike all others, not austere" (815), "In uncompassionate anger do not so" (818), and "Bear not too sensibly, nor still insist" (913). Furthermore, a number of her definitions are also negatively constructed: "irreligious / Dishonourer" and "I see thou art implacable . . . / Thy anger, unappeasable, still rages, / Eternal tempest never to be calm'd" (960–64) are examples of this.

Because of her extremely high use of negatives, Dalila creates an imprecise, ill-defined reality. We know why things are not, but we really don't know why things are. She leaves us unsure of her and thereby unsure of the reality she offers us in the play. Because of this hedging and because she defines in order to shirk responsibility, Dalila weakens herself as a definer.

When we compare the types of realities defined and how they are created (negatively for Dalila), we see that Samson's definitions are stronger than Dalila's. Although Samson initially "misdefines" his "crime" and does so to avoid accepting responsibility for his actions, as the play progresses his definitions become more accurate and precise, and he uses them to acknowledge and accept responsibility for his actions. Dalila justifies our dismissal of her reality because her sole purpose in defining is to shift the responsibility for her actions elsewhere and to redefine them to the point where they are virtually unrecognizable. Furthermore, her highly concentrated use of negatives and negative constructions creates for us a reality so indefinite that it is difficult for us to say just what it is exactly.

From this study I conclude that Milton uses syntax to define and differentiate the characters in *Samson Agonistes;* data from the running of Potter's programs clearly demonstrate this. My research supports some of the existing interpretations of the poem but for the first time on a "scientifically" provable basis. The programs reveal that Milton has assigned the syntax of dominance to Samson, which supports my intuition of Samson's dominance.

Samson's dominance is reflected in the type of syntax that characterizes his speech and in the quality of that syntax, which becomes stronger as the play progresses. Early in the play Samson's questions, imperatives, and definitions are comparatively weak: his early questions, although attempting to explore, are usually used to complain; his imperatives are few and weak; and his definitions, when not providing background information, are used to evade responsibility for his actions and to "misdefine" the nature of his "crime." In the middle of the play Samson's questions are challenging and accusative; his imperatives are frequent and forceful; and his definitions, now more accurate, are used to acknowledge and to accept responsibility for his actions. At the end of the play Samson's dominance is reflected not only in the continued use of the stronger types of questions, imperatives, and definitions characteristic of his encounters with Dalila and Harapha, but also in his position as someone able to provide reassurance to others.

The use of the mainframe system has made possible a closer examination of the text of *Samson Agonistes* than has previously been done. Potter's programs have allowed me objectively to support my understanding of the character of Samson. The computer is a very useful tool in literary criticism in that it invites a new perspective to be taken on older literature; it brings to our attention things previously hidden in our texts and makes new what we once thought so familiar.

Notes

1. Quotations of Milton are from *The Complete English Poetry of John Milton*, ed. John T. Shawcross (New York: New York University Press, 1963).

References

Milton, John. *The Complete English Poetry of John Milton*. Ed. John T. Shawcross. New York: New York University Press, 1963.
Potter, Rosanne G. (1980). "Toward a Syntactic Differentiation of Period Style in Modern Drama: Significant Between-Play Variability in 21 English-Language Plays." *Computers and the Humanities* 14:187–96.
——— (1981). "Character Definition Through Syntax: Significant Within-Play Variability in 21 Modern English-Language Plays." *Style* 15, 4:415–34.
——— (1982). "Reader Responses and Character Syntax." *Computing in the Humanities*. Ed. Richard W. Bailey. Amsterdam: North Holland, 65–78.

APPENDIX

Although I was able to apply the COMP STYLE package to *Samson Agonistes*, I wish to report several difficulties that arose. Segmenting the text for entry into the mainframe system caused numerous problems. Potter has established a 500-character maximum for text entry. This has allowed her "the freedom to use one sentence when that sentence was free-standing and interpretable, and more when it was not sufficient for rhetorical analysis" (1980, 189). All too frequently, however, the 500-character maximum proved too short to handle a rhetorical unit of Milton's poem, and frequently it proved too short to cover a Miltonic sequence. If the passage did not fit the 500-character maximum, I first looked for full stop punctuation, either a period or question mark. If unable to locate either of those,

I next looked for, in descending order, a semicolon, a colon, or finally an independent clause separated from another independent clause by a coordinating conjunction. Although this produced some rather artificial rhetorical units, the procedure worked adequately most of the time. For *Samson Agonistes,* a 1000-character maximum for text entry should be more than adequate to cover any rhetorical unit in the poem.

The definition program was not very helpful on this particular project because it gave me back most of the text simply sorted by character. If categories of definition were established, the different types of definitions could be given symbols that the computer could read, sort, and count by category. For example, in this poem definitions could be categorized by character, situation, and reality. Such categorization would greatly reduce the amount of hand sorting for this particular variable.

Several programs (exclamations, comparisons, and fragments and pauses) did not produce results in accordance with Potter's work on twenty-one English-language plays. Milton rarely uses exclamations; when he does, they do not define excitability in characters. Comparisons in modern drama suggest a poetic nature of the character, but in a poem characters speak poetically, comparisons being part of poetic language, so this particular program was not very helpful. High use of fragments and pauses in modern drama frequently marks a character who is dominated by others. This feature is not part of Milton's syntax—there is only one fragment in the play. More research would show whether the absence of this feature and the extremely high use of definition is related to the nature of poetry and poetic language, or whether it is related to the period in which the poem was written.

Much work needs to be done on older drama to understand how earlier dramatists use syntax to define characters and how their use differs from that of modern dramatists. Research on earlier playwrights such as Shakespeare, Marlowe, Jonson, Webster, Ford, Wycherley, and others could perhaps identify other syntactical variables worth looking at. Such research might also lead to a better understanding of the nature of audience expectations of characters and how this expectation has/has not changed over the centuries. Research on Milton's other poem-play, *Comus,* and on Marlowe's *Doctor Faustus* might also reveal interesting differences in the way early dramatists used syntax in poem-plays as opposed to prose plays.

>> 9

Speech Acts and the Art of the Exemplum in the Poetry of Chaucer and Gower

EUGENE GREEN

In presenting issues of commitment and prudential conduct, the medieval exemplum bears some direct resemblance to speech acts. Whether the speech act is
a command, a promise, or a request, its utterance, if sincere, constitutes a commitment, a desire to have fulfilled what is said. Likewise, the exemplum is a brief
narrative that typically, as in the poetry of Chaucer and Gower, concerns itself
with the sincerity of utterances, with whether a character is willing to have his
words count as genuine in meaning and purpose.[1] So in comparable exempla,
those in Gower's *Confessio Amantis* and Chaucer's *Legend of Good Women* as
well as in the Canterbury group—*The Man of Law's Tale*, *The Physician's Tale*,
and *The Wife of Bath's Tale*—the force of what is expressed requires some
study.[2] Instances are numerous: in the account of Florent or in *The Wife of Bath's
Tale* the motives of the hag in requesting marriage as recompense for her aid are
central to matters of prudential action; in the tale of Ariadne the promises of the
imprisoned Theseus illustrate the difficulties of deciding what is sincere. Clearly,
if the nature of motives and prudential conduct characterizes the exemplum and
the speech act, then one question that this correspondence invites has to do with
the poetic practices of Chaucer and Gower, with the ways that they depict their

many uses of commands, requests, and promises. That the two poets drew upon similar sources for the work of re-creation, that they both enclosed their exempla in frames—a prologue for the *Legend of Good Women,* an epilogue, too, for *Confessio Amantis*—offers an excellent opportunity for a stylistic approach, for a computational analysis of the speech acts in their exempla.[3] The argument is that in designing exempla from a variety of sources, in shaping narratives that contain problematic speech acts, Chaucer and Gower each exhibit traits of style precisely suited to their separate purposes.[4]

An initial procedure in identifying speech acts for analysis in Chaucer's and Gower's poetry is to enter as data all the instances in the texts of performative verbs, verbs in the imperative mood, and the modal auxiliaries *shal* and *wol* that have first person pronouns (*I* and *we*) as subjects. The second step is to apply criteria for winnowing out inappropriate examples. To begin, a verb or verb phrase counts as a performative if within an utterance it implies that it is expressing (or has expressed) a command, a promise, or a request. For example, in the utterance, "I prey yow hoold your argumentz in pees," the verb *prey* counts as a performative, because it is finite, appears in the present tense, indicative mood, active voice, and has a first person singular subject. The overall effect of the utterance is to express a request: the performative verb *prey,* combined with the proposition *yow hoold your argumentz in pees,* constitutes a speech act. As forms of narrative, moreover, Chaucer's and Gower's exempla often contain instances of performative verbs, verbs of different tenses, moods, and voices; and these may have grammatical subjects of different person and number. For these instances, the following criteria help to distinguish appropriate from inappropriate utterances.

I. Appropriate Uses Other Than Those Already Indicated
   A. Tenses
      1. Present emphatic as in
         This wold I for my laste word beseche / That thou mi love aquite as I deserve. . . .
      2. Present perfect tense as in
         I . . . ofte have prayed, / That it mot be the grettest prys [reward]
      3. Past tense as in
         And in myself this convenaunt made I tho [then], / That ryght swich as ye felten, . . . / The same wolde I fele. . . .
   B. Nonfinite forms as in
      I me recommande [commit myself] / To him which al me may comande, / Preyende . . . / That his corone longe stonde.
   C. Passive Voice as in
      To every wight [person] comanded was silence.

    D. Grammatical Subjects other than *I* as in

> Of that thou hast me preid, . . . I schal / . . . Conseil upon thi nede. I can me
> wel acorde / . . . to telle as ye me bidde.
> Sche cleped him and bad abide.
> And thus for me thei preiden alle. . . .

II. Inappropriate Uses

    A. Future tense as in

> He shal sweren to you . . . , / He shal no more agilten (offend). . . .

    B. Nonfinite forms

       1. The infinitive form as subject as in

> Allas! to bidde a woman gon [to go] by nyghte. . . .

       2. The infinitive form in a clause of indefinite time as in

> For whan . . . / I have . . . / Of love to beseche hire . . . / I am concluded
> with a nay.

    C. Subjunctive Mood in a noun clause, as in

> My will is that thou besieche / And preie . . . for the pes [peace]. . . .

    D. Indefinite Subjects as in

> A kynge to kepe his lyges [subjects] in justice; / . . . And therto is a kyng
> . . . ysworn. . . .

    E. Clause Structure

       1. Interrogative as in

> Who bad the foure spirites of tempest / . . . "Anoyeth, neither see, ne land,
> ne tree"?

       2. Conditional as in

> And if I profre yow . . . / To ben youre page. . . .

The difference between a "normal" form of a speech act and those that fall within the appropriate categories listed above is one of immediacy. The "normal" form presents the speaker at the moment of commitment. But utterances that have performative verbs, mostly in the past tense, often with grammatical subjects other than that of the first person, report rather than enunciate speech acts. Since in almost all instances a reader can easily enough transpose reported speech acts into a "normal" form, they, too, contribute to a computational analysis.

Three other forms of utterance, identified as indirect speech acts, complete the categories open to study. These include expressions in the imperative mood (a large group) as well as less frequent instances of the subjunctive mood and the modal auxiliary *shal* or *wol* as part of the verb phrase. None of the utterances in this group need occur with a performative verb, yet each, supported by its immediate context, is expressive of a command, a promise, or a request.

Typically, the Middle English verb in the imperative mood has in its plural form the inflections *-eth* or *-e; -e* also appears in the singular form, as does the bare stem. The second person pronouns *thou* and *ye* occasionally accompany the verb. Almost all instances of the imperative pass muster as speech acts. Exceptions such as "Drede the nat, for I am here!"—indicative of reassurance rather than a request or command—occur sporadically. The word *let* or *lat,* appearing before an infinitive form, recurs throughout the exempla: *let,* as in "This Tereus let make his shipes yare [ready]," exemplifies the past tense form of the imperative and stands as an example of a reported speech act. A final, incidental form of the imperative has the pronoun *thou* and the auxiliary verb *shalt,* as in "Thou shalt no longer in thyn hous hir save [keep]." In the lines "And lat us speke of wyves . . . ; / Preyse everyman his owene," the verb *preyse,* in the subjunctive mood and accompanied by the imperative *lat,* helps to express a request. Such a use of the subjunctive, however, is infrequent in Chaucer and Gower's exempla.

The utterance "in youre servise thus I wol endure," one of several promises that Theseus makes to Ariadne, also depends on context to distinguish it from the customary use of "I wol" to express an intention that is not yet a commitment. So in the utterance "Bot now this thing mai be non other, / I wole a lettre unto my brother," Canace expresses an intention—not a promise—although one can, upon a moment's reflection, supply a suitable context to convert her utterance into a speech act.

The grammatical and contextual properties of the utterances that in Chaucer and Gower's exempla express commands, promises, and requests imply the possibility of having a computer read and identify in texts a substantial number of appropriate forms. Surely, a computer program, supplied with a glossary, can locate and record many utterances containing performative verbs and *lat* or *let.* A program for identifying forms in the imperative mood is a greater challenge, requiring at least a capacity to distinguish principal clauses that have both subjects and predicates from those that have the verb alone. In this study, all data in the computer underwent coding first by hand. What follows are results drawn from entering more than four hundred instances of speech acts as logical records for the purpose of creating a data base.

The number of verbs in each exemplum and in the poets' prologues (Gower's epilogue, too) is insufficient for statistical analysis of each; so the data under study constitutes a pool of forms garnered from the several texts and used to examine the overall practices of Chaucer and Gower. Then, too, this pool of data, already characterized by forms of speech act (command, promise, request), by forms of verb (performative, imperative, auxiliary, and subjunctive), and by modes of presentation (direct address, reported utterance) presents a first level of entry into a statistical analysis. Table 1 lists the poets' use of speech acts: commands, promises, and requests.

A brief glance at the table tells much about the poets' preference for different kinds of speech act. Since Chaucer and Gower hardly mirror each other in recre-

TABLE 1. INCIDENCE OF COMMANDS, PROMISES, AND REQUESTS

	Commands	Promises	Requests
Chaucer	80	53	79
Gower	92	41	98

ating similar narratives (the prologues are different, and four of the exempla are not directly comparable), the numbers under each heading are bound to vary. The question is whether the variance is sufficiently large to show that the poets differ significantly. A first impression, based on Gower's less frequent use of promises (his total number of speech acts is greater—231), might imply a significant difference. A chi-square test compares the poets' observed, actual choices in each cell to a number which would be expected in each cell if the poets did not differ. (One step in the test is to determine the expected frequencies.) The result of this comparison shows that the apparent variance in Chaucer's and Gower's practice, if marked, nonetheless does not differ significantly from the expected pattern. Thus Chaucer's promises comprise .25 of the speech acts in his row; the proportion for Gower is .18. If the poets were fully in accord with the possible, expected frequencies, the ratio of promises for each would be .21. If they were significantly different, then the proportion of Chaucer's promises would be about .26, and of Gower's, .16. The results of the chi-square test for Table 1 are $X^2 = 3.59$, $df = 2$, which yields a probability of .85 difference, short of the .95 difference established as at least requisite for a significant finding.

The different ways of expressing these speech acts, however, help to specify some significant difference between the poets. One way is to express a speech act by different forms of the verb or verb phrase. Table 2 describes the poets' choices among the possibilities.

The contrasting preferences shown in this table are striking. If it is true that a ranking of the columns for Chaucer and Gower results in concurrence (performative verbs as first for both poets), the proportions indicate a sharp contrast in preference. Whereas, for instance, verbs in the imperative mood comprise for Gower a small porportion of his total number (.16), the ratio for Chaucer is .38, a difference in itself substantial enough to yield a significant result in a chi-square test. The relative difference in the ratio of performative verbs is even greater. The consequence is that the similarity in the choice of verb forms is no closer than a probability of .001 ($X^2 = 35.72$, $df = 2$). So if Chaucer and Gower are moderately alike in the choices of commands, promises, and requests, their enunciation of these speech acts through the use of particular patterns of verb is significantly different.

Lastly, the poets' narratives (both the exempla and the prologues) rely on the use of direct address and reported utterances. So if Chaucer has Jason directly

TABLE 2. PATTERNS OF VERBS EXPRESSING SPEECH ACTS

	Performative verbs	Verbs in the imperative mood	Other patterns of verbs
Chaucer	107	80	25
Gower	180	38	13

TABLE 3. DIRECT ADDRESS AND REPORTED UTTERANCES AMONG PERFORMATIVE VERBS

	Direct address	Reported utterances
Chaucer	39	68
Gower	31	149

promise Medea, "Youre man I am," Gower reports that Jason "faire . . . behihte [promised] / That . . . he scholde hire take for his wif. . . ." Table 3 summarizes the poets' use of direct address and reported utterance in regard only to performative verbs (instances of reported utterances containing verbs in the imperative—he "let the peple calle"—are too few for statistical analysis).

Although for both poets the instances of direct address comprise fairly small ratios (.36 for Chaucer, .17 for Gower), the difference is again significant; the result of a chi-square test is $X^2 = 13.77$, $df = 1$, and the likelihood of similarity is less than .001. In sum, the results of these three tests indicate that the poets agree in their choice of speech acts, but not in the ways to express them.

Yet these results prompt other questions responsive to statistical analysis, questions directly concerned with the genre of the exemplum as well as with matters of grammar and pragmatics. Of the exemplum as a genre, Burrow says that the poets "were interested not so much in the history of an individual, a court or a nation, as in moral ideas. Hence we might expect to find a preponderence of single-episode stories, given the relative ease with which the moral bearing of such tales can be controlled and limited."[5] To adopt Burrow's view, then, is to ask how Chaucer and Gower used speech acts to illuminate moral ideas in the exempla under study, whether their modes of presentation repay statistical analysis. Throughout the tales and prologues at least one moment is concerned with moral issues and offers some prospect for computational work: such moments include a lover's vow of fidelity (typically deceptive), a woman's effort to avert disaster (usually desertion, rape, or murder) or to realize her desires (a marriage or the protection of God), and instances of apostrophe, as it were, during which a figure all alone discloses a sense of distress or hope. In these moments the characters in the exempla are likely to enter into promises, to issue commands, to utter requests, or else to concern themselves with the commitments of others, desired, unfulfilled, or betrayed. Table 4 outlines the occurrence of these three moments in the poetry compared.

TABLE 4. RECURRENT MOMENTS OF CHALLENGE AND REFLECTION

Tale	Poet	Moments		
		Deception	Womanly risk and challenge	Solitude
Aeneas, Dido	Chaucer	Aeneas accused	Dido's plea	Her suicide
	Gower	———	Dido's letter	
Albinus, Rosemound	Gower	Albinus's feast	Rosemound's revenge	———
Ariadne, Theseus	Chaucer Gower	Theseus's pledge	Ariadne's eloping	Ariadne forsaken
Canace, Machaire	Gower	———	Canace as victim	Her letter to Machaire
Cleopatra	Chaucer	———	Cleopatra bereft	Her pledge to Antony
Constance	Chaucer Gower	Queens' plots	Her survival and reunion	Her prayers
Wife of Bath Florent	Chaucer Gower	———	Hag's espousal and wooing	———
Hypermnestra	Chaucer	Egistes' plot	Her resistance	Her decision to save Lyno
Jason, Medea	Chaucer Gower	Jason's desertion	Medea's espousal	Medea bereft Medea prays
Lucrece	Chaucer Gower	———	Lucrece's rape	———
Phyllis, Demophoon	Chaucer Gower	Demophoon's pledge	Phyllis's espousal	Phyllis's complaint
Pyramus, Thisbe	Chaucer Gower	———	Thisbe's flight	Thisbe's mourning
Virginia	Chaucer Gower	Apius's plot	Virginia's slaying	———
Prologue Prologue	Chaucer Gower	———	———	The poets' prayers.

The commentary under each heading applies to both poets' versions, except in instances of a repeated name—see Jason, Medea under Solitude; ——— indicates the absence of a relevant moment.

The idea of a moment in Table 4 does not refer to a particular instance or episode (although a moment in a tale may appear in only one episode) but to an essential or constituent element in a tale or prologue. The hag's effort to marry and woo Florent recurs in more than one episode; Phyllis's complaint before death is a single apostrophe of considerable force. The episodes in these moments contain speech acts expressed directly or reported, and these, in turn, appear frequently enough to repay statistical analysis, an analysis, too, that helps to demonstrate how performative verbs and verbs in the imperative mood contribute—together with other features of style—to the power of the exemplum as a genre that engaged Chaucer and Gower's audiences. Just how the audiences responded to these moments in the poetry is also an issue that statistical analysis helps to clarify. The discussion that follows examines, to begin, moments of deception in the poetry.

Since Chaucer and Gower's exempla address problematic commitments—the narratives of betrayal, rape, and murder surely exceed those with satisfactory outcomes—the stylistic challenge is to acknowledge the audience's familiarity with the traditional tales (from Ovid and elsewhere) yet to evoke a heightened sense of engagement, a sense that misplaced trust is not merely an old story but is rather always disturbing for human affairs. Chaucer relies on two techniques to bestir his audience. The first is that of narrative commentary, a device that enables him to enlist what the audience already knows of a traditional character's treachery. Together, Chaucer's narrator and the audience join in denouncing the villain of an exemplum, and often the denunciation accompanies the utterance of a speech act. So in *The Legend of Phyllis,* the narrator says of Demophoon,

> For unto Phillis hath he sworen thus,
> To wedden hire, and hire his trouthe plyghte,
> And piked of hire al the good he myghte . . . ,
> (516.2465–67)

a verbal irony few could miss.[6]

The second technique draws the audience to the immediate exchanges between characters in an exemplum. Instead of the narrator's commentary, one hears a Jason or a Tereus swear fidelity and has the opportunity to decide (as if one were a direct participant) how to respond. Typically what colors such instances of immediate exchange, many of them promises, is the presence of adverbial modifiers of time, manner, or condition, each a commonplace yet subtly overstated in a particular context. Thus when Tereus addresses Pandion, promising that his daughter Procne

> ". . . shal come to yow ageyn anon,
> Myself with hyre I wol bothe com and gon,
> And as myn hertes lyf I wol hire kepe,"
> (514.2276–78)

one has both a double commitment to consider—a pledge to escort and to safeguard Philomela—and the force of the vows themselves, whether the adverb of time *anon* "at once" and the adverb of manner *as my hertes lyf* are revealingly excessive.

In Gower's exempla an acknowledgement of the audience's familiarity and a use of immediate exchanges likewise result in instances of commentary and direct address. Since Gower generally does not have his narrator Genius intrude himself upon the exempla presented (as Chaucer's narrator continually does), the commentary often expresses views from within, like those offered by Philomela's parents, who have their reservations about her journeying to Thrace yet feel compelled to honor Tereus' request:

> The fader and the moder bothe
> To leve here douhter weren loth,   [daughter]

> Bot if thei were in presence;   [in attendance]
> And natheles at reverence
> Of him, that wolde himself travaile,
> Thei wolden noght he scholde faile
> Of that he preide, and yive hire leve. . . .
> (99.5.5605–11)

Whereas Chaucer's narrator counts on the audience's accord as he satirically exposes Demophoon, Gower's asks for a reflection on motives—the hypotactic style of the passage presenting the views of Philomela's parents patently encourages a weighing of their thoughts and alternatives. Like Chaucer, Gower has instances of direct address that demand of the audience an attention to the words of a speech act, an evaluation of its integrity. In the tale of Constance, for example, King Allee's mother Domilde forges her son's letter to the royal court and thereby has his retainers suppose that he has commanded his wife's exile:

> I charge you and bidde this,
> That ye the same Schip vitaile,   [victual]
> In which that sche tok arivaile,
> Therinne and putteth bothe tuo,
> Hireself forthwith hire child also,
> And so forth brought unto the depe
> Betaketh hire the See to kepe.
> (158.2.1030–36)

The implicit question here is whether the audience, .. presented such a letter, could have wiser heads than those at Allee's court. The quotation has two performative verbs of command, an adverb of time, *forthwith,* and the colorless adverb of manner *so.* Despite the love of Allee for his queen (evident from the onset of their marriage and the promise of his newly born son), the style of the letter—its direct orders—convinces the court to act.

Now these two techniques of commentary and direct address recur throughout the exempla, usually at the outset of a tale in Gower's poetry, at a climactic moment in Chaucer's. Table 5 records the incidence of speech acts directly addressed or reported in moments of deception.

TABLE 5.   MODES OF ENUNCIATING SPEECH ACTS IN MOMENTS OF DECEPTION

	Direct address	Reported utterances
Chaucer	16	8
Gower	8	10

A chi-square test of the poets' choices yields a significant difference, and so $X^2 = 4.17$, $df = 1$, $p = .05$.[7] This significant difference underscores, moreover, the value of reported utterance and direct address for the poets. Although both present direct address in episodes of duplicitous commitment (fake promises, misleading commands, spurious requests), implying that the abuse of language is hard to detect, Chaucer is especially skillful in his demonstration that the ear cannot reliably tell, even at crucial moments, the genuine from the fraudulent. As for instances of reported utterances, Chaucer has his narrator spurn the villains of the exempla, whereas Gower explores the effects of guile on the generous impulses of decent collaborators. What is more, this statistical result accords with the poets' overall preferences (see Table 3). Thus the pattern of enunciating speech acts directly or by means of report in regard to moments of deception illustrates a specific use of characteristic style. That deception affects the responses of the poets' audiences testifies to one essential use of speech acts in the exempla.

A second moment in the poetry, fully characteristic of *Confessio Amantis* and the *Legend of Good Women*, concerns matters of decision and crisis, particularly those that find women requesting justice or commitment (as in *The Wife of Bath's Tale*) or else facing loss or harm. Some of these moments immediately follow acts of deceptive commitment—as when in *The Legend of Dido* Aeneas's false promise to marry and his sailing for Rome compel Dido's urgent, unmediated appeal:

> "Have mercy! and let me with yow ryde!
> These lordes, which that wonen me besyde,   [dwell]
> Wole me distroyen only for youre sake.
> And, so ye wole me now to wive take,
> As ye han sworn, thanne wol I yeve yow leve   [give you leave]
> To slen me with youre swerd now sone at eve!
> For thanne yit shal I deyen as youre wif.
> I am with childe, and yeve my childe his lyf!
> Mercy, lord! have pite in youre thought!"
> (503–04.1316–24)

Other poignant moments portraying women in distress include Canace's fruitless request that her father Eolus have compassion, despite her incestuous affair with Machaire:

> And sche began merci to crie,
> Upon hire bare knes and preide,
> And to hire fader thus sche seide:
> "Have mercy! fader, thenk I am
> Thi child, and of thi blod I cam.
> That I misdede yowthe it made,

And in the flodes bad me wade,
Wher that I sih no peril tho;
But now it is befalle so,
Merci, my fader, do no wreche!"   [vengeance]
And with that word sche loste speche. . . .
                    (232.3.222–32)

Neither Dido's nor Canace's pleas, both surely meant to win the audience's compassion, succeed in averting catastrophe. Chaucer has Dido remind Aeneas of his sworn word as she utters her requests (the use of the imperative mood heightens the sense of crisis) that he protect her and her child. Indeed the contradictions in her speech contribute to the poignancy of her lot. On the other hand, Gower's presentation of Canace combines almost all the techniques at his command to depict women in distress. He introduces the pleas with the formal gesture "Upon hire bare knees" and couples the performative verb *preide* with the verb *seide*. He has Canace attribute her incest to the bidding of "yowthe," a power whose command she could not refuse. Gower also has her request forgiveness ("do no wreche!") and depicts her loss of speech as she swoons. The force of the rhetoric wins over the audience—who would not help these women?—and also prompts outrage at Aeneas's indifference and at Eolus's cruelty. In such episodes Chaucer and Gower elicit a righteousness born of their audience's strong feelings and decency.

Elsewhere in the exempla the techniques that the poets have for mustering support for women in need correspond quite well with those used for depicting Dido and Canace. Remarkably, Chaucer relies on the imperative mood in legend after legend, in his tale of Custance, and in presenting the Wife of Bath's hag, whose efforts govern her forms of speech before Guenevre's court and in bed with the knight whom she asks to decide what sort of spouse she is to be. The departures from the uses of the verb are also revealing. Threatened by Tarquin, Chaucer's Lucretia like Canace falls silent—"No word she spak" (509.1796)—and then, summoning strength, she "axeth grace and seyth al that she can" (509.1804). Clearly the use of comment rather than the imperative mood is appropriate; that Tarquin has Lucretia by the throat and a sword at her heart makes the indirect allusion to her words harrowing, not melodramatic.

Still another stylistic variant that Chaucer presents in *The Legend of Hypermnestra* is the qualifying of a promise. Confronted by her father Egiste, the newly wed Hypermnestra responds to his demand for full obedience; she tries to accommodate him even as she is mindful of her obligations to her husband:

"Lord and fader, al youre wille,
After my myght, god wot, I shal fulfille,   [knows]
So it to me be no confusioun."
                    (518.2650–51)

The adverbs of condition (the phrase "After my myght," the clause "So it to me be no confusioun") stand as rebukes to the deceptive promises that villains in the exempla make, but what Hypermnestra learns is that integrity has no value for a father bent on his own mad schemes. In sum, of twenty episodes that Chaucer presents of women hoping to withstand antagonism and to maintain their sense of propriety, fourteen contain instances of requests in the imperative mood, and six evidence forms of the performative verb.

Gower makes very little use of the imperative mood, and in no other instance is it as moving as in his account of Canace. Instead, he depends on varieties of description and direct address. The accounts of Lucretia, Thisbe, and Ariadne include their speechlessness or swooning; the suffering of Dido and the death of Virginia each appear in a brief two- or three-line summary. Performative verbs occur in the other moments, including the instructive episode that portrays Florent's wife, who achieves (as Constance also does in her story) some satisfaction. What Gower has the hag show (she is actually the king of Cizile's daughter) is a rhetorical skill that helps her attain her newly wedded husband's love. Even before her metamorphosis from a hag to a lovely princess she requests that Florent spend the night with her—the first step in winning his acquiescence:

> My lord, go we to bedde,
> For I to that entente wedde,
> That thou schalt be my worldes blisse
> (83.1.1769–71)

Directly after, the new bride, still a hag,

> spak and preide,
> And bad him thenke on that he seide,
> Whan that he tok hire to the hond.
> (84.1.1795–97)

From a request in the subjunctive mood which Florent reluctantly fulfills to a summarized series of further requests, this time through the use of performative verbs, Gower prepares his audience's attention for a powerful instance of the bride's persuasiveness. For when Florent turns to find his bride transformed (she encourages him to turn to her) Gower advances their union with a still further use of speech acts:

> And as he wolde have take hir nyh,   [drawn her close]
> Sche put hire hand and be his leve
> Besoghte him that he wolde leve,   [wait]
> And seith that forto wynne or lese
> He mot on of tuo thinges chese,

Wher he wol have hire such on nyht,
Or elles upon daise lyht,
For he schal noght have bothe tuo.
    (84 – 5.1805 – 13)

The performative verb *besoghte* accomplishes two purposes: to restrain the passionate Florent and to have him consider alternatives, neither of them quite desirable. Aroused by his bride, he checks his impulses and complies with her requests. The entire sequence of requests, indeed, is in sum as splendid as it is exceptional in the exempla. Compared to the recurrent failures of women in Gower's other narratives, this episode depicting a woman successful in her requests demonstrates with some deftness the necessary art, even in the instance of approaching an honorable knight. And very likely the women in Gower's audience would have agreed. So, altogether, Gower's sparing use of the imperative and subjunctive mood in these episodes for making requests—five in all—and his array of other techniques, whether or not they include performative verbs—nineteen instances—argues a demonstrable contrast with Chaucer's practices. Table 6 illustrates the difference.

A chi-square test of the poet's choices yields a significant result: $X^2 = 7.75$, $df = 1$, $p = .01$.[8] Moreover, a comparison of results for this moment to the results of Table 9.2 underscores how strongly committed to the use of the imperative mood Chaucer is in the making of requests. Thus the effect of these significantly different practices is that Chaucer emphasizes the urgency in the voice of women, whereas Gower responds diversely to the dilemmas and challenges that women in his exempla face. Surely Canace's plea and the requests of Florent's bride present two extraordinary rhetorical moments in his stories.

Throughout the poems under comparison moments recur of characters entirely alone whose utterances either reveal their steadfastness (as Cleopatra's for Antony, Thisbe's for Pyramus), their distress or betrayal (as Ariadne's, Dido's), or their commitment to the divine (as Custance's, Chaucer's narrator in the Prologue to the *Legend of Good Women*). Seventeen separate examples of such moments appear in Chaucer's poetry, sixteen in Gower's, and in at least half of these each poet includes a request or promise; their practice shows no statistical difference.[9]

The comparability of the poets' use of promises and requests in moments of

TABLE 6. MOMENTS OF FEMININE CHALLENGE AND RISK

	Verbs in the imperative mood	Performative verbs and other expressive elements
Chaucer	14	6
Gower	5	19

isolated speech prompts an effort to determine whether their techniques of presentation are also similar. A review of these passages indicates that the verbs for promising and requesting, in fact, have different effects. Quite often Gower couples verbs such as *preide, makth a vou,* and *bidde* with others in order to introduce passages of characters expressing themselves, whereas Chaucer includes performative verbs directly in their speeches.[10] So to begin Medea's requests to the gods, Gower has "Sche preide, and seide" (48.5.3739); the muted Philomela has her complaint introduced by Gower's remarking, "Thogh sche be mouthe nothing preide, / Withinne hir herte thus sche seide" (103.5.5739–40); Procne, apprised of her sister's fate, "to Venus and Cupide / preide, and furthermor sche cride / Unto Appollo the hiheste, / And seide . . . " (106.5.5843–46). In general, this coupling of verbs to introduce speech in isolation occurs in ten of fifteen instances for Gower, in only five of seventeen for Chaucer (and in none of the introductions does he use a performative verb). Thus, although the poets do not differ significantly in the ratio of passages that have performative verbs, their place in relation to the speeches varies markedly. Table 7 outlines instances of coupled verbs.

A chi-square test of the ratios for coupled verbs, as illustrated above, yields a significant result of $X^2 = 4.43$; $df = 1$, $p = .05$. Now one effect of this coupling, whether or not it includes a specific performative such as *preide* to introduce a passage, is to suggest a frame, as if Gower had as his purpose the setting of a speech for his audience to contemplate.

A passage from the story of Demophoon and Phyllis illustrates Gower's coupling of verbs to create a frame and to present a speech as if it were an inscription for study; in Chaucer's version Phyllis speaks in a manner quite different. In Gower's exemplum, the audience hears Phyllis as she addresses the absent Demophoon, pauses, and then resumes her complaint:

So as sche mihte and evere in on	[was able over and again]
Sche cleped upon Demophon,	[called]
And seide, "Helas, thou slowe wiht,	[person]
Wher was ther evere such a knyht,	
That so thurgh his ungentilesce	
Of Slowthe and of foryetelnesse	[negligence]
Ayein his trowthe brak his stevene?"	[broke his word]
And tho hire yhe up to the hevene	[eyes]

TABLE 7. PATTERNS OF VERBS TO INTRODUCE APOSTROPHES IN MOMENTS OF ISOLATION

	Single verbs	Coupled verbs
Chaucer	12	5
Gower	5	10

Sche caste, and seide, "O thou unkinde,
Hier schall thou thurgh thi Slowthe finde,
If that thee list to come and se,   [you are moved]
A ladi ded for love of thee,
So as I schal myselve spille;
Whom, if it hadde be thi wille,
Thou migtest save wel ynowh."
(324.4.842–55)

The speech begins after the coupling of *clepede* and *seide,* the verbs linked to emphasize an effect of formality, quite like that associated with frames. And, indeed, Phyllis's speech comports with the sense of a formal frame established by the two pair of verbs. As the first part of her complaint ends, her sorrow is quite apparent from the final words "brak his stevene" in the rhetorical question. Demophoon's failure of fidelity, an abrogating of his pledge reported earlier in the exemplum, accounts for her isolation and influences the manner of her complaint. For in the first part, Phyllis's verbs (they are *was* and *brak*) help to suggest a portrait of Demophoon as a figure of negligence—a "slowe wiht, / Where was ther evere such a knyht"—who characteristically abandons his commitments, who against "his trowthe brak his stevene." The second part of the complaint portrays Phyllis as a distraught woman, about to take her life. The verb *finde* in the independent clause has the meaning "perceive," suggesting that just as Phyllis would have Demophoon contemplate her condition, so Gower would have his audience also reflect, also consider her as a victim of neglect or indifference.

Chaucer's presentation of isolated characters who speak out has effects, not of portraiture, but decidedly of action. His presentation of Phyllis's complaint has an unmistakable vibrancy. Whereas Pearsall notes that at his best Gower reveals "the complex meaningfulness of human behavior . . . ," the initial impact of a speech like that designed by Chaucer for Phyllis is to have her voice, as Kiser says, "dominate her own legend." [11] Her letter to Demophoon in Chaucer's version shows this immediacy:

She seyde, "Thy saylis come nat agen,   [sails]
Ne to thy word there is no fey certeyn;   [faith]
But I wot why ye come nat," quod she,
"For I was of my love to yow to fre.
And of the goddes that ye han forswore,
Yif hire vengeaunce falle on yow therfore,
Ye be nat suffisaunt to bere the peyne.
To moche trusted I, wel may I pleyne,
Upon youre lynage and youre fayre tonge,
And on youre teres falsly out yronge.
How coude ye wepe so by craft? quode she.
Now certes, yif ye wol have in memorye,

It oughte be to yow but lyte glorye
To han a sely mayde thus betrayed!   [innocent]
To God," quod she, "preye I, and ofte have prayed,
That it mot be the grettest prys of alle,
And most honour that evere the shal befalle!
And whan thyn olde auncestres peynted be,
In which men may here worthynesse se,
Thanne preye I God thow peynted be also
That folk may rede, forby as they go,
'Lo! this is he, that with his flaterye
Bytraised hat and don hire vileyne
That was his trewe love in thought and dede!' "
                    (516.2518–42)

Although Chaucer's speech for Phyllis is longer than Gower's (in fact, not all of it appears above), the verb *seyde* alone introduces it. And if in Gower's version the effect is that of a portrait, in Chaucer's the use of the performative verb *preye* in Phyllis's complaint is to request that the gods deny Demophoon any honor as great as that she accorded him and that they depict him as an example of scorn for future generations. What is more, Chaucer encourages a sense of dynamic speech both by repeating the verb *quod* three times and by intensifying Phyllis's sense of request in such an expression as "preye I, and ofte have prayed," practices that Gower does not follow. Phyllis's complaint is, then, as Frank says, "not so much about herself and her feelings as about Demophoon—*his* promises, *his* false tears, *his* oaths to the gods." [12] Chaucer's Phyllis is not a model; on the contrary, she is actively imploring the gods to make Demophoon an example of someone to scorn. Thus Chaucer does not couple introductory verbs, as Gower does, to frame complaints such as Phyllis's, but instead uses devices quite his own to encourage a sense of voice, not one preserved from antiquity but one actively engaged with an audience of the fourteenth century. To engage oneself in Phyllis's cause is to close the distance between a figure of antiquity and Chaucer's time.

The three moments chosen from analysis in this essay exhibit both the relation of speech acts to the exemplum as a genre and the value of computational analysis. Clearly, the deceptive uses of speech acts that have catastrophic effects or the efforts of women to realize their desires, and the speech of those who find themselves alone are vital to Chaucer's and Gower's poetry. Performative verbs, utterances in the imperative mood, and their propositions all contribute to the structure of the genre. The linking of the exemplum and speech acts also helps to establish a line of questioning directly applicable to literary analysis, for by requiring a statistical test for claims of correlation concerning speech acts in a genre, one gains some insight into subtle, indispensable attributes of style and structure. The result of examining Chaucer's and Gower's exempla, through the use of speech acts and statistics, provides, in fact, an appreciation that is new. Moreover, the results of statistical analysis enable a sense of how general patterns throughout the exempla (Tables 1, 2, 3) apply to particular moments critical to moral issues (Tables 5, 6, 7).

In this essay, too, the statistical method consistently at work is that of testing hypotheses. The null hypothesis assumes that a test of stylistic difference will show a high degree of comparability in the work of Chaucer and Gower. For Table 9.1 the null hypothesis holds true for the uses of speech acts. Yet the null hypothesis fails to account for the significant results that statistical tests provide of generic moments in the exempla. In regard to moments of deception Gower and Chaucer differ significantly in the use of direct address and reported utterances. The women of Chaucer's exempla, whether distraught or hopeful of achievement, are much more likely to express themselves in the imperative mood (a significant finding) than Gower's women—and this result also has the advantage of placing modes of speech act within a larger array of techniques for depicting a crucial moment in the poetry. On the other hand, the null hypothesis holds true for speech expressed in isolation, inasmuch as the poets use speech acts in comparable ratios. Yet even so, the placing of performative verbs in relation to these acts reveals a significant difference: for Gower's coupling them with other verbs achieves a formal effect of framing quite different from Chaucer's purposes. In short, literary and statistical analyses complement each other and benefit from computational coding, arrangement, and testing.

Finally, these hypotheses are fruitful in illuminating some aspects of aesthetic concern. For Gower, such a concern has to do with the encouraging of reflection, of relating art directly to matters of moral commitment. His exempla invite an audience to weigh the substance of his stories, to have a regard for the commitments made, maintained with some difficulty, often broken. And the power of such reflection, if sufficiently moving, is that it can help to effect reform. Maybe the best instance of Gower's moral aesthetic appears in the *Confessio Amantis,* near the close of the epilogue.

> Homward a softe pas y wente   [I]
> Wher that with al my hol entente
> Upon the point that y am schryve   [confessed]
> I thenke bidde whil y live.
>
> *Parce precor, Criste, populos quo gaudit iste;*
> *Anglia ne triste subeat, rex summe, resiste.*
> *Corrige quosque status, fragiles absolue reatus;*
> *Vnde deo gratus vigeat locus iste beatus.*
>   (467–68.8.2967–70ff.)[13]

The stylistic devices here all reflect practices associated with the foregoing analysis: a performative verb to introduce the Latin prayer, spoken in isolation, the verbs of which are mostly in the imperative mood. Even more, the prayer itself is reflective of Gower's hopes for a reform of spirit, a reform that the exemplum as a genre advocates. As Gower prays that God respond to his request, so he would have his audience do likewise.

In the Prologue to the *Legend of Good Women* Chaucer as narrator prays to his inspiring daisy, whom he serves with whatever "wit or myght" (484.83F) he has. Turning from an audience of lovers to seek her guidance, he says to her,

> The hert in-with my sorwfull brest yow dredeth
> And loveth so sore that ye be verrayly
> The maistresse of my wit, and nothing I.
> My word, my werk ys knyt so in youre bond
> That, as an harpe obeieth to the hond
> And maketh it soune after his fyngerynge,
> Ryght so mowe ye out of myn herte bringe
> Swich vois, ryght as yow lyst, to laughe or pleyne.
> Be ye my gide and lady sovereyne!
> As to myn erthly god to yow I calle,
> Bothe in this werk and in my sorwes alle.
> (484.86–96F)

The attributes of this passage are plainly Chaucerian. Chaucer has no performative verb like Gower's *bidde* to introduce a prayer, no matter how formal it is. Instead the verb *calle* at the close emphasizes his dedication. In the prayer, too, the clause "My word, my werk ys knyt so in youre bond" reaffirms rather than constitutes a speech act that he soon after expresses in the mood of the imperative: "Be ye my gide and lady sovereyne!" The force of this prayer, moreover, as Peck argues, "is a celebration of the imagination. Imagination operates on two levels. [Chaucer's] initial response is to the daisy's beauty, which he intuits enthusiastically. But what strikes him more than its surface beauty is its operative beauty or the *way* it imitates the sun. He loves most of all to see *how* the daisy behaves, *how* it deliberates." [14]

In the act of observing his muse, in imagining her acts, Chaucer also displays an aesthetic of verbal acts as he re-creates from his Ovidian and other sources. For in the shaping of his art he manifests a fidelity of spirit that in itself is an act of moral commitment. Thus, if Gower shapes his exempla as a public poet who implicitly urges self-reflection as an appropriate response for his audience, Chaucer reveals what the act of artistic creation as a commitment means. This difference in the poets' mode of imagination results, as the statistical analysis helps to show, in complementary perceptions: Gower invites his readers to contemplate the morality of antiquity as vital to them; Chaucer's art supposes that moral passions expressed by women of the past can find convincing expression in four-teenth-century England.

Notes

1. J. A. Burrow, *Ricardian Narrative* (New Haven, Conn.: Yale University Press, 1971), 91, says that "the meaning of an 'ensample' depends not on its content but on the variable 'entente' of the people who use it. Alceste dismisses this very Chaucerian argument rather impatiently ('Lat be thyn arguynge'), and demands, as a 'penance,' simply that Chaucer write about women who, unlike Criseyde, were faithful in love. Thus she dictates the content of the Legends, but leaves the poet free in the critical matter of 'entente.'" Burrow's statement of faithfulness, whether or not a lover's commitments are sincere, implies forms of expression that correspond to speech acts. Yet not every instance of a speech act throughout the course of an exemplum has immediate significance for its governing ideas or intentions.

2. Burrow, 82, includes the *Legend of Good Women* and *Confessio Amantis* as collections that "illustrate in story or *exemplum* some truth or concept concerning human life and conduct," topics that count prudence as a virtue. Although *The Man of Law's Tale, The Physician's Tale,* and *The Wife of Bath's Tale* have other generic properties, they, too, have meanings and intentions that fall within the spirit of the exemplum. D. W. Robertson, Jr., in *A Preface to Chaucer* (Princeton, N.J.: Princeton University Press, 1962), 276, says that in *The Canterbury Tales* the narrators' recital and interpretations "contribute to the thematic development of . . . [the poem] as a whole. This rather subtle arrangement is made possible by the fact that the tales have an exemplary force."

3. Chaucer has two narratives, "The Legend of Cleopatra" and "The Legend of Hypermnestra," for which Gower has no comparable analogue. For the purposes of this study two other exempla—Gower's "Tale of Albinus and Rosemund" and "The Tale of Canace and Machaire" (each very little longer than Chaucer's poems)—have their speech acts included.

4. The shared heritage of the poems under comparison include the Ovidian Pyramus and Thisbe, Jason and Medea (Chaucer also has a legend of Hypsipyle), Tarquin and Lucrece, Theseus and Ariadne, Tereus and Philomela, Demophoon and Phyllis. From Livy's history Chaucer and Gower take the story of Virginia; from Nicholas Trivet's *Anglo-Norman Chronicle* (ca. 1335) they draw their stories of Custance; and the story of Florent (Chaucer's knight is anonymous) has its roots in folklore, its immediate sources unknown. Geoffrey Chaucer, *The Works of Geoffrey Chaucer,* ed. F. N. Robinson, 2nd ed. (Boston: Houghton Mifflin, 1957), 692, 702–03, 727, 847–53, outlines the sources of each tale or legend. John Gower, *Confessio Amantis,* ed. Russell A. Peck (Toronto: University of Toronto Press, 1980), 494–523 has full bibliographic detail.

5. Burrow, 82.

6. Citations, like that for the lines quoted, differ for the poetry of Chaucer and Gower. For Chaucer's work the page numbers appear before a period, line numbers after. For Gower's work page numbers appear first, book numbers after the first period, line numbers after the second period. The Robinson edition has the texts of Chaucer for this study; for Gower the work used is John Gower, *John Gower's English Works,* ed. G. C. Macaulay, 2 vols. (London: Kegan Paul, Trench, Trubner, 1900).

7. Two moments of deceptive promising in Chaucer's poetry are neither commentary nor direct address but instances of a narrated exchange: 146.142–46 and 507.1635–50. Since these two resemble most instances of direct address, they appear with that group. Even if these are deleted from the sample, the results are significant: $X^2 = 3.12$, $df = 1$, $p = .05$ in a one-tail nest (the direction depends on the significant pattern established by

Table 3.). Listed for Gower under direct address is 41.5.3456–61, also an instance of indirect speech, not direct address.

8. Gower's "Go we to bed" contains a verb in the subjunctive mood that closely resembles in function verbs in the imperative mood that are used for making requests. So for this analysis "go" contributes to the count for verbs in the imperative mood in Table 9.6.

9. Since moments may comprise more than one episode in a tale, it is worthwhile identifying their occurrences. Passages of Chaucerian characters, in isolation, expressing themselves:

Promises or requests		Other purposes of speech	
67.449–62	499.890–912	71.811–9	516.2495–512
69.638–44	506.1567–68	71.825–33	518.2689–705
71.844–61	506.1571–75	499.832–40	504.1354–65
484.84–96	513.2211–17	507.1672–77	
497.681–95	516–7.2518–54		

Passages of Gower's characters, in isolation, expressing themselves:

Promises or requests	Other purposes of speech
233.3279–306;204.4.114–15	148.2 643–49
204.4.114–15;158–59.1057–76	265.3.1429–33
158–59.2.1057–76;48–49.5.3738–40	266.3.1459–81
48.49.5.3738–40;55.5.3978–86	324.4.849–55
55.5.3978–86;95.5.5444–61	103.4.5.5787–68
103.5.5739–52;105–6.5816–41	
106.5.5844–60;446–48.8.2224–2300	
467–68.8.2966–70ff.	

10. The following list indicates Gower's coupling of performative verbs throughout his exempla (Chaucer has nothing quite comparable):

Requests

151.2.760–62 (criende, bad, preide, seide);
232.3.222–24 (began to crie, preide, seide);
46.5.3650–51 (besoghte, seide);
48.5.3739 (preide, seide)
55.5.3977–83 (clepe, calle, preide, hield up, crie, seide);
100.5.5634 (began to crie and preie);
103.5.5739–40 (preide, seide);
105.5.5820 (preide, seide);
106.5.5844–46 (preide, cride, seide).

11. Derek Pearsall, *Gower and Lydgate,* ed. Geoffrey Bullough (Harlow, Essex: Longmans, Green, 1969), 18. Lisa J. Kiser, *Telling Classical Tales: Chaucer and the Legend of Good Women* (Ithaca, N.Y.: Cornell University Press, 1983), 121–22.

12. Robert Worth Frank, Jr., *Chaucer and the Legend of Good Women* (Cambridge, Mass.: Harvard University Press, 1972), 153. It is worth noting that part of the intensity in the speech Chaucer designs for Phyllis derives from the choice and spacing of verbs. Chaucer has her begin with a verb and complement *is no fey,* a preparation for a shift to the present perfect tense *han forswore* (in a short relative clause) that becomes a part of a

perfective infinitive clause *To han a sely mayde thus betrayed* before introducing the performative verbs in "To God . . . preye I, and ofte have prayed. . . ." This sequence from a stative verb to the perfect tense, to a present active indicative form, itself reinforced, dramatizes a good part of the verbal attack that Phyllis mounts before turning upon herself and concluding that her drowning will not move a Demophoon, hard as stone.

13. Peck, 522, has the English, prepared by Alfred Geier, for the following quotation: "Spare, I beg, O Christ, this people's joy; resist England's grievous demise, O highest King. Set right all conditions and rank, set free those weakly accused; then this land, pleasing to God, will grow strong and blessed."

14. Russell A. Peck, "Chaucerian Poetics and the Prologue to the *Legend of Good Women*," in *Chaucer in the Eighties*, ed. J. N. Wasserman and R. J. Blanche (Syracuse, N.Y.: Syracuse University Press, 1986), 45.

>> 10

Gender Patterns
in Henry James:

A Stylistic Approach to Dialogue in Daisy Miller, The Portrait of a Lady, and The Bostonians

EUNICE MERIDETH

The impetus for Henry James to explore the role of the "American girl" lies in his concern about the rigid constraint of social roles in late nineteenth-century America. Disenchanted with the American male focus on business and money, he considered the "situation of women, the decline of the sentiment of sex, and agitation on their behalf the most salient and peculiar point in our social life" (Matthiessen, xvii). The precursor of the feminist character, James's "American girl" emerges as an eager young woman who develops her own personality by struggling against the restrictions of society. For James, she was the American spirit following the Civil War—freedom-loving and adventurous, chafing at the rules by which society allowed adventure and defined freedom. Such a woman and the man who interacts with her provide a rich rhetorical field for analysis of male and female roles and definitions.

This study approaches that field through computational stylistics, analyzing one medium of James's message—his characters' language—in order to identify the difference in rhetorical patterns of style used in creating male and female characters in *Daisy Miller, The Portrait of a Lady,* and *The Bostonians.* The analysis of these stylistic gender patterns is accomplished by investigating the "primary rhetoric" of fictional characters using variables which have rhetorical implications in writing and speaking and which are easily identifiable: questions, imperatives, exclamations, pauses, fragments, conditionals, definitions, negatives, universals, adverbs, and comparisons. By focusing on a rhetorical unit (dialogue) that is clearly defined, the context as well as the content of a character's speech may be studied to determine how stylistic structure defines character. What is said is certainly significant, but how it is said is a direct function of style. From the perspective of gender, then, the study of stylistic patterns poses two important questions: What effect does the syntax of a character have on his/her definition as male or female, heroine or hero? Are male characters empowered by their speech characteristics while female characters are undercut by the speech characteristics they are assigned?

The stylistic devices explored herein do not include all the components of style in the classical sense. Rather, they are the syntactic and semantic variables that make up COMP STYLE, a package of computer programs designed by Rosanne G. Potter of Iowa State University. The COMP STYLE package provides for text entry, text segmentation, sorting, counting, and printing. The results offer an accurate identification and classification of simple syntax that may be applied to the language of speakers. COMP STYLE also contains programs for statistical analysis. These functions of COMP STYLE are not employed in this study, however, because of the relatively small size of this sample.

The important numerical distinction in this study lies in the difference between the actual variable usage and the variable usage that can be projected from total dialogue. In this case, the best statistical method for deciding significance is the chi-square "goodness of fit" test—a statistical test which determines whether the distribution of the frequencies across a set of categories differs from a set of expected frequencies. There are two conditions necessary for this type of test to be valid: all items must be independent of each other (they must appear in one and no more than one of the cells), and no item must be counted more than once. In this study, the eleven variable programs are run independently of one another but on the same data set. Therefore, the two conditions for validity in the chi-square tests are met as long as each variable is tested individually.

The statistical significance of variables established by the "goodness of fit" test is one point from which the investigation of important differences in stylistic usage can begin. However, while numbers that denote variable usage and significance are important pieces of evidence that confirm or refute critical interpretation, they are also indicators that need careful evaluation. For example, the difference between Daisy's and Winterborne's observed frequency of questions in *Daisy Miller* is significant at the .10 level, but if the frequency scores differed by only 1, the results would be significant at the .05 level. Further, critical significance is affected by the role the characters are thematically assigned to play—a factor for which numbers cannot account. Examining the content of a variable file, therefore, adds depth and validity to the interpretation of a variable which a study of the numbers alone cannot supply.

Potter explains how the assignment of variables specific to COMP STYLE helps define character: "My theory is that our judgments and expectations about characters are causally related to the syntactic choices made by playwrights" ("Toward a Syntactic Differentiation," 187). The dialogue in plays, the subject of Potter's study, differs from the dialogue in novels in that playwrights communicate with their audiences chiefly through the dialogue of their characters. Whereas fictional characters, like characters in a drama, can be said to define themselves to others largely through their speech, they are also a product of the narration surrounding their speech. This study, however, intentionally focuses on the "primary rhetoric" of the characters—their dialogue. I apply Potter's programs and methods to the speech of James's characters to identify any rhetorical patterns of style that emerge from James's choices in constructing dialogue. This is obviously an exploratory study: it does not present a wide cross-section of James's characters and works; it does, however, offer a unique approach to a representative sample of male and female characters in thematically related texts.

Besides their obvious value as classics, these particular works by James lend insight into any gender study because they focus on the plight of his "American girl." All the novels present a female character who may be labeled a "new woman" of the late nineteenth century. This type of woman is the precursor of contemporary feminist characters. All the novels feature a woman as the protagonist and deal with the power of money and the power of men and women in society. All the novels outline the same basic plot: a young woman comes to challenge the restrictions placed on her gender, but is unsuccessful and is eventually sacrificed or suppressed. In addition, these three novels illustrate James's progression from his early work, *Daisy Miller,* through his middle work. Including his "masterpiece," *The Portrait of a Lady,* and the work that he designated as his last "American girl" novel, *The Bostonians* (Eakin, 195). Following *The Bostonians,* James felt that he had exhausted the possibilities of this character; he was not to visit his "American girl" again until late in his career in *The Wings of the Dove* and *The Golden Bowl.*

DAISY MILLER

An immediate literary success, Daisy Miller was, in Henry James's own words, a character of "pure poetry" (*The Art of the Novel,* 270). Hers was a charm enhanced by physical beauty and innocent playfulness. Her charm was flawed, however, by a lack of mature and intelligent judgment—a flaw associated with childhood that relegated her to the perpetual position of "girl." Elizabeth Allen observes that "The most intelligent of James's women survive by learning and understanding the world of social codes and forms by using language—that primary means of signifying—with consummate skill" (43). Daisy does not learn

TABLE 1.   NUMERICAL RESULTS IN *DAISY MILLER*

	Daisy			Winterborne			
	Obv	Exp	Cell	Obv	Exp	Cell	Chi-square
Ques	42	50.55	1.28	41	32.45	2.00	3.28*
Imp	15	16.44	.05	12	10.56	.08	.13
Excl	76	62.12	2.88	26	39.88	4.49	7.37***
Paus	21	18.27	.27	9	11.73	.42	.69
Frag	3	4.25	.13	4	2.74	.21	.34
Cond	17	15.23	.11	8	9.78	.17	.28
Def	116	121.19	.18	83	77.81	.28	.46
Neg	128	120.58	.40	70	77.42	.62	1.02
Univ	29	22.53	1.58	8	14.47	2.46	4.04**
Adv	21	30.45	2.63	29	19.55	4.10	6.73***
Comp	3	3.65	.01	3	2.35	.01	.02

Percentage of Dialogue: Daisy = 60.9%; Winterborne = 39.1%

* = critical significance to the .1 level.
** = critical significance to the .05 level.
*** = critical significance to the .01 level.

or accept the European social codes and forms, so Daisy does not survive. Her failure to control, her very uncertainty, can be illustrated by the variable usage in her syntax.

Following is an illustration of the computer's searching and sorting by variable for *Daisy Miller*. Table 1 depicts the numerical results, listing the observed frequency of variable use, the expected frequency of variable use, and the statistical significance of the difference between the two frequencies. A character (such as Daisy) with 60.9 percent of the total dialogue, for example, would have an expected frequency of 50.55 questions, 60.9 percent of the total questions. Daisy's observed frequency of question use, however, is 42. With her ability to question weakened, Daisy is reinforced in her social role as the more submissive character—the one who is questioned. As the character who has a larger frequency of questions than was expected, Winterborne exhibits an aura of authority as the one who questions, the one who demands an explanation.

The variables in Table 1 are arranged in order to conform to earlier studies by Potter indicating that questions, imperatives, exclamations, pauses, fragments, and conditionals are "reliable and independent measures of difference between characters" ("Reader Responses," 65). A dominant character, for example, will exhibit a high use of questions, definitions, and imperatives, a low use of fragments. Other variables in the order—definitions, negatives, universals, adverbs, and comparisons—are variables that all offer unique ways of "defining." Through such variables, characters can say what "things" or people are, what they are not, what they are like, or how they are like something, establishing both definition and motivation for action.

Table 1 illustrates the syntax of a young woman who does not use the language of dominance. Daisy has a low use of questions and definitions. She is also assigned variables which, in this study, reveal excitability and uncertainty: exclamations and conditionals. Winterborne's syntax is another story. His syntactical usage clearly establishes dominance in language: a high use of questions and definitions as well as a higher use of imperatives. The questioning a character employs affects dominance because questions are linguistic strategies that are related to corresponding answers. Suzanne Langer has reported that "the way a question is formed determines in part the answer that can be given" (Spender, 7). A rhetorical question, for example, does not require an answer but simply emphasizes an idea with which the addressee can be expected to agree. A direct question, on the other hand, requires an answer but may be submissive (May I please go?) or accusative (Did I not tell you to go?). Winterborne typically asks aggressive questions that demand acquiescence or justification: "Couldn't you get some one to stay—for the afternoon—with Randolph?" ("Daisy Miller," 278). "And what is the evidence you have offered?" (297). "Do you mean to speak to that man?" (300). "Why the devil did you take her to that fatal place?" (321). Winterborne seeks an explanation and exhibits power by holding the person questioned accountable to him personally.

Daisy's questions, on the other hand, seek information or are coy: "Have you been to that old castle?" (277). "But did you really mean what you said just now: that you would like to go up?" (278). "You won't back out?" (279). "Did you ever hear anything so quaint?" (297). The difference between Daisy's and Winterborne's questions, however, is not just a difference of tone. Ferenc Kiefer explains that "the meaning of a question is the set of all its true answers" (1). The "yes-no" question that Daisy uses contains only two propositions, one the negation of the other. Winterborne's questions are more complicated: they go beyond the simple two-proposition question by demanding an account of another's behavior, thereby assuming the power to judge.

The possession of power can also be registered through imperatives, statements which issue commands or give directions. According to Bennison Gray, "Imperatives imply existence of powerful forces or standards" (62). Certainly in literary discourse the imperative implies power—the power to give an order or state what "should be." For example, Daisy's use of imperatives delineates the line of power in her family as ten of her fifteen imperatives are directed to Randolph, her mother, and Eugenio. She is most aggressive with her younger brother: "You had better wait till you are asked" (272). "Ask him his name" (274).

Toward Winterborne, Daisy is more subtle and couches her imperatives in a flattering manner: "Do wait over till Friday, and I will go down to the landing and see her arrive" (292). "Tell me if Mr. Giovanelli is the right one" (301). In both of the latter examples, Daisy wants a response from Winterborne but does not have the power to direct that response. She must therefore mask her directive in a polite structure and attempt to gain indirectly that which she cannot order outright. On the other hand, Daisy's last request is both direct and made more dramatic by the use of a double imperative, revealing the importance of the message to the dying girl. She orders her mother, *"Mind* you *tell* Mr. Winterborne" (320).

Winterborne's imperatives are notable because they all direct action and imply judgment. He again expresses his authority over Daisy (an authority established by virtue of being male) when he asserts, "You certainly won't leave me" (300). "Pray understand, then, that I intend to remain with you" (300). He feels he knows best and uses the imperative form to try to control Daisy's behavior: "Don't do that" (309). "I should advise you to drive home as fast as possible and take one" (319). Moreover, his last words to Daisy are expressed as a negative imperative: he conceals his real concern and expresses doubt about her seriousness with a single command: "Don't forget Eugenio's pills" (319). Winterborne's imperative usage assumes a position of power over both Daisy and Eugenio that intersects gender and social class.

Whereas questions and imperatives can indicate power or strength, exclamations that reveal strength of emotion may also create an impression of weakness. The exclamation variable is an important part of James's strategy in *Daisy Miller* as it appears in 17% of the sentences used. In addition, the difference in exclamatory usage between the two characters is statistically significant to the .01 level.

Among the three heroines studied, Daisy has the highest usage of exclamations, including "gossipy" rejoinders such as: "Well, I declare!" (295) and "Gracious Me!" (298, 303). Another use of the exclamation by Daisy occurs in three separate incidents, in a "building" pattern when she is trying to get Winterborne to do or believe something. Daisy uses eleven exclamations when she wants "a little fuss" (289) about a boat ride, nine when she is defending her friendship with Giovanelli to Winterborne, and six when she is discovered at night in the Colosseum. In all three incidents, her closing exclamation—her parting shot—starts with "well": "Well, I hope it won't keep you awake!" (289). "Well, then—I am not!" (316). "Well, I have seen the Colosseum by moonlight!" (319). This reoccurring exclamatory pattern, coupled with her immediate exit, makes her seem like a petulant child whose exclamations can be dismissed as immature behavior—temper tantrums that trivialize the seriousness of the later consequences.

Winterborne's use of the exclamation is much less frequent, but the content is stronger. He uses the structure to curse: "Damn his good looks!" (301). "The servants be hanged!" (305). The exclamation is also used to stress an important point that the reader should note: "I suspect, Mrs. Walker, that you and I have lived too long at Geneva!" (305). Winterborne's low use of this variable is consistent with his portrayal as a calm, controlled person. When Winterborne uses an exclamation, he is expressing frustration, an emotional reaction that he, a man "born of winter," normally avoids.

Daisy's high use of exclamations does not in itself make her a weak or flighty character. There is an important distinction in recognizing a difference "between" two characters as opposed to a difference "from" a strong character. Winterborne's manner should not be the standard against which Daisy is judged. She defines him, after all, as "stiff as an umbrella" (316). Rhetorical strength does not require the absence of emotion but the control of emotion.

Female characters in James's fiction usually exhibit stormy emotions as well as a hidden fund of willpower. In a limited sense, these emotions contribute to a stereotypic female "power" because males are not often considered emotional. However, in a recent study of the perceptions of female and male speech, Cheris Kramer demonstrates that emotional and enthusiastic forms of speech, stereotyped as "female" characteristics, are not valued: "When they are combined with the other perceived traits of female speech, that mode of delivery appears ineffectual" (159).

Power gained through emotion becomes self-defeating for James's Daisy Miller when, by expressing emotion, she appears to lose self-control, to be easily overcome. While excitability through exclamatory structure is a way for Daisy to force others to become more aware of her interests, it also is a characteristic that gives the impression of being less logical, less intelligent, and less able to make decisions. Daisy's story is supported, but her role is subordinated in this manner by her syntax and the signals that her syntax sends. Carol Pearson and Katherine Pope explain how Daisy's lack of strength affects the female:

> James's story [*Daisy Miller*] is conventionally (and rightly) interpreted as a study in the deleterious effects of American innocence. But it is also a specifically *female* innocence—in Daisy and her mother. Daisy Miller does not want the protected life of the conventional woman, but she has been given neither the knowledge or the strength to deal with the world on her own. . . . James's novel might discourage unconventional behavior in women, as it reinforces the idea that women who deviate from cultural norms die. (110)

The linguistic weakness in Daisy's questions and exclamations mirror the lack of knowledge and strength that Pearson and Pope find in her action.

All the variables collected in this study do not contribute equally to character differentiation, but they all offer insight. Consider the signals that Daisy's and Winterborne's adverb use send. Daisy's adverbs are often repetitive and negative. She uses "dreadfully" four times, "awfully" twice, as well as "fearfully," and "disagreeably." Her positive adverbs are assigned to Giovanelli: "He's tremendously clever" (298), and "He's perfectly lovely" (298).

Winterborne's adverbs are both positive and assertive. He uses "certainly" four times, "wonderfully" twice, as well as "earnestly," "happily," "perfectly," "absolutely," "evidently," "intellectually," and "exactly." His adverb

usage signals confidence; Daisy's signals insecurity. Emotionality and polite social deference in Daisy's dialogue further compound her insecure signals so that
neither the character nor her message is taken seriously. Whereas Daisy scan-
dalizes society with her unconventional behavior, her syntax models the conventional linguistic stereotype—the submissive female. Daisy is, therefore, a heroine
sent forth on a mission to challenge cultural norms but without the verbal means
of success.

THE PORTRAIT OF A LADY

Like Daisy Miller, Isabel Archer sets out on a social adventure in an unfamiliar
culture. Isabel, however, enjoys more personal development and independence
than Daisy; her syntax reflects these qualities. Of the four males who revolve
around her, I have chosen to compare Isabel's dialogue with Ralph Touchett's
because he becomes her mentor, provider, and judge and is the only male who
appears throughout the book. Isabel's and Ralph's observed and expected frequencies of variable usage, based on percentage of total dialogue (Isabel, 66%,
Ralph, 34%), are depicted in Table 2.

"In the language of *The Portrait of a Lady,*" Elizabeth Allen finds "the more
powerful subjects are those who watch, observe, and spectate" (59). Ralph, the
major spectator, assumes a passive role, yet his influence is all the more powerful
because of its subtlety. Ralph sets up the canvas and attempts to construct a portrait of the lady he wishes Isabel to become through his use of imperatives and
definitions.

TABLE 2. NUMERICAL RESULTS IN *THE PORTRAIT OF A LADY*

	Isabel			Ralph			
	Obv	Exp	Cell	Obv	Exp	Cell	Chi-square
Ques	309	304.92	.04	153	157.08	.08	.12
Imp	100	109.56	.75	66	56.44	1.45	2.20
Excl	139	144.54	.18	79	74.46	.22	.40
Paus	141	154.44	1.08	93	79.56	2.11	3.19*
Frag	13	13.20	.00	7	6.80	.00	.00
Cond	126	114.84	.99	48	59.16	1.92	2.91*
Def	639	650.76	.20	347	335.24	.38	.58
Neg	782	732.60	3.26	328	337.40	6.34	9.60***
Univ	125	132.00	.32	75	68.00	.62	.94
Adv	221	244.20	2.11	149	125.80	4.10	6.21**
Comp	12	20.46	3.10	19	10.54	6.01	9.11***

Percentage of Dialogue: Isabel = 66%; Ralph = 34%

* = critical significance to the .1 level.
** = critical significance to the .05 level.
*** = critical significance to the .01 level.

By assigning the higher proportion of definition use of Ralph, James gives him the power to explain, to present alternatives, to offer guidance—in short, to be the major source of wisdom: "I call people rich when they're able to meet the requirements of their imaginations" (*The Portrait of a Lady,* 158). "Yes, but everything is relative: one ought to feel one's relation to things—to others" (286). "There's nothing makes us feel so much alive as to see others die" (469). "Dear Isabel, life is better: for in life there's love" (470). In these few passages, one can trace the plot of *The Portrait of a Lady* and see James's "observer" carefully, patiently explaining the lessons to be learned, not only to Isabel, but to the reader as well.

For Isabel, the definition is a more personal structure, focusing on "I am." According to Tony Tanner, "James has so selected and arranged his realistic data . . . that Isabel's journey is also an analogue of the journey of the inquiring self seeking realization and identity" (68). Isabel is not so much interested in defining the world she journeys through as in finding her place in that world. Her self-conscious search for that identity is present in her speech: "Very likely: I'm affected by everything" (90). "It's not only that, but I'm not sure I wish to marry any one" (98). "I'm absorbed in myself—I look at life too much as a doctor's prescription" (189). "I'm rather ashamed of my plans: I make a new one every day" (222).

Isabel's internal journey peaks in the fireside scene of chapter 42. After that point, her definitions of self change: "I'm very sure of that" (381). "I'm not an angel of any kind" (393). "Yes. I'm wretched" (399). "No, I'm not simple enough" (442). Isabel has come to know herself, her husband, and, most importantly, her limited realm of possibilities. James himself in his *Notebooks* defines Isabel as "that poor girl, who has dreamed of freedom and nobleness, who has done, as she believes [sic] a generous, natural, clear-sighted thing, finds herself in reality ground in the very mill of convention" (15). James assigns his own words to Ralph when he defines Isabel thus: "You wanted to look at life for yourself—but you were not allowed: you were punished for your wish. You were ground in the very mill of convention" (470).

The author's voice is also present in Ralph's use of the imperatives which he uses to encourage and philosophize: "Don't question your conscience so much—it will get out of tune like a strummed piano" (189). "Spread your wings, rise above the ground" (189). "Judge people as critics, however, and you'll condemn them all" (211). "And remember this, that if you've been hated you've also been loved" (471). The authority inherent in the imperative structure supports Ralph's wisdom, which arises from his experience and ability to observe.

Isabel's imperatives change tone to reflect her favor with a character. With Ralph, she is charming and polite: "Imagine one belonging to an English class!" (58). "Pray do; but I don't say I shall always think your remonstrance just" (67).

"By no means, you're very tired: you must go home and go to bed" (133). Ralph's opinion is very important to her, so she qualifies her directions so that she does not give offense, a stereotypic female strategy. Her reluctance to direct Ralph leaves him free to ignore her imperatives—which he does. Robin Lakoff explains this linguistic phenomenon: "For surely we listen with more attention the more strongly and forcefully someone expresses opinions, and a speaker unable—for whatever reason—to be forceful in stating his views, is much less likely to be taken seriously" (51).

Isabel's interaction with Casper Goodwood exemplifies Lakoff's theory. She seriously wants him to leave, so she employs a more forceful tone: "Think of me or not, as you find most possible: only leave me alone" (136). "Well then, as you have companions in misfortune, make the best of it" (139). "Don't be an infant!" (140). Her rejection of Goodwood mellows with experience, however. Her final dismissal, also accomplished with imperatives, has intense emotional content but none of the anger and sting of earlier scenes: "Do me the greatest kindness of all" (481). "As you love me, as you pity me, leave me alone" (482). When Isabel recognizes Goodwood as an important and potentially dangerous force in her life, her imperatives lose their commanding tone, and she reverts to an inoffensive pleading.

Helping to set the larger tone of the work, negatives reveal the attitude of the characters. The highest usage of this variable (significant to the .01 level) is assigned to Isabel, a fact that confirms H. Lee Gershuny's findings of negativity in females: "The female stereotype is negative and inferior by definition. . . . Behavior described in a man as assertive is described in a woman as pushy, bitchy, or castrating" (55). Moreover, it is the female who is punished by society for her repudiation of cultural norms.

Isabel expresses her feelings of inferiority as she uses the negative: "I don't know—I can't judge" (29). "I haven't the least idea" (35). But she also recognizes that her early opportunities arise from what she is NOT: "I'm not in my first youth" (141). "I've neither father nor mother: I'm poor and of a serious disposition: I'm not pretty" (141). "I'm therefore not bound to be timid and conventional; indeed I can't afford such luxuries" (141). What freedom she has occurs because the social conventions of family, age, and physical beauty have been negated. "Yet the central irony of the novel emerges," Virginia C. Fowler states, "from the discrepancy between the high expectations of Isabel held by her friends and herself and the actual powerlessness that inheres in her simply being a woman" (66).

Isabel feels guilty for refusing Warburton and Goodwood, guilty that Ralph does not share her good health, and accepts marriage even as she recognizes that it is, for her, a negative state. Ralph warns her that in accepting marriage to Osmond, "You're going to be put into a cage" (282). But she replies, "If I like my cage, that needn't trouble you" (282). Fowler notes that "Though Isabel has at this moment no understanding of how little to her liking will be the particular cage that marriage to Osmond will provide her, she registers no surprise or outrage at Ralph's prediction" (69). Syntactically, she does not use her negatives to deny the charges but rather to suppress Ralph's reaction and rationalize what she recognizes to be true. Moreover, once she has accepted the social restrictions of the convention of marriage, even her negative freedom is lost.

Trapped and isolated, Isabel confides her desolation through negatives: "I don't know what great unhappiness might bring me to; but it seems to me I shall always be ashamed" (400). The very social conventions that she thought of as "luxuries" now control her identity. She cannot denounce her husband because in doing so she would negate her life and her choice: "I don't like him. But that's enough; I can't announce it on the housetops. I can't publish my mistake. I don't think that's decent" (400). Again, we see a stylistic pattern emerging: the restless but ultimately submissive female reinforced in that role by syntax that is stereotypically inhibiting.

THE BOSTONIANS

The properties of speech are especially important in *The Bostonians* because James's heroine of this work, Verena, is, by trade and talent, a public speaker. Although Olive is also a strong female character in this book and a fascinating study in her own right, Verena is the pivotal figure. Further, James named Verena as the heroine when he indicated to his brother William that, in lieu of a better title, he might have to call the book "*Verena: The Heroine*" (Matthiessen, xvii).

Verena as a heroine, however, lacks the personal appeal of Daisy or the self-realization of Isabel. She is closely identified with the social movement for women's rights, but her syntax does not reveal the variable strength we might expect from a character who has "the gift of expression" ("The Bostonians," 493). Following is Table 3, which plots both Verena's and Basil's observed and expected frequencies based on their respective percentage of dialogue (Verena, 47%; Basil, 53%).

Like Ralph in *The Portrait of a Lady*, Verena affects a passive role, but she does not act as the artist, as observer and judge. She is at once a receptacle and reflection of others' ideas: she acts through the direction of any strong personality. Her role as a woman's advocate is hampered both by the lack of dominant syntax and by the high usage of exclamations and conditionals in her personal speech. As her father's and later Olive's spokeswoman, she gives moving lectures, but without strength in her own language she is not in herself a strong personality.

TABLE 3. NUMERICAL RESULTS IN *THE BOSTONIANS*

	Verena			Basil			
	Obv	**Exp**	**Cell**	**Obv**	**Exp**	**Cell**	**Chi-square**
Ques	99	136.77	10.16	192	154.23	9.01	19.17***
Imp	28	30.55	.14	37	34.45	.12	.26
Excl	129	106.69	4.52	98	120.31	3.95	8.47***
Paus	113	96.82	2.54	93	109.18	2.26	4.80**
Frag	7	7.52	.00	6	5.48	.00	.00
Cond	76	56.87	6.10	45	64.13	5.41	11.51***
Def	223	224.19	.00	254	252.81	.00	.00
Neg	244	237.37	.70	261	267.65	.14	.84
Univ	85	70.03	2.99	64	78.97	2.65	5.64**
Adv	92	85.54	.42	90	96.46	.37	.79
Comp	26	21.15	.90	19	23.85	.79	1.69

Percentage of Dialogue: Verena = 47%; Basil = 53%

* = critical significance to the .1 level.
** = critical significance to the .05 level.
*** = critical significance to the .01 level.

Basil, on the other hand, is absolute to the point of arrogance. His syntax pattern does indeed confirm a position of strength with the high use of questions and a higher use of imperatives and definitions. Basil's contempt for the feminist movement is evident in his questions. He does not seek information to counter his ignorance. He demands to know how any intelligent person can be involved in the woman's movement and trivializes such interest: "Do you mean your sister's a roaring radical?" (426). "Do you really believe all that pretty moonshine you talked last night?" (486). "What do they care for you but to gape and grin and babble?" (740).

In addition, Basil uses the question in a contradictory manner first to suggest that women have great power and then to suggest that the woman's movement is powerless. "The Abolitionists brought it on [the Civil War] and were not the Abolitionists principally females?" (487). "Do you think any movement is going to stop that—or all the lectures from now to doomsday?" (507). Obviously, Basil believes that women who have the power to start a war do not need a movement.

Verena's questions, on the other hand, seek approval through a "tag" structure that betrays uncertainty: "You would stay if you liked it, wouldn't you?" (516). "And didn't feel the want of a vote to-day at all, did you?" (535). "They trust me, they trust me, don't they, father?" (739). The impression such a structure gives, according to Lakoff, is that the speaker is "not really sure of himself, of looking to the addressee for confirmation, even of having no views of his own. This last criticism is, of course, one often leveled at women" (55). Furthermore, Verena's last three questions are typical of both her concern and confusion: "I don't understand—where shall we go?" (744). "Where will you take me?" (744). "And what will the people do?" (744). She asks for direction to act, but, more importantly, she asks to be excused from decision making.

Because questions constitute Basil's most significant variable (.01 level), they are important to his character definition. In contrast, Verena's most significant variable (.01 level) is the conditional. Identified in this study by the word "if," the conditional can describe conditions that precede action or indicate uncertainty. Potter states, "such sentences posit contingencies: they are often speculative in nature" ("Toward a Syntactic Differentiation," 194).

Verena's use of the conditional is indeed speculative, but it is speculation born of a desire to please: "I know you like me to speak so much—I'll try to say something if you want me to" (515). "I'll do it alone, if you prefer" (515). "Now mind, if you don't like what's inside, it isn't my fault" (596). "But it will still come back, if you will leave me" (744).

Basil uses the conditional within the Aristotelian device of a hypothetical argument to set up enthymemes: "If, as you say, there is to be a discussion, there will be different sides, and of course one can't sympathise with both" (436). "If you regard me as the enemy, it's very kind of you to receive me" (584). "She's mine or she isn't, and if she's mine, she's all mine!" (741). This argumentative format serves Basil, the lawyer, well, for it carries a legalistic mystique that makes the argument sound logical and the speaker sound intelligent.

Verena's and Basil's perceptions of their situations in *The Bostonians* help explain the roles they adopt and the action they pursue. Their perceptions of themselves, as illustrated by the "definition" variable, evidence their self-concept and explain their motivation in adopting those roles. For example, the definitions that are rooted in "I am" in the first 500 lines of dialogue in *The Bostonians* establish Basil as a man of action and confidence as he states that he is very ambitious, very sure, sure, a man, always delighted, able to interpret history, glad, very rich, one of them, not so bad, very familiar, coming out. Verena defines herself in these same 500 lines when she says that she is just a girl, only a girl, a simple American girl, like Mrs. Farrinder, young, afraid, glad, not naturally concentrated.

Basil's definition of the female role is also clearly stated: "The use of a truly amenable woman is to make some honest man happy" (594). Verena initially has a different idea: "We [women] are the heart of humanity, and let us have the courage to insist on it" (614). But Basil persists: "Dear Miss Tarrant, what is most agreeable to women is to be agreeable to men" (665). Verena, the champion of women, shows little respect for her gender or confidence in herself when she states, "That's fortunate for us poor creatures" (904).

One has only to examine Verena's syntax in this manner to discover why she was suppressed: her will could not match Basil's will when her self-concept was so negative. It's hard to act and speak like a mature woman when you see yourself as only a "simple American girl" (466). Verena, then, becomes a victim, not a heroine. Her lofty speeches have little impact on her own actions because she has neither internalized the ideals of the movement nor found the strength to assert herself in her personal speech. In *The Bostonians,* James renews the now-

familiar pattern of women using language that intrinsically assigns them submissive social roles.

James's appreciation of the power of language is not questioned; for him the
speech act was vital.

> The imparting of a coherent culture is a matter of communication and response—each
> of which branches of an understanding involves the possession of a common lan-
> guage, with its modes of employment, its usage, its authority, its beauty, in working
> form; a medium of expression, in short, organized and developed.
>
> (*The Question of Our Speech*, 6)

But when the "medium of expression" used to challenge cultural stereotypes is,
in fact, the medium of that culture and faithful to its stereotypes, the challenger
is trapped, is not able to develop outside the culture. James's heroines in *Daisy
Miller, The Portrait of a Lady,* and *The Bostonians* are indeed trapped by the
restrictions of society, and each is punished for her challenge. Daisy is dead,
Isabel sentenced to a loveless marriage, and Verena subdued and silenced. James
uses the victimization of these three women to make a social statement, but they
are victims nonetheless.

STYLE IN HENRY JAMES

The rhetorical gender patterns identified through variable use and analysis exemplify Henry James's style; therefore, these variable data sets may also be used
to trace stylistic patterns of James the author. Table 4 lists numerically the percentage of the total dialogue assigned to each variable in the books studied; Figure 1 plots the same results.

From the visualization in Figure 1, a "styleprint" of James's syntactic struc-

TABLE 4.   NUMERICAL RESULTS ILLUSTRATED IN FIGURE 1

Variable	Total percentage of variable use		
	Daisy	Lady	Bostonians
Questions	14.0	15.0	19.7
Imperatives	4.5	5.4	4.4
Exclamations	17.0	7.0	15.0
Pauses	5.0	7.6	13.9
Fragments	1.0	.6	.8
Conditionals	4.2	5.6	8.2
Definitions	33.0	33.0	32.3
Negatives	33.0	36.0	34.0
Universals	6.0	6.5	10.0
Adverbs	8.4	11.7	12.3
Comparisons	1.0	1.1	3.0

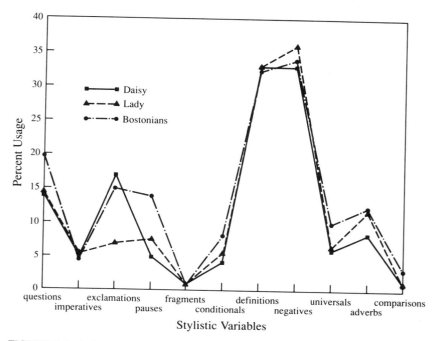

FIGURE 1. Style in Henry James

ture emerges: the peaks and valleys trace a very low fragment use but the high use of definitions and negatives. The low fragment use is consistent with James's "end-linking" as described by Ralf Norrman: "Cohesion, in any text, is achieved both through a rational ordering of linguistic units in relation to each other and through a rational ordering of whatever they refer to. In James, the former takes precedence over the latter" (66). Fragments that interrupt, or leave a linguistic unit hanging, have very little use in this type of "building" style.

Definitions and negatives, on the other hand, are extremely important structures for James both in frequency and semantic impact. James obviously understands the need for his characters to define, for he uses such statements, generally identified by an "x is y" formula, in one out of every three sentences of dialogue in all three works. J. A. Ward notes that "When James composes a novel he is not so much interested in dramatizing what will happen to the protagonist as he is in dramatizing who the protagonist is" (35). Relationships become paramount and hinge on what or who a character *is* as well as what he/she *is not*.

To know Daisy and understand the dynamics of her relationship with Winterborne, it is necessary to appreciate the interaction of definition and negative when she states, "I'm a fearful, frightful flirt! Did you ever hear of a nice girl that was not?" ("Daisy Miller," 308). Daisy must accept the negative self-definition of "flirt" in order to maintain the positive identity of a "nice girl." The same moral and sexual standards, however, do not apply to males. Ironically, Winterborne, who judges Daisy so severely for being a flirt, confides, "My dear aunt, I am not so innocent"("Daisy Miller," 282). Yet this self-definition does not lower his ethos; conversely, through this definition, Winterborne appears sophisticated.

In this study, definitions cause conflict for the females who seek self-identification even while they function as "signs" of femininity for male subjects. Elizabeth Allen explains that since the "sign" is an abstract property made up of the signifier (Daisy, Isabel, Verena) and the signified (the American girl), the existence of a preordained sign (femininity) causes a conflict in seeking a sense of self: " 'Feminine,' " like 'woman,' is a signifier attached to a range of signifieds to create signs which bear a very arbitrary relation to the woman herself—arbitrary from her point of view, that is, not from her society's" (12).

James assigns definitions to his female heroines that present a paradox for these women who, as the agents of change, must also be the keepers of culture with its attending characteristics of art, beauty, tradition, and, most important, social conventions. Daisy is the new American culture for Winterborne, attractive but "completely uncultivated" ("Daisy Miller," 282). Isabel is a "collectible" for Osmond and a specimen for Ralph, a female who is written into art. Verena is the virgin to-be-possessed, so it is important that Basil feel that she is "all mine" ("The Bostonians," 741).

The most noticeable variations in James's "styleprint" are in the exclamation and pause variables. This deviation is most pronounced in *The Portrait of a Lady,* where James assigns proportionately more exclamations to the male than the female yet proportionately less exclamations than in the other two works. In other words, when James does assign exclamations to the male, he uses a significantly lower percentage of that syntactic variable.

The stylistic structure studied in these three works cannot begin fully to describe James's style, nor does it picture a static phenomenon. This exploratory study, however, does present evidence that James uses the stylistic variables of questions, imperatives, fragments, conditionals, definitions, and negatives in a similar manner in different works. This evidence also establishes patterns which present males' speech as direct, clear, and commanding, while reinforcing the notion of "weak" or submissive female speech. Some movement toward a stronger syntax for the female in *The Portrait of a Lady* confirms most critical judgment of Isabel as a stronger heroine than Daisy or Verena. Isabel asks more questions, and her lower use of exclamations downplays the impression of excitability or emotion often assigned to women.

Through his stylistic choices in *Daisy Miller, The Portrait of a Lady,* and *The Bostonians,* James portrays lively but inexperienced "girls" who are syntactically weaker than the males in the three works. This lack of linguistic power contributes to their failure to realize their needs, their failure to succeed. We must credit James as a novelist who uses his talent to probe as well as validate the real psychological need of his heroines to establish their own identities. Yet his unconscious syntactic choices often undercut the challenge to cultural norms that his stories present. James writes with concern about the situation of women, and his heroines do, at least, challenge social norms. James's stylistic choices, however, reinforce the stereotypic image of women that makes that challenge necessary.

References

Allen, Elizabeth. *A Woman's Place in the Novels of Henry James.* London: Macmillan, 1984.

Banta, Martha. "Women in Post-Bellum American Literature." In *What Manner of Woman.* Ed. Marlene Springer. New York: New York University Press, 1977, 235–70.

Corbett, Edward P. J. *Classical Rhetoric for the Modern Student.* New York: Oxford University Press, 1965.

Eakin, Paul John. *The New England Girl.* Athens: University of Georgia Press, 1976.

Fowler, Virginia C. *Henry James's American Girl: The Embroidery on the Canvas.* Madison: University of Wisconsin Press, 1984.

Gershuny, H. Lee. "Language and Feminist Research." In *Women in Print I.* Ed. Joan E. Hartman and Ellen Messer-Davidow. New York: The Modern Language Association of America, 1982, 47–65.

Gray, Bennison. *The Grammatical Foundations of Rhetoric.* New York: Mouton, 1977.

James, Henry. "The Bostonians." In *The American Novels and Stories of Henry James.* Ed. F. O. Matthiessen. New York: Knopf, 1947, 424–746.

———. "Daisy Miller." In *The Turn of the Screw and Other Short Fiction by Henry James.* New York: Bantam Books, 1981, 269–321.

———. *The Notebooks of Henry James.* New York: Oxford University Press, 1947.

———. *The Portrait of a Lady.* Boston: Houghton, 1969.

———. "Preface to *Daisy Miller.*" In *The Art of the Novel.* New York: Charles Scribner's ner's Sons, 1962, 267–87.

———. *The Question of Our Speech.* Folcroft, Pa.: Folcroft Press, 1969.

Klefer, Ference, ed. *Questions and Answers.* Boston: D. Reidel, 1983.

Kramer, Cheris. "Perceptions of Female and Male Speech," *Language and Speech* 20 (1977): 151–61.

Lakoff, Robin. "Language and Women's Place." *Language and Society* 2 (1973): 45–80.

Matthiessen, F. O. "Introduction." In *The American Novels and Stories of Henry James.* New York: Knopf, 1947.

Norrman, Ralf. *The Insecure World of Henry James's Fiction.* London: Macmillan, 1982.

Pearson, Carol and Katherine Pope. *The Female Hero.* New York: R. R. Bowker, 1981.

Potter, Rosanne G. "Reader Responses and Character Syntax." In *Computing in the Humanities.* Ed. Richard W. Bailey. Amsterdam: North-Holland, 1982, 65–78.

———. "Character Definition Through Syntax." *Style* 15 (Fall, 1981): 415–34.

———. "Toward a Syntactic Differentiation of Period Style in Modern Drama: Significant Between-Play Variability in 21 English-Language Plays." *Computers and the Humanities* 14 (1980): 187–96.

Spender, Dale. *Man Made Language*. Boston: Routledge & Kegan Paul, 1980.

Springer, Mary Doyle. *A Rhetoric of Literary Character.* Chicago: University of Chicago Press, 1978.

Tanner, Tony. "The Fearful Self." In *Twentieth Century Interpretations of The Portrait of a Lady,* ed. Peter Buietenhuis. Englewood Cliffs, N.J.: Prentice-Hall, 1968, 67–82.

Ward, J. A. *The Search for Form*. Chapel Hill: University of North Carolina Press, 1967.

>> 11

Reliable Narration
in The Good Soldier

C. RUTH SABOL

Scholars interpret literary texts differently because as readers they rely on individual psychological processes and cultural conditioning to make the intuitive
judgments that affect their interpretations.[1] However, the computer can provide
data to corroborate or question those judgments. Using information obtained
from the computer-produced *A Concordance to Ford Madox Ford's* The Good
Soldier,[2] I have used linguistic evidence to argue that Dowell, the narrative voice
in *The Good Soldier*, is a reliable narrator.

COMPUTER-PRODUCED DATA

The computer programs of the Wisconsin Old Spanish Dictionary Project* per-
mitted Todd Bender and me to generate a concordance, a verbal index, and a
field of reference to *The Good Soldier*. A concordance alphabetically lists each
occurrence of every word and cites the page and line number of each occurrence.
A verbal index alphabetizes all the words and provides a total count for each
word. A field of reference reproduces the entire text, numbering each page and
line. Certainly, concordances alone are but raw data to which scholars must apply
their interpretive judgments. However, concordances need not provide scholars
with mere exercises in what a latter-day Dr. Johnson might complain to be count-

ing the streaks of the tulip. Because more computer-produced concordances are becoming accessible to literary scholars, the information available from such tools should be used to assist them to expand their knowledge of texts, to sharpen their critical judgments, and to provide additional verification for that knowledge and those judgments.

One of the first uses of computer-produced concordances was to show statistical deviance in the language between texts (or between authors). It is essential, however, to distinguish between deviance in the language of a text and language that is merely impressionistically striking.[3] For example, the deviance between one language feature of Ford's *The Good Soldier* and Joseph Conrad's *Lord Jim* is that *The Good Soldier* contains nearly three times as many occurrences of *that* as does the much longer *Lord Jim*. Such deviation in the basic language of a text is a clear indication of differences in style or in meaning or both.

Impressionistically striking language, on the other hand, may not distinguish sufficiently between the characteristic language of one text and another. For example, F. R. Leavis in *The Great Tradition* faulted Conrad for overworking such impressionistically striking words as *inscrutable, inconceivable,* and *unspeakable* in *Heart of Darkness*.[4] Yet, "A Concordance to *Heart of Darkness*"[5] shows that the words were used four, six, and three times, respectively. Although striking, they are certainly not "overworked." And if one were concerned with stylistic differences between, say, Conrad's *Heart of Darkness* and Ford's *The Good Soldier,* a scholar would certainly not rely on so few as thirteen occurrences of three words.

In fact, texts may be better distinguished by the less striking diction, the function words, such as *a, an, the,* or *that.* (Doubters need only read Halliday's 1962 lecture notes on the anaphoric *the* in "Leda and the Swan."[6]) Isolating such function words, obviously, is easy using a computer. By contrast, who among us would plod through an entire text of even so few as 74,000 words to list every occurrence of *that?* Fortunately, once we have accurately reproduced the text in machine-readable form (certainly, time-consuming drudgery for those of us without access to reliable optical scanners or text archives), computer programs easily isolate the data we need.

I scrutinized the occurrences of *that* in *The Good Soldier* because the verbal index in the concordance showed an unusually high total contrasted with the total in other, longer texts (such as Conrad's *Lord Jim,* Charlotte Brontë's *Jane Eyre,* and Emily Brontë's *Wuthering Heights*[7]). I then focused on the nominal complement *that*-clause used so frequently by the Dowell narrator because it is semantically complex and accessible to linguistic analysis. I took a 10,000-word spread sample of the text[8] and located in the field of reference each nominal complement *that*-clause in the sample. Each clause was then analyzed and interpreted. This process provided a new way of looking at *The Good Soldier*. (Working from the printed concordance and field of reference, I took the spread sample and located the nominal complement *that*-clauses in the field of reference by hand. With a copy of the computer tape, available from the University of Wisconsin, I could have used the computer programs at Wisconsin to print out the spread sample and to isolate the contexts of all the *thats*. Distinguishing any one use of *that* from a possible six uses is most accurately a task for human interpretation, however.)

RELIABLE NARRATION

Certainly, Wayne Booth's distinction between reliable and unreliable narration has been useful in advancing the critical understanding of the complexities of texts. In a version expanded from the well-known chapter in *The Rhetoric of Fiction,* Booth clearly asserts that the mark of an unreliable narrator is neither the potential for deception, nor the use of difficult irony, nor the instances of lying. An unreliable narrator is either mistaken or pretending by speaking as if he had certain qualities which the implied author denies him.[9] But when a narrator like Dowell "speaks," the degree to which he is certain of the truth of his utterances varies markedly. Dowell's degree of certitude is indicated by the semantic nature of the predicates that he uses. For example, take these utterances:

but I *know* that Luther and Bucer were there (44.08);[10]

But I *thought* that perhaps that would not be quite English good form . . . (260.10);

But I *guess* that I myself, in my fainter way, come into the category of the passionate, of the headstrong, and the too truthful (257.11). [Italics added.]

The predicates *know, thought,* and *guess* reveal that Dowell is more convinced of the truth of some *that*-clause complements than others. Only the predicate *know* (a linguistic factive) indicates that Dowell fully believes the truth of the complement. *Thought* and *guess* (linguistic nonfactive predicates of propositional attitude)[11] indicate no presupposition of truth. Therefore, the degree of certitude may vary from strong to weak:

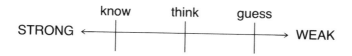

Thus, predicates such as *know, think,* or *guess* indicate varying mental states or modes of speaking that imply the degree of a speaker's conviction that an utterance is true. A speaker's strength of conviction is called *truth conditions,* and the existing truth conditions determine a speaker's choice of predicates. Certain factives like *know* reveal that a speaker absolutely believes the truth of what he speaks. *Know* is described linguistically as a strong factive (in most contexts); *think* and *guess* are not factives at all.[13] That is, when a speaker uses *know,* that speaker believes the truth of the following proposition, whereas when a speaker uses *think* or *guess,* the truth conditions are less strong. Furthermore, to assert the truth of a proposition, such as

> It is, however, certain that the fourth of August always proved a significant date for her [Florence] (79.12),

does not linguistically carry the force of semantic presupposition—that is, it does not presuppose (or imply) that Dowell believes that the fourth of August did indeed always prove a significant date for Florence. He may believe the assertion, or he may not believe it. A reader cannot know from the semantic nature of the language since the truth is not presupposed in the semantic structure of the language that Dowell has chosen. For example, one may say, "I am certain that it is Tuesday" to mean either that the speaker believes that it probably is Tuesday or that one is not at all sure that it is Tuesday as in "I am certain that it is Tuesday, isn't it?" Even though the tag question "isn't it?" may not appear in the surface structure of the language, it may be held implicitly by the speaker. On the other hand, unless one were purposely lying or attempting to deceive, one would not say, "I know that it is Tuesday" and be uncertain that it is Tuesday. Therefore, to assert the truth of a proposition using "certain" is semantically distinct from presupposing the truth of the same proposition using "know" (as it is distinct from truth entailed by a proposition).[14] Clearly then, when Dowell "speaks," he speaks through a variety of utterances that bear different semantic features which must be taken into account when a reader assesses his reliability.

To establish Dowell's narrative reliability, then, we need not rely on merely intuitive judgments. By examining the semantic features of the predicates that introduce the *that*-clause complements, we can distinguish three types of utterances: (1) utterances of fact based upon the use of factive predicates that presuppose the truth of their *that*-clause complements (e.g., "I *know* that it is Tuesday" means the speaker is convinced the complement is true); (2) utterances counter to fact (called *counterfactuals*) based on the occurrences of so-called world-creating predicates which presuppose the opposite of their *that*-clause complements (e.g., "I *dreamed* that it was Tuesday," [15] which means the speaker was convinced that the complement was not true); and (3) utterances of assertion that express varying degrees of certitude but do not presuppose truth (e.g., "I *think* that it is Tuesday" or "I *guess* that it is Tuesday," which means the speaker is not convinced whether or not the complements are true).

Several other semantic principles affect a narrator's reliability. Only Dowell's voice narrates; therefore, when in indirect discourse he utters a factive predicate imputing the utterance to another character, such as Leonora Ashburnham, the truth of the utterance is presupposed in Dowell's belief world.[16] At the same time, when Dowell uses a world-creating predicate to communicate a proposition imputed to another character, Dowell presupposes the opposite in his belief world (a linguistic counterfactual indicating that the proposition is counter to fact). Therefore, with assertions imputed to other characters by the narrator, two considerations determine whether or not the narrator shares the degree of certitude expressed by the other characters: (1) the narrator chooses the language expressing certitude and (2) the narrator may or may not have access to actual sources of knowledge. For example, when Dowell says,

And she [Nancy Rufford] was more *certain*
that Edward did not love Leonora and
that Leonora hated Edward (223.03), [Italics added.]

Dowell probably shares Nancy Rufford's certitude since, in indirectly reporting Nancy's assertion, Dowell chooses *certain* rather than some other term. He could have used, for example, a world-creating predicate like

She *imagined*
that Edward did not love Leonora and
that Leonora hated Edward,

which presupposes that Dowell does not believe the complement of *imagined* (as in "He imagined a world without war," a counterfactual which presupposes that, in fact, the world does have war). On the other hand, were Dowell to have said,

She *knew*
that Edward did not love Leonora and
that Leonora hated Edward,

he clearly would have expressed his belief in the truth of the complements.

Not only Dowell's choice of predicates in indirect discourse, but also his access to information held by third person subjects help us to judge his degree of certitude.[17] Take, for example:

He [Edward] had not any idea that Florence could have committed suicide without writing at least a tirade to him. The absence of that made him *certain* that it had been heart disease (132.32). [Italics added.]

Dowell does not share Edward Ashburnham's certainty that Florence died of heart disease. Edward is mistaken. Dowell knows that Edward is mistaken because Dowell knows that Florence did not suffer from heart disease. Dowell has access to such knowledge; Ashburnham does not. Therefore, when Dowell has access to the same knowledge as the third person subject, he likely holds the same degree of certitude. But when he has access to more reliable knowledge, then he may not share the subject's certitude.

In order to analyze the nominal *that*-clause complements to show whether Dowell's utterances are either fact, counterfact, or merely assertion, I have grouped them in eleven categories. The facts (based on factive predicates), counterfacts (based on world-creating predicates), and assertions (based on either performative or mental predicates) are included in (1) Dowell's utterances to a dramatic audience, (2) Dowell's utterances about the relationship between the Dowells and the Ashburnhams, (3) Dowell's utterances coming indirectly from Leonora Ashburnham about Edward Ashburnham's affairs, (4) Dowell's utterances coming indirectly from Leonora about the relationship between her and Dowell, (5) Dowell's utterances about Florence Dowell, (6) Dowell's utterances coming indirectly from Nancy Rufford and Edward Ashburnham about the relationship between Leonora and Edward, (7) Dowell's utterances coming indirectly from Nancy and Edward about their relationship, (8) Dowell's utterances coming indirectly from Edward about Florence, (9) Dowell's utterances about the relationship between Florence and Leonora, (10) Dowell's utterances about his relationship to Edward, and (11) Dowell's utterances of historical fact.

First, Dowell's utterances to the dramatic audience addressed as "you" include

It occurs to me [i.e., I remember] that
I [Dowell] have never told you anything about my marriage (79.29);

One remembers . . . that
one has forgotten to mention them [the events] in their proper places and that one may have given, by omitting them, a false impression (187.11);

(. . . you must remember that
I have been writing away at this story now for six months and reflecting longer and longer upon these affairs.) (188.06);

It suddenly occurs to me [i.e., I remember] that
I have forgotten to say how Edward met his death (258.25);

You remember that
peace had descended upon the house; that Leonora was quietly triumphant and that Edward said his love for the girl had been merely a passing phase (258.26).

The predicate *remember* introducing all five of these complement *that*-clauses is factive; that is, it asks the dramatic audience to remember events that the narrator knows to be true. We know that Dowell believes that he has not told his silent listener the details of his marriage to Florence (because he has not) and that he has not mentioned how Edward Ashburnham met his death. No evidence contradicts that Dowell is concerned that he not give the listener a false impression or that he has been writing for six months and reflecting upon events. Finally, Dowell believes that Leonora's quiet triumph in sending Nancy Rufford away is accompanied by external peace and Edward's denial of any lasting love for Nancy Rufford. No counterfacts or assertions indicate that Dowell is mistaken. Therefore, the utterances by Dowell to the dramatic audience must be taken to be reliable. He is neither mistaken nor pretending by speaking as if he had certain qualities, in this case knowledge, which the implied author denies him.

Dowell's utterances about the Dowell-Ashburnham relationship are equally consistent. Based on the factive verbs introducing the *that*-clauses, Dowell says,

You will perceive [i.e., be aware] . . . that
our friendship [the friendship between and Dowells and the Ashburnhams] has been a young-middle-aged affair . . . (4.20).

However, by using the counterfactive *supposing* to say,

Supposing [i.e., make believe] . . . that,
as human affairs go, we were an extraordinarily safe castle (5.24),

Dowell makes clear that he believes the complement is not true. Then, when Dowell asserts,

I swear [i.e., say] to you that
the breaking up of our little four-square coterie was such another unthinkable event (5.22)

and

. . . the more certain I become [i.e., believe] that
Florence was a contaminating influence—she depressed and deteriorated poor Edward; she deteriorated, hopelessly, the miserable Leonora (188.10),

Dowell is neither mistaken nor pretending by speaking as if he had certain qualities which the implied author denies him. He says that the Dowell-Ashburnham relationship involved young-middle-aged characters. And, even though Dowell asserts that the breaking up of the four-square coterie was unthinkable, still the counterfactual shows that Dowell knew that the "extraordinarily safe castle" was not safe at all. Dowell asserts that Florence was the contaminating and deteriorating influence on the group members. Intuitively, readers might judge Dowell to be mistaken, hence unreliable, in this assertion. But the assertion is neither contradicted nor supported by any fact or counterfact. The implied author does not deny Dowell any knowledge that Dowell claims to have.

The utterances about Edward Ashburnham's affairs come from Dowell and indirectly through Dowell from Leonora Ashburnham, a third-person grammatical subject. They are based on the factives *to be aware, to see,* and *to realize,* indicating Dowell believes the complements are true. He says,

> . . . she could not but be aware that
> both Mrs. Basil and Maisie Maidan were nice women (182.13);

> The curious, discounting eye . . . did not prevent her seeing that
> Mrs. Basil was very good to Edward and Mrs. Maidan very good for him (182.15);

> . . she realized that
> she [Leonora] had not, before, been afraid of husbands and of scandals, since, then, she did her best to keep Maisie's husband unsuspicious (183.30).

On the other hand, based on his use of the world-creating predicate *imagined,* Dowell believes the opposite of the complements when he says,

> She imagined that
> Edward was carrying on intrigues with other women—with two at once; with three (182.04);

> Leonora, indeed, imagined that
> she [Leonora] could manage this affair [with Maisie Maidan] all right (184.14);

> . . . she imagined that
> if she [Leonora] could take Maisie and Edward to Nauheim, Edward would see enough of her to get tired of her pretty little chatterings, of the pretty little motions of her hands and feet (184.16);

> And Leonora imagined that
> when poor Maisie was cured of her heart and Edward had seen enough of her, he would return to her [Leonora] (184.29).

Finally, on the basis of predicates of propositional attitude, Dowell expresses varying degrees of certitude as he says,

> It was quite literally the case that
> his [Edward's] passions—for the mistress of the grand-duke, for Mrs. Basil, for little Mrs. Maidan, for Florence, for whom you will—these passions were merely preliminary canters compared to his final race with death for her [Nancy Rufford] (117.18);

> She was certain that
> he [Edward] was not trying to seduce that poor child [Maisie] (191.07);

> She was certain that
> hitherto they [Edward's affairs] had consisted of the short passion for the Dolciquita, the real sort of love for Mrs. Basil, and what she deemed the pretty courtship of Maisie Maidan (193.10).

Taken together, the truth conditions of all of these utterances are not contradictory. Dowell is neither proved mistaken nor does he claim to know truths that the implied author denies him: Edward's affair with Dolciquita was relatively trivial; Edward's affairs with Mrs. Basil and Mrs. Maidan were probably good for him, yet preliminary to his final affection for Nancy Rufford; and Leonora constantly misjudged her ability to understand and manage Edward's affairs. Leonora imagines Edward carrying on two or three affairs at once, a counterfactual indicating Dowell's disbelief. The consistency of all these related facts, counterfacts, and assertions shows, once again, Dowell's reliability.

Dowell's utterances about the relationship between himself and Leonora Ashburnham show that Dowell believes the complements by saying:

> . . . I discovered that
> the pain in my [Dowell's] left wrist was caused by Leonora's clutching it:
> "I can't stand this," she said with a most extraordinary passion; "I must get out of this" (44.26);

> But I know that
> when I came out of it she was saying: "Oh, where are all the bright, happy, innocent beings in the world?" (45.25);

> And Leonora . . . had . . . a sense [i.e., felt] that
> that hotel room was cleared, that there were no papers on the table, that there were no clothes on the hooks, and that there was a strained silence (74.14);

> And then she saw that
> Maisie's boxes were all packed, and she began a search for Mrs. Maidan herself—all over the hotel (75.02);

> The odd thing is [i.e., it is odd] that
> what sticks out in my [Dowell's] recollection of the rest of that evening was Leonora's saying:
> "Of course you might marry her," and, when I asked whom, she answered:
> "The girl" (105.03);

> . . . it was the actual fact that—
> Leonora with an odd English sense of decency had determined to wait until Edward had been in his grave for a full week before she spoke (107.29).

Dowell utters no conterfactives, but he does assert,

> And I suppose—no I am certain that
> she never had it [the sex instinct] towards me (32.07).

The bases for Dowell's convictions of the truth of the *that*-clauses reside in the principle that sense perceptions, such as *to see, to hear,* or *to feel,* are taken to be true unless that truth is contradicted. Dowell reports pain in the left wrist caused by Leonora and reports Leonora's words to him. He also reports what Leonora saw: a cleared hotel room and Maisie's boxes all packed. Finally, he reports Leonora's "odd English sense of decency" as fact. On the other hand, that there was no sexual interest between him and Leonora is asserted. The implied author, again, does not present any knowledge to contradict Dowell. Therefore, Dowell must be taken to be reliable in his utterances about his relationship with Leonora.

The certain information Dowell relates about his wife Florence, although sparse, is also consistent. Dowell believes the complements by saying,

> . . . that was the first knowledge I had [i.e., knew] that
> Florence had committed suicide (108.08).

Yet he believes the opposite of the complement when he says,

> They probably imagined that
> the mere associations of the steamer might have effects on Florence's nerves (91.22)

since this is only "imagined" by Florence's doctors. Finally, Dowell asserts that

> (. . . there was no mistaking) . . . that
> Florence was coldly and calmly determined to take no look at any man who could not
> give her a European settlement (82.01).

The fact that Dowell knows Florence was not ill with heart disease and hence died by suicide, not heart disease, is consistent with the counterfactual "imagined" by Florence's doctors: the steamer trip might affect Florence's nerves. Dowell knows that Florence's nerves were not vulnerable to the effects of a trans-Atlantic steamer crossing. Finally, the assertion of Florence's determination to "take no look at any man who could not give her a European settlement" presents us with no information that questions Dowell's reliability.

On the basis of the factivity of the predicates that introduce the *that*-clauses, Dowell believes these complements revealing the relationship between Edward and Leonora Ashburnham:

> And she was quite aware that,
> at that date, the hottest she [Leonora] could have made it for him [Edward] would
> have been to refuse, herself, ever to see him again (102.21);
>
> She began to perceive [i.e., see] that
> Edward was extravagant in his largesses (143.34);
>
> . . . he was even hurt that
> Leonora's confessor did not make strenuous efforts to convert him [Edward] (145.11);

. . . the knowledge had come to her [i.e., she knew] that
Edward did not love Leonora and that Leonora hated Edward (220.11).

At the same time, Dowell does not hold true the counterfactuals "imagined" by Leonora.

She imagined that,
by now, she [Leonora] understood him [Edward] better, that she understood better his vanities and that, by making him happier, she could arouse his love (185.02).

Dowell asserts

It is, at any rate, certain that
Edward's actions were perfectly—were monstrously, were cruelly—correct. He sat still and let Leonora take away his character, and let Leonora damn him to deepest hell, without stirring a finger (250.03);

and he also does not contradict Nancy Rufford as he reports,

And she was more certain that
Edward did not love Leonora and that Leonora hated Edward (223.03).

Clearly, Dowell perceives enmity between Edward and Leonora: Leonora considers refusing "ever to see [Edward] again," Leonora's confessor did not make the expected effort to convert Edward, and Leonora knew that Edward was extravagant. All of these presupposed truths culminate in the fact that "Edward did not love Leonora and Leonora hated Edward," which Nancy Rufford states indirectly. Besides these presupposed truths, Dowell believes that Leonora only "imagined" she understood Edward; in fact, she did not. Yet, Edward was at fault for allowing Leonora to "take away his character." Here again, Dowell is not mistaken and does not claim knowledge denied him by the implied author.

There are neither factives nor counterfactuals to describe the relationship between Edward Ashburnham and Nancy Rufford, only assertions based on mental predicates like *be certain*. Dowell states,

But I am pretty certain that
I [Dowell] am right in the case of Nancy Rufford—that she had loved Edward Ashburnham very deeply and tenderly (248.17).

Because Nancy Rufford claims that

. . . she was certain that
he [Edward] was drinking too much . . . (227.22),

Dowell thinks so, too. And Dowell asserts, with Edward Ashburnham, that

He [Edward] was certain that
if she [Nancy] had once submitted to him she would remain his forever (245.23).

Nancy's concern for Edward and Edward's certainty that if Nancy "had submitted to him she would remain his forever" are consistent with Dowell's assertion that Nancy "loved Edward Ashburnham." Dowell is not shown to be mistaken or denied by the implied author knowledge that Dowell claims to have.

Dowell asserts what he thinks is Ashburnham's eventual tiring of Florence and what he thinks is Florence's deteriorating effect on Leonora by saying,

But I am convinced [i.e., believe] that
he [Edward] was sick of Florence within three years of even interrupted companionship and the life that she led him (101.09);

There is no doubt [i.e., I do not doubt] that
she [Florence] caused Leonora's character to deteriorate (188.13).

Dowell also asserts,

He [Edward] had not any idea that
Florence could have committed suicide without writing at least a tirade to him. The absence of that made him certain that it had been heart disease (132.32).

Dowell thinks that Edward "was sick of Florence," that Edward mistakenly thought Florence had died of heart disease, and that Florence had a deteriorating effect on Leonora. Although no factives presuppose Dowell's conviction of the truth of these assertions, still there is no evidence that Dowell is mistaken or that the implied author denies Dowell knowledge he pretends to have.

In contrast to Florence's relationship to Ashburnham and her effect on Leonora, which is all based on assertion, Dowell's relationship with Edward Ashburnham is presented to us through factive predicates. Dowell says,

In Ashburnham's face I know that
there was absolute panic (44.24);

For I can't conceal from myself the fact [i.e., I know] that
I [Dowell] loved Edward Ashburnham—and that I loved him because he was just myself (257.14);

. . . he could see in my eyes that I [Dowell] didn't intend to hinder him (259.28);

When he saw that
I [Dowell] did not intend to interfere with him [so] his eyes became soft and almost affectionate (260.03).

Dowell knows that he could read the emotional response of panic on Edward's face, that Edward could see that Dowell did not intend to hinder his committing suicide, and that Edward's eyes became affectionate. Dowell, in fact, knows because Dowell and Ashburnham are psychological doubles sharing the same self. Dowell clearly knows that Edward Ashburnham "was just myself." This belief in the duality of self is not merely asserted; it is presupposed in the semantic structure of the language of factivity used by Dowell.

Finally, Dowell "knows" these historical incidents:

> . . . I know that
> Luther and Bucer were there (44.08);
>
> I understand that
> rabbits do a great deal of harm to the short grass in England (107.13);
>
> I understand also that
> those years—the nineties—were very bad for farming (146.06).

He also asserts,

> It is, however, certain that
> the fourth of August always proved a significant date for her [Florence] (79.12).

These snippets of events create a broad overview of English history from Luther's Protest to the time when rodents begin to nibble away the tidy English country life—"the short grass of England"—and the cultivated growth of farming begins to stagnate during the 1890s. All of these subtle but significant events culminate in "the fourth of August" and England's involvement in The Great War. Dowell is reliable.

Dowell's use of factive predicates, like *know*, which presuppose the truth of the *that*-clause complements; of world-creating predicates, like *imagine*, which create counterfactuals that presuppose the opposite of what they state; and of predicates of propositional attitude, like *think*, which do not presuppose the truth of the *that*-clause complements, are all consistent in pointing out that the Dowell narrator is reliable. Reliable and unreliable narration may be distinguished in these terms:

> A narrator may be called *reliable* when that narrator's assertions of certitude are consistent with the truth of propositions presupposed by the language which the speaker (author) uses.
>
> A narrator is *unreliable* when that narrator's assertions express a particular set of norms (judgments of belief) throughout a novel which conflict with the norms (judgments of truth) of the implied author discernible through an analysis of factivity and semantic presupposition.

In limited narration, normative judgment resides linguistically in the utterances of factivity which semantically presuppose the truth of their complements and in the counterfacts linguistically marked by the use of world-creating predicates. An author selecting language automatically selects (consciously or unconsciously) the semantic structure that necessarily controls the meaning of a text. Therefore, analyzing and judging the factives and the counterfactuals is another means of arriving at the normative judgment of the implied author. A narrator is reliable when the assertions are consistent with the presupposed facts, unreliable when the assertions are inconsistent or in conflict with the presupposed facts. A narrator like Dowell is not unreliable, as Booth agrees, because he lies or even because he may be a madman. Nor is a narrator like Dowell unreliable when he merely thinks, guesses, or imagines. *To think* or *to guess* wrong is not sufficient to brand a narrator unreliable. To be unreliable, a narrator must present himself as if he had qualities which the author denies him. Therefore, only a thorough semantic analysis of the truth conditions of a narrator's assertions can give a reader hard evidence of a narrator's reliability or unreliability.

The many literary scholars who have concluded that Dowell is an unreliable narrator have done so by intuitive judgments. The data necessary to provide the linguistic evidence to either corroborate or contradict those judgments were not easily available until the computer became accessible to scholarship. In *The Good Soldier,* the computer that Dowell never knew has provided data that have shown him to be more reliable than intuitive judgments have.

Notes

* I am grateful to the University of Wisconsin Old Spanish Dictionary Project directed by John Nitti and Lloyd Kasten and to computer programmers Jean Anderson and Jurgen Patau. The Project (funded by grants from the Research Tools Division of the National Endowment for the Humanities) made possible the computer-generated concordances that provided the basic data for this study.

1. Michael Riffaterre, "Criteria for Style Analysis," *Word* 15 (1959): 163.

2. C. Ruth Sabol and Todd K. Bender, *A Concordance to Ford Madox Ford's* The Good Soldier (New York: Garland, 1981).

3. Nils E. Enkvist, "On the Place of Style in Some Linguistic Theories," in *Literary Style: A Symposium,* ed. Seymour Chatman (New York: Oxford University Press, 1971), 63.

4. F. R. Leavis, *The Great Tradition* (1948; reprint, New York: New York University Press, 1967), 177.

5. Sibyl C. Jacobson, "Structure of *Heart of Darkness:* A Study in Narrative Technique and a Concordance to *Heart of Darkness* " (Ph.D. dissertation, University of Wisconsin-Madison, 1972), 129.

6. Michael A. K. Halliday, "Descriptive Linguistics in Literary Studies," in Angus McIntosh and M. A. K. Halliday, *Patterns of Language* (Edinburgh, 1964; reprint, Bloomington: Indiana University Press, 1966), 58.

7. See C. Ruth Sabol and Todd K. Bender, *A Concordance to Brontë's Jane Eyre* (New York: Garland, 1981), 331; *A Concordance to Brontë's Wuthering Heights* (New

York: Garland, 1984), 214; and James W. Parins et al., *A Concordance to Conrad's Lord Jim: Verbal Index, World Frequency Table and Field of Reference* (New York: Garland, 1976), 178.

8. G. Udny Yule, "Theory of the Word-distribution, with an Exordium on Sampling: the Characteristic," *The Statistical Study of Literary Vocabulary* (Cambridge, 1944; reprint, n.p.: Archon Books, 1968), 35–56; for a discussion of the medium-size samples (4,000 to 50,000 words) preferred by statisticians see Rebecca Posner, "The Use and Abuse of Stylistic Statistics," *Archivum Linguisticum* 15 (1963): 124.

9. Wayne C. Booth, "Distance and Point-of-View: An Essay in Classification," *Essays in Criticism* 11 (1961): 72.

10. Numbers in parentheses refer to page and line numbers in Ford Madox Ford, *The Good Soldier: A Tale of Passion* (1915; reprint, New York: Albert and Charles Boni, 1927).

11. Since Paul and Carol Kiparsky's 1970 publication of "Fact" (in *Semantics: An Interdisciplinary Reader in Philosophy, Linguistics, and Psychology*, ed. Danny D. Steinberg and Leon A. Jakobovits [Cambridge: Cambridge University Press, 1971]; reprinted from *Progress in Linguistics*, ed. M. Bierwisch and K. Heidolph [The Hague: Mouton, 1970]), the notion of factivity and the term *factive* have been accepted by linguists and applied to predicates like *know* as a way of talking about the truth value of a complement utterance. Predicates like *know* indicate a speaker's full commitment to the truth value of a complement. Other predicates like *think* are non-factive; that is, they lack a speaker's full commitment to the truth value. *Think* and *know* also express a mental attitude toward a proposition rather than an action, called a performative (like *say*). *To know* or *to think* expresses a mental attitude; *to say* expresses performance or action.

12. Marc S. Rosenberg, "Counterfactives: A Pragmatic Analysis of Presupposition," (Ph.D dissertation, University of Illinois at Urbana-Champaign, 1975), 130.

13. I have listed some predicates according to the semantic features and terminology which are commonly accepted in linguistics:

Factive verbs

	Mental	Sensory
Emotive	regret resent be odd be sad	
Nonemotive	know be aware realize[a] understand forget	see hear perceive[b] sense notice

Performative verbs

accuse announce ask blame criticize declare	excuse inquire justify mention order promise	request say scold tell warn

Mental verbs of propositional attitude

believe be certain be possible be true	doubt fear guess hope	suspect think want

World-creating verbs

be joking	dream	pretend
be kidding	imagine[c]	wish
be mistaken	make believe	

[a] *Realize* is classified here as a nonemotive factive; see Rosenberg, 80–91; Lauri Karttunen, "Some Observations on Factivity," *Papers in Linguistics* 4 (1971), 64–65; and Jerry L. Morgan, "Presupposition and Representation of Meaning: Prolegomena" (Ph.D. diss., University of Chicago, 1973), 82.

[b] Ann Borkin discusses *perceive* as a sensory factive. See "*To Be* and Not *To Be*," *Papers from the Ninth Regional Meeting of the Chicago Linguistics Society* (Chicago: University of Chicago Press, 1973), 44–56.

[c] *Imagine* is classified here as a world-creating verb although its semantic nature is the subject of some disagreement.

14. Linguists (and philosophers) distinguish between assertion and the truth conditions of assertion which may be either conditions of entailment or presupposition. For example (from Wilson):

Assertion:	Archibald is a man.
Entails:	(a) Archibald is a person.
	(b) Archibald is a male.
	(c) Archibald is adult.

And (from Paul and Carol Kiparsky):

Assertion:	I regret that the door is closed.
Presupposes:	The door is closed.

Horn expresses the logical difference between presupposition and entailment as:

Whenever Sentence 1 is true and Sentence 2 is true and whenever Sentence 1 is not true and Sentence 2 is true, then Sentence 1 presupposes Sentence 2. On the other hand, whenever Sentence 1 is true and Sentence 2 is true and whenever Sentence 1 is not true and Sentence 2 is not true, then Sentence 1 entails Sentence 2. I have restated in natural language what Horn states in logical symbols:

If $(S \rightarrow S')$ and $(-S \rightarrow S')$, then S presupposes S'.

If $(S \rightarrow S')$ and $(-S \rightarrow -S')$, then S entails S'.

Hence, although both entailment and presupposition express truth conditions, the nature of the relationship of the truth conditions to the assertion differs. That difference is seen in negation.

See Deirdre Wilson, *Presupposition and Non-Truth-Conditional Semantics* (New York: Academic Press, 1975); Paul Kiparsky and Carol Kiparsky, "Fact"; and Laurence R. Horn, "A Presuppositional Analysis of *Only* and *Even*," *Papers from the Fifth Regional Meeting of the Chicago Linguistics Society*, ed. Binnick et al. (Chicago: University of Chicago Press, 1969), 98; see also Lauri Karttunen, "Presupposition of Compound Sentences," *Linguistic Inquiry* 4 (Spring 1973): 171.

Some linguists distinguish between semantic presupposition and pragmatic presupposition. Rosenberg, 62–66, explains semantic presupposition based on factive predicates in this fashion:

Form a sentence with a putative factive predicate in the matrix and a *that*-complement following. If one concludes that the *that*-complement must be true whether the factive verb is affirmed or negated, then the predicate is factive.

But, in order for the restated form to apply to any specific sentence (or utterance), a question like this has to be asked: Can a speaker ever utter a statement like "John isn't aware that Helen speaks German," if the presupposition, "Helen speaks German," does not hold? Yes, because pragmatic factors (the context of speech events) must be considered. For example in the context: "John isn't aware that Helen speaks German, because she doesn't," the tag makes any claim to the truth of "Helen speaks German" absurd.

George Lakoff points out that "Natural language is used for communication in a context and every time a speaker uses a sentence of his language to perform a speech act . . . he is making certain assumptions about that context." Therefore, the notion of presupposition is not simply that certain predicates called factives automatically presuppose that a speaker believes the complement proposition to be true and that the hearer accepts the proposition to be true within the belief world of the speaker. But normally, the so-called factive predicates do indeed presuppose their complements, and to argue otherwise requires hard linguistic or contextual evidence to the contrary—intuitive judgments alone are not enough; see George Lakoff, "Linguistics and Natural Logic," *Synthèse: An International Journal for Epistemology, Methodology, and Philosophy of Science* 22 (Dec. 1970): 175.

15. See David K. Lewis, *Counterfactuals* (Oxford: Basil Blackwell, 1973).
16. See Jerry L. Morgan's Free Pass Principle, cited in Rosenberg, 53.
17. Rosenberg, 185.

>> 12

Changes in Shaw's Dramatic Rhetoric:

Mrs. Warren's Profession, Major Barbara, *and* Heartbreak House

ROSANNE G. POTTER

Bernard Shaw began his dramatic career late but continued writing rhetorically powerful plays well into his seventies. The length of his career alone encourages a longitudinal study of Shaw's dramatic rhetoric. Such a study might involve statistical analysis of semantic data culled from the ten-volume *Concordance to the Plays and Prefaces of Bernard Shaw* [1] or of syntactic data gained by parsing randomly selected passages from the seven-volume *Bodley Head Bernard Shaw: Collected Plays.* [2] Although I shall use some statistically derived terms in my analysis of Shaw's work, I do not here choose to approach the issue of changes in Shaw's dramatic rhetoric from the perspective of a literary statistician, but rather from that of a literary critic.

Statistical analysis demands the inspection of a wide range of independent variables chosen from passages selected randomly out of a comprehensive sample. The analysis of dramatic rhetoric, on the other hand, demands the inspection of a narrow band of sometimes interdependent variables in passages of rhetorical importance selected from a coherent set of works. [3]

Instead of looking at Shaw's entire canon, I analyze here three major plays written in successive decades: *Mrs. Warren's Profession* (1893), when Shaw was thirty-seven; *Major Barbara* (1905), when he was forty-nine; and *Heartbreak House* (1916), when he was sixty. I explore two questions: how do several important Shaw plays develop from first to last act? and what changes emerge from a study of Shaw's early, middle, and late dramatic rhetoric?

Lacking a formal university education, Shaw learned practical rhetoric on Hyde Park corner and practiced it to great effect during the 1880s as one of the founding members of the Fabian Society. Thus when, after writing five unsuccessful novels, Shaw turned to drama in the nineties (because, according to St. John Ervine, he had "the gift of dialogue"[4]), his oratorical skills became his stock in trade. As a militant socialist, internationalist, pacifist, vegetarian, and teetotaler, Shaw always stood in strenuous opposition to conventional values.[5]

When he came to write plays, the literary works most dependent on the public, he faced the problem of purveying unconventional messages without being dismissed as a crank. An inveterate flouter of sentimental conceptions of the world, Shaw saw solutions to human problems where the public simply saw irreverence.[6] Since his moral sense differed so greatly from his audience's, his resolutions were usually found aesthetically unsatisfying. This blurring of ethical questions into aesthetic attacks should not surprise. The standard (though usually unexpressed) maxim is surely something like this: "When a work is realistic in design, it had better *be* realistic, or it is badly made." Even now, the originality of Shaw's morality places his resolutions at risk of being judged as aesthetically unsatisfying. Most critics agree that Shaw's expositions are flawless and his complications engage, but that his resolutions rarely convince.[7] A study of changes in Shaw's dramatic rhetoric shows how he attempted to meet this criticism.

CRITICAL PREMISES

This study rests on two critical premises. The first connects Shaw's conception of reality and the resolutions of his plays: Shaw's unconventional definition of reality means that he must persuade audiences to accept his resolutions. The second premise postulates that the dialogue of plays is the primary means of persuasion and thus should be the primary object of study in the rhetorical analysis of drama. Thus, to understand Shaw's problems with resolutions, I study his ways of assigning dialogue to characters.

That character relationships, portrayed mainly through dialogue, create expectations in the theatre-goer or reader is self-evident. That the fulfilling or thwarting of expectation is highly implicated in successful or unsuccessful resolutions of plays I shall attempt to prove by example. This is not to assert a one-to-one relationship between fulfilled expectations and successful resolutions, but rather to point out the problematic link between the two concepts. A playwright who plans to thwart expectations that have been created by the very language of the work will have to work harder than one who follows a more predictable path to resolution.[8]

As a critic, I chose to gather together and count obvious syntactic features assigned to characters because I am convinced that these stylistic choices affect both character definition and readers' responses. The counted features enable me to give a precise description of the comparative rhetorical effectiveness of the characters in scenes. Computer methods allow the gathering and rearranging of dialogue for analysis by character within feature. My previous computer studies of the relationships between character definition and syntax also justify focusing tightly on those items of syntax that contribute to readers' judgments of *dominance*.[9]

In my 1982 study of reader responses and character syntax, *dominance* proved the trait most reliably measured and significantly correlated to a certain syntactic profile: high use of imperatives, questions, and definitions and low use of sentence fragments. This essay assumes that the character trait which readers perceive as *dominance* correlates to that cluster of simple syntax.

SCENES AND STRUCTURE

Shifts in dominance emerge best if we recognize the scene as the primary unit of analysis. Although conventionally divided into acts, modern plays should, I believe, be investigated by scenes. One traditional way of defining scenes uses the eighteenth-century French convention of declaring a new scene as soon as a character enters or leaves the stage. This convention breaks plays, especially those with many characters, into a very large number of very small units. The common dictionary definition of *scene* is equally inadequate; several respected dictionaries define a scene as "A sub-division of an act in a dramatic presentation in which the setting is fixed and the time is continuous."[10] This generalization may be fine for describing Shakespearean drama, but for modern drama it errs in the opposite direction from the classical French definition. If we used the dictionary as a guide, most modern plays (where the place and time rarely change except at act breaks) would then have scenes coequal with acts, i.e., with no subdivisions.

Both definitions leave the researcher with unmanageable units: one too small, the other too large. Instead of forcing analysis of dramatic rhetoric into either of these models, I propose this definition of scene: a scene consists of all the action and representation between two rhetorically determined moments in an act. The rhetoric of the work determines the line after which one may say that a new scene has begun. Since critics may differ about "the rhetoric of the work," the two rhetorically determined moments may also differ. However, once specific scene boundaries have been defined by listing the first line and the last line, other critics will at least know the field under analysis; they may question the divisions, accept them and attempt replication of the earlier critic's work, or accept them in order to draw other inferences from them. (See Appendix 1 for the first and last lines of the thirty scenes in the three plays.)

Rhetorical analysis, at least analysis which attempts to compare speakers, requires all major characters to be present and capable of speaking within the same period of time. This realization impelled my first decision to subdivide the acts of Shaw's plays; I wanted to find the passages where major characters were interacting. In the process of marking these scenes out of the larger acts, I found that all three plays could be easily divided into ten scenes. This structure (which first surfaced when I was looking for the crucial scenes in *Mrs. Warren's Profession*, and then reappeared, without forcing, during the analysis of *Major Barbara*) encouraged me to devise a table for the comparison of quantities within scenes and acts. (See Table 1.)

Table 1 shows that the number of characters on stage and the number of lines per play increase as the years pass.[11] In *Mrs. Warren's Profession*, all six characters are on stage during only one scene; the mean is 3.6 characters per scene. In *Major Barbara*, with fifteen named characters (six of these characters appear only in Act 2), six or more characters are on stage during five scenes; the highest number on stage at once is nine; the mean is 5.8 characters per scene. In *Heartbreak House* the ten named characters all share the stage during two scenes. Eight or more characters are on stage during four scenes; the mean is 6.3. The actual number of important roles increases from five in *Mrs. Warren's Profession* to seven in *Major Barbara* to eight in *Heartbreak House*. If presenting a larger number of characters both simultaneously and in a larger number of scenes is a sign of increasing dramatic skill, then Shaw clearly grew more skillful as he grew older.

In Table 1, the shifts in the number of scenes per act show another area of increased complexity in Shaw's later plays. In *Mrs. Warren's Profession*, Shaw presents his ideas within a very simple structure of pairs. Three of the four acts consist of two scenes per act; the second act, which initially looks like four scenes, is actually two pairs of scenes. The play presents the conflict between two characters in the context of four other characters. Two-character scenes begin and end the play; the midpoint consists of a pair of them.

Shaw alternates between scenes that focus on two characters and scenes that present the central characters in the context of the others. Act I provides a short two-scene exposition: it consists of a two-character introduction followed by a group scene in which all the other characters are presented. Act II establishes

Characters per Scene*

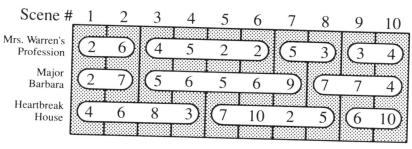

Units per Scene†

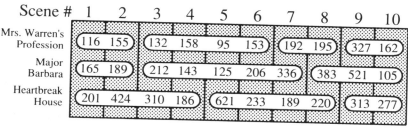

Units per Act	1	2	3	4	Total
Mrs. Warren's Profession	271	538	387	489	= 1685
Major Barbara	354	1022	1009		= 2385
Heartbreak House	1121	1263	590		= 2974

* White space links the number of characters (or units) into acts to emphasize changes in balance between acts in the three plays.

† A "Unit" is, in common language, a line of dialogue, usually a sentence. When more than one sentence is required for analysis, speeches are segmented rhetorically.

TABLE 1. Numerical data on characters and units per scene and act in thirty scenes from three plays by Bernard Shaw

how like Frank and Mrs. Warren are in the first and second scenes; then the third and fourth scenes, the exact midpoint of the play, show Vivie and Mrs. Warren taking turns at dominance. Act III continues the complication started in Scenes 3 and 4 of Act II by giving Vivie more information about her mother while toying with the various possible melodramatic resolutions in two brief scenes focused first on Frank and Vivie, then on Vivie and Crofts. Act IV continues the two-scenes pattern, but reverses it; here the larger cast resolves itself into a final conflict between the two central characters. Shaw gives each of the three important male characters an opportunity to display himself in relation to each of the central female characters. The design of the play reveals itself easily. The play could serve as a model for beginning students of dramatic structure.

In *Major Barbara,* the obvious chaining of scenes has disappeared; now a quite short two-scene first act leads into a very long five-scene second act, and is followed by an almost equally long three-scene third act. At the core of this play is the number *three:* the primary action pits the members of a triangle (father, daughter, and fiancé) against one another. As Undershaft says:

> I am a millionaire; you are a poet; Barbara is a savior of souls. What have we three to do with the common mob of slaves and idolaters? (120–21).[12]

> We three must stand together above the common people: how else can we help their children to climb up beside us? Barbara must belong to us, not the Salvation Army (121).

The action occurs in three settings: Wilton Crescent (Lady Britomart's world), the West Ham Shelter (Barbara's world), and Perivale St. Andrews (Undershaft's world). The three worlds represented are drawn to three different, and progressively larger, scales: the indoor salon, pictured in feet, expands into the outdoor but enclosed yard, measured in yards, and both are dwarfed by the view of the village from the open parapet, apparently encompassing miles.

The larger numbers of scenes per act and units per scene reflect the increasing complexity of the positions presented in each act. The consistent pattern in the play is that each person acts through the agency of a second to get to a third. Lady Britomart reintroduces Undershaft to his family through a discussion with Stephen. Barbara tries to convert her father through saving Bill's soul. Undershaft shows Barbara that the Army is for sale by giving a check to Mrs. Baines. Undershaft wins Barbara over to the munitions work by convincing Cusins to accept his offer.

The expositions and complications of these first two plays show some similarities, but greater differences. The first scene in both presents two characters discussing the initial situation of the drama; the second scene introduces the other characters. In *Mrs. Warren's Profession,* however, one of the main characters appears in Scene 1; while in *Major Barbara* none of the principal characters appears until Scene 2. The complications of the two plays also differ: *Mrs. Warren's* two settings, two acts, and six scenes, as opposed to *Major Barbara's* one setting, one act, and five scenes. The length of space devoted to the complication (measured here by units of dialogue, i.e., 925 versus 1,022), however, shows only a moderate increase from the earlier to the later play. A notable difference is the introduction of six new characters in Act II of *Major Barbara.*

Contrasting the final acts of the two plays reveals major structural differences. In *Major Barbara* the resolution takes three scenes instead of two, and is more than twice as long as the resolution of *Mrs. Warren's Profession;* the number of characters increases from four to seven in the group scenes, and from two to four in the final scenes. Even at this, the simplest level of investigation (counting the number of characters and contrasting the length of scenes and acts), Shaw's problem with resolutions begins to emerge.

Although signs of development can be seen between the expositions and complications of these plays, the resolutions are quite different in kind. The last act of *Mrs. Warren's Profession* is simple and unadorned; the resolution of *Major Barbara* is complicated by set changes and increased numbers of characters appearing in more scenes, speaking more lines. By *Heartbreak House* the proportions are reversed: a very long, four-scene first act leads to a still longer, four-scene second act; both are followed by a comparatively short, two-scene third act. Shaw has clearly changed strategies in allocating scenes and characters within scenes. The first act exposition is almost as long (both in number of scenes and length of scenes) as the second act complication. The third act resolution, on the other hand, is now back to two scenes and is proportionally shorter than in either of the earlier plays.

Whether the movement to the short last act resulted from a conscious or subconscious decision to deemphasize resolutions hardly matters; a clear shift away from attempts to convince in the resolution can be seen by contrasting the last acts of the earlier plays with *Heartbreak House.* The differences in relative lengths and numbers of characters show a distinct tendency to undercut the emotional impact of the resolution.[13]

The relationship between the context characters and the central characters reverses; the opening up of the focus in the final act of *Heartbreak House* is radically different from the more standard narrowing down to the most important characters in *Mrs. Warren's Profession* and *Major Barbara*. All ten characters return to the stage during the last scene of *Heartbreak House;* the obvious consequence is a diluting of rhetorical effect. Instead of two (or three) characters going at each other head-to-head, arguing about whose position is correct, six characters sit about talking in a mostly desultory way, until they (and the other four) are briefly stirred up by an outside threat but almost as quickly subside back into somnolence. Shaw clearly structured this last act quite differently from the last acts of important earlier plays.

As the number of characters increases, so does the number of scenes needed for an understanding of the resolution. In *Mrs. Warren's Profession,* three confrontation scenes suffice. By *Major Barbara* one must analyze four scenes; and no less than five scenes must be examined for an understanding of *Heartbreak House.*

SYNTAX AND CHARACTER

After these descriptions of structural characteristics of the three plays (and suggestions about their possible impact on the resolutions), let us now look at the dialogue, the primary ground for objective research on dramatic literature. This research on Shaw's rhetoric follows earlier studies of syntax in the first acts of twenty-one English-language plays; it assumes that the correlations between syntactical items and character traits discussed in those studies exist. As in the other projects, I have accumulated data on eleven syntactic variables; however, here I have chosen to present the results on only five: questions, imperatives, and definitions (because of their importance in readers' judgments of the character trait *dominance*), as well as exclamations and adverbs (because of their usefulness as guides to *excitability* and *education*).[14]

My previous research has shown all five variables to be independent measures; however, I have chosen these five syntactic items for critical, not statistical, reasons. I worked with all eleven until it became clear to me that these five revealed most about character differentiation. Counts on the five traits allow the presentation of a high level of information unencumbered by too many details. Figures 1–12 show the plotted scores and the raw numbers for each character's use of the five variables.[15] Looking at the plots for the three plays, one can see at a glance the increasing complexity.

MRS. WARREN'S PROFESSION

The resolution of *Mrs. Warren's Profession* leaves Vivie having contentedly dismissed her mother (and her erstwhile lover) in exchange for work as an actuary and an occasional cigar. My working hypothesis for this play is that Vivie's strength of character, measured by her use of dominant syntax, enables her to dismiss her mother and go on to live her own life. In order to gauge the relative strengths of the two characters, we look at the scenes where the two characters talk alone to see if the hypothesis matches the actual resolution. These conversations occur at the end of Act II and Act IV.

The end of Act II naturally divides into two scenes at the point where, according to both the stage directions and the tone of the dialogue, a new Mrs. Warren emerges.

> You! youve no heart. [*She suddenly breaks out vehemently in her natural tongue—The dialect of a woman of the people—with all her affectations of maternal authority and conventional manners gone, and an overwhelming inspiration of true conviction and scorn in her*] (309)

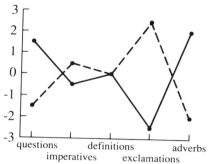

Figure 1
Act II, Scene 3

	que	imp	def	exc	adv
Vivie	18	5	15	2	4
Mrs. Warren	15	6	15	7	0

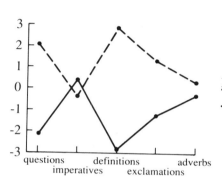

Figure 2
Act II, Scene 4

	que	imp	def	exc	adv
Mrs. Warren	27	4	46	17	10
Vivie	6	8	17	4	7

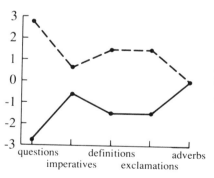

Figure 3
Act IV, Scene 2

	que	imp	def	exc	adv
Mrs. Warren	34	13	51	12	9
Vivie	12	8	39	0	9

FIGURES 1–3. *Mrs. Warren's Profession*

Breaking the scene here brings the power shift from Vivie (in the first half of the conversation) to Mrs. Warren (in the second) into sharp focus. As Figures 1 and 2 show, Vivie is the stronger during the beginning of the conversation when she conducts her accusatory interrogation of her mother, but Mrs. Warren is the stronger when she defends her choices.

Figure 1

Vivie begins Act II, Scene 3 by asking a series of rhetorical questions designed to inform her mother that she considers herself independent.

> Why? Do you expect that we shall be much together?
>
> You and I, I mean? (305)
>
> Do you think my way of life would suit you? (306)
>
> Has it really never occurred to you, mother, that I have a way of life like other people? (307)

Mrs. Warren's initial responses are of shocked disbelief and "motherly" superiority; she makes several belittling assertions about Vivie's attempt at independence, first in the form of rhetorical questions and then in the form of a piece of advice, phrased as a negative imperative, complete with a double put-down:

> Y o u r way of life! What do you mean? What nonsense is this youre trying to talk? Do you want to show your independence, now that youre a great little person at school? Dont be a fool, child. (306)

As the third scene progresses, Mrs. Warren expresses vacillating emotions: she is at first galled by Vivie's indifference, then infuriated by the silent responses to her assertions of authority. She querulously attempts to assert her rights as Vivie's mother, then passes through a stage of weepy recriminations, and finally is driven to express herself, as Shaw indicates in the stage directions, *wildly* and *passionately*. But we would recognize these emotional shifts without the stage directions, since the syntax expresses them just as clearly. Vivie's cold, analytic questioning and distant asserting provoke intensely emotional reactions which reverberate through Mrs. Warren's sentences.

> Dont keep on asking me questions like that. Hold your tongue . . . Your way of life will be what I please, . . .
>
> You young imp! Take care. I shall do something I'll be sorry for after, and you too. (306)

Oh, my darling, how can you be so hard on me? Have I no rights over you as your mother?

Oh no, no. Stop, stop. I a m your mother: I swear it.

Oh, you cant mean to turn on me—my own child! it's not natural. You believe me, dont you? Say you believe me. (307)

You dont know what youre asking. I cant tell you.

My God, what sort of woman are you? (308)

The pressure of Mrs. Warren's warning and begging imperatives, her attempted assertions of authority, and her disbelieving questions keep Vivie from winning audience sympathy despite her obvious right to seek the identity of her father. As Figure 1 shows, Mrs. Warren just barely exceeds Vivie on imperative use and matches her in definition use. Thus, though Vivie's strength is apparent, Mrs. Warren's side of the debate is strongly presented even in this, the weakest of her scenes.

Figure 2

In Act II, Scene 3 both characters define the world equally; in Scene 4 Mrs. Warren does almost all the defining. The high and low uses of four variables shift: where before Vivie asked more questions and Mrs. Warren used more imperatives, here Mrs. Warren is much higher on questions and uses fewer imperatives. They also exchange places on adverbs; the only consistency between the characters' syntactical usages is that Mrs. Warren still uses a commanding majority of exclamations. Few would dispute that the scene where Mrs. Warren justifies her choices in life (and simultaneously Vivie comes to respect her) reveals Mrs. Warren at her strongest. Her arguments convince. She draws a clear and circumstantial account of her youth, of the choices offered to her by the world she was born into, and of her feelings about prostitution as a realistic profession for poor women.

Rhetorically, Shaw equips her with every syntactic and semantic tool in his kit to win over both Vivie and the audience to her vision of the realities of prostitution in the world as it is presently constituted. Her pragmatic reasoning on this subject comes from solid good sense mixed with a real regret that poor women are faced with such limited chances.

It's far better than any other employment open to her. I always thought that oughtnt to be. It c a n t be right, Vivie, that there shouldnt be better opportunities for women. I stick to that: it's wrong. But it's so, right or wrong; and a girl must make the best of it. (314)

Mrs. Warren's impact on Vivie is palpable, and by the end of the act Vivie admits her defeat.

> My dear mother: you are a wonderful woman: you are stronger than all England. (315)
>
> You have got completely the better of me tonight, though I intended it to be the other way. Let us be good friends now. (316)

However, we should not fail to note Shaw's implicit comment on the change wrought in Vivie. Her act-closing embrace of her mother, both verbal and physical, is ironically contrasted with Mrs. Warren's sentimental sequence of wheedling tag questions and exclamations.

> I brought you up well, didn't I, dearie? And you'll be good to your poor old mother for it, wont you? Blessings on my own dearie darling! a mother's blessing! (316)

Figure 3

When we move from this scene of Mrs. Warren triumphant (but hinting of her fears about the future) to Act IV, Scene 2, we see a remarkable difference between the action of the scene and the shape of the contrasting lines in Figure 3. Although Vivie is firmly in charge during the dismissal scene, she speaks fewer lines and uses fewer of all the sentence types than does her mother; Vivie matches Mrs. Warren only on adverb use. I must therefore consider whether the Act IV, Scene 2 numbers refute my analytic presuppositions.

The variable usage table and Figure 3, which represents the numbers graphically, would seem to indicate that Mrs. Warren is far and away the stronger of the two, yet the action of the last act of the play shows Vivie winning her point and Mrs. Warren being summarily dismissed. Either the plotted points reveal nothing about who the dominant character is or, as I will argue, the shape of the plotted line reveals why readers and audiences have difficulty with the resolution of this play. The quantity and power of Mrs. Warren's speech, though totally consistent with her character, make it difficult for audiences to accept Shaw's eminently practical resolution of the action. Mrs. Warren's speech habits should adequately establish her dominance, but Shaw imposes a reasoned outcome on an emotional dilemma. Vivie is "right" in asserting that:

> I am my mother's daughter. I am like you: I must have work, must make more money than I spend. But my work is not your work, and my way not your way. We must part. (353)

This resolution makes perfect sense but still is not emotionally convincing. Audiences come with too much emotional baggage about mothers and daughters, and about fairness (Vivie owes Mrs. Warren duty in exchange for being brought up as a respectable woman) to be able to accept either Vivie's hardness or Mrs. Warren's utter rout. In addition to what the audience brings, Shaw's own depiction of Mrs. Warren's vitality and rhetorical strength creates expectations that Shaw refuses to fulfill. Vivie overwhelms her mother into agreement using two exclamations and an agreement-seeking question:

> No: right to get rid of you! I should be a fool not to! Isnt that so? (355)

Mrs. Warren grudgingly admits that Vivie is right, but not without noting:

> But Lord help the world if everybody took to doing the right thing! (355)

The percentage of readers and audiences who agree with her has not been studied objectively. But, from early to contemporary, almost all critics comment on Vivie's "coldness"; I believe that the "warmth" of Mrs. Warren's language (as reflected in Figure 3) contributes significantly to this judgment.

People are rarely as reasonable, farsighted, and cool in their dealings with one another as characters in Shaw's plays. Here, as it would in a number of later plays, Shaw's poetics conflict with his rhetoric. He paints Mrs. Warren as rhetorically powerful even in the last scene of the play when Vivie dismisses her. His dramatic sense about Mrs. Warren forbids inconsistency; had he been more a dogmatist, less a dramatist, he could have portrayed Vivie as greatly stronger, Mrs. Warren weaker.[16]

The resolution in this play does not convince because Shaw insists that the pragmatic solution take precedence over the emotional realities signified by the syntax. Mrs. Warren, given that she speaks more lines and employs a more energetic syntax, should emerge triumphant at the end of the play. As it is, Shaw wants to have his dramatically consistent cake and make the public eat his moral vision too. That combination works for Shaw, but rarely for readers or audiences.[17]

MAJOR BARBARA

In the second play of the sample, four scenes must be analyzed and three characters must be included on the plotted representation of the four scenes. When only two characters are plotted, as in *Mrs. Warren's Profession,* the peak of one character, by definition, matches the valley of the other. The picture shows only where the two are closely related and where exceedingly differentiated. When a third character contributes to the sums, the numerical interrelations and therefore the plotted pictures change.

Shaw's goals in *Major Barbara* are to clarify the relations between money and arms and to show why the armorers always win over the religious and the intellectuals. This means first educating the audience about the real relations between armorers and society—through the education of both Barbara and Cusins—and then demonstrating why these two representatives of the positive forces in society end up working for a munitions maker. The actual resolution of the play—Barbara and Cusins ecstatically agreeing to work in Undershaft's village—can be explained by an analysis of the scenes in which they interact.

Figure 4

The plot debate begins in Act I, Scene 2 when Barbara and Undershaft make a bargain: each promises to visit the other's work place and take the chance of being converted to the other's values:

UNDERSHAFT. May I ask have you ever saved a maker of cannons?

BARBARA. No. Will you let me try?

UNDERSHAFT. Well, I will make a bargain with you. If I go to see you tomorrow in your Salvation Shelter, will you come the day after to see me in my cannon works?

BARBARA. Take care. It may end in your giving up the cannons for the sake of the Salvation Army.

UNDERSHAFT. Are you sure it will not end in your giving up the Salvation Army for the sake of the cannons?

BARBARA. I will take my chance of that.

UNDERSHAFT. And I will take my chance of the other. [They shake hands on it.] (91)

From this beginning one might suspect another two-character struggle for the power to define; however, as the play progresses, Cusins, who was initially identified merely as Barbara's highly educated fiancé, becomes an important player. Though named after Barbara in her capacity as a major in the Salvation Army, the play really focuses on Undershaft's desire to find a successor to manage the munitions works; that person turns out to be Cusins.

Once one knows what the play is about, discovering the scenes where the essential relationships are revealed is easy. Act I, Scene 2 shows Undershaft controlling the conversation on his first visit with his estranged family (and the two fiancés, Cholly and Dolly). Figure 4 demonstrates, however, that his control is not absolute: Barbara outdoes Undershaft and Cusins on both imperatives and exclamations (the two men share second place on these variables). Undershaft uses the critical indicators of dominance (questions and definitions) at a markedly

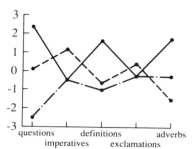

Figure 4
Act I, Scene 2

	que	imp	def	exc	adv
Undershaft	15	2	18	0	11
Barbara	8	7	11	2	1
Cusins	0	2	10	0	5

questions imperatives definitions exclamations adverbs

Figure 5
Act II, Scene 4

	que	imp	def	exc	adv
Cusins	21	5	49	5	8
Undershaft	17	5	42	5	3
Barbara	7	3	14	2	2

questions imperatives definitions exclamations adverbs

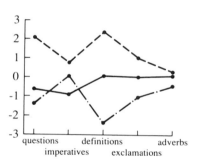

Figure 6
Act II, Scene 5

	que	imp	def	exc	adv
Barbara	15	10	26	13	4
Undershaft	4	3	17	9	3
Cusins	1	7	7	5	1

questions imperatives definitions exclamations adverbs

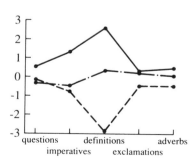

Figure 7
Act III, Scene 2

	que	imp	def	exc	adv
Undershaft	30	41	113	23	19
Cusins	14	8	72	21	13
Barbara	17	2	13	9	3

questions imperatives definitions exclamations adverbs

FIGURES 4–7. *Major Barbara*

higher level than either Cusins or Barbara; he also makes a notably high use of adverbs. This last is somewhat striking, as this variable usually correlates with educated, intellectual characters. Although Undershaft goes out of his way to identify himself as "not a gentleman; and . . . never educated," his speech patterns belie his protestations and show him to be a conscious rhetorician. Undershaft appeals to Cusins, the professor, by admitting his own lack of education, while simultaneously demonstrating that refined intelligence can come from sources other than being a gentleman.

Figure 5

In Act 2, Scene 4, when Cusins shows up as the syntactically primary character, Undershaft is actually seducing Cusins with his redefinition of the functions of religion and preparing the audience for the principal action of Act II—the "buying" of the Army.

> UNDERSHAFT. Barbara must belong to us, not to the Salvation Army.
>
> CUSINS. Well, I can only say that if you think you will get her away from the Salvation Army by talking to her as you have be talking to me, you dont know Barbara.
>
> UNDERSHAFT. My friend: I never ask for what I can buy.
>
> CUSINS. [in a white fury] Do I understand you to imply that you can buy Barbara?
>
> UNDERSHAFT. No; but I can buy the Salvation Army.
>
> CUSINS. Quite impossible.
>
> UNDERSHAFT. You shall see. All religious organizations exist by selling themselves to the rich (121).

From here on Undershaft proceeds to demolish every argument that Cusins offers in defense of the Army by pointing out how the Army "draws their [the poor's] teeth" and thus benefits "a man of business."

Both Cusins and Undershaft appear on the high side of the plot in Figure 5; Barbara (not on stage for much of the scene) can only come up with negative numbers on this plot. Cusins speaks more lines and uses more questions, definitions, and adverbs than either of the others. In this case the secondary character (Undershaft) matches the principal speaker (Cusins) only on imperatives and exclamations. Shaw's restraint in his portrayal of Undershaft's rhetorical strength I take to be a very subtle example of his debating skill: the cagey rhetorician lures unwary opponents out into the open by letting them seem to "win" in the early encounters.

Figure 6

In Act II, Scene 5, Barbara's line stands out at the top of the plot. The points on this plot visually represent both Barbara's syntactic superiority and her solitude above the alliance of Undershaft and Cusins. She outstrips the two males in the use of all variables; they merely interact with each other below the mean. The end of Act II is tragic for Barbara; however, her tragedy is strongly undercut by the representation of the league between Undershaft and Cusins, who leave Barbara to go marching out to "the great meeting" with drum and trombone.

> BARBARA. Dolly: you are breaking my heart.
>
> CUSINS. What is a broken heart more or less here? Dionysos Undershaft has descended. I am possessed. (135)

Barbara's response to Undershaft's buying of the Army and Cusins's ironic possession is an emotionally intense loss of faith in the Army.

> I can't pray now. Perhaps I shall never pray again. [*almost delirious*] I can't bear any more. Quick march! Drunkenness and Murder! My God, why hast thou forsaken me? (136)

By echoing Christ's words on the cross, Barbara connects her sufferings to his; for a religious person, no words could point to tragedy more emphatically than these. However, the rest of the play does not build on this emotion. In Act III Scene 2, Undershaft admonishes Barbara not to "make too much of your little tinpot tragedy." (170) Out of such emotional redefinitions is the Shavian rhetorical world built.

Barbara's Act II, Scene 5 (Figure 6) tragedy compares interestingly with Undershaft's Act III, Scene 2 rhetorical appeals to Cusins to succeed him at the munitions works (Figure 7). Both figures reflect the power of the central characters' speech, despite the differences in the emotions imputed to those characters. The high use of all five syntactic variables can work in vastly different emotional contexts. In this case, a statistical test prevents any further elaboration of the similarity between the shape of the two plotted lines. The cell chi-square statistic serves as an objective warning that the differences in the language assigned to the characters in Act II, Scene 5 are not significant, whereas those in Act III, Scene 2 are.[18]

Figure 7

In Act III, Scene 2, Undershaft triumphs over Barbara's emotions with his emotional arguments:

BARBARA. And will he be the better for that?

UNDERSHAFT. You know he will. Dont be a hypocrite, Barbara. He will be better fed, better housed, better clothed, better behaved . . . It is cheap work converting starving men with a Bible in one hand and a slice of bread in the other. I will undertake to convert West Ham to Mahometanism on the same terms. Try your hand on my men: their souls are hungry because their bodies are full.

BARBARA. And leave the East End to starve?

UNDERSHAFT. [his energetic tone dropping into one of bitter and brooding remembrance] I was an east ender. I moralized and starved until one day I swore that I would be a full-fed free man at all costs; that nothing should stop me except a bullet, neither reason nor morals nor the lives of other men. (173)

Readers may notice that he has not responded to Barbara's basic question about her (or anyone's) responsibilities to the poor of the East End, but on stage Barbara accepts his personal testimony as an answer. Soon after he uses Cusins's breadth of historical knowledge as a lever against him.

UNDERSHAFT. Vote! Bah! When you vote, you only change the names of the cabinet. When you shoot, you pull down governments, inaugurate new epochs, abolish old orders and set up new. Is that historically true, Mr Learned Man, or is it not?

CUSINS. It is historically true. I loathe having to admit it. I repudiate your sentiments. I abhor your nature. I defy you in every possible way. Still it is true. But it ought not to be true.

UNDERSHAFT. Ought! ought! ought! ought! ought! Are you going to spend your life saying ought, like all the rest of our moralists? Turn your oughts into shalls, man. (174/175)

These passages and Figure 7, in their different ways, demonstrate the primary fact about this scene: Undershaft speaks constantly. He uses an impressively high number of all syntactic items and, in passage after passage, other characters speak single lines while he discourses in paragraphs. Whether readers or audiences are convinced by Undershaft's blazing rhetoric, Act III, Scene 2 represents an internally satisfying debate. Cusins and Barbara are persuaded that the best venue for their respective talents is Perivale St. Andrews and the munitions factory.

The same question arises with *Major Barbara* as arose in the resolution of *Mrs. Warren's Profession:* why doesn't this resolution universally convince (or better, satisfy) readers and audiences? Shaw uses almost all of Act I to prepare us for Undershaft's strength;[19] in Act II and earlier in Act III, he shows us the great need of both Barbara and Cusins to find work that satisfies them spiritually. Shaw has certainly put much more rhetorical skill into preparing audiences and readers for his resolution here than he used in the earlier play, yet critics starting with Gilbert Murray (the original for Cusins) have disputed the meaning of the play's ending.[20]

The critical tendency has been to accept the play's resolution, but to assert that it doesn't mean Undershaft has won; rather, that Barbara and Cusins will eventually triumph by bringing the values of religion and culture to Undershaft's world.[21] Such a sentimental reading arises out of the conventional certainty that attractive, idealistic characters will prevail. Shaw's pragmatic values represent a world where the strong win, not because they are better but because they are stronger. There can be little doubt that Undershaft is the strongest character in this trio. He is the main subject of discussion before his first entrance. His high use of questions and definitions (two of the leading indicators of dominance) as well as his high use of adverbs (the sign of intellectual power) make him stand out during his first appearance. The play ends after a scene in which he completely dominates on all variables; in the final scene Barbara and Cusins also admit to being won over to his "religion."

Shaw indicates clearly in his letters that he does not want readers and audiences to like this resolution, but rather to learn from it.[22] But regardless of what Shaw says in his letters, the internal message behind all the idealistic raptures of Barbara and Cusins at the end of the play is that in a world constituted as a collection of nation-states bickering over supremacy, the munitions maker will always, as Undershaft had told Lady Britomart and Stephen earlier in Act III, "pay the piper and call the tune." Undershaft defines himself as the strongest character in the play, the one who has to win; he has something to offer Barbara—a place where "souls are hungry because their bodies are full"—and she has nothing to give him (other than the opportunity to win over Cusins).

In this case, Shaw's rhetoric matches his purposes completely: Undershaft is the winner of the plot debate, and Undershaft uses the syntax of dominance. The problem with this resolution is not inconsistency between the morality espoused by the play and the language assigned to the winning character. The complexity of the issues explored (money and munitions, the powers of good and the powers of evil) and the more traditional plot elements (boy, girl, inheritance) work against each other. Shaw undermines the play's resolution by making the losing characters an unconventional but attractive young couple. Audiences who have gotten emotionally involved with Barbara and Cusins in Act II have a hard time accepting a resolution in which the young couple not only decide to join Undershaft in the making of munitions but also go off joyfully to find a house in the village as if in a "they-lived-happily-ever-after" fairy tale.[23]

There are two ways out of this dilemma: either blink out the business (murder and mutilation) they are joining or blink out Undershaft's superior strength and imagine a triumphant trinity of forces (power, religion, and poetry). Both solutions fly in the face of the clear arguments of the third Act, but they have been the standard ways of trying to be content with the resolution. Thus has the ending been sentimentalized despite Shaw's complete deployment of his mature rhetorical skills.[24]

HEARTBREAK HOUSE

The analysis of *Heartbreak House* proves more complicated than that of either earlier play. Determining which scenes need study is, in itself, somewhat difficult. I have chosen Act I, scenes 2 and 4, because they respectively represent Hesione's public (to the guests) and private (to her father and husband) faces. These two scenes (taken together) reveal many things the three inhabitants of the house hide from their guests.[25] Scene 1 of Act II consists of Ellie's interview with Mangan, Hesione and Ellie's discussion of Mangan while he is hypnotized, and his later reactions to that discussion. The last vestiges of the traditional "education of a young girl" plot promised in Act I dissolve in Act II, Scene 1. These three scenes first set up, then knock down, conventional expectations. Since the rest of Act II only hints at the play's direction or meaning, both scenes of Act III must be analyzed if the resolution of the play is to be understood.

When looking at plays that exist primarily at the literal level (like *Mrs. Warren's Profession* and *Major Barbara*), issues of dominance revolve around two or three characters who really are fighting to define reality. The action and meaning of *Heartbreak House* are, however, primarily metaphoric. The battles here are more diffused; the characters, since they represent allegorical virtues or vices, are dominant only as needed to establish the play's definition of reality. The relationship between character and dominance in this play can be summed up in these three assertions: the inhabitants of *Heartbreak House* and their visitors take turns being briefly, and therefore ineffectually, dominant. The shifts in dominance embody the central metaphor of the play: England, like this house, is a ship without a skipper heading for the rocks.

The plots of the primary speakers in the five crucial scenes direct attention to the differences between this late play and the two earlier ones. Initially, the first three plots for *Heartbreak House,* Figures 8, 9, and 10, may look similar to the three-character scenes in *Major Barbara;* however, a closer inspection shows that six characters count as major in these three scenes. Only one character, Hesione, reappears in all three scenes; another, Ellie, appears in two; and four others, Ariadne, Shotover, Hector, and Mangan, appear only once. The last two scenes (Figure 11 and 12) exemplify the differences even more clearly. The first of these requires the plotting of four characters, the second of five characters. All told, seven different characters are momentarily dominant (Hesione and Ellie, as well as Ariadne, Mangan, Hector, Shotover, and Mazzini), so must be represented on one or more plots.

Figure 8

Hesione dominates the action in Act I, Scene 2; she uses the most questions, imperatives, and exclamations and shares with Ellie the high use of definitions. Ariadne's presence, but lack of importance, in the scene is reflected by her negative scores on all variables; Ellie, on the other hand, manages to use considerably more adverbs than Hesione and to match her in defining. In this combination of syntax Ellie resembles Vivie in Act II, Scene 3 of *Mrs. Warren's Profession*. Each of these younger women holds her own in the battle for definition against the older woman while clearly asserting her own superior education. However, each, in her own way, is dominated by the older woman's stronger use of the syntax of dominance. Vivie manages to ask a few more questions and, as was noted earlier, they are powerful ones, but Mrs. Warren still outdoes her in imperatives. Ellie's three imperatives hardly emerge against the background of Hesione's thirteen.

The most striking syntactic feature of Figure 8 is, in fact, Hesione's extraordinarily high use of both questions and exclamations. No other character in the thirty scenes of this sample, including several that are much longer (See Table 1 for the number of lines in Scene 9 of *Major Barbara* and Scene 5 of *Heartbreak House*) exceeds Hesione in number of questions and exclamations. Hesione dominates Act I of *Heartbreak House* by appearing in three of its four scenes and speaking the highest number of lines; her speech habits also correspond to those of dominant characters. The play starts by giving the strong impression that Hesione will be the principal character. As the other plots show, however, she re-emerges as a character in competition for dominance (with Mangan) in only one other scene (Act II, Scene 1).

Shaw used a similar approach in Act I, Scene 1 of *Major Barbara*, where Lady Britomart's syntactic dominance overwhelms Stephen. There, the apparently dominant character functions to introduce the truly dominant character, Undershaft. In this play, where no play-dominating character ever does emerge, Hesione's early dominance only functions to establish her occasional power in the world of *Heartbreak House;* her lack of dominance in the last scene of Act I prepares us for the erratic power shifts that define the world of pre-World War I England as Shaw presents it in this play.

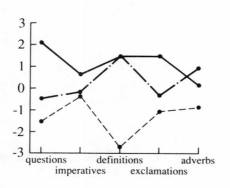

Figure 8
Act I, Scene 2

Hesione	48	13	60	35	15
Ellie	17	3	60	14	24
Ariadne	4	1	10	5	3
	que	imp	def	exc	adv

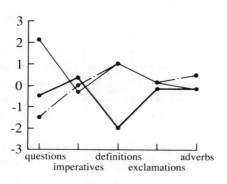

Figure 9
Act I, Scene 4

Hector	19	2	30	6	2
Shotover	8	3	30	6	4
Hesione	11	4	21	5	2
	que	imp	def	exc	adv

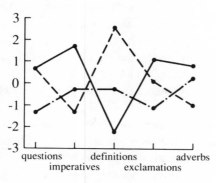

Figure 10
Act II, Scene 1

Hesione	39	28	65	23	18
Mangan	39	13	89	18	9
Ellie	29	18	75	12	15
	que	imp	def	exc	adv

FIGURES 8–12. *Heartbreak House*

Figure 9

Figure 9 reflects the antiphonal dialogue in Act I, Scene 4—the strange, private exchange between the three permanent inhabitants of the house: Hesione,

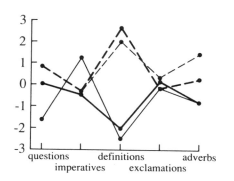

Figure 11
Act III, Scene 1

	que	imp	def	exc	adv
_Ariadne	21	6	42	11	14
_Mangan	21	6	46	8	7
_Hesione	16	5	18	10	1
_Hector	6	15	15	8	1

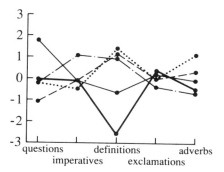

Figure 12
Act III, Scene 2

	que	imp	def	exc	adv
Mazzini	4	1	32	4	10
_Hector	14	3	22	5	4
Shotover	4	9	30	2	1
_Ariadne	0	3	31	4	6
_Hesione	5	3	12	6	2

FIGURES 8–12. (*cont.*)

Hector, and Captain Shotover. The plotted lines cluster tightly on three variables; in fact, two characters share the same number of definitions, of exclamations, and of adverbs, but not always the same two characters. Hector comes closest to being dominant on this chart: he uses as many questions as the other two combined, and as many definitions and exclamations as Captain Shotover. Shotover also uses the highest number of adverbs; but the numbers are so small (4, 2, and 2) that they indicate very little. Hesione, markedly down from her Act I, Scene 2 dominance, shows up as high on imperatives only; however, again the differences are so small (between 4, 3, and 2) that they hardly merit attention.

The real business of this scene is to reveal the intimate concerns of the inhabitants of the house; all three, to different degrees, care more about the relations between power and money (a theme that is central for Shaw in all three plays) than about the sexual dalliances that appear to motivate them in the public scenes. Hector and Shotover discuss winning "the powers of life and death" over the

Mangans and Randalls of this world, who are "strangling [their] souls." The sound of this scene is more like a trio of matched voices than a conflict between contrasting voices. The scene emphasizes similarities, instead of differences, among the three inhabitants of the house, as can easily be seen by contrasting this plot to the others in the sample.

Figure 10

Act II, Scene 1 as represented in Figure 10 shows Hesione back to her earlier strengths, highest on imperatives, exclamations, and adverbs and equaling Mangan on questions. Ellie, who appears to be demonstrating her new power both with Mangan and with Hesione in this long and crucial scene, still shows up to be much weaker than either of them when the items of syntax are counted. This weakness is especially striking because Ellie speaks more lines than anyone else in Act II.

An obvious explanation of this underemphasized speech can be found by anyone sensitive to the tone of Ellie's reaction to her Act I heartbreak: she expresses her depression though the use of low-intensity, i.e., essentially unmarked, language. Ellie's use of all the variables that have to do with dominance is exactly predictable, that is, it matches her role size. Her use of the variables that correlate with judgments of excitability (exclamations and fragments) is notably low (7 and 13 percent, respectively, below what could be predicted given the size or her role). Thus, though the semantic content of her speeches tells us that she can manipulate Mangan and Hesione as well as Hesione manipulated her in Act I, an investigation of her syntax shows her surpassed by both Mangan and Hesione on questions and exclamations, by Hesione on imperatives and adverbs, and by Mangan on definitions.

The real struggle for control, mirrored in the syntax, goes on between Hesione and Mangan. Mangan's importance in this scene is noteworthy since he is represented as hypnotized (i.e., mute) during 340 lines of this 620-line scene. Even so, he manages to define the situation at a markedly higher level than either of the women, one of whom (Ellie) is on stage and speaking throughout the scene. Mangan gets in fifty-six definitions before Ellie puts him under and thirty-three after she wakes him up. He also matches Hesione in questions, though semantically his are more truculent than dominant.

Figure 11

Act III, Scene 1 presents the characters sitting, or wandering around, outside the house. Figure 11 is the first chart to reflect the syntax usage of four characters and, as might be expected, the extra character makes the chart look more complicated. Ariadne uses the highest number of exclamations and adverbs and shares the highest question use with Mangan. Ariadne speaks so much more than any other character in Scene 1 that she ends up being the principal speaker of the entire act. Considering Shaw's earlier habit of giving the largest share of the dialogue to the rhetorically dominant character, the assignment of so many lines to a rather unimportant outsider is surprising. Ariadne does explain what is wrong with the house (no stables), thus introducing the contrast between Horseback Hall and Heartbreak House. It is at this point that the play begins veering away from the drawing-room-comedy tradition of sexual intrigues and into its own unabashedly allegorical vein.

The other highly noticeable character is Mangan; he defines more than any other character and is a high questioner. Again, as an outsider who is the butt of much ill-treatment, Mangan hardly seems an appropriate definer of the issues as the play winds down to its symbolic ending. In Scene 1, after all discuss Mangan's engagement to Ellie, he tells the truth about money and no one believes him, which leads into a discussion first of who will save England, then to Mangan's attempts to tear off his clothes, and finally to Ellie's revelation that she does not intend to hold Mangan to their engagement.

The only thing remotely like a physical action is Mangan's abortive attempt to strip. The spiritual action is dilatory and diffuse: many subjects arise, are discussed briefly, and then submerge in the darkness of the evening. In terms of the traditional definitions of play structure, the breaking of the engagement between Ellie and Mangan is the only dramatic action; this action completes the plot on its simplest level. The breaking of the engagement, however, is finally accomplished not, as the first act had led us to expect, by Hesione's machinations, but by Ellie's report of her spiritual marriage with the Captain.

Figure 12

Act III, Scene 2 takes the action much further into the realm of symbolism. The allegory in the previous scene might be ignored by playgoers trying desperately to hang onto the literal weekend-at-a-house-in-the-country level of the play, but no such illusions can be cherished in this last scene. Figure 12, the most cluttered plot, represents the primary syntax of the five characters with the largest roles in Act III, Scene 2. Four characters break the surface of the net of lines by being the highest users of at least one variable. Each of the connections between an item of syntax and a character is important.

In an ensemble scene like this one, Shaw must define each character's part in the represented action. He helps readers and audiences to hold all the strands of the rambling conversation together by assigning each character a keynote. Mazzini, Ellie's father and a mild-mannered fighter for freedom, who has been decidedly secondary and quite unprepossessing until the last scene, emerges as the final definer of the whole company at *Heartbreak House:*

> Surely, if I may say so, rather a favorable specimen of what is best in our English culture. You are very charming people, most advanced, unprejudiced, frank, humane, unconventional, democratic, free-thinking and everything that is delightful to thoughtful people. (173)

Later in a series of calm, yet devastating, definitions, Mazzini sums up his view of the political realities.

> Every year I expected a revolution, or some frightful smash-up: it seemed impossible that we could blunder and muddle on any longer. But nothing happened except, of course, the usual poverty and crime and drink that we are used to. Nothing ever does happen. It's amazing how well we get along, all things considered. (175)

This fatalistic summary of the practical consequences of life without a point leads Hector, who is the prominent questioner, to seek answers from Shotover who, as the embodiment of ancient wisdom, gives advice and issues injunctions.

> CAPTAIN SHOTOVER. It is the man who lies drinking in his bunk and trusts to Providence that I call the drunken skipper, though he drank nothing but the waters of the River Jordan.
>
> HECTOR. And this ship we are all in? This soul's prison we call England?
>
> CAPTAIN SHOTOVER. . . . Do you think the laws of God will be suspended in favor of England because you were born in it?
>
> HECTOR. Well, I dont mean to be drowned like a rat in a trap. I still have the will to live. What am I to do?
>
> CAPTAIN SHOTOVER. . . . Learn your business as an Englishman. . . . Navigation. Learn it and live; or leave it and be damned. (176–77)

Hesione continues looking for and finding excitement in everything; even at the end of the play, after the unexpected aerial bombing attack, she reacts with an exclamation of pleasure:

> But what a glorious experience! I hope theyll come again tomorrow night. (181)

When Shaw designed a play to make a large social statement about England before the first World War, he had to decide whether or not to present his major characters against a background of stereotypes (i.e., characters not requiring elaboration because they represent socially recognizable types). Like Chekhov in *The Cherry Orchard,* Shaw in *Heartbreak House* creates a metaphor that encapsulates a major historical and social change in complex personal interrelations. Both Chekhov and Shaw use obvious stereotyping in minor characters, but both also foreground a large group of important characters, rather than focusing on only two or three. Plays that attempt to depict a whole society at a significant moment of historical and social change take on a structurally challenging task. Structurally challenging, because many characters, representing a wide spectrum of positions, must be created with a relatively small number of lines.

Shaw presents the five major speakers as if members of an operatic company all singing at once in their different registers and producing an extravagant closing quintet. No character's truth is privileged as the play ends; all contribute their pieces to the puzzle. Every speaker has some of the truth about the sophisticated, urbane, gracious inhabitants of England as World War I approaches. No one character presents Shaw's message. All of the characters, taken together, paint a picture of a civilization heading mindlessly into the future. Although a meaning must be pieced together out of Shotover's "scraps and leavings," the resolution of *Heartbreak House* is surely the most successful of the three in this sample. Exactly because Shaw has created a world where many characters share bits of the truth, but no character is rhetorically strong enough to "win" over the others, he has finally created a play where the resolution truly enacts the theme, is consistent with the rhetorical strategies, and leaves no room for sentimentalizing or misreading.

CONCLUSIONS

The twelve plots reveal that characters in these three plays are assigned syntax more to accord with their roles in specific scenes rather than because of depicted speech habits. Occasionally a character will be associated with a particular feature (i.e., Hesione and exclamations), but even when this co-occurrence happens frequently, it is not likely to supersede a functional need for a high use of that feature in the role of another character (see Ariadne in Figure 11). Minor characters, like Lomax in *Major Barbara*, can be given speech gestures ("Oh, I say!" fourteen times in the play), but the major characters tend to use the syntax of dominance when they are dominant, and not when they are not.

Relative position (who's up, who's down) can be gauged first and foremost by the most obvious measure—number of lines. Once that most primary feature has been established, the next obvious question concerns the complexity of the action: is it two-way, three-way, four-way, or more? The number of characters interacting in a play by Shaw (or for that matter by any other dramatist) affects the emotional impact. Two characters locked in head-to-head conflict display their syntactical differences more sharply than three disputants do. Once a third character is added to a scene, very frequently the dynamics of triangles begin to be seen. Just as all triangles are not equilateral, most threesomes become two-against-one relationships. The Shaw plots graphically display the frequency with which two of the lines appear to match each other, while the third line stands alone, either above the other two (as in Figures 6 and 7) or below (as in Figures 5 and 8). In rare cases (most notably in Figure 10) do we see three characters sharing the floor as competitors of more or less equal strengths.

Shaw appears able to add any number of additional minor roles (five in Act II of *Major Barbara,* and seven in Act II of *Heartbreak House*) without any diminution of the power of his major characters; the minor characters provide a busy background against which the major characters perform. However, when the number of important characters in a scene reaches four or five, the effective strength of each character tends to diminish; the multiplication of speakers divides the impact of any speaker. Each complication of the foreground by another presence, another voice, means both more artistic work for Shaw in differentiation and more intellectual work for the audience or reader. Since a play can occupy only a finite amount of time, Shaw must make each character's position clearer and thus, by consequence, less complicated; he must communicate more in a smaller number of lines.

With computer-aided stylistic analysis, a critic can classify syntactic details and generalize about how characters are differentiated and about how dramatists attempt to accomplish their rhetorical goals. Through this study of twelve scenes in three Shaw plays, I have identified how Shaw could go wrong in the creation of his characters. Vivie triumphs at the end of Act III, Scene 2, while using low levels of marked syntax; she speaks comparatively little and uses a high level of adverbs only. Mrs. Warren, on the other hand, soars above Vivie on all the features which correlate both to dominance and excitability.

Shaw can assert through the plot resolution that Vivie is more powerful than her mother even though he assigns her low-intensity language, but it is a very big risk. Audiences have historically tended to dismiss Vivie as "cold" and the ending as "unbelievable." This kind of analysis can also show Shaw at his rhetorical heights, in Undershaft's immensely powerful appeals to Barbara and Cusins; but even when he is doing everything necessary to surmount a recognized problem, he cannot prevent audiences from sentimentalizing the meaning of resolutions that do not satisfy their emotional needs. Rhetoric, no matter how carefully employed, cannot persuade audiences whose emotions have become engaged by the rhetoric and who therefore seek emotionally satisfying resolutions.

My research on these three plays contributes to several generalizations about what Shaw seems to have learned through the repeated "misreadings" of his endings.[26] In his later plays, Shaw moved away from characters who would arouse the emotions of readers and audiences toward more obvious debates between representatives of conflicting positions. Shaw's getting rid of the power of emotionally convincing characters was like Barbara's getting "rid of the bribe of bread." When Shaw learned that audiences would listen simply for the pleasure of his language, he could stop introducing the dynamite of emotional engagement. So the messages got more complex, the number of characters and crucial scenes increased, and the danger of emotional misreading decreased.

Notes

1. Compiled and edited by E. Dean Bevan (Detroit: Gale Research, 1971). This concordance is unfortunately not based on the most authoritative edition of Shaw's works.

2. Edited by Dan Laurence (London: Max Reinhardt, The Bodley Head, 1970–1972).

3. For examples of work done from the perspective of the literary statistician, see essays by Ross, Stevenson, and Goldfield in this volume. For other examples of work done primarily from the perspective of the literary critic, see the essays in this volume by Fortier, Sabol, Waggoner, and Merideth.

4. St. John Ervine, *Bernard Shaw, His Life, Work, and Friends* (New York: William Morrow, 1956), 71.

5. Richard Ohmann, *Shaw: The Style and the Man* (Middletown, Conn.: Wesleyan University Press, 1962), 71–108, characterized Shaw's nondramatic style as marked by "the posture of opposition." Ohmann excluded the plays from his study, so he does not assert about them; however, a syntactic examination of the dialogue and of the rhetorical challenges Shaw sets for himself shows that the same stylistic stance also characterizes his dramatic writings.

6. I am indebted to R. J. Kaufmann for this insight. See his "Introduction" to *G. B. Shaw, A Collection of Critical Essays* (Englewood Cliffs, N.J.: Prentice-Hall, 1965), especially pages 1–5, for the best general summary of the emotional relations between Shaw and the public.

7. The formulation is mine, but support for various parts of it can be found in: Henry L. Mencken, *George Bernard Shaw, His Plays* (New York, 1905), 8; William Archer quoted in T. F. Evans, *Shaw: The Critical Heritage* (London: Routledge & Kegan Paul, 1976), 63, 116–19, and an unsigned notice, *Morning Post* (op. cit.), 167; Maurice Valency, *The Cart and the Trumpet* (New York: Oxford University Press, 1973), 167; and Nicholas Grene, *Bernard Shaw: A Critical View* (London: Macmillan, 1984), 41, 101.

8. Of course, a whole class of serious twentieth-century drama consists of plays that flout conventional morality. These plays do not attempt to manage the rhetoric because they are not in the business of persuading but rather of shocking. The plays of Shaw's middle period are of quite a different kind; they still hope to convince despite their assault on powerful, extra-literary forces.

9. That three-part project studied eleven syntactic variables in twenty-one first acts and made statistically significant assertions about between-play variability, within-play variability, and correlations between syntax and reader response. For complete details on the variables selected, their reliability for measuring within- and between-play variability, and regression analysis of syntactic contributions to reader responses, see my essays: "Toward a Syntactic Differentiation of Period Style in Modern Drama: Significant Between-Play Variability in 21 English-Language Plays," *Computers and the Humanities* 14 (1980):187–96; "Character Definition Through Syntax: Significant Within-Play Variability in 21 Modern English-Language Plays," *Style* 15, 4 (1981):415–34; "Reader Responses and Character Syntax," in *Computing in the Humanities*, ed. Richard W. Bailey (Amsterdam, New York, Oxford: North-Holland, 1982), 65–78. I do not re-argue the statistical case here; I assume the validity of discoveries described in those studies. See Appendix 2 for a brief discussion of COMP STYLE, the programs designed for this project.

10. Quoted from *American Heritage Dictionary of the English Language*, ed. William Morris (Boston: American Heritage and Houghton-Mifflin, 1971), 1160; almost the same wording appears in *Webster's Third New International Dictionary of the English Language*, unabridged, ed. Philip Babcock Gove (Springfield, Mass.: G. and C. Merriam, 1965).

11. The computer assists the critic here by numbering the lines and thereby encouraging a quantitative approach to the dimensions of the text that would probably not have emerged using more traditional, verbal methods.

12. All quotations from Shaw's plays are from *The Bodley Head Bernard Shaw: Collected Plays with Their Prefaces*, 7 vols., ed. Dan H. Laurence (London, Sydney, Toronto: Max Reinhardt, The Bodley Head, 1970–1972). *Mrs. Warren's Profession* appears in vol. 1 (1970); *Major Barbara* in vol. 3 (1971); *Heartbreak House* in vol. 5 (1972). Shaw's idiosyncratic orthography (e.g., contractions without apostrophes) and use of letter-spacing to indicate emphasis have been retained.

13. The order of presentation of these structural assertions does not follow the order of discovery. The data were originally collected and analyzed by acts; these results were statistically encouraging, but they presented critically unmanageable information. Only after deciding to segment the acts into scenes and to recount those variables that seemed most pertinent did I arrive at reportable results. This process, painful as it was for me, should probably be expected by anyone wishing to use computer-generated analysis of text to make useful critical statements. A literary critic cannot simply apply software to a text and report results; computer criticism requires the extensive use of trial and error methods until the approach matches the text under analysis.

14. Judgments of the character trait *dominance* were elicited with this question: To what extent does the character control the action and/or the other characters? Readers had to respond within a forced-choice five-item scale (i.e., markedly dominant, moderately dominant, neither dominant nor dominated, moderately dominated, and markedly dominated) and were asked to contrast the characters by responding to one trait at a time.

15. The quantitative results could have been represented in many different ways. I wanted a visual device that would enable contrasting the pertinent syntactic facts about one scene with those about another, about one play with those about another. Since some facts will inevitably be highlighted in one presentation and submerged in another, constructing a visual representation requires many decisions about the most informative quantitative data and about the least important information. I chose to represent the numerical relations on a multi-character plot around a zero midpoint because this way of presenting the information facilitated making contrasts between Shaw's early, middle, and late methods of creating characters and achieving resolutions. The process of plotting each character's variable use required collecting the actual number of occurrences per character per scene and figuring the comparative mean scores for array on a $+3$ to -3 table. Scaling the frequencies allowed me to reduce the impact of the differences in raw numbers between heavily occurring variables (like definitions) and infrequently occurring variables (like adverbs or exclamations) and also to reduce the importance of scene length so that comparisons were easier to perceive.

16. Shaw told Janet Achurch in a letter (September 4, 1893) that "I have made the daughter the heroine . . . the great scene will be the crushing of the mother by the daughter." It is interesting to note that he made these assertions when the second act was "half finished," that is, before Mrs. Warren's voice of a "woman of the people" first emerged. See Stanley Weintraub's *Bernard Shaw: The Diaries 1885–1897* (University Park and London: Pennsylvania State University Press, 1986), Vol. 2, 963–66, 970–71, 974–75, 977, 979, 983–85 for Shaw's statements about the play as he was composing it.

17. Shaw was already responding to attacks on the emotional truth of Vivie's dismissal of her mother as early as 1902 in a new preface to the play (*Collected Plays*, vol. 1, 252).

18. According to the chi-square test, the differences in variable use between charac-

ters in this scene are not statistically significant. A quick look at the raw numbers shows why; the differences between one character and another show up only moderately on questions and definitions. Information about the statistical test performed on the frequency counts from each scene (showing which met the "statistically significant" test) can be found in Appendix 5. I do not discuss these results in this essay.

19. For a detailed analysis of how Shaw uses the first act to prepare audiences for the unexpected resolution (Undershaft's winning the plot debate), see my essay "The Rhetoric of a Shavian Exposition: Act One of *Major Barbara,*" *Modern Drama* 26, 1 (1984): 62–74.

20. See Shaw's response to Murray's letter in *Bernard Shaw, Collected Letters, 1898–1910*, ed. Dan H. Laurence (New York: Dodd, Mead, 1972) 565–66.

21. One of the best proponents of this position is Bernard F. Dukore in *Bernard Shaw, Playwright, Aspects of Shavian Drama* (Columbia: University of Missouri Press, 1973), 246–48.

22. *Letters, 1898–1910,* 566.

23. See Dukore, 193–203. Dukore gives an excellent description of Shaw's revisions of the third act to inject brutality into the representation of Undershaft and to strengthen the portrayal of Cusins.

24. The most effective way of avoiding the issues raised in *Major Barbara* and of dismissing Shaw's resolution is to say that the third act is too "talky." The 1941 Gabriel Pascal movie version drops most of the talk in exchange for panoramas of splendid (not specifically military) foundry scenes (sparks flying, molten steel being poured, crashing sounds of heavy machinery) and ends with energetic workers (including a cleaned-up, sober Bill) marching happily by to upbeat music.

25. The contrast between these two scenes exemplifies one of the primary image clusters in the play: masking and unmasking, dressing up and undressing.

26. Shaw's consciousness of, and eventual irritation with, misinterpretations and misreadings can be seen in many of his prefaces (especially those to *Mrs. Warren's Profession, Major Barbara,* and *Pygmalion*).

APPENDIX 1

Scene Boundaries in the Acts of the Three Plays by Shaw:

		First words	Last words
Mrs. Warren's Profession			
Act I			
1	Scene 1	I beg your pardon.	It's very difficult; but—
2	Scene 2	Here they are.	you see my daughter there?
Act II			
3	Scene 1	Oh Lord! I dont know which is	To gain or lose it all.
4	Scene 2	Wherever have you been, Vivie?	Goodnight, dear Mrs. Warren.
5	Scene 3	Did you ever in your life	You! youve no heart.
6	Scene 4	Oh, I wont bear it: I wont put	darling! a mother's blessing!
Act III			
7	Scene 1	Half-past eleven. Nice hour	Vivvums, ring the gate bell.
8	Scene 2	Pleasant young fellow that,	I say—wait—dash it!
Act IV			
9	Scene 1	Come in It's not locked.	—oobye!
10	Scene 2	Well, Vivie, what did you go	And goodbye, Frank.

Major Barbara

Act I
1 Scene 1 What's the matter? but I dont shew it.
2 Scene 2 Are Dolly and Cholly to come in No. Certainly not.

Act II
3 Scene 1 Feel better arter your meal, a fool like you would do.
4 Scene 2 Good morning. expect to be sought after.
5 Scene 3 Oh, there you are, Mr Shirley! to papa: I havnt time.
6 Scene 4 I fancy you guess something be delighted, my dear.
7 Scene 5 Major! Major! heres that man in the proper spirit, miss!

Act III
8 Scene 1 Youve left off your uniform! have outgrown your mother.
9 Scene 2 Well? proud of my father. I—
10 Scene 3 Barbara: I am going to accept in the morning, Euripides.

Heartbreak House

Act I
1 Scene 1 God bless us! that he really forgets.
2 Scene 2 Ellie, my darling, my pettikins I'm quite cured.
3 Scene 3 One second more, and she would Fool! Goat!
4 Scene 4 Your sister is an extremely is not made in the light.

Act II
5 Scene 1 What a dinner! I dont call it thing in this menagerie.
6 Scene 2 Help! Help! A burglar! Help! take a book. Goodnight.
7 Scene 3 Does nothing ever disturb you, Why did you spoil it?
8 Scene 4 I beg your pardon. We did not women! Fall. Fall and crush

Act III
9 Scene 1 What a lovely night! the man. We are all fools.
10 Scene 2 Oh! Here comes the only man Oh, I hope so.

APPENDIX 2

COMP STYLE (the package of programs developed as a result of my studies of between- and within-play variability) finds similar syntactic items, sorts and lists them chronologically by character, and presents tables containing simple comparative numbers about each speaker's use of each variable. COMP STYLE does not give statistical answers to any critical questions about individual works. The package does provide some descriptive statistics about individual works which, when added to descriptive statistics about other, similar works, can answer some statistical, and ultimately some critical, questions.

A statistician confronted with data on eleven syntactic and semantic variables assigned to 132 characters in twenty-one first acts immediately thinks of within- and between-play variability. A critic faced with statistics about variability may wonder how to use this information to answer critically interesting questions. Eventually, translations became obvious. Within-play variability measures differences between characters in a work and can lead to assertions about how characters are defined by their dialogue. Between-play variability measures differences between works and can, when these works are arranged along a time line, lead to descriptions of changes across periods. The character definition data can also be correlated with reader responses to the same works to reveal how reader judgments about certain character traits (primarily dominance and excitability) correlate with the characters' syntax.

APPENDIX 3

The first acts of these twenty-one plays were the sample for my original research project on simple syntax in twenty-one English-language plays.

Author	Title	Year
Shaw	*Mrs. Warren's Profession*	1893
Wilde	*The Importance of Being Earnest*	1895
Shaw	*Major Barbara*	1905
Synge	*The Playboy of the Western World*	1907
O'Casey	*Juno and the Paycock*	1924
Rice	*Street Scene*	1928
Hellman	*The Children's Hour*	1934
Saroyan	*The Time of Your Life*	1939
O'Neill	*Long Day's Journey into Night*	1941
Williams	*A Streetcar Named Desire*	1947
Miller	*Death of a Salesman*	1949
Eliot	*The Cocktail Party*	1949
Beckett	*Waiting for Godot*	1953
Osborne	*Look Back in Anger*	1956
Wesker	*Chicken Soup with Barley*	1958
Hansberry	*A Raisin in the Sun*	1959
Albee	*Who's Afraid of Virginia Woolf?*	1962
Pinter	*The Homecoming*	1965
Stoppard	*Rosencrantz and Guildenstern Are Dead*	1967
Gray	*Butley*	1970
Rabe	*Sticks and Bones*	1972

APPENDIX 4: THE CHI-SQUARE CONTRIBUTION TO THIS STUDY

The chi-square statistic shows that the frequencies (the number of questions, imperatives, definitions, exclamations, and adverbs spoken by the characters) are contingent on the items of syntax used by characters at very significant levels in eight of the twelve scenes. The procedures used to figure these significance levels follow.

The deviations from the mean (created by those characters in that scene) is figured first. The formula is $A1 - (A1 + A2 + \ldots) / X$, where the As stand for each character's use of a feature and X for the number of characters being plotted. Frequently, the answers fall between $+3$ and -3 and are plotted without further transformation. If the raw numbers are large (usually because the scene is long), the highest and lowest answers will fall outside of the +3 to −3 range. In these cases, all results for that scene are divided by whatever divisor will bring them into the +3 to −3 range. This scaling device reduces the impact of scene length, so allows comparison of the shape of characte profiles across scenes and between plays. Had the scaling not been performed, one of the plots would have gone from +43 to −53. I was not interested in allowing the comparative lengths of scenes to interfere in the depiction of the comparative differences between characters within each scene.

Although scaling was used to represent the data on the figures, the actual counts were used in the chi-square tests. I am not a great believer in letting statistical tests tell literary critics what is significant, but I provide Table 2 for those who are. As Table 2 shows, most scenes meet the chi-square test resoundingly; only Act II, Scene 3 of *Mrs. Warren's Profession,* Act II, Scenes 4 and 5 of *Major Barbara,* and Act I, Scene 4 of *Heartbreak House* do not. Since my decisions about the scenes to study proceed from critical principles rather than statistical tests, I did not (on getting these results) dismiss the four scenes from consideration. Statistical analysis confirms that significant variability occurs in two-thirds of the scenes; but it cannot assert that study of the other four scenes is worthless. As it happens, my critical sense coincides with the results of this statistical test; not one of the four scenes bears any crucial weight in my assessment of changes in Shaw's dramatic rhetoric.

		DF	CELL CHI^2 VALUE	PROB	LIKELIHOOD RATIO CHI^2	PROB
Mrs. Warren's	Act II, Scene 3	**4**	7.131	**0.129**	8.840	**0.065**
Profession	Act II, Scene 4	**4**	12.559	**0.014**	11.690	**0.020**
	Act IV, Scene 2	**4**	12.319	**0.015**	16.320	**0.003**
Major	Act I, Scene 2	**8**	22.279	**0.004**	28.076	**0.000**
Barbara	Act II, Scene 4	**8**	3.933	**0.863**	3.948	**0.862**
	Act II, Scene 5	**8**	10.609	**0.225**	10.461	**0.234**
	Act III, Scene 2	**8**	38.964	**0.000**	36.145	**0.000**
Heartbreak	Act I, Scene 2	**8**	23.882	**0.002**	24.373	**0.002**
House	Act I, Scene 4	**8**	6.168	**0.628**	6.261	**0.618**
	Act II, Scene 1	**8**	15.670	**0.047**	16.260	**0.039**
	Act III, Scene 1	**12**	42.399	**0.000**	37.867	**0.000**
	Act III, Scene 2	**16**	45.349	**0.000**	47.845	**0.000**

TABLE 2. Cell chi-square analysis of variable frequencies in twelve scenes from three plays by Bernard Shaw

SELECTED BIBLIOGRAPHY OF THEORETICAL AND PRACTICAL WORKS RELATED TO LITERARY COMPUTING

Since this part of the book is designed to aid newcomers to the field of literary computing, the main bibliography is prefaced with an introductory section on general articles, guides, and reference books. These works are widely recognized, recommended by most specialists, and easily available. They are here annotated only if their titles are not self-explanatory or if my reasons for including them might not be obvious. I note reviews when they appeared in the principal specialist journals: *Style, Computers and the Humanities* (*CHum*), and the various incarnations of the Association of Literary and Linguistic Computing (*ALLC Bulletin, ALLC Journal, Literary and Linguistic Computing*).

Four generous scholars—Joseph Rudman, Nancy Ide, Susan Hockey, and Robert Tannenbaum—made their much larger personal bibliographies available to me; without their help I would not have attempted to devise this selected bibliography. I thank them all and, of course, absolve them of responsibility for my selections and additions.

General Articles, Guides, and Reference Books

Most works in this category can be annotated with the same general comment: "Technically outdated, but a useful introduction to the basic issues involved in . . ." The statistical texts (Thompson, Brainerd, and Kenny) are least subject to this caveat. Changes resulting from improved hardware (more powerful microcomputers) and software (more user-friendly interfaces to large statistical packages, etc.) are occurring constantly. Nevertheless, it is still worth a beginner's time to approach the field as it was five or even ten years ago; these earlier syntheses explain the issues facing humanists who compute.

Brainerd, Barron. *Weighing Evidence in Language and Literature: A Statistical Approach.* Toronto: University of Toronto Press, 1974. Review by Dolores M. Burton in *Style* 11 (1977): 407–09.

Burton, Dolores M. "Automated Concordances and Word Indexes" (in four parts): "The Fifties," *CHum* 15 (1981): 1–14; "The Early Sixties and the Early Centers," *CHum* 15 (1981): 83–100; "The Process, the Progress, and the Product," *CHum* 15 (1981): 139–54; "Machine Decisions and Editorial Revisions" *CHum,* 16 (1982): 195–218. Probably the first contact most humanists have with computing is with a printed concordance. These essays give both an historical and a theoretical discussion of the problems and realities of concordance creation.

Garside, Roger, Geoffrey Leech, and Geoffrey Sampson, eds. *The Computational Analysis of English: A Corpus-Based Approach.* London and New York: Longman, 1987. This collection of essays, by the editors and others, is a polemic in favor of corpus-based analysis of English. Though apparently distant from literary criticism, the insights sought by practical linguists can be essential to those interested in differentiating authors and genres.

Hockey, Susan. *A Guide to Computer Applications in the Humanities.* Baltimore: Johns Hopkins University Press, 1980. Review by F. E. Knowles in *ALLC Bulletin* 8 (1980): 280–81; by Raoul N. Smith in *CHum* 16 (1982): 126–27.

———. "OCR: The Kurzweil Data Entry Machine." *Literary and Linguistic Computing* 1 (1986): 63–67. Describes the realities of "reading" text into computer memory with an optical character recognition machine.

Howard-Hill, T. H. *Literary Concordances, A Complete Handbook for the Preparation of Manual and Computer Concordances.* Oxford: Pergamon, 1979. Review by Serge Lusignan in *CHum* 14 (1980): 129–30.

Kenny, Anthony. *The Computation of Style, An Introduction to Statistics for Students of Literature and the Humanities.* Oxford: Pergamon Press, 1982.

Kučera, Henry, and W. Nelson Francis. *Computational Analysis of Present-day American English.* Providence, R.I.: Brown University Press, 1967. A description of "the Brown Corpus"—a randomly selected, million-word collection of edited English (published in 1962 by authors identified as American). Corpus-based research attempts to make generalizations about features of a language by contrasting usage across carefully devised genre divisions. These generalizations may be useful as standards for measuring literary usage.

Johansson, Stig. "The LOB Corpus of British English Texts: Presentation and Comments." *ALLC Journal* 1 (1980): 25–36. A brief description of the Lancaster-Oslo-Bergen corpus designed to match the Brown Corpus and thus to enable contrasts between the two forms of English.

Oakman, Robert L. *Computer Methods for Literary Research.* 2nd ed. Athens, University of Georgia Press, 1984. Review by V. M. De Feu in *ALLC Bulletin* 13 (1985): 59–60; by Peter C. Patton in *CHum* 15 (1981): 245–46.

Thompson, N. D. "Literary Statistics" (in six parts): "On the Small Print of Statistics," *ALLC Bulletin* 1 (1973): 10–14; "On Probability Distributions," *ALLC Bulletin* 2 (1974): 10–15; "On Estimation," *ALLC Bulletin* 2 (1974): 42–47; "On Hypothesis Testing," *ALLC Bulletin* 2 (1974): 55–61; "Correlation and Regression," *ALLC Bulletin* 3 (1975): 29–35; "On the Future of Literary Statistics," *ALLC Bulletin* 3 (1975): 166–71.

Computer Criticism

COLLECTIONS OF ESSAYS

Books appear in this section if they contain *many* essays of specific literary critical interest: lists of authors' names and short titles follow. There are many collections containing edited papers from a variety of conferences on humanities and literary computing that have not been included here; relevant essays from such collections are cited under Individual Works.

Bailey, Richard W., ed. *Computing in the Humanities*. Amsterdam: North-Holland, 1982. Ralph E. Griswold, "Icon Programming Language"; C. Ruth Sabol, "Focus and Attribution in Ford and Conrad"; Todd K. Bender and Sue M. Briggum, "Quantitative Stylistic Analysis in Ford and Conrad"; Rosanne G. Potter, "Reader Responses and Character Syntax."

Bessinger, Jess B., Stephen M. Parrish, Jr., and Harry F. Arader, eds. *Literary Data Processing Conference*. White Plains, N.Y.: IBM, 1964. Ephim G. Fogel, "The Humanist and the Computer: Vision and Actuality"; Alan Markman, "Asking Meaningful Questions of the Computer"; Louis Milic, "Use and Abuse of Computing in Literary Studies"; Roberto Busa, "An Inventory of Fifteen Million Words"; W. Nelson Francis, "A Standard Corpus of Edited Present-Day American English"; Sally Sedelow, "Parameters for Computational Stylistics"; Joseph Raben, "A Study of Milton's Literary Influence on Shelley"; also early discussions of optical character recognition, standards for machine readable texts, automatic content analysis.

Brunet, Étienne, ed. *Méthodes quantitatives et informatiques dans l'étude des textes/Computers in Literary and Linguistic Research: En hommage à Charles Muller*. 2 vols. Geneva and Paris: Slatkine-Champion, 1986. Barron Brainerd, "Three Issues Related to the Topic of the Conference"; Thomas N. Corns, "Literary Theory and Computer-based Criticism"; Michel Lenoble, "Le Marriage imposible?"; Louis T. Milic, "A Priori Questions in Stylistics"; Klaus M. Schmidt, "Concept versus Meaning. The Contribution of Computer-Assisted Content Analysis and Conceptual Text Analysis to this Disputed Area."

Derval, Bernard, and Michel Lenoble, eds. *La Critique Littéraire et l'Ordinateur / Literary Criticism and the Computer*. Montreal, 1985. Essays by Paul Fortier, "Using the Computer for Literary Criticism"; Susan Hockey, "Literature and the Computer at Oxford University"; John Smith, "ARRAS System for Literary Text Analysis"; Rosanne G. Potter, "Messy Data Sets"; Étienne Brunet, "Le phrase de Zola."

Doležel, Lubomír, and Richard W. Bailey, eds. *Statistics and Style*. New York: American Elsevier, 1967. Bailey's "A Framework for the Statistical Analysis of Style" is especially useful. Other important essays by: Paul R. Bennett, "Yule's Statistic Applied to *Julius Caesar* and *As You Like It*"; E. P. J. Corbett, "Swift's *A Modest Proposal*"; C. B. Williams, "On Sentence Length as a Criterion of Literary Style"; and Karl Kroeber, "The Perils of Quantification: Jane Austen's *Emma*."

Hamesse, Jacqueline, and Antonio Zampoli, eds. *Computers in Literary and Linguistic Computing/L'Ordinateur et les recherches littéraires et linguistiques*. Proceedings of the Eleventh International Conference. Université Catholique de Louvain (Louvain-la-Neuve) 2–6 April 1984. Paris and Genève: Champion-Slatkine, 1985. Elaine F. Nardocchio, "Structural Analysis of Drama: A Québécois Example"; Robert L. Oakman, "Computers and Surface Structures in Prose Style: The Case of Carlyle"; Klaus M. Schmidt, "An Algorithmic Approach to a Parser for Automatic Disambiguation of Homographs in Middle High German On the Basis of the Conceptual Dictionary Project"; Hillel Weiss, "Toward a Computerized Mapping of Literary Texts."

Jones, Alan, and R. F. Churchhouse, eds. *The Computer in Literary and Linguistic Research*. Cardiff: University of Wales Press, 1976. Paul Fortier and Colin McConnell, "French Prose Fiction Text Analysis"; Kenneth Kemp, "Cautions on the Use of Quantitative Linguistics"; Joseph Leighton, "Rhetorical Devices in 17th C. German Sonnets"; Joseph Raben and David Lieberman, "Text Comparison"; David Tallentire, "Confirming Intuitions about Style using Concordances."

King, Margaret, ed. *Parsing Natural Languages, Proceedings of the Second Lugano*

Tutorial, July 6–11, 1981. London: Academic Press, 1983. Eleven essays at an advanced level. Of interest to anyone who wants to understand the issues in parsing as seen by theoretical linguists and artificial intelligence experts. For the past twenty-five years, literary computing has sought reliable methods of automated parsing; when the linguists and AI experts finally achieve this goal, syntactic analysis of literary texts will no longer be dependent on the onerous, and subjective, work of hand-tagging.

Leed, Jacob, ed. *The Computer and Literary Style, Introductory Essays and Studies.* Kent, Ohio: Kent State University Press, 1966. Essays by Sally Yeates Sedelow and Walter A. Sedelow, Jr., "A Preface to Computational Stylistics"; Ivor S. Francis, "An Exposition of the Statistical Approach to the *Federalist* Dispute"; Louis Milic, "Unconscious Ordering in Swift"; Josephine Miles and Hanan C. Selvin, "Factor Analysis and Vocabulary of 17th Century Poetry"; H. H. Somers, "Statistical Methods in Literary Analysis"; and Andrew Q. Morton, "Indications of Authorship in Greek Prose."

INDIVIDUAL WORKS

A few unannotated French titles are included on the recommendations of specialists in this field.

Adamson, Robin. "The Colour Vocabulary in *L'Étranger*." *ALLC Bulletin* 7 (1979): 221–37. Uses a concordance and frequency counts to examine the thematic context of color terms; their importance in relation to the structure of the novel; their relevance in an interpretation of the personality of Meursault and in achieving an effect of stylistic distancing. But, also see Isabel Forbes's "Letter to the Editor," *ALLC Bulletin* 8 (1980): 209–10, for a criticism of the lack of contextualization of this study in either color terms research or available linguistic control group information (the computer corpus: *Trésor de la langue français* and the *Dictionnaire des fréquences du TLF*).

Beatie, Bruce A. "Measurement and the Study of Literature." *CHum* 13 (1979): 185–94. A summary of what a "scientific" study of literature would be, including a brief review of various attempts; ends with the assertion that "we still only have hypotheses, not replication." Based on a survey of the topics treated in *CHum* from 1966 to 1971 (vols. 1–6).

Brunet, Étienne. *Le Vocabulaire français de 1789 à nos jours.* 3 vols. Geneva and Paris: Slatkine/Libraire Champion, 1981. Review by Richard L. Frautschi in *CHum* 15 (1982): 257–59.

Burrows, J. F. *Computation into Criticism: A Study of Jane Austen's Novels and an Experiment in Method.* Oxford: Clarendon Press, 1987. A study of the thirty most common words in Austen's novels and argument for their importance in a literary critical analysis of Austen's style and the styles of her many characters. Certainly the most convincing literary critical demonstration that function words are worth serious study.

Burton, Dolores M. *Shakespeare's Grammatical Style: A Computer-Assisted Analysis of* Richard II *and* Antony and Cleopatra. Austin and London: University of Texas Press, 1973. Review by Barron Brainerd in *CHum* 9 (1975): 40–44. The aim of this excellent book is "to develop a theory and method of literary study at once value based and formal." Burton develops her theory out of a consideration of the basic issues in stylistic analysis (as raised by Ohmann, Riffaterre, Barthes, and Lacan, among others), then describes a method based on applying "the well-defined abstractions of mathematics" to a wide range of grammatical variables. The analysis of the two Shakespeare plays, the central core of the book, reveals the usefulness of linguistic and quantitative categories for stylistic analysis.

Chisholm, David. "Phonology and Style: A Computer-Assisted Approach to German Verse." *CHum* 15 (1981): 199–210. Chisholm's analysis of Goethe's prose and poetry and of 100 sonnets by nineteenth and early twentieth century German poets leads him to generalizations about vertical patterning in German verse. Of particular interest to those seeking computer methods of analyzing sound features in poetry; knowledge of prosodic and statistical terminology assumed.

Cluett, Robert. "Robertson Davies: The Tory Mode." *CHum* 11 (1977):13–23. A study of Robertson's style as measured across thirty word-class and syntactic features and among eleven other twentieth-century English-speaking (male) writers. The scores on the fifteen most revealing variables are presented in tables and discussed briefly.

Crosland, Andrew. "The Concordance as an Aid in the Historical Study of Style." *Style* 11 (1977):274–83. Excellent summary of early uses.

Fortier, Paul A. *Décor et dualisme: l'Immoralist d'André Gide.* Stanford French and Italian Studies. Saratoga, Calif.: Anma Libri, 1988.

———. *Le Métro émotif: Etude du fonctionnement des structures thématiques dans* Voyage au bout de la nuit *de Céline.* Paris: Minard, 1981.

———. *Structures et communication dans* la Jalousie *d'Alain Robbe-Grillet.* Sherbrooke. Naaman, 1981.

Galloway, Patricia. "Narrative Theories as Computational Models: Reader-Oriented Theory and Artificial Intelligence." *CHum* 17 (1983):169–74. An excellent article. Galloway contends that researchers in Artificial Intelligence and in narrative theory share many common interests and problems. She points out the similarity between Wolfgang Iser's concept of the reader's knowledge base meeting the implied author's knowledge base and the similar AI concept of frames and inferencing: processing memory (data structures) with syntactics and pragmatic procedures..

Greenblatt, Daniel L. "Using Statistics for the Historical Study of Style." *Style* 11 (1977):251–61. A demonstration of the use of statistics to place Marvell in relation to the Metaphysical Poets using the Halle-Kyser theory of metrical complexity.

Guinn, Dorothy Margaret. "The Making of a Masterpiece: Stephen Crane's *The Red Badge of Courage.*" *CHum* 14 (1980):231–39. Changes made by Stephen Crane from a draft to the final manuscript analyzed using HAWKEYE. Primarily examples of differences between the two texts; little explanation of what computerized grammatical analysis contributes.

Hiatt, Mary. *Artful Balance, The Parallel Structure of Style.* New York and London: Teacher's College Press, Columbia University, 1975. Review by Susan W. Tiefenbrun in *CHum* 10 (1976):358; by Barron Brainerd in *Style* 11 (1977):410–11. A computer-assisted study of parallelism and other rhetorical devices of repetition occurring in contemporary informative and imaginative prose, based on the Brown Corpus. Hiatt carefully discriminates among a large number of types of parallelism and points out the problems of using this very general corpus as the basis for a study of rhetorical figures.

Jaynes, Joseph. "A Search for Trends in the Poetic Style of W. B. Yeats." *ALLC Journal* 1 (1980):11–18. Asserts that statistical stylistics gives little support to the generally accepted critical description of syntactic differences between Yeats's early and late poems; some indications of changes in diction do emerge.

Joyce, James. "Stepping Back to Get Closer: Computing as a Semiotic Tool." *ALLC Bulletin* 7 (1979):130–35. Brief discussion of the computer and semiotic model-making in a project on rhyming words in Middle English poetry.

Kroeber, Karl. *Style in Fictional Structure: The Art of Jane Austen, Charlotte Brontë, George Eliot.* Princeton, N.J.: Princeton University Press, 1971. A computerized approach by a literary critic who has serious doubts about the usefulness of statistical analysis of literary texts. The book is unfortunately vague on the sampling techniques and statistics used. I include it because Kroeber does not gloss over his doubts about the applicability of computer techniques to the specific question of fictional structures. We need to recognize that many valid literary critical questions cannot be appropriately formulated for statistical analysis.

Logan, Harry M. "The Computer and Metrical Scansion." *ALLC Journal* 3 (1982):

9–14. Useful explanation of a four pass procedure for assigning, and correcting, metrical stress. The method not only automates scansion but also allows Logan to rank poets and poems on a scale of metrical complexity.

Martindale, Colin. "The Evolution of English Poetry." *Poetics* 7 (1978):231–48. Starting from a psychological perspective, Martindale argues that the basic trends in the history of an art form are a product of the continual necessity to regress from normal abstract waking consciousness to an associative or primary process state of consciousness. If this generalization is true, Martindale asserts that literary vocabulary should become more saturated with words indicative of primary process thought. This theory is tested by a content analysis study of eighty-eight English poets born between 1490 and 1949 along with a control group of non-literary prose written between 1770 and 1970.

———. "Evolutionary Trends in Poetic Style: The Case of the English Metaphysical Poetry." *CHum* 18 (1984):3–21. An elaborate study of content analysis passed through a dictionary for the rating of each dimension found in the texts; a highly statistical account using factor analysis and regression analysis for comparing the lexical items in the poetry of a matched sample of metaphysical and non-metaphysical seventeenth century English poets.

Miles, Josephine. *Eras and Modes in English Poetry.* 2nd rev. ed. Berkeley and Los Angeles: University of California Press, 1964. One of Miles's many numerical studies of both the semantics and the syntax of English poetry. Complete with many fascinating though difficult-to-read tables.

Milic, Louis Tonko. *A Quantitative Approach to the Style of Jonathan Swift.* The Hague and Paris: Mouton, 1967. The earliest full length application of computational and statistical approaches to the study of style in a major author. Milic's work is substantial and has stood the test of time; it applies the tools of authorship attribution studies to literary critical purposes.

———. "Contra Fish: The Arrogance of Misreading." *Style* 19 (1985):117–33. A review of *Is There a Text in This Class? The Authority of Interpretive Communities* in which Milic defends himself, and computational stylistics, against Stanley Fish's 1973 attack. (See below under Freeman in the section on Stylistic, Rhetorical, and Discourse Analysis.)

Oakman, R. L. "Carlyle and the Machine: A Quantitative Analysis of Syntax in Prose Style." *ALLC Bulletin* 3 (1975):100–10. Using a sample of 1,000 sentences randomly selected from the 26 volumes of Carlyle's prose (60,000 words in 200 paragraphs), Oakman applied computerized parsing routines to output masses of quantitative information on syntactic features. Oakman had to do much of the work manually because the parser could not handle the length of Carlyle's sentences. This experience is another example of the practical limitations of machine parsing; it should remind beginners of how much still needs to be done before true syntactic analysis can be expected.

Potter, Rosanne G. "Character Definition Through Syntax: Significant Within-Play Variability in 21 Modern English-Language Plays." *Style* 15, 4 (1981):65–78.

———. "Literary Criticism and Literary Computing: The Difficulties of a Synthesis." *CHum* 22, 2 (1988):91–97.

———. "Toward a Syntactic Differentiation of Period Style in Modern Drama: Significant Between-Play Variability in 21 English-Language Plays." *CHum* 14 (1980): 187–96.

Ross, Donald. "Beyond the Concordance: Algorithms for Description of English Clauses and Phrases." In *The Computer and Literary Studies.* Ed. A. J. Aiken, R. W. Bailey, and N. Hamilton-Smith. Edinburgh: Edinburgh University Press, 1973. Ross is one of the pioneers in automated parsing of literary texts.

Schmidt, Klaus M. "Conceptual Glossaries: A New Tool for Medievalists." *CHum* 12 (1978):19–26. A discussion of how computerized content analysis might assist literary critics. Schmidt discusses then dismisses co-occurrence methods of content analysis; he argues instead for a thesaurus method in which glossaries are built manually from the texts. (A useful bibliography for content anaysis.)

Small, Ian. "Computational Stylistics and the Construction of Literary Readings: Work in Progress." *Prose Studies* 7.3 (1984): 250–60. Small compares Lionel Johnson's 1894 assertions about Pater's vocabulary with Edmund Chandler's 1958 *Pater on Style* in order to contrast both accounts of Pater's alleged vocabulary with computer concordances of his works. In the process, some fascinating questions arise about the importance of the percentage of uniquely (or doubly, or triply) occurring words in the vocabulary of a literary work. The book ends with a call for advice and suggestions on a corpus of nineteenth-century critical texts designed to provide an external standard against which the vocabularies of specific writers could be measured.

Smith, John B. "Image and Imagery in Joyce's *Portait:* A Computer-Assisted Analysis." In *Directions in Literary Criticism: Contemporary Approaches to Literature.* Eds. Stanley Weintraub and Philip Young. University Park and London: Pennsylvania State University Press, 1973, 220–27. In this presentation, intended for a literary critical audience, Smith places his research in the tradition of Caroline Spurgeon's and discusses his thirteen-hundred word list of images, which was plotted against the units of the text to map the richness of the imagery.

———. *Imagery and the Mind of Stephen Dedalus: A Computer-assisted Study of Joyce's* Portrait of the Artist as a Young Man. Lewisburg, Pa.: Bucknell University Press, 1980. Well-balanced study of Joyce's use of images to create Stephen and Smith's use of computing to map imagery in *Portrait.*

———. "Thematic Structure and Complexity." *Style* 9 (1975): 32–54. Summary essay on the use of "state diagrams" to show associative patterns by gathering together seemingly random experiences (of Stephen Dedalus in *A Portrait of the Artist as a Young Man*) or of images in four sermons. These diagrams reflect the simplicity or complexity of the thematic structure. This study is briefly referenced in Smith's more theoretical essay in this volume.

Vanderbok, Judith A. "Growth Patterns in E. E. Cummings's Sonnets: A Quantitative Approach." *ALLC Bulletin* 6 (1978): 42–52. Use of statistics to test F. O. Matthiessen's assertion that Cummings did not mature in depth of vision, style, or technique.

Wittig, Susan. "The Computer and the Concept of Text." *CHum* 11 (1978): 211–15. Wittig argues that computer users analyze texts from a New Critical definition of the text as linear, completed (confined to graphic representation on the printed page), and meaningful in and of itself. Following Culler and Iser, Wittig asserts that text acquires meaning only in the act of reading and in the creative interaction with the reader; she calls on computer critics to stop focusing on the signal and instead focus on the reader's act of signification.

Zwaan, Rolf A. "The Computer in Perspective." *Poetics* 16, 6 (1987): 553–68. Follows from Wittig's premise that most computer studies of literature have been based within the narrow framework of New Criticism and structuralism. Argues that an artificial intelligence model, i.e., the creation of an expert system for the simulation of the cognitive process, should be the direction of those interested in the empirical study of literature. Zwaan's three-stage computer simulation is designed to produce experimentally testable predictions. First, the computer acts as a heuristic device and guides researchers to a theory; then, a part of the theory is stated in algorithmic form; finally, the running of the program tests the theory for structural deficiencies.

Books and Essays Related to Literary Computing

THEORETICAL WORKS

Many works in the next two sections have nothing explicit to do with literary computing. The theoretical works are by philosophers of language, speech act theorists, generative grammarians, discourse analysts, socio-linguists, and pragmaticists. Their work can help literary critics to ask better questions about how language works in literature.

What literary computing most needs is theoretical clarity about language. The computer has enforced methodological rigor; but too many computer-using critics start from literary texts without having placed the language used in those texts within any larger framework. This lack of a frame of reference often leads to thoughtless counting, statistical analysis, and reporting of every linguistic feature of the text. In the next section of this bibliography I attempt to provide, on a modest scale, a set of possible contexts for thought about language. Following the principle used throughout, I annotate at greater length if the titles are not self-explanatory or if the reasons for inclusion might not be self-evident.

Austin, John L. *How to Do Things with Words*. New York and London: Oxford University Press, 1962. The unpretentious book about the philosophy of ordinary language that announced speech act theory.

Banfield, Ann. *Unspeakable Sentences: Narration and Representation in the Language of Fiction*. Boston: Routledge & Kegan Paul, 1982. Banfield says she is "not attempting a taxonomy of narrative sentences" but rather "an explanation of how a style and from it an entire genre develops linguistically and the nature of its rapport with language itself" (18). Chapters on: the expression of subjectivity and the sentences of direct and indirect speech; the sentence of represented speech and thought; communication and the sentence of discourse; the sentences of narration and discourse; the sentence representing nonreflective consciousness and the absence of the narrator; the historical development of narrative style; and narration and representation: the knowledge of the clock and the lens. Banfield demonstrates the differences among direct speech, indirect speech, and represented speech.

Christensen, Francis. *Notes Toward a New Rhetoric: Six Essays for Teachers*. New York, Evanston, and London: Harper and Row, 1967. This book, though designed for teachers of composition, provides a method for describing the various grammatical layers within sentences and paragraphs. Christensen's methods of assigning and tagging levels to additions in sentences, and to coordinated and subordinated material in paragraphs, could be translated into algorithms for rhetorical analysis.

Cole, Peter, and Jerry L. Morgan, eds. *Syntax and Semantics*. Vol. 3, *Speech Acts*. New York: Academic Press, 1975. Contains many important essays, especially H. P. Grice's "Logic and Conversation" (41–58) and John R. Searle's "Indirect Speech Acts" (59–82).

Coulthard, Malcolm. *An Introduction to Discourse Analysis*. New ed. London: Longman, 1985. See especially Chapter 9 on "The Analysis of Literary Discourse" for excellent analysis of *Othello* and *The Dumb Waiter*.

Dijk, T. A. van, ed. *Handbook of Discourse Analysis*. 4 Vols. New York: Academic Press, 1985. Vol. 1: *Disciplines of Discourse;* Vol. 2: *Dimensions of Discourse;* Vol. 3: *Discourse and Dialogue;* Vol. 4: *Discourse Analysis in Society*. This large international, interdisciplinary collection presents a survey of and an introduction to discourse analysis emphasizing the diversity of approaches in this field. The editorial position guiding the collection is that the essays be "accessible to advanced and interested students in all disciplines of the humanities and the social sciences, and not only to specialists in some area of research." (xiv) The strength of these volumes is their jargon free presentation of the issues; the only weakness is the daunting length.

Goffman, Erving. *Forms of Talk*. Philadelphia and Oxford: University of Pennsylvania Press and Basil Blackwell, 1981. See especially the excellent chapters on "Replies and Responses" and "Response Cries."

Gray, Bennison. *The Grammatical Foundations of Rhetoric: Discourse Analysis*. The Hague, New York, and Paris: Mouton, 1977. Review by F. Knowles in *ALLC Bulletin* 8 (1980):203. About the skills needed for written composition, this book takes the position that in order "to convey meaning without the aid of responsive listeners" (3), writers must create an implied dialogue of questions and answers. Gray does some very fascinating work on the definition of a sentence and on implications and relations between assertions.

Kelly, Edward F., and Philip J. Stone. *Computer Recognition of English Word Senses*. Amsterdam: North-Holland, 1975. Review by Kenneth W. Staggs in *CHum* 11 (1977): 176–77. An excellent explanation of one of the primary methods of computer-aided content analysis (using the dictionary look-up method of tagging words with category descriptors). Contains a disambiguation dictionary and other useful tables ("multi-step suffix removals").

Levinson, Stephen C. *Pragmatics*. Cambridge: Cambridge University Press, 1983. After lengthy investigation of possible definitions for pragmatics, Levinson finally resigns the effort and says the rest of the book will give "an overview of the central tasks that pragmaticists wrestle with." Chapters on "Truth-conditions"; "Utterance Entailments"; "Conversational Implicatures"; "Presuppositions"; "Felicity Conditions"; and "Inferences Based on Conversational Structures."

Masterman, Margaret. "Rhetorical Punctuation by Machine." In *Advances in Computer-Aided Literary and Linguistic Research*. Ed. D. E. Ager, F. E. Knowles, and Joan Smith. Birmingham: University of Aston in Birmingham, 1979. 289–320. An impressive and very clear discussion of algorithms for automated marking of rhetorical units in English sentences.

Ohmann, Richard. "Generative Grammars and the Concept of Literary Style." *Word* 20 (1964):423–39. Ohmann first lists all the kinds of critical methods which attempt to approach the subject of "style"; then dismisses them as inadequate to the task. This sets up his solution, generative grammar. A germinal work in the field of stylistics.

———. "Instrumental Style: Notes on the Theory of Speech as Action." In *Current Trends in Stylistics*. Ed. Braj B. Kachru and F. W. Stalkke. Edmonton, Alberta, and Champaign, Ill.: Champaign Linguistic Research, 1972. The essay in which Ohmann states his move into speech act theory as an explanatory substructure for stylistic analysis.

———. "Speech Acts and the Definition of Literature." *Philosophy and Rhetoric* 4 (1971):1–19. In an attempt to answer the question "what the genus of literature is and what its differentia are " (2) Ohmann argues that the genus of literature is discourse, but discourse whose sentences lack the illocutionary force that would normally attach to them. Its illocutionary force is mimetic.

Osgood, Charles E., George J. Suci, and Percy H. Tannenbaum. *The Measurement of Meaning*. Urbana, Chicago, and London: University of Illinois Press, 1957. An early computerized study of semantic differentials as instruments of measurement in psychological research. Anyone doing semantic, thematic, or content analysis would be well advised to investigate this basic statistical research on sets of polar terms ("good-bad," "strong-weak," "active-passive," etc.).

Pratt, Mary Louise. *Toward a Speech Act Theory of Literary Discourse*. Bloomington and London: Indiana University Press, 1977. Pratt takes on the Structuralist poetics position that "literary discourse is different in kind" from ordinary language and devotes the book to showing that it is merely different in use. This book popularized Searle and Grice for literary critical use.

Riffaterre, Michael. "Criteria for Style Analysis." *Word* 15 (1959):154–74. An early attempt to approach literary texts objectively. Riffaterre suggests that the stylistician focus on the decoder; he posits the term AR (average reader) as a label for the places in texts which have elicited value judgments of past critics. The AR criteria for measuring SDs (stylistic devices) allow the analysis of just those passages which can be shown to be stylistic stimuli regardless of the response they have evoked. Once value judgments have been disregarded, Riffaterre asserts that the analysis of SDs can proceed objectively.

Searle, John R. "The Logical Status of Fictional Discourse." *New Literary History* 6 (1975):319–32. Essential reading for anyone planning to use speech act theory as a theoretical model.

———. *Speech Acts: An Essay in the Philosophy of Language.* Cambridge: Cambridge University Press, 1969. Divided into two parts. Part 1, "A Theory of Speech Acts," includes chapters on "Method and Scope," "Expressions, Meaning and Speech Acts," "The Structure of Illocutionary Acts," and "Predication". Part 2, on "Some Applications of the Theory," has chapters on "Three Fallacies in Contemporary Philosophy," "Problems of Reference," and "Deriving 'Ought' from 'Is'."

Searle, John R., Ferenc Kiefer, and Manfred Bierwisch, eds. *Speech Act Theory and Pragmatics.* Vol. 10, Synthesis Language Library. Dordrecht Holland: D. Reidel, 1980. A collection of fourteen essays around the general subject of the distinction "between speaker's meaning and sentence meaning . . . that distinction is the same as the distinction between context-free meaning (semantics) and context-dependent meaning (pragmatics)." These essays can be taken in sum to point out how philosophically risky it is to perform any analysis at the semantic or syntactic level. Not addressed to computer-using critics, but probably should be read by them before beginning as a necessary and salutary warning about the oversimplification induced by many computer applications to texts.

Stone, Philip J., Dexter C. Dunphy, Marshall S. Smith, and Daniel M. Ogilvie. *The General Inquirer: A Computer Approach to Content Analysis.* Cambridge, Mass. and London: MIT Press, 1966. Defines content analysis as "any research technique for making inferences by systematically and objectively identifying specified characteristics within texts" (5). The authors engaged in psychological research by analyzing texts for related words or idioms that reflected role relations or states of emotion in writers. The content analysis process is dependent on a pre-computational stage, category construction; once the dictionary of concepts has been established, then the computational translations and statistical analyses follow mechanically. The computational means discussed here are out of date; this kind of research is, however, quite alive.

Wardhaugh, Ronald. *How Conversation Works.* Oxford and New York: Basil Blackwell, 1985. Chapters on "The Social Basis of Talk"; "Locating an Agenda"; "Cooperation and Playing the Game"; "Beyond and Behind Words"; "The Importance of Context"; "Getting Started and Keeping Going"; "Topics, Turns, and Terminations"; "Requesting, Informing, Advising, Agreeing, Apologizing, Promising"; "Samples of Conversation"; "Consequences."

Yule, G. Udny. *The Statistical Study of Literary Vocabulary.* Cambridge: Cambridge University Press, 1944. An essential early explanation of appropriate applications of statistical analysis to vocabulary in literary texts.

STYLISTIC, RHETORICAL, AND DISCOURSE ANALYSIS

This subsection points in the opposite direction, toward non-computer-using analysts whose work is all but tumbling into computer applications. These critics are asking many of the same questions, thinking along the same lines, but have not turned to computer methods for assistance in their endeavors. The moment of synthesis may come when all the counters, critics, and analysts of language can meet in some great congress of the lovers of language. In the meantime, it is a good idea at least to remember that others are out there.

Burton, Deirdre. *Dialogue and Discourse: A Sociolinguistic Approach to Modern Drama Dialogue and Naturally Occurring Conversation.* London: Routledge & Kegan Paul, 1980. An excellent attempt to apply the insights of discourse analysis and linguistics to the dialogue of modern plays. Burton seeks a principled method of analyzing the impact of discourse rules on our understanding of what is implicated by lines of dialogue. An analysis of style in literature "must show how stylistic features build the fictional world of the literary work."

Chatman, Seymour. *The Later Style of Henry James.* Oxford: Basil Blackwell, 1972. Chatman considers James's later style under eighteen stylistic headings that enable him to distinguish quite specifically between a good parody (by Max Beerbohm) and a fairly bad one (by W. H. D. Rouse). Non-computerized, but could have been. What would have happened to the effectiveness and length (135 pages) of this book, had it been?

———, ed. *Literary Style: A Symposium.* London and New York: Oxford University Press, 1971. Major collection: includes essays by Barthes, Miles, Todorov, Wellek, Doležel, Levin, Wimsatt, Starobinski, and Sauce. Those of most use to readers of this book, however, are by Louis T. Milic, "Rhetorical Choice and Stylistic Option"; Stephen Ullmann, "Stylistics and Semantics"; Richard Ohmann, "Speech, Action, and Style"; and M. A. K. Halliday, "Language of William Golding's *The Inheritors.*"

D'Haen, Theo, ed. *Linguistics and the Study of Literature,* Amsterdam: Rodopi, 1986. Essays by Ronald Carter, "A Question of Interpretation: An Overview of Some Recent Developments in Stylistics"; Donald C. Freeman, "Syntax, Agency, and the Imagination: Keats' 'Ode to Psyche' and 'Ode on a Grecian Urn'"; G. N. Leech, "Music in Metre: 'Sprung Rhythm' in Victorian and Georgian Poetry"; Michael H. Short, "Literature and Language Teaching and the Nature of Lnaguage"; Roger Fowler, "Studying Literature as Language"; Andre Lefebvere, "On the Processing of Texts, or What is Literature?"; Willie van Peer, "Pulp and Purpose: Stylistic Analysis as an Aid to a Theory of Texts."

Freeman, Donald C., ed. *Essays in Modern Stylistics.* London: Methuen, 1981. Essays by Paul Kiparsky, "The Role of Linguistics in a Theory of Poetry"; Jonathan Culler, "Literary Competence"; Stanley Fish, "What is Stylistics . . . ?"; Mary Louise Pratt, "Literary Cooperation and Implicature."

Iser, Wolfgang. *The Implied Reader: Patterns of Communication in Prose Fiction from Bunyan to Beckett.* Baltimore and London: Johns Hopkins University Press, 1974. A collection of fourteen essays on Fielding, Smollett, Scott, Thackeray, Faulkner, Compton-Burnett, Joyce, Beckett, and "The Reading Process." Iser offers a radical investigation of the reader's role in fiction; he asserts that writers leave gaps in the text which give the readers motivation and opportunity to bring conflicting material together. Iser describes "the process of anticipation and retrospection" as what "leads to the formation of a virtual dimension, which in turn transforms the text into an experience for the reader." (281) Iser's position has elements both amenable and inimical to computer analysis.

Leech, Geoffrey N., and Michael H. Short. *Style in Fiction: A Linguistic Introduction to English Fictional Prose.* English Language Series, No. 13. London and New York: Longman, 1981. This textbook based on the New Stylistics will also be useful to researchers interested in quantitative approaches. See Chapters Two, "Style, Text, and Frequency," and Three, "A Method of Analysis and Examples," for a checklist of linguistic and stylistic features that can be investigated heuristically and then counted; also Chapter Five, "The Rhetoric of the Text," for useful application of pragmatics.

Lodge, David. *The Language of Fiction: Essays on Critical and Verbal Analysis of the English Novel.* London: Routledge & Kegan Paul, 1966. Summary on stylistics

(52–87) is useful background reading on Spitzer, Ullmann, and others. Despite his own interest in repetitions, Lodge insists that criticism has to do with values and cannot be made numerical.

Mair, Christian. "The 'New Stylistics': A Success Story or the Story of Successful Self-Deception?" *Style* 19 (1985):117–33. A review article on four stylistics textbooks, actually an assessment of the relations between linguistic analysis and literary criticism, with more than a passing glance at things computational. Assesses the impact of Fish's attack on Milic, Ohmann, Riffaterre, Doležel, and Halliday. Says that statistical, computer-aided approaches to style had their heyday in the 1960s and are "no longer regarded as the safest approach to the phenomenon of style."

Steinmann, Martin, Jr., ed. *New Rhetorics*. New York: Scribners, 1967. Essays by Francis Christensen, "A Generative Rhetoric of the Paragraph"; James Sledd, "Coordination and Sub-ordination"; Richard E. Young and Alton L. Becker, "A Tagmemic Contribution to a Modern Theory of Rhetoric."

Bibliographies

"Annual Bibliography for 1979 and Supplement to Previous Years." *CHum* 13 (1979): 172–83.

Bailey, Richard, and Dolores Burton, eds. *English Stylistics: A Bibliography*. Cambridge, Mass.: MIT Press, 1968. Annual updates in *Style*.

Bailey, Richard W., and Lubomír Doležel, eds. *An Annotated Bibliography of Statistical Stylistics*. Ann Arbor: University of Michigan Press, 1968.

Rudman, Joseph. "Selected Bibliography for Computer Courses in the Humanities." *CHum* 21 (1987):235–54. A small section of Rudman's exhaustive bibliography, all of which will eventually be published under specific categories in *CHum*.

Waite, Stephen V. F. "Annual Bibliography for 1974." *CHum* 9 (1975):127–44; "Annual Bibliography for 1975." *CHum* 10 (1976):101–21; "Annual Bibliography for 1976." *CHum* 11 (1977):100–18. See especially the Language and Literature sections.

Books on Programming

Many literary critics will be content to use the increasing number of commercial text analysis (e.g., Micro ARRAS, designed by John B. Smith) or concordance packages (e.g., Micro OCP, the Oxford Concordance Program, or Word Cruncher, originally the BYU [Brigham Young University] Concordance Package). Others, however, will wish to learn programming to gain more control of their research. I include the citations below because these books discuss the three languages primarily used by researchers in the humanities computing; each is the standard text.

Griswold, Ralph E., and Madge T. Griswold. *The ICON Programming Language*. Englewood Cliffs, N.J.: Prentice-Hall, 1983. Review by F. E. Knowles in *ALLC Bulletin* 12 (1984):66–67.

Hockey, Susan. *SNOBOL Programming for the Humanities*. Oxford: Clarendon Press, 1985. Review by Barron Brainerd in *CHum* 21 (1987):137–38; by W. J. Jones in *Literary and Linguistic Computing* 3 (1988):56–57.

Ide, Nancy. *PASCAL for the Humanities*. Philadelphia: University of Pennsylvania Press, 1986. Review by C. Michael Sperberg-McQueen in *CHum* 21 (1987):261–64.

INDEX

CONTRIBUTORS

RICHARD W. BAILEY
Department of English, University of Michigan at Ann Arbor

PAUL A. FORTIER
Department of French, University of Manitoba at Winnipeg

JOEL D. GOLDFIELD
Department of Foreign Languages, Plymouth State College at Plymouth, New Hampshire

EUGENE GREEN
Department of English, Boston University

NANCY IDE
Department of Computer Science, Vassar College at Poughkeepsie, New York

EUNICE MERIDETH
Department of Education, Loras College at Dubuque, Iowa

ROSANNE G. POTTER
Department of English, Iowa State University at Ames

DONALD ROSS, JR.
Department of English, University of Minnesota at Minneapolis

C. RUTH SABOL
Department of English, West Chester University at West Chester, Pennsylvania

JOHN B. SMITH
Department of Computer Science, University of North Carolina at Chapel Hill

BARBARA STEVENSON
Department of English, Kennesaw College at Marietta, Georgia

JULIA WAGGONER
School of Library Science, University of Iowa at Iowa City